READINGS
IN
CLASSICAL
CHINESE
PHILOSOPHY

Third Edition

READINGS IN CLASSICAL CHINESE PHILOSOPHY

Third Edition

Edited by

Philip J. Ivanhoe
Georgetown University

and

Bryan W. Van Norden
Vassar College

Hackett Publishing Company, Inc.
Indianapolis/Cambridge

26 25 24 23   1 2 3 4 5 6 7

For further information, please address
    Hackett Publishing Company, Inc.
    P.O. Box 44937
    Indianapolis, Indiana 46244-0937

    www.hackettpublishing.com

Cover design by E. L. Wilson
Composition by Aptara, Inc.

Library of Congress Control Number: 2022941889

ISBN-13: 978-1-64792-108-8 (pbk.)
ISBN-13: 978-1-64792-109-5 (PDF ebook)

The paper used in this publication meets the minimum requirements of American
National Standard for Information Sciences—Permanence of Paper for Printed
Library Materials, ANSI Z39.48–1984.

∞

CONTENTS

Preface   *vii*
Comparative Romanization Table   *ix*
Map of China during the Spring and Autumn Period   *x*
Introduction   *xi*
Selective Bibliography   *xviii*

CHAPTER ONE
Kongzi (Confucius), *Analects*   3
   Introduction and Translation by Edward G. Slingerland

CHAPTER TWO
Mozi   57
   Introduction and Translation by Philip J. Ivanhoe

CHAPTER THREE
Yangist Writings   111
   Introduction and Translation by Paul Kjellberg

CHAPTER FOUR
Mengzi (Mencius)   119
   Introduction and Translation by Bryan W. Van Norden

CHAPTER FIVE
The School of Names   161
   Introduction and Translation by Bryan W. Van Norden

CHAPTER SIX
Laozi, *Daodejing*   171
   Introduction and Translation by Philip J. Ivanhoe

CHAPTER SEVEN
Shen Dao   213
   Introduction and Translation by Eirik L. Harris

CHAPTER EIGHT
Zhuangzi   223
   Introduction and Translation by Paul Kjellberg

CHAPTER NINE
Xunzi   269
    Introduction and Translation by Eric L. Hutton

CHAPTER TEN
Han Feizi   323
    Introduction and Translation by Eirik L. Harris

CHAPTER ELEVEN
Great Learning and *Mean*   383
    Introduction and Translation by Bryan W. Van Norden

CHAPTER TWELVE
Nature Comes from the Mandate   391
    Introduction and Translation by Philip J. Ivanhoe

APPENDICES
Important Figures   *401*
Important Periods   *407*
Important Texts   *409*
Important Terms   *411*

Image Credits   420

PREFACE

The first edition of *Readings in Classical Chinese Philosophy* introduced the seven most familiar, widely read, and important thinkers of the "classical period" of Chinese philosophy (roughly the sixth to the end of the third century BCE): Kongzi (Confucius), Mozi, Mengzi (Mencius), Laozi, Zhuangzi, Xunzi, and Han Feizi. The second edition added selections to illustrate two critically important but often neglected intellectual trends of this period (Yangism and the School of Names). This third edition includes additional selections for each chapter, selections from Shen Dao (an influential but under-studied figure from this era), a completely new translation of the writings of Han Feizi, partial translations of two texts that became highly influential in later Chinese philosophy (the *Great Learning* and *Mean*), and one recently rediscovered text (*Nature Comes from the Mandate*). Each of the sections of this volume begins with a brief introduction to the work and thinker it concerns and concludes with a short and lightly annotated selective bibliography. The volume is intended to serve as an introduction to and source book for these texts, not as a philosophical primer for the thought of these authors. Introductory and interpretive material is kept to a minimum, but the volume includes four appendices—*Important Figures, Important Periods, Important Texts,* and *Important Terms*—that describe mythical and historical figures, periods of time, classical texts, and specialized terms that regularly appear in the texts translated here. Preceding the introduction is a *Map of China during the Spring and Autumn Period*, which shows the approximate locations of the major states and rivers. Readers are encouraged to turn to these reference materials whenever they encounter terms or names in the text that are not explained in footnotes. Explanatory notes are provided at the bottom of each page in cases of a single occurrence of an obscure term or name, or when more explanation appeared to be warranted. Those who wish to pursue additional secondary literature in English concerning the texts and thinkers included in this reader are encouraged to consult the Title Support Page that is maintained for this volume at https://www.hackettpublishing.com/rccp-support.

Knowledge of the Chinese language is in no way required for making full and thorough use of this volume. However, Chinese characters are provided for important references and terms of philosophical art in order to help the beginning student of Chinese and for the common edification of all. We do not provide characters for textual emendations or other textual notes, as these issues require advanced facility in the classical Chinese language and other basic research languages of sinology. Readers interested in pursuing textual issues are encouraged to consult the appropriate sections of the web page mentioned above.

We have used the Pinyin romanization system throughout this volume and added tone marks where the romanization is accompanied by Chinese characters. We have chosen to romanize the common formal names of Chinese thinkers—their surnames and the honorific title zǐ 子 (literally "Master")—as one word rather than two. So, for example, Zhuang Zi (literally "Master Zhuang") is written as Zhuangzi and Han Fei Zi ("Master Han Fei") appears as Han Feizi. All romanizations in the bibliographies and notes remain in their original form in order to facilitate locating these sources. We have provided a complete table comparing the Pinyin and older Wade-Giles systems of romanization following this preface. Since this book deals with traditional Chinese thought, we have chosen to use the traditional or long-form versions of Chinese characters, rather than the short-form versions in common use today.

We, the editors, have tried to balance a desire for consistency in the use of specialized terms with the variety of senses many of these terms have within the range of texts presented here, as well as with the different sensibilities and styles of the individual translators. In cases where a certain important term of art is rendered in different ways, we have provided notes alerting readers and directing their attention to the other occurrences and translations.

We would like to thank the contributors to this volume for their work and their patience with us throughout the editorial process. Edward G. "Ted" Slingerland III (Philosophy Department, University of British Columbia) translated selections from the *Analects* of Kongzi (Confucius); Paul Kjellberg (Philosophy Department, Whittier College) contributed the selections from Zhuangzi and on the thought of Yang Zhu; Eric L. Hutton (Philosophy Department, University of Utah) translated parts of Xunzi's writings; and Eirik L. Harris (Philosophy Department, Colorado State University) contributed selections from Shen Dao and Han Feizi. We, the editors, contributed the remaining translations of Mozi, Mengzi (Mencius), Laozi (*Daodejing*), *Great Learning, Mean, Nature Comes from the Mandate*, as well as the selections representing the thought of the School of Names.

We would like to thank Robert B. Rama and Jeremy R. Robinson for their help in preparing the manuscript for the second edition of this volume, and Laura Clark and Marie Deer for their help in preparing the manuscript for the third edition of this volume. Mark Csikszentmihalyi, Shari Ruei-hua Epstein, T. C. "Jack" Kline III, Pauline Chen Lee, Shuen-fu Lin, and Eric Schwitzgebel offered very helpful corrections and comments on various parts of earlier drafts of the manuscript.

COMPARATIVE ROMANIZATION TABLE

The following conversion table is provided in order to allow the reader to keep track of and convert between the Pinyin and Wade-Giles systems of romanization.

Pinyin	Wade-Giles
b	p
c	ts'/tz'
ch	ch'
d	t
g	k
-ian	ien
j	ch
k	k'
-ong	ung
p	p'
q	ch'
r	j
si	ssu/szu
t	t'
x	hs
you	yu
yu	yü
z	ts/tz
zh	ch
zhi	chih
zi	tzu

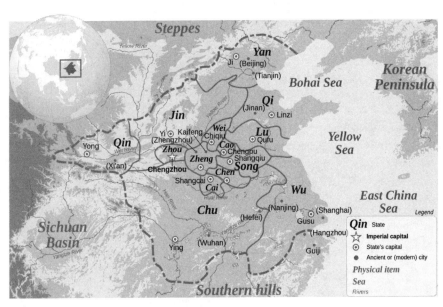

Map of China during the Spring and Autumn Period

INTRODUCTION

Chinese history and thought extend much farther back in time than the period covered in this volume, though it is fair to say that philosophy—in the sense of self-conscious reflection upon, modification of, and defense of one's views—begins with the debate between Kongzi and Mozi. Nevertheless, a general sense of the trajectory of Chinese thought prior to this period and some understanding of the shape of the intellectual landscape on the eve of the age represented here will help the reader to appreciate more deeply the views of the thinkers presented.

The earliest substantial written documents we have from China are carved onto bone and shell or etched onto ritual vessels of bronze. These incised inscriptions, together with other modern archaeological discoveries, have allowed scholars to reconstruct speculative yet intriguing pictures of very early Chinese society and culture.[1] Most of the surviving "oracle bone inscriptions" date from around the twelfth to mid-eleventh century BCE, the closing years of the Shang dynasty.[2] They record the queries of royal diviners—often the king himself—who sought the advice and assistance of various ancestral and nature spirits. Ritual vessel inscriptions, which date from the Shang and continue, in their high form, on down through the eighth century BCE, in the period known as the Western Zhou dynasty, also provide a wealth of information concerning very early Chinese elite culture, particularly many of its religious views.[3]

These sources describe a precarious world, saturated with unruly and unpredictable spiritual powers. Above there was Shàng Dì 上帝, "The Lord on High," a powerful and only vaguely understood spirit who controlled the forces of nature and largely determined the fate of human beings. Unlike ancestral spirits and even

---

1. The best introductions to this period of Chinese civilization are Kwang-chih Chang, *Shang Civilization* (New Haven: Yale University Press, 1980) and David N. Keightley, ed., *The Origins of Chinese Civilization* (Berkeley: University of California Press, 1983). Two useful surveys of Chinese history from the earliest times through the period we cover in this book are Michael Loewe and Edward L. Shaughnessy, eds., *The Cambridge History of Ancient China: From the Origins of Civilization to 221 B.C.* (New York: Cambridge University Press, 1999) and John S. Major and Constance Cook, *Ancient China: A History* (New York: Routledge, 2017). For a general overview of all of Chinese history, see Harold M. Tanner, *China: A History* (Indianapolis: Hackett Publishing, 2009).

2. For a remarkably edifying introduction to Shang oracular inscriptions, see David N. Keightley, *Sources of Shang History: The Oracle-Bone Inscriptions of Bronze Age China* (Berkeley, CA: University of California Press, 1978).

3. The most illuminating and thorough introduction to early bronze inscriptions is Edward L. Shaughnessy, *Sources of Western Zhou History: Inscribed Bronze Vessels* (Berkeley, CA: University of California Press, 1991).

the spirits of Nature, *Shang Di* was so remote from human concerns and so far from human understanding that he could not be approached directly. Other spirits and particularly ancestral spirits, though, could appeal to *Shang Di* on behalf of their living descendants and solicit his support for their all-too-human endeavors.

The majority of oracular and bronze-vessel inscriptions record attempts by the ruling members of Shang and Zhou society to influence the spirits through ritual supplication and sacrifice. Those appeals that are directed specifically at ancestral spirits are among the clearest early expressions of "ancestor worship," and, given our concern with the development of philosophy, it is interesting that even at this early stage we find an explicit concern with the inner life of the worshipper. For these inscriptions make clear that sacrifice was not simply an external behavior; in order for one's sacrifice to be accepted by the appropriate spirit, one had to offer it with the proper inner attitudes and feelings of respect and reverence. Moreover, it was thought that with enough effort of the right sort, the appropriate attitudes and feelings could be cultivated.

In early Chinese religious thought, ancestral spirits bridge what in other traditions often looms as an abyss between the spiritual and human worlds. There is no fundamental metaphysical rupture in the cosmos; at the very least, living human beings have concerned representatives in the spiritual world who can temper and appeal to the more remote and recalcitrant forces. This gives early and even later Chinese religious thought a distinctively "this-worldly" orientation, and it had a profound influence on the shape and style of later philosophical reflection.

Another fascinating and productive aspect of this complex of beliefs, attitudes, and practices is the attention early diviners paid to keeping track of their past interactions with the spiritual world. Shang diviners kept extensive records of their oracular activities; these included notes concerning the consequences that resulted from following the advice derived through divination. K. C. Chang argues that these records were kept in the belief that by studying these past records, thoughtful individuals could discern the most reliable patterns of productive human-spirit interaction.[4] He further suggests that such practices deeply influenced later Chinese conceptions of and attitudes toward history and in particular the value and role of historical precedent.

Together, these beliefs about the role of ancestral spirits and the wisdom of history laid the foundation for beliefs and attitudes that shaped and endured throughout the Chinese tradition, particularly in the tradition of the Rú 儒 ("Erudites" or "Confucians"). They in particular preserved and elaborated on the idea that by keeping the lessons of the past in one's mind and the ancestors in one's heart, one

---

4. See Chang, *Shang Civilization*, 90.

could find a way through a dangerous and unpredictable world. These ideas find various expressions in the later philosophical literature. Different thinkers defend tradition on a variety of grounds, extending from a fundamental faith in a past golden age preserved in traditional cultural forms, to more subtle defenses of the accumulated authoritative force of efficacious precedents. As Benjamin Schwartz has pointed out, the unique part the ancestors played as mediators between the human and spiritual worlds lent itself to a form of life in which finding and fulfilling one's designated familial and social roles—whatever these might be in a particular case—allowed one to take one's proper place in a harmonious universal scheme that worked for the benefit of all.[5] The fact that such family-based roles also appeared to be "natural" further reinforced this general conceptual scheme and opened up a way—that was taken by some of the thinkers we present here—to provide a more naturalized account of this early conception of the good human life.

When the Shang were overthrown and their conquerors founded the Zhou dynasty, we find the beginning of a tendency to naturalize and in a certain sense domesticate aspects of earlier Shang belief.[6] We use "naturalization" to refer to a preference for accounts of actions and events in terms of systematic, natural phenomena rather than spiritual power. For example, while the early Zhou rulers appear to have promoted the idea that their supreme deity Tiān 天 (literally "Heaven" or "sky") was identical to the earlier *Shang Di*, with the passage of time *Tian* came to be thought of as the structure or disposition of the universe itself, as opposed to an entity or being with consciousness and intention. This transition is clear in texts like the *Analects*, where one finds conceptions of Heaven both as an active agent and as the natural order of things. Another idea that manifests what we are calling the trend toward naturalized accounts is the notion of Tiānmìng 天命, "Heaven's Mandate," which the Zhou invoked to justify their conquest of the Shang. The idea was that Heaven confers its "mandate" to rule on those who best represent its interests and concerns for humankind. The Zhou portrayed the last Shang kings

---

5. Benjamin I. Schwartz, *The World of Thought in Ancient China* (Cambridge, MA: Harvard/Belknap Press, 1985), 23.

6. Chinese historical dates prior to the Han dynasty (202 BCE–220 CE) are often uncertain, and those prior to the Eastern Zhou dynasty (770 BCE) are especially speculative. Many textbooks still follow the *History of the (Former) Han Dynasty* in dating the origin of the (Western) Zhou dynasty to 1122 BCE, but most contemporary scholars agree that this date is too early. David S. Nivison and David W. Pankenier have plausibly argued that the founding of the (Western) Zhou dynasty was within twenty years of a conjunction of the planets noted by Chinese astronomers that occurred in 1059 BCE. (See Pankenier, "Astronomical Dates in Shang and Western Zhou," *Early China* 7 [1981–1982]: 2–37.) We tentatively give 1045 BCE as the date of founding of the (Western) Zhou dynasty, as suggested by Nivison in "The Dates of Western Zhou," *Harvard Journal of Asiatic Studies* 43, no. 2 (December 1983): 481–580.

as drunken, self-serving despots who had forsaken their role-specific obligations and indulged their passions, thus bringing chaos to the world. As a consequence of this ethically reprehensible behavior, they were stripped of the mandate to rule.[7] This naturalized the earlier scheme in the sense that now an individual's intentional actions and chosen way of life directly defined their relationship with the spirit world and determined who secured and maintained Heaven's favor. The shift to a new conception of Heaven and the appeal to Heaven's Mandate also domesticated earlier Shang beliefs, in the sense of opening up the workings of the world to broader human understanding and control. In Shang times, the spirit world was largely beyond direct human understanding; oracular inquiries were like scouting parties, sent out into potentially hostile territory in search of strategically useful information. And even such indirect knowledge and partial control of the spiritual world was limited to royal diviners. In the emerging Zhou world view, however, anyone was potentially capable of understanding and harnessing the ethical power of Heaven.[8]

Later thinkers offered very different and at times conflicting accounts of the Western Zhou and its exemplary individuals, but there was broad agreement that this period was largely one of remarkable internal stability, peace, and prosperity. According to traditional accounts, the fall of the Western Zhou was the result of its last king's lack of virtue. It seems that King You was deeply enamored of his concubine Bao Si and indulged himself by amusing her. Bao Si in turn was terribly fond of having the king light the series of beacon fires that were supposed to be used to summon his vassals from surrounding territories in times of attack. And so, even though there was no danger of attack, he would have the fires lit for her amusement. His vassals would gather their forces and rush to the capital, only to find that it was a false alarm. After a number of such false alarms, they stopped coming and hence were not there when the real attack came, toppled his regime,

---

7. This idea can still be seen in the modern Chinese word for "revolution," which is gémìng 革命, "stripping the mandate." For excerpts from the *History* in which the Zhou rulers rationalize their conquest of the Shang, see the Title Support Page for this volume at www.hackettpublishing.com/rccp-support.

8. Early Chinese society restricted women to primarily domestic vocations. However, there were exceptions to this general rule, and there was a developed literature on woman's virtue quite early in Chinese history. See Lisa Raphals, *Sharing the Light: Women and Virtue in Early China* (Albany, NY: SUNY Press, 1999) and Robin R. Wang, ed., *Images of Women in Chinese Thought and Culture* (Indianapolis: Hackett Publishing Company, 2003). For representative writings by women in later Confucian thought, see Ann A. Pang-White, *The Confucian Four Books for Women: A New Translation of the "Nü Sishu" and the Commentary of Wang Xiang* (New York: Oxford University Press, 2018). Interestingly, in pre-Han China one finds no explicit arguments giving reasons why women could not develop complete forms of virtues, of the kind that one finds, for example, in the writings of Aristotle.

and forced the remnants of the Zhou court to flee and found a new capital far to the east.[9] From this we are to see how self-indulgence weakens the power of a ruler, and that eventually such conduct will result in the loss of Heaven's Mandate to rule. Political failure follows closely upon the heels of moral decay, and both are regarded as being largely within an individual's control.[10] These distinctive characteristics of Zhou religious, ethical, and political thought became central features of much of later Chinese philosophy.

From the perspective of the present work, the Eastern Zhou marks the dawn of the "classical period" of Chinese philosophy. It begins with Kongzi (better known in the West by the Jesuit Latinization of his name, "Confucius"), in a period when China consisted of a number of increasingly independent states, and culminates with Han Feizi, with the unification of central China under a new dynasty known as the Qin.[11] Of the thinkers covered in this volume, three—Kǒngzǐ 孔子, Mèngzǐ 孟子, and Xúnzǐ 荀子—are from what came to be called the Rújiā 儒家 ("Confucian School") and two—Lǎozǐ 老子 and Zhuāngzǐ 莊子—are from the more loosely affiliated group of thinkers later called the Dàojiā 道家 ("Daoist School").[12] In addition, there are selections from Mòzǐ 墨子, founder and leader of the fascinating, powerful, and highly organized movement known as the Mòjiā 墨家 ("Mohist School"), from Gōngsūn Lóngzǐ 公孫龍子 and Huìzǐ 惠子, who were later categorized as members of the Míngjiā 名家 ("School of Names"), from a "Yangist" text (one influenced by the thought of Yáng Zhū 楊朱), and from Shèn Dào 慎到 and Hán Fēizǐ 韓非子, two incisive, influential, and original thinkers who were later classified as representatives of the Fǎjiā 法家 ("Legalist School"). For this third edition, in addition to including more selections from the preceding figures and movements, we have also included selections from two works that later became immensely influential in the Confucian tradition, the *Great Learning* (Dà Xué 大學) and *Mean* (Zhōngyōng 中庸), along with a recently excavated text that illustrates Chinese thinking from around 300 BCE, *Nature Comes from the Mandate* (Xìng zì Mìng Chū 性自命出).

---

9. For a discussion of Bao Si, see Raphals, *Sharing the Light*, 64–66.

10. Uncontrollable and inexplicable factors could still affect one's overall destiny, but as these were beyond one's choice and conscious control, they received very little attention in the developing literature.

11. It is from "Qin" that we get our name "China."

12. Most of these labels were invented in the Han dynasty (by Sima Tan and popularized by his son, Sima Qian). There is evidence that the Confucians and Mohists were organized movements in the Zhou dynasty, but the other "schools" are only (sometimes) useful labels for grouping thinkers whose ideas are similar in some respects. For brief descriptions of these "schools" of thought, see *Important Terms* in the appendices.

As will be clear from the notes and appendices included in this volume, this selection of writings by no means exhausts or even fully represents the range of thinkers who lived, thought, argued, and wrote during this period.[13] There was a remarkably wide variety of thinkers active during this time in early China, a fact reflected in another name for this age: the bǎijiā 百家, "hundred schools," period. Even among the thinkers we present here, one finds a broad range of philosophical views. There are reflective defenders of tradition, ethical sensibility theorists, nature mystics, consequentialists, and egoists as well as those who present a purely political theory of state organization and control. One finds a variety of visions of the good life, ranging from those who insist that only the right kind of society presents human beings with a way to live complete and satisfying lives, to those who argue that any self-conscious attempt to produce a good life will inevitably be contaminated and undermined by that effort. For proponents of this latter view, the only solution is to stop trying to find a solution and allow oneself to fall back into the preexisting harmony of Nature. Many of these different views rest on explicit or implied views about the character of human nature, and here again we see remarkable variety. This is true even in the case of the founder and first two most eminent defenders of Confucianism—Kongzi, Mengzi, and Xunzi—who shared a significant number of commitments and looked to a common historical and textual heritage.

The thinkers of the hundred schools period disagreed not only in theory but also with each other. That is to say, not only were their views in conflict, but they themselves often argued with one another. Such exchanges led to greater philosophical sophistication, with thinkers responding to and often adapting each other's views in order to enhance their own positions. The careful reader will be able to see numerous examples of such disagreement and mutual borrowing in the selections presented here, and understanding this aspect of the philosophical life of this period is important for a full appreciation of the lively and creative spirit of the time.

The intellectual variety seen among the early philosophers represented here did not stop with this first classical period. Throughout subsequent history, Chinese thinkers continued to produce philosophical views of stunning originality and power. While certain early schools of thought died out, their influence remained and is clearly reflected in the thought of their longer-lived competitors.[14] Over time, other, non-Chinese traditions of thought came and profoundly influenced

---

13. This is true even if one counts only the thinkers for whom we have at least some samples of their work. Extant bibliographies and references in texts that we do have point, in addition, to an immensely rich and extensive literature that is either lost or has not yet come to light.

14. For example, the Mohist School died out around the time of the Qin conquest, but it left a deep and indelible influence on both Daoist and Confucian thought.

indigenous traditions. Buddhism, for example, which arrived in China sometime around the first century CE, generated a fundamental and enduring transformation of every active philosophical school. (See the selective bibliography below for a few of the many good secondary works on classical Chinese philosophy, along with some books with which to start learning about the later history of Chinese thought.)

The most important lesson to take away from this rich and complex history is that "Chinese philosophy" is not a single theory, thinker, or tradition but rather a diverse and lively conversation that has been going on for more than twenty-five hundred years and is still active and evolving in our own time. Thus, *Readings in Classical Chinese Philosophy* might more accurately be entitled *Readings in Classical Chinese Philosophies*. It is the hope of the editors and other contributors to this volume that this work serves to facilitate an engagement with and appreciation of the wealth of philosophical ideas found in early China.

Philip J. Ivanhoe
Washington, DC

Bryan W. Van Norden
Poughkeepsie, NY

June 2005; revised July 2022

SELECTIVE BIBLIOGRAPHY

Angle, Stephen C., and Justin Tiwald. *Neo-Confucianism: A Philosophical Introduction.* Malden, MA: Polity Press, 2017.

Csikszentmihalyi, Mark, trans. *Readings in Han Chinese Thought.* Indianapolis, IN: Hackett Publishing, 2006.

Graham, Angus C. *Disputers of the Tao.* La Salle, IL: Open Court Press, 1989.

Ivanhoe, Philip J. *Confucian Moral Self Cultivation*, rev. ed. Indianapolis, IN: Hackett Publishing Company, 2000.

———, trans. *Master Sun's Art of War.* Indianapolis, IN: Hackett Publishing, 2011.

Legge, James, trans. *The Chinese Classics. 5 vols.* 1895. (Reprinted many times. Includes translations of the *Analects, Mencius [Mengzi], Great Learning, Doctrine of the Mean, History [The Shoo King], Odes*, and the *Spring and Autumn Annals* with the *Zuozhuan [Zuo's Commentary]*.)

Munro, Donald J. *The Concept of Man in Early China.* Stanford, CA: Stanford University Press, 1969.

Nivison, David S. *The Ways of Confucianism*, ed. Bryan W. Van Norden. Chicago, IL: Open Court Press, 1996.

Pang-White, Ann A., trans. *The Confucian Four Books for Women: A New Translation of the "Nü Sishu" and the Commentary of Wang Xiang.* New York, NY: Oxford University Press, 2018.

Raphals, Lisa. *Sharing the Light: Women and Virtue in Early China.* Albany, NY: SUNY Press, 1999.

Schwartz, Benjamin I. 1985. *The World of Thought in Ancient China.* Cambridge, MA: Harvard/Belknap Press, 1985.

Tiwald, Justin, and Bryan W. Van Norden, eds. *Readings in Later Chinese Philosophy: Han Dynasty to the Twentieth Century.* Indianapolis, IN: Hackett Publishing Company, 2014.

Van Norden, Bryan W. *Introduction to Classical Chinese Philosophy.* Indianapolis, IN: Hackett Publishing Company, 2011.

Wang, Robin R., ed. *Images of Women in Chinese Thought and Culture.* Indianapolis, IN: Hackett Publishing Company, 2003.

READINGS
IN
CLASSICAL
CHINESE
PHILOSOPHY

CHAPTER ONE

KONGZI (CONFUCIUS)

Analects

Introduction

The *Analects* (*Lúnyǔ* 論語—literally, the "Classified Teachings") purports to be a record of the teachings of Kǒngzǐ 孔子 or "Confucius" (551–479 BCE) and his disciples.[1] Kongzi believed that the Golden Age of humankind had been realized during the height of the Zhou dynasty, from ca. 1045 to 771 BCE (the so-called Western Zhou period).[2] Typified by the cultural heroes King Wen (d. ca. 1050 BCE), his son King Wu (r. 1045–1043), and the virtuous regent, the Duke of Zhou (r. ca. 1042–1036 BCE), the early Zhou rulers established and maintained a special relationship with Tiān 天, "Heaven," by properly and sincerely observing a set of sacred practices collectively referred to as the lǐ 禮, "rites" or "rituals." The scope of the rites was quite vast, including everything from grand state ceremonies to the proper way to sit or fasten one's lapel—details that we might think of today as issues of etiquette. In return for such formal obedience to Heaven in all matters great and small, the Zhou royal line was rewarded

---

1. Some scholars have questioned the traditional view of the text as a unified work, arguing that it represents many different chronological strata and even incompatible viewpoints. The Chinese have nevertheless read it as a coherent whole for thousands of years, and this is the perspective on the text that we adopt here. This said, the reader will note that our selection gives greater weight to those portions of the text generally agreed to be earlier and most authoritative, books 1–9.

2. On the uncertainty of dates in the Western Zhou dynasty, see note 6 in the Introduction to this volume. Dates here follow Edward L. Shaughnessy, "Western Zhou History," in *The Cambridge History of Ancient China: From the Origins of Civilization to 221 B.C.*, eds. Michael Loewe and Edward L. Shaughnessy (New York: Cambridge University Press, 1999), 292–351.

with a Mìng 命, "Mandate,"[3] to rule China, manifested in the form of a charismatic Dé 德, "Virtue," or power.[4]

By Kongzi's time, the Zhou kings had been reduced to mere figureheads, and real political power was in the hands of various local rulers. In Kongzi's eyes, the "scholars" of his day—those who should properly have been motivated by a love for learning and a devotion to the culture of the Zhou—were interested only in self-aggrandizement and sensuous pleasures, and the people, who were thereby bereft of moral leadership and had grown unruly, could only be controlled through strict laws and harsh punishments. But despite the bleakness of this world, Kongzi believed that there was still hope for humanity, because the traditional Zhou ritual forms and written classics—which had been carefully preserved by a small group of cultural specialists, the Rú 儒, "Erudites" or "Confucians"[5]—could serve as a sort of blueprint for rebuilding the lost Golden Age. Kongzi thus dedicated his life to both transmitting these cultural forms to his contemporaries and striving to embody them in his own person, hoping in this way to lead his fallen world back to the Dào 道, "Way," of Heaven.

Kongzi's Way, which involves lifelong and sincere devotion to traditional cultural forms, eventually culminates in a kind of intuitive mastery of those forms, and one who has attained this state of consummate mastery—the jūnzǐ 君子, "gentleman"—is said to possess the supreme virtue of Rén 仁, "Goodness." Originally referring to the strong and handsome appearance of a noble warrior, *Ren* designates for Kongzi the quality of the perfectly realized person—one who has so completely mastered the Way that it has become a sort of second nature.[6] Such a state of spiritual perfection is referred to as wúwéi 無為, "effortless action" or "nonaction":

---

3. By the time of the *Analects,* the term *ming* had taken on the additional meaning of "fate" or "destiny," but was thought to be similarly decreed by Heaven. For a discussion of this term, see Edward Slingerland, "The Conception of *Ming* in Early Chinese Thought," *Philosophy East & West* 46, no. 4 (1996): 567–81.

4. On the Confucian understanding of "Virtue" (Dé 德) see David S. Nivison, "The Paradox of 'Virtue,'" in *The Ways of Confucianism: Investigations in Chinese Philosophy,* ed. Bryan W. Van Norden (Chicago, IL: Open Court Press, 1996), 31–43.

5. For *ru,* see *Important Terms* in the appendices and *Analects* 6.13 for Kongzi's criticism of the "petty *Ru.*"

6. Part of Goodness is caring for or love of others (*Analects* 12.22). Later philosophers emphasized this aspect of Goodness, so in later chapters the same character is translated "benevolence." See also *Ren* under *Important Terms* in the appendices.

a state of spontaneous harmony between individual inclinations and the sacred Way of Heaven.[7] Through the power of Virtue accruing to one so perfectly in harmony with Heaven, this state of individual perfection will lead to the spontaneous and effortless ordering of the entire world. There will be no need for raising armies, instituting laws, or issuing governmental decrees, for the entire world will be as inexorably drawn to a ruler with true Virtue as the heavenly bodies are bound to their proper circuits in the sky (cf. *Analects* 2.1).

Book One

1.1 The Master said, "To learn, and then have occasion to practice what you have learned—is this not satisfying? To have friends arrive from afar—is this not a joy? To be patient even when others do not understand—is this not the mark of the gentleman?"

1.2 Master You[8] said, "A young person who is filial and respectful of his elders rarely becomes the kind of person who is inclined to defy his superiors, and there has never been a case of one who is disinclined to defy his superiors stirring up rebellion.

"The gentleman applies himself to the roots. 'Once the roots are firmly established, the Way will grow.' Might we not say that filial piety and respect for elders constitute the roots of Goodness?"

1.3 The Master said, "A clever tongue and fine appearance are rarely signs of Goodness."[9]

---

7. Although the term "nonaction" is often associated with Daoism, it is found in the *Analects* (15.5) and is arguably an important concept for many early thinkers. See Edward Slingerland, *Effortless Action: Wu-wei as Conceptual Metaphor and Spiritual Ideal in Early China* (New York: Oxford University Press, 2003).

8. A disciple of Kongzi.

9. Cf. 15.11 and 16.4 below. A suspicion of those who are overly glib or outwardly pleasing is a common theme in the *Analects*, which is very much concerned with distinguishing genuine virtue from "counterfeit virtue"—that is, the outward appearance of virtue without the inner substance.

1.4 Master Zeng[10] said, "Every day I examine myself on three counts: in my dealings with others, have I in any way failed to be dutiful? In my interactions with friends and associates, have I in any way failed to be trustworthy? Finally, have I in any way failed to put into practice what I teach?"

1.6 The Master said, "A young person should be filial when at home and respectful of his elders when in public. Conscientious and trustworthy, he should display a general care for the masses but feel a particular affection for those who are Good. If he has any strength left over after manifesting these virtues in practice, let him then devote it to learning the cultural arts."

1.9 Master Zeng said, "Take great care in seeing off the deceased and sedulously maintain the sacrifices to your distant ancestors, and the common people will sincerely return to Virtue."

1.10 Ziqin asked Zigong,[11] "When our Master arrives in a state, he invariably finds out about its government. Does he actively seek out this information? Surely it is not simply offered to him!"

Zigong answered, "Our Master obtains it through being courteous, refined, respectful, restrained, and deferential. The Master's way of seeking it is entirely different from other people's way of seeking it, is it not?"[12]

1.11 The Master said, "When someone's father is still alive, observe his intentions; after his father has passed away, observe his conduct. If for three years he does not alter the ways of his father, he may be called a filial son."

1.12 Master You said, "When it comes to the practice of ritual, it is harmonious ease that is to be valued. It is precisely such harmony that makes the Way of the Former Kings so beautiful. If you merely stick rigidly to ritual in all matters, great and small, there will remain that which you cannot accomplish. Yet if you know enough to value harmonious ease but try to attain it without being regulated by the rites, this will not work either."

---

10. A disciple of Kongzi.

11. Both disciples of Kongzi.

12. That is, Kongzi does not actively pry or seek out information but rather is so perfected in Virtue that what he seeks comes to him unbidden.

1.15 Zigong said, "Poor without being obsequious, rich without being arrogant—what would you say about someone like that?"

The Master answered, "That is acceptable, but it is still not as good as being poor and yet joyful, rich and yet loving ritual."

Zigong said, "An ode says,

'As if cut, as if polished;
As if carved, as if ground.'

"Is this not what you have in mind?"[13]

The Master said, "Zigong, you are precisely the kind of person with whom one can begin to discuss the *Odes*. Informed as to what has gone before, you know what is to come."

Book Two

2.1 The Master said, "One who rules through the power of Virtue is analogous to the Pole Star: it simply remains in its place and receives the homage of the myriad lesser stars."[14]

2.2 The Master said, "The *Odes* number several hundred, and yet can be judged with a single phrase: 'Oh, they will not lead you astray.'"[15]

2.3 The Master said, "If you try to guide the common people with coercive regulations and keep them in line with punishments, the common people will become evasive and will have no sense of shame. If, however, you guide them with Virtue, and keep them in line by means of ritual, the people will have a sense of shame and will rectify themselves."

---

13. *Odes* (Mao # 55) (see *Odes* under *Important Texts* in the appendices). Zigong's point is that this ode seems to describe metaphorically a person who has been shaped and perfected by a long, arduous process of self-cultivation.

14. On the Confucian understanding of "Virtue" (Dé 德) see David S. Nivison, "The Paradox of 'Virtue,'" in *The Ways of Confucianism: Investigations in Chinese Philosophy,* ed. Bryan W. Van Norden (Chicago, IL: Open Court Press, 1996), 31–43. See also the online Title Support Page for this volume at www.hackettpublishing .com/rccp-support for an image of the apparent motion of the fixed stars around the Pole Star.

15. *Odes* (Mao # 297). The original reference is to powerful war horses bred to pull chariots, who are trained not to swerve from the desired path. The metaphorical meaning is that one committed through study to the *Odes*—"yoked" to them, as it were—will not be led astray.

2.4 The Master said, "At fifteen I set my mind upon learning; at thirty I took my place in society;[16] at forty I became free of doubts;[17] at fifty I understood Heaven's Mandate;[18] at sixty my ear was attuned; and at seventy I could follow my heart's desires without overstepping the bounds of propriety."

2.7 Ziyou[19] asked about filial piety. The Master said, "Nowadays 'filial' means simply being able to provide one's parents with nourishment. But even dogs and horses are provided with nourishment. If you are not respectful, wherein lies the difference?"

2.8 Zixia[20] asked about filial piety. The Master said, "It is the demeanor that is difficult. If there is work to be done, young people shoulder the burden, and when wine and food are served, elders are given precedence, but surely filial piety consists of more than this."

2.9 The Master said, "I can talk all day long with Yan Hui[21] without him once disagreeing with me. In this way, he seems a bit stupid. And yet when we retire and I observe his private behavior, I see that it is in fact worthy to serve as an illustration of what I have taught. Hui is not stupid at all."

2.10 The Master said, "Look at the means a man employs, observe the basis from which he acts, and discover where it is that he feels at ease.[22] Where can he hide? Where can he hide?"

2.11 The Master said, "Both keeping past teachings alive and understanding the present—someone able to do this is worthy of being a teacher."

2.12 The Master said, "The gentleman is not a vessel."[23]

---

16. That is, through mastery of the rites; cf. *Analects* 8.8, 16.13, and 20.3.

17. Cf. *Analects* 9.29.

18. Cf. *Analects* 16.8, 20.3.

19. A disciple of Kongzi.

20. A disciple of Kongzi.

21. Kongzi's favorite disciple, who died, tragically, at an early age (cf. *Analects* 5.9, 6.3, 6.7, 6.11, and 11.9).

22. Cf. *Analects* 4.2.

23. Qì 器, literally a ritual vessel designed to serve a particular function, is also used by extension to refer to officials who are specialized in one particular task. The gentleman is not a narrow specialist (cf. *Analects* 5.4, 6.13, 9.2, 9.6, 13.4, and 19.7).

2.15 The Master said, "If you learn without thinking about what you have learned, you will be lost. If you think without learning, however, you will fall into danger."

2.17 The Master said, "Zilu,[24] remark well what I am about to teach you! This is wisdom: to recognize what you know as what you know, and recognize what you do not know as what you do not know."

2.19 Duke Ai asked, "What can I do to induce the common people to be obedient?"

Kongzi replied, "Raise up the straight and apply them to the crooked, and the people will submit to you. If you raise up the crooked and apply them to the straight, the people will never submit."

2.21 Some people said of Kongzi, "Why is it that he is not participating in government?"[25]

[Upon being informed of this,] the Master remarked, "The *History* says,

'Filial, oh so filial,
Friendly to one's elders and juniors;
[In this way] exerting an influence upon those who govern.'[26]

Thus, in being a filial son and good brother one is already taking part in government. What need is there, then, to speak of 'participating in government'?"

Book Three

3.1 Kongzi said of the Ji Family, "They have eight rows of dancers performing in their courtyard. If they can condone this, what are they *not* capable of?"[27]

3.3 The Master said, "A man who is not Good—what has he to do with ritual? A man who is not Good—what has he to do with music?"[28]

---

24. A disciple of Kongzi.

25. Lit., "doing government" (wéizhèng 為政). The reference is to Kongzi's lack of an official position.

26. See James Legge, trans., *The Shoo King*, vol. 3 of *The Chinese Classics* (Oxford: Clarendon Press, 1871; Taipei: SMC Publishing 1991), 535.

27. The Ji Family had usurped power from the rightful authorities in Kongzi's home state of Lǔ 魯 and was for Kongzi representative of the ritual, moral, and political improprieties of his age. Later ritual texts describe the "eight rows of dancers" as a ritual prerogative of the emperor; presumably in Kongzi's time it was viewed as the prerogative of the Zhou kings. In either case, the Ji Family's use of eight rows of dancers is obviously an egregious violation of ritual propriety.

28. Cf. *Analects* 3.12 and 17.11. *Analects* 3.3 is probably also directed at the head of the Ji Family criticized in 3.1.

3.4 Lin Fang[29] asked about the roots of ritual.

The Master exclaimed, "What a noble question! When it comes to ritual, it is better to be spare than extravagant. When it comes to mourning, it is better to be excessively sorrowful than fastidious."

3.8 Zixia asked, "[The *Odes* say,]

> 'Her artful smile, with its alluring dimples,
> Her beautiful eyes, so clear,
> The unadorned upon which to paint.'[30]

"What does this mean?"

The Master said, "The application of colors comes only after a suitable unadorned background is present."

Zixia said, "So it is the rites that come after?"[31]

The Master said, "It is you, Zixia, who has awakened me to the meaning of these lines! It is only with someone like you that I can begin to discuss the *Odes*."

3.11 Someone asked for an explanation of the *di* sacrifice.[32] The Master said, "I do not understand it. One who understood it could handle the world as if he had it right here," and he pointed to the palm of his hand.

3.12 "Sacrifice as if [they were] present" means that, when sacrificing to the spirits, you should comport yourself as if the spirits were present.

The Master said, "If I am not fully present at the sacrifice, it is as if I did not sacrifice at all."[33]

---

29. Lin Fang is usually identified as a man of Lu and presumably shares Kongzi's concern that his fellow countrymen were neglecting the "roots" and attending to the superficial "branches" of ritual practice.

30. The first two lines appear in the present version of the *Odes* (*Mao* # 57), while the third does not.

31. That is, the adornment provided by the rites is meant to build upon appropriate native emotions or tendencies. Just as all the cosmetics in the world are of no avail if the basic lines of the face are not pleasing, so too is the refinement provided by ritual practice of no help to one lacking in zhì 質, "native substance." Cf. *Analects* 3.4, 5.10, and 6.18.

32. An important sacrifice to the earliest known ancestor of the reigning dynasty, the performance of which was the prerogative of the presiding ruler. By Kongzi's time, the performance of this rite had degenerated to the point that he could no longer bear to look upon it.

33. Although some commentators take "not fully present" in the literal sense (i.e., not being physically present at the sacrifice, and sending a proxy in one's stead), the preceding comment would suggest that what is at issue is psychological or spiritual presence.

3.14 The Master said, "The Zhou gazes down upon the two dynasties that preceded it.[34] How brilliant in culture it is! I follow the Zhou."

3.17 Zigong wanted to do away with the practice of sacrificing a lamb to announce the beginning of the month.[35]

The Master said, "Zigong! You regret the loss of the lamb, whereas I regret the loss of the rite."

3.18 The Master said, "If in serving your lord you are careful to observe every detail of ritual propriety, people will [wrongly] think you obsequious."[36]

3.19 Duke Ding asked, "How should a lord employ his ministers? How should a minister serve his lord?"

Kongzi replied, "A lord should employ his ministers with ritual, and ministers should serve their lord with dutifulness."

3.20 That Master said, "The 'Cry of the Ospreys'[37] expresses joy without becoming licentious, and expresses sorrow without falling into excessive pathos."

3.23 The Master was discussing music with the Grand Music Master of Lu. He said, "What can be known about music is this: when it first begins, it resounds with a confusing variety of notes, but as it unfolds, these notes are reconciled by means of harmony, brought into tension by means of counterpoint, and finally woven together into a seamless whole. It is in this way that music reaches its perfection."[38]

3.24 A border official from the town of Yi requested an audience with the Master, saying, "I have never failed to obtain an audience with the gentlemen who have passed this way." Kongzi's followers thereupon presented him.

---

34. That is, the Xia and Shang dynasties.

35. Apparently, this sacrifice had originally been part of a larger ritual to welcome the new moon. By Kongzi's time the ritual itself had fallen into disuse in Lu, whereas the sacrifice—being the responsibility of a particular government office—had survived. Zigong does not see the point of continuing this vestigial, materially wasteful practice in the absence of its original ritual context.

36. Ritual practice had so degenerated by Kongzi's age that a proper ritual practitioner was viewed with suspicion or disdain.

37. The first of the *Odes,* and sometimes used to refer to the *Odes* as a whole.

38. Music thus serves as a model or metaphor for the process of self-cultivation: starting in confusion, passing through many phases, and culminating in a state of perfection.

After emerging from the audience, the border official remarked, "You disciples, why should you be concerned about your Master's loss of office? The world has been without the Way for a long time now, and Heaven intends to use your Master like the wooden clapper for a bell."[39]

Book Four

4.1 The Master said, "To live in the neighborhood of the Good is fine. If one does not choose to dwell among those who are Good, how will one obtain wisdom?"[40]

4.2 The Master said, "Without Goodness, one cannot remain constant in adversity and cannot enjoy enduring happiness.

"Those who are Good feel at home in Goodness, whereas those who are wise follow Goodness because they feel that they will profit from it."

4.3 The Master said, "Only one who is Good is able to truly love others or despise others."

4.4 The Master said, "Merely set your heart sincerely upon Goodness and you will be free of bad intentions."

4.5 The Master said, "Wealth and social eminence are things that all people desire, and yet unless they are acquired in the proper Way I will not abide them. Poverty and disgrace are things that all people hate, and yet unless they are avoided in the proper Way I will not despise them.

"If the gentleman abandons Goodness, how can he merit the name? The gentleman does not go against Goodness even for the amount of time required to finish a meal. Even in times of urgency or distress, he necessarily accords with it."

4.6 The Master said, "I have yet to meet a person who truly loved Goodness or hated a lack of Goodness. One who truly loved Goodness could not be surpassed, while one who truly hated a lack of Goodness would at least be able to act in a

---

39. That is, to wake up the fallen world. Some commentators believe that the bell referred to is the kind used by itinerant collectors and transmitters of folk songs, and that the border official's point is thus that Heaven has deliberately caused Kongzi to lose his official position so that he might wander throughout the realm, spreading the teachings of the Way.

40. Other translators would give the sense as, "With regard to neighborhoods, it is the presence of those who are Good that makes them desirable. How could someone who does not choose to dwell in Goodness be considered wise?"

Good fashion, insofar as he would not tolerate that which is not Good being associated with his person.

"Is there a person who can, for the space of a single day, simply devote his efforts to Goodness? I have never met anyone whose strength was insufficient for this task. Perhaps such a person exists, but I have yet to meet him."

4.7 The Master said, "People are true to type with regard to what sort of mistakes they make. Observe closely the sort of mistakes a person makes—then you will know his character."

4.8 The Master said, "Having in the morning heard the Way [was being put into practice], one could die that evening without regret."

4.9 The Master said, "A scholar who has set his heart upon the Way but who is still ashamed of having shabby clothing or meager rations is not worth engaging in discussion."

4.10 The Master said, "With regard to the world, the gentleman has no predispositions for or against [any person]. He merely seeks to be on the side of [those he considers] right."

4.12 The Master said, "If in your affairs you abandon yourself to the pursuit of profit, you will arouse much resentment."

4.13 The Master said, "If a person is able to govern the state by means of ritual propriety and deference, what difficulties will he encounter? If, on the other hand, a person is not able to govern the state through ritual propriety and deference, of what use are the rites to him?"

4.14 The Master said, "Do not be concerned that you lack an official position, but rather concern yourself with the means by which you might become established. Do not be concerned that no one has heard of you, but rather strive to become a person worthy of being known."

4.15 The Master said, "Zeng! All that I teach can be strung together on a single thread."[41]

"Yes, sir," Master Zeng responded.

---

41. The word rendered here as "teach" (Dào 道) also means "the Way," and a double entendre is almost certainly intended: "all that I teach" is also "my Way."

After the Master left, the disciples asked, "What did he mean by that?"

Master Zeng said, "All that the Master teaches amounts to nothing more than dutifulness [zhōng 忠] tempered by sympathetic understanding [shù 恕]."[42]

4.16 The Master said, "The gentleman understands rightness, whereas the petty person understands profit."

4.17 The Master said, "When you see someone who is worthy, concentrate upon becoming their equal; when you see someone who is unworthy, use this as an opportunity to look within yourself."

4.18 The Master said, "In serving your parents you may gently remonstrate with them. However, once it becomes apparent that they have not taken your criticism to heart you should be respectful and not oppose them, and follow their lead diligently without resentment."

4.19 The Master said, "While your parents are alive, you should not travel far, and when you do travel you must keep to a fixed itinerary."

4.20 The Master said, "One who makes no changes to the Ways of his father for three years[43] after his father has passed away may be called a filial son."

4.21 The Master said, "You must always be aware of the age of your parents. On the one hand, it is a cause for rejoicing, on the other a source of anxiety."

4.22 The Master said, "People in ancient times were not eager to speak, because they would be ashamed if their actions did not measure up to their words."

4.23 The Master said, "Very few go astray who comport themselves with restraint."

---

42. To be *zhong,* "loyal" or "dutiful," involves fulfilling the duties and obligations proper to one's ritually defined role (see *Analects* 5.19 below for a description of someone deemed *zhong* by Kongzi). This virtue is to be tempered by the virtue of *shu,* "sympathetic understanding": the ability, by means of imaginatively putting oneself in the place of another, to know when it is appropriate or yì 義, "right," to bend or suspend the dictates of role-specific duty. (This interpretation is developed in Philip J. Ivanhoe, "The 'Golden Rule' in the *Analects,*" in *Confucius Now: Contemporary Encounters with Confucius,* ed. David Jones [Open Court Press, 2008], 81–107.) Cf. *Analects* 5.12, 6.30, 12.2, 15.3, and 15.24; *Mean* 13 (in chapter 11 of this volume).

43. The length of the mourning period for parents, equivalent to twenty-five months by Western reckoning. Cf. *Analects* 17.21 and note 157 to that passage.

4.24 The Master said, "The gentleman wishes to be slow to speak, but quick to act."

4.25 The Master said, "Virtue is never solitary; it always has neighbors."[44]

Book Five

5.1 The Master said of Gongye Chang, "He is marriageable. Although he was once imprisoned as a criminal, he was in fact innocent of any crime." The Master gave him his daughter in marriage.[45]

5.4 Zigong asked, "What do you think of me?"
    The Master replied, "You are a vessel."
    "What sort of vessel?"
    "A precious ritual vessel."[46]

5.8 Meng Wubo[47] asked, "Is Zilu Good?"
    The Master replied, "I do not know."
    Meng Wubo repeated his question.
    The Master said, "In a state of one thousand chariots, Zilu could be employed to organize the collection of military taxes, but I do not know whether or not he is Good."
    "What about Ran Qiu?"
    "In a town of one thousand households, or an aristocratic family of one hundred chariots, Ran Qiu could be employed as a steward, but I do not know whether or not he is Good."
    "What about Zihua?"
    "Standing in his proper place at court with his sash tied, Zihua could be employed to converse with guests and visitors, but I do not know whether or not he is Good."

---

44. The reference is to the attractive power of Virtue.

45. The social stigma attached to former criminals in early China was enormous and inescapable, since criminals were prominently branded or tattooed. In giving his daughter in marriage to a former criminal, Kongzi is flouting conventional mores and making a powerful statement concerning the independence of true morality from conventional social judgments.

46. Cf. *Analects* 2.12 and see the note to that passage.

47. The son of a minister of Lu, who also appears in *Analects* 2.6 (not in this volume). The three figures he asks about—Zilu, Ran Qiu, and Zihua—are all disciples of Kongzi.

5.9 The Master said to Zigong, "Who is better, you or Yan Hui?"

Zigong answered, "How dare I even think of comparing myself to Hui? Hui learns one thing and thereby understands ten. I learn one thing and thereby understand two."

The Master said, "No, you are not as good as Hui. Neither of us is as good as Hui."

5.10 Zai Wo was sleeping during the daytime. The Master said, "Rotten wood cannot be carved, and a wall of dung cannot be plastered. As for Zai Wo, what would be the use of reprimanding him?"[48]

The Master added, "At first, when evaluating people, I would listen to their words and then simply trust that the corresponding conduct would follow. Now, when I evaluate people, I listen to their words but then closely observe their conduct. It is my experience with Zai Wo that has brought about this change."

5.12 Zigong said, "What I do not wish others to do unto me, I also wish not to do unto others."

The Master said, "Ah, Zigong! That is something quite beyond you."[49]

5.13 Zigong said, "The Master's cultural brilliance is something that is readily heard about, whereas one does not get to hear the Master expounding upon the subjects of human nature or the Way of Heaven."[50]

---

48. That is, Zai Wo, a disciple of Kongzi, obviously lacks the zhì 質, "native substance" (see *Analects* 6.18), that serves as the background upon which the "color" of Confucian self-cultivation is to be applied (see *Analects* 3.8).

49. Zigong's aspiration—what has been referred to as the "negative Golden Rule"—is a formulation of the virtue of *shu*, "sympathetic understanding": the ability to temper the strict dictates of loyalty to one's *zhong*, "duty," by imaginatively placing oneself in another's place. (See *Analects* 4.15 on these concepts.) Zigong's aspiration to the virtue of *shu* is particularly amusing to Kongzi because Zigong is the most unimaginative and rigid of all the disciples. In *Analects* 5.4, for instance, his fastidious adherence to the rites leads Kongzi to dub him a "ritual vessel" of limited capacity, and in *Analects* 14.29 he is criticized by Kongzi for being too strict and judgmental with others (i.e., for not moderating his duty-defined demands upon others with understanding). Zigong thus functions in the *Analects* as an excellent example of how the virtue of loyalty goes awry when not tempered with sympathetic understanding, and this is perhaps why Kongzi singles out Zigong in *Analects* 15.24 for his message that "sympathetic understanding" is the one teaching that can serve as a lifelong guide.

50. That is, in his teachings Kongzi did not concern himself much with such theoretical, esoteric subjects as human nature or the Way of Heaven, but rather tried to focus his disciples' attention upon the task at hand, acquiring the cultural refinement necessary to become gentlemen. For a discussion of other interpretations of this passage and how it relates to *Analects* 17.2 (later in this chapter), see Philip J. Ivanhoe, "Whose Confucius? Which *Analects*?" in *Confucius and the "Analects": New Essays*, ed. Bryan W. Van Norden (New York: Oxford University Press, 2002), 119–33.

5.19 Zizhang[51] said, "Prime Minister Ziwen[52] was given three times the post of prime minister, and yet he never showed a sign of pleasure; he was removed from this office three times and yet never showed a sign of resentment. When the incoming prime minister took over, he invariably provided him with a complete account of the official state of affairs. What do you make of Prime Minister Ziwen?"

The Master said, "He certainly was dutiful."

"Was he not Good?"

"I do not know about that—what makes you think he deserves to be called Good?"

"When Cuizi assassinated the Lord of Qi, Chen Wenzi—whose estate amounted to ten teams of horses—abandoned all that he possessed and left the state.[53] Upon reaching another state, he said, 'The officials here are as bad as our Great Officer Cuizi,' and thereupon left that state. Again, after going to another state, he said, 'The officials here are as bad as our Great Officer Cuizi,' and thereupon left that state as well. What do you make of Chen Wenzi?"

The Master said, "He certainly was pure."

"Was he not Good?"

"I do not know about that—what makes you think he deserves to be called Good?"

5.22 When the Master was in the state of Chen, he sighed, "Oh, let us go home! Let us go home! Our young followers back in Lu are wild and ambitious—they put on a great show of brilliant culture, but they lack the means to prune and shape it."[54]

5.26 Yan Hui and Zilu were in attendance. The Master said to them, "Why do you not each speak to me of your aspirations?"

Zilu answered, "I would like to be able to share my carts and horses, clothing and fur with my friends and associates, without feeling regret."

Yan Hui answered, "I would like to avoid being boastful about my own abilities or exaggerating my accomplishments."

Zilu then said, "I would like to hear of the Master's aspirations."

The Master said, "To bring comfort to the aged, to inspire trust in my friends, and be cherished by the youth."[55]

---

51. A disciple of Kongzi.

52. A prime minister of the state of Chu who was renowned for his integrity and devotion to the state.

53. Cuizi and Chen Wenzi were both officials in the state of Qi. The former is said to have assassinated Lord Zhuang of Qi in 548 BCE.

54. Cf. *Mengzi* 7B37 (in chapter 4 of this volume).

55. Cf. the more elaborate version of a similar conversation in *Analects* 11.26.

5.27 The Master said, "I should just give up! I have yet to meet someone who is able to perceive his own faults and then take himself to task inwardly."

5.28 The Master said, "In any village of ten households there are surely those who are as dutiful or trustworthy as I am, but there is no one who matches my love for learning."

Book Six

6.3 Duke Ai[56] asked, "Who among your disciples might be said to love learning?"

Kongzi answered, "There was one named Yan Hui who loved learning. He never misdirected his anger, and never made the same mistake twice. Unfortunately, his allotted lifespan was short, and he has passed away. Now that he is gone, there are none who really love learning—at least, I have yet to hear of one."

6.5 When Yuan Si was serving as steward, he was offered a salary of nine hundred measures of millet, but he declined it.

The Master said, "Do not decline it! [If you do not need it yourself], could you not use it to aid the households in your neighborhood?"[57]

6.7 The Master said, "Ah, Yan Hui! For three months at a time his heart did not stray from Goodness. The rest could only sporadically maintain such a state."

6.10 Boniu[58] fell ill, and the Master went to ask after his health. Grasping his hand through the window, the Master sighed, "That we are going to lose him must be due to fate! How else could such a man be afflicted with such an illness, and we left with nothing we can do?[59] How else could such a man be afflicted with such an illness?"

---

56. Duke Ai (r. 494–468 BCE) was the nominal ruler of Lu, which was in fact controlled by the Ji Family.

57. In light of the many injunctions against seeking office for the sake of material benefit that are found in Kongzi's teachings, the disciple Yuan Si no doubt expected to be praised by the Master for declining to be paid a salary. Kongzi's response reflects the fact that the proper course of action cannot be determined by a simple formula but should rather be the result of careful reflection and consideration of the needs of others. The Master may also have detected a note of spiritual pride in Yuan Si's grandiose gesture and seen the need to deflate his feeling of self-importance.

58. A disciple of Kongzi.

59. The latter half of the sentence is not present in the received text of the *Analects* but is present in the Dingzhou version, and it is also part of the *Records of the Historian* version of this story.

6.11 The Master said, "What a worthy man was Yan Hui! Living in a narrow alley, subsisting upon a basket of grain and gourd full of water—other people could not have borne such hardship, yet it never spoiled Hui's joy. What a worthy man was Hui!"

6.12 Ran Qiu said, "It is not that I do not delight in your Way, Master, it is simply that my strength is insufficient."

The Master said, "Someone whose strength is genuinely insufficient collapses somewhere along the Way. As for you, you deliberately draw the line."[60]

6.13 The Master said to Zixia, "Be a gentlemanly *Ru*. Do not be a petty *Ru*."[61]

6.17 The Master said, "Who is able to leave a room without going out through the door? How is it, then, that no one follows this Way?"

6.18 The Master said, "When native substance overwhelms cultural refinement, the result is a crude rustic. When cultural refinement overwhelms native substance, the result is a foppish pedant. Only when culture and native substance are perfectly mixed and balanced do you have a gentleman."

6.20 The Master said, "One who knows it is not the equal of one who loves it, and one who loves it is not the equal of one who takes joy in it."[62]

6.21 The Master said, "You can discuss the loftiest matters with those who are above average, but not with those who are below average."

6.22 Fan Chi[63] asked about wisdom.

The Master said, "Working to ensure social harmony among the common people, respecting the ghosts and spirits while keeping them at a distance—this might be called wisdom."

He then asked about Goodness.

---

60. That is, Ran Qiu has already decided he cannot do it, and so he does not even try.

61. For the general term Rú 儒, see the introduction to this chapter, as well as *Ru* under *Important Terms* in the appendices. The phrase "petty *Ru*" refers to someone content to serve as a narrow technician or "vessel" (*Analects* 2.12) or to a moral hypocrite such as the "village worthy" (*Analects* 17.13).

62. "It" is presumably the Way.

63. One of Kongzi's younger disciples.

The Master said, "One who is Good sees as his first priority the hardship of self-cultivation, and only after thinks about results or rewards. Yes, this is what we might call Goodness."

6.23 The Master said, "The wise take joy in rivers, while the Good take joy in mountains. The wise are active, while the Good are still. The wise are joyful, while the Good are long-lived."[64]

6.25 The Master said, "A *gu* that is not a proper *gu*—is it really a *gu*? Is it really a *gu*?"[65]

6.27 The Master said, "Someone who is broadly learned with regard to culture, and whose conduct is restrained by the rites, can be counted upon to not go astray."

6.28 The Master had an audience with Nanzi, and Zilu was not pleased.[66] The Master swore an oath, saying, "If I have done anything wrong, may Heaven punish me! May Heaven punish me!"

6.29 The Master said, "Acquiring Virtue by applying the mean—is this not best? And yet among the common people few are able to practice this for long."

---

64. This is a famously cryptic passage. Perhaps the most plausible interpretation is provided by the Han dynasty commentator Bāo Xián 包咸: "The wise take joy in actively exercising their talent and wisdom in governing the world, just as water flows on and on and knows no cease. The Good take joy in the sort of peace and stability displayed by mountains, which are naturally inactive and yet give birth to all of the myriad things." Cf. *Analects* 9.17.

65. A gū 觚 was a ritual drinking vessel, and commentators generally agree that Kongzi's sigh of displeasure was provoked by the fact that the sort of *gu* being used by his contemporaries was not a proper *gu* (i.e., not in accordance with Zhou dynasty standards), although there is disagreement over the question of what precisely was wrong—some claiming that the offending *gu* was not of the proper shape, others that it was not of the proper size. In any case, this passage serves to illustrate Kongzi's strict adherence to ancient practices, his dissatisfaction with the practices of his contemporaries, and his concern for the proper use of names (cf. *Analects* 13.3). For an image of a *gu*, see the Title Support Page for this volume at www.hackettpublishing .com/rccp-support.

66. Nanzi was the wife of Lord Ling of Wei, and a woman of ill repute. Zilu was not pleased that Kongzi would seek an audience with such a person. As many commentators point out, however, it is likely that ritual dictated that when arriving in a state one request an audience with certain minor local officials. In having an audience with Nanzi upon arriving in Wei, Kongzi was therefore merely observing the dictates of ritual propriety, which is more important than avoiding unsavory company. Zilu might thus—like Chen Wenzi in *Analects* 5.19 above—be characterized as "pure," but such rigid fastidiousness falls rather short of Goodness.

6.30 Zigong said, "If there were one able to bestow much upon the common people and bring succor to the multitudes, what would you make of him? Could such a person be called Good?"

The Master said, "Why stop at Good? Such a person should surely be called a sage! Even someone like Yao or Shun would find such a task daunting. Desiring to take his stand, one who is Good helps others to take their stand; wanting to realize himself, he helps others to realize themselves. Being able to take what is near at hand as an analogy[67] could perhaps be called the method of Goodness."

Book Seven

7.1 The Master said, "I transmit rather than innovate. I trust in and love the ancient ways. I might thus humbly compare myself to Old Peng."[68]

7.2 The Master said, "Remaining silent and yet comprehending, learning and yet never becoming tired, encouraging others and never growing weary—these are tasks that present me with no difficulty."

7.3 The Master said, "That I fail to cultivate Virtue, that I fail to inquire more deeply into that which I have learned, that upon hearing what is right I remain unable to move myself to do it, and that I prove unable to reform when I have done something wrong—such potential failings are a source of constant worry to me."

7.4 In his leisure moments, the Master was composed and yet fully at ease.

7.5 The Master said, "How seriously I have declined! It has been so long since I last dreamed of meeting the Duke of Zhou."[69]

7.6 The Master said, "Set your heart upon the Way, rely upon Virtue, lean upon Goodness, and explore widely in your cultivation of the arts."

---

67. This sounds like a formulation of the virtue of *shu*, "sympathetic understanding." (See *Analects* 4.15.)

68. The most plausible explanation of this reference is that of Bao Xian: "Old Peng was a great worthy of the Yin dynasty who was fond of transmitting ancient tales. In comparing himself to Old Peng, Kongzi indicates his reverence for those who merely transmit [and do not innovate]."

69. Ideally, one's immersion in the culture of the Zhou is to be so complete that it penetrates even one's dream life.

7.7 The Master said, "I have never denied instruction to anyone who, of their own accord, offered up as little as a bundle of silk or bit of cured meat."[70]

7.8 The Master said, "I will not open the door for a mind that is not already striving to understand, nor will I provide words to a tongue that is not already struggling to speak. If I hold up one corner of a problem, and the student cannot come back to me with the other three, I will not attempt to instruct him again."

7.9 When the Master dined in the company of one who was in mourning, he never ate his fill.

7.12 The Master said, "If wealth were something worth pursuing, then I would pursue it, even if that meant serving as an officer holding a whip at the entrance to the marketplace. Since it is not worth pursuing, however, I prefer to follow that which I love."

7.14 When the Master was in the state of Qi he heard the Shao music, and for three months after did not even notice the taste of meat. He said, "I never imagined that music could be so sublime."[71]

7.16 The Master said, "Eating plain food and drinking water, having only your bent arm as a pillow—certainly there is joy to be found in this! Wealth and eminence attained improperly concern me no more than the floating clouds."[72]

7.17 The Master said, "If I were granted many more years, and could devote fifty of them to learning, surely I would be able to be free of major faults."

7.18 The Master used the classical pronunciation when reciting the *Odes* and the *History*, and when conducting ritual. In all of these cases, he used the classical pronunciation.[73]

---

70. There is some debate over the exact meaning of this passage, with some (such as the Han commentator Zhèng Xuán 鄭玄) claiming that it refers to the fact that Kongzi would not deny instruction to anyone over fifteen years of age, and others arguing that the term shùxiū 束修 (usually taken to mean "bundle of silk and cured meat" or "bundle of cured meat") actually refers to the *bearing* of the person seeking instruction—that is, an attitude of respect and self-discipline. In either case, the point is that Kongzi does not select students on the basis of their wealth or social standing.

71. The Shao is the court music of the sage-king Shun.

72. "Improperly" is literally in a "not right (yì 義)" fashion.

73. Chinese characters are not directly phonetic in the manner of an alphabet, and the same character can be pronounced differently by speakers of different dialects. In Kongzi's age, people were apparently aware that

7.19 The Duke of She asked Zilu about Kongzi. Zilu had no reply.

[Upon Zilu's return], the Master said, "Why did you not just say: 'He is the type of person who is so passionate that he forgets to eat, whose joy renders him free of worries, and who grows old without noticing the passage of the years'?"

7.20 The Master said, "I am not someone who was born with knowledge. I simply love antiquity, and diligently look there for knowledge."

7.22 The Master said, "When walking with two other people, I will always find a teacher among them. I focus on those who are good and seek to emulate them, and focus on those who are bad in order to be reminded of what needs to be changed in myself."

7.23 The Master said, "It is Heaven itself that has endowed me with Virtue. What have I to fear from the likes of Huan Tui?"[74]

7.24 The Master said, "Do you disciples imagine that I am being secretive? I hide nothing from you. I take no action, I make no move, without sharing it with you. This is the kind of person that I am."

7.28 The Master said, "No doubt there are those who try to innovate without acquiring knowledge, but this is a fault that I do not possess. I listen widely, and then pick out that which is excellent in order to follow it; I see many things, and then remember them. This constitutes a second-best sort of knowledge."

7.30 The Master said, "Is Goodness really so far away? If I simply desire Goodness, I will find that it is already here."

7.32 Whenever the Master was singing in a group and heard something that he liked, he inevitably asked to have it sung again, and only then would harmonize with it.

---

the spoken languages of the various regions of China differed significantly from the "classical pronunciation," which Liu Baonan argues must have been the dialect spoken in the Western Zhou capital. We must assume that knowledge of these pronunciations was kept alive, at least in the state of Lu, through use in formal and ritual contexts. This passage suggests, though, that Kongzi's contemporaries had begun to ignore this tradition and eschew the classical pronunciations in favor of local dialect—a Christian analogy would be the abandonment of Latin in favor of services in the vernacular. This represents a departure from the Way of the Zhou that Kongzi characteristically resists.

74. Huan Tui was a minister in the state of Song who apparently wished to do Kongzi harm; cf. *Analects* 9.5 and 14.36.

7.33 The Master said, "There is no one who is my equal when it comes to cultural refinement, but as for actually becoming a gentleman in practice, this is something that I have not yet been able to achieve."[75]

7.34 The Master said, "How could I dare to lay claim to either sageliness or Goodness? What can be said about me is no more than this: I work at it without growing tired and encourage others without growing weary."

Gong Xihua observed, "This is precisely what we disciples are unable to learn."

7.35 The Master was seriously ill, and Zilu asked permission to offer a prayer.

The Master said, "Is such a thing done?"

Zilu said, "It is. The *Eulogy*[76] reads, 'We pray for you above and below, to the spirits of Heaven and of earth.'"

The Master said, "In that case, I have already been offering up my prayers for some time now."[77]

7.37 The Master said, "The gentleman is self-possessed and relaxed, while the petty man is perpetually full of worry."

7.38 The Master was affable yet firm, awe-inspiring without being severe, simultaneously respectful and relaxed.

Book Eight

8.2 The Master said, "If you are respectful but lack ritual you will become exasperating; if you are careful but lack ritual you will become timid; if you are courageous but lack ritual you will become unruly; and if you are upright but lack ritual you will become inflexible.

"If the gentleman is kind to his relatives, the common people will be inspired toward Goodness; if he does not neglect his old acquaintances, the people will honor their obligations to others."

---

75. This is perhaps merely a polite demurral (cf. *Analects* 7.34), but it serves to emphasize the difficulty of obtaining in practice the proper balance between wén 文, "cultural refinement," and zhì 質, "native substance" (cf. *Analects* 6.18), and is no doubt meant as a warning against falling into "foppish pedantry"—the more insidious and common of the two failings described in *Analects* 6.18 above.

76. The title of a traditional prayer text.

77. That is, through his life's work. Any sort of direct appeal for Heaven's aid or bartering with Heaven is unnecessary.

8.7 Master Zeng said, "A scholar-official must be strong and resolute, for his burden is heavy and his Way [Dào 道] is long. He takes up Goodness as his own personal burden—is it not heavy? His way ends only with death—is it not long?"

8.8 The Master said, "Find inspiration in the *Odes*, take your place through ritual, and achieve perfection with music."

8.9 The Master said, "The common people can be made to follow it, but they cannot be made to understand it."

8.12 The Master said, "It is not easy to find someone who is able to learn for even the space of three years without a thought given to official salary."

8.13 The Master said, "Be sincerely trustworthy and love learning, and hold fast to the good Way until death. Do not enter a state that is endangered, and do not reside in a state that is disordered. If the Way is being realized in the world, then show yourself; if it is not, then go into reclusion. In a state that has the Way, to be poor and of low status is a cause for shame; in a state that is without the Way, to be wealthy and honored is equally a cause for shame."

8.19 The Master said, "How great was Yao as a ruler! So majestic! It is Heaven that is great, and it was Yao who modeled himself upon it. So vast! Among the common people there were none who were able to find words to describe him.[78] How majestic in his accomplishments, and glorious in cultural splendor!"

Book Nine

9.2 A villager from Daxiang[79] remarked sarcastically, "How great is Kongzi! He is so broadly learned, and yet has failed to make a name for himself in any particular endeavor."

When the Master was told of this, he said to his disciples, "What art, then, should I take up? Charioteering? Archery? I think I shall take up charioteering."[80]

---

78. That is, the influence of Yao's Virtue was so subtle and pervasive that the people were transformed naturally, without being aware of what was happening. Cf. *Analects* 17.19, where Heaven is said to rule without the need for words. For the sage-king Yao, see under *Important Figures* in the appendices.

79. The name of a small hamlet.

80. Kongzi's response is equally sarcastic, expressing his contempt for limited or merely technical skills. Cf. *Analects* 2.12, 9.6, and 19.7.

9.3 The Master said, "A ceremonial cap made of linen is prescribed by the rites, but these days people use silk. This is frugal, and I follow the majority. To bow before ascending the stairs is what is prescribed by the rites, but these days people bow after ascending. This is arrogant, and—though it goes against the majority—I continue to bow before ascending."[81]

9.5 The Master was surrounded in Kuang.[82] He said, "Now that King Wén 文 is gone, is not culture [wén 文] now invested here in me? If Heaven intended this culture to perish, it would not have given it to those of us who live after King Wen's death. Since Heaven did not intend that this culture should perish, what can the people of Kuang do to me?"

9.6 The Prime Minister asked Zigong, "Your Master is a sage, is he not? How is it, then, that he is skilled at so many menial tasks?"

Zigong replied, "Surely Heaven not only intends him for sagehood, but also gave him many other talents."

When the Master heard of this, he remarked, "How well the Prime Minister knows me! In my youth I was of humble status, so I became proficient in many menial tasks. Is the gentleman broadly skilled in trivial matters? No, he is not."[83]

9.10 Whenever the Master saw someone who was wearing mourning clothes, was garbed in full official dress, or was blind, he would always rise to his feet, even if the person was his junior. When passing such a person, he would always hasten his step.[84]

9.11 With a great sigh Yan Hui lamented, "The more I look up at it the higher it seems; the more I delve into it, the harder it becomes. Catching a glimpse of it before me, I then find it suddenly at my back.[85]

"The Master is skilled at gradually leading me on, step by step. He broadens me with culture and restrains me with the rites, so that even if I wanted to give up I could not. Having exhausted all of my strength, it seems as if there is still something

---

81. Kongzi is referring to ascending the stairs when approaching a ruler or other superior. To bow after ascending puts one on the same level as one's superior and hence is less respectful.

82. The most common explanation is that the target of the Kuang troops was a certain Yang Hu, who had in the past caused some trouble in the state of Kuang. Kongzi apparently physically resembled Yang Hu and—to add to the confusion—one of Kongzi's disciples was a known associate of Yang Hu's.

83. Cf. *Analects* 2.12, 9.2, and 19.7.

84. As a sign of respect.

85. "It" refers to the Way.

left, looming up ahead of me. Though I desire to follow it, there seems to be no way through."

9.12 The Master was gravely ill, and Zilu instructed his fellow disciples to attend Kongzi as if they were his ministers.[86]

During a remission in his illness, the Master [became aware of what was happening and] rebuked Zilu, saying, "It has been quite some time now, has it not, that you have been carrying out this charade! If I have no ministers and yet you act as if I have, who do you think I am going to fool? Am I going to fool Heaven?[87] Moreover, would I not rather die in the arms of a few of my disciples than in the arms of ministers? Even if I do not merit a grand funeral, it is not as if I would be left to die by the side of the road!"

9.13 Zigong said, "If you possessed a piece of beautiful jade, would you hide it away in a locked box, or would you try to sell it at a good price?"

The Master responded, "Oh, I would sell it! I would sell it! I am just waiting for the right offer."[88]

9.14 The Master expressed a desire to go and live among the Nine Yi Barbarian tribes. Someone asked him, "How could you bear their uncouthness?"

The Master replied, "If a gentleman were to dwell among them, what uncouthness would there be?"[89]

9.17 Standing on the bank of a river, the Master said, "It passes on like this—does it not? Never stopping day or night!"[90]

---

86. That is, following the rites proper to a minister attending to a ruler—which, of course, Kongzi was not.

87. As the Jin dynasty commentator Lǐ Chōng 李充 notes, Kongzi's concern over the ritual abuses of the Ji Family—who were usurping the ritual prerogatives of the Zhou kings in an attempt to impress their contemporaries and curry favor with Heaven (see *Analects* 3.1)—no doubt accounts for some of the harshness in his rebuke of Zilu.

88. The gentleman should surely share his Virtue with the world by taking public office. Kongzi, however, refuses to actively peddle his wares on the market, but rather waits for his Virtue to be recognized by the right ruler.

89. The Yi were a group of "barbarians" (i.e., non-Chinese) who lived along the east coast of what is now present-day China. Kongzi's comment is a testament to the transformative power of the gentleman's Virtue. Cf. *Xunzi* chapter 2 (in chapter 9 of this volume).

90. Many traditional commentators take this passage to be a lament on the passage of time (and perhaps a reflection of Kongzi's sense of personal failure). Others see the river's unremitting and thorough progress toward the sea as a metaphor for the ideal student's progress toward Goodness. Cf. *Mengzi* 4B18 (in chapter 4 of this volume).

9.18 The Master said, "I have yet to meet a man who loves Virtue as much as he loves sex."

9.19 The Master said, "[The task of self-cultivation] might be compared to the task of building up a mountain: if I stop even one basketful of earth short of completion, then I have stopped completely. It might also be compared to the task of leveling ground: even if I have only dumped a single basketful of earth, at least I am moving forward."[91]

9.22 The Master said, "Surely there are some sprouts that fail to flower, just as surely as there are some flowers that fail to bear fruit!"

9.23 The Master said, "We should look upon the younger generation with awe, because how are we to know that those who come after us will not prove our equals? Once, however, a man reaches the age of forty or fifty without having learned anything, we can conclude from this fact alone that he is not worthy of being held in awe."

9.24 The Master said, "When a man is rebuked with exemplary words after having made a mistake, he cannot help but agree with them. However, what is important is that he change himself in order to *accord* with them. When a man is praised with words of respect, he cannot help but be pleased with them. However, what is important is that he actually *live up* to them. A person who finds respectful words pleasing but does not live up to them, or agrees with others' reproaches and yet does not change—there is nothing I can do with one such as this."[92]

9.28 The Master said, "Only after Winter comes do we know that the pine and cypress are the last to fade."

9.29 The Master said, "The wise are not confused, the Good do not worry, and the courageous do not fear."

---

91. A bit of encouragement to balance out Yan Hui's lament in *Analects* 9.11.

92. Nominal assent to the Way is insufficient—one must *love* the Way and strive to embody it in one's person. The problem is what is the teacher to do with a student who intellectually understands or superficially agrees with the Way but cannot summon up the genuine commitment required of the gentleman. Cf. *Analects* 5.10, 6.12, 9.18, and 15.16.

Book Ten[93]

10.2 At court, when speaking with officers of lower rank, he was pleasant and affable; when speaking with officers of upper rank, he was formal and proper. When his lord was present, he combined an attitude of cautious respect with graceful ease.

10.3 When called upon by his lord to receive a guest, his countenance would become alert and serious, and he would hasten his steps. When he saluted those in attendance beside him—extending his clasped hands to the left or right, as their position required—his robes remained perfectly arrayed, both front and back. Hastening forward, he moved smoothly, as though gliding upon wings. Once the guest had left, he would always return to report, "The guest is no longer looking back."

10.10 He would not instruct while eating, nor continue to converse once he had retired to bed.[94]

10.11 Even though a meal was only of coarse grain or vegetable broth, he invariably gave some as a sacrificial offering, and would do so in a grave and respectful manner.

10.12 He would not sit unless his mat was straight.

10.17 One day the stables burned. When the Master returned from court, he asked, "Was anyone hurt?" He did not ask about the horses.[95]

---

93. Based upon their style, lack of explicit subject, and parallels to be found in other early ritual texts such as the *Record of Ritual* or *Book of Etiquette and Ritual,* scholars have concluded that most of the passages in this book were probably culled from a lost ritual text that provided anonymous guidelines and injunctions for the aspiring gentleman. From earliest times, however, this book has been viewed by commentators as an extended description of the ritual behavior of Kongzi in particular, and it was in fact probably intended by the editors of the earliest stratum of the *Analects* (books 1–10) to be understood that way. Seen as an actual description of the Master's behavior rather than a set of impersonal ritual guidelines, book 10 serves as a sort of capstone for the first half of the *Analects*, providing a series of descriptions of the Master effortlessly embodying in his words, behavior, and countenance the lessons imparted throughout the rest of the text. What is being emphasized in this book is the ease and grace with which the Master embodies the spirit of the rites in every aspect of his life—no matter how trivial—and accords with this spirit in adapting to new and necessarily unforeseeable circumstances.

94. That is, he remained thoroughly focused in all of his activities.

95. Considering that horses were quite valuable commodities and stable hands easily replaceable, Kongzi's response is both unexpected and moving.

10.19 When he was sick, and his lord came to visit him, he would lay with his head to the east, draped in his court robes, with his ceremonial sash fastened about him.[96]

10.20 When summoned by his lord, he would set off on foot, without waiting for his horses to be hitched to the carriage.[97]

10.21 Upon entering the Grand Ancestral Temple, he asked questions about everything.

10.23 When receiving a gift from a friend—even something as valuable as a cart or a horse—he did not bow unless it was a gift of sacrificial meat.[98]

10.25 When he saw someone fasting or mourning, he invariably assumed a changed expression, even if they were an intimate acquaintance. When he saw someone wearing a ritual cap or a blind person, he would invariably display a respectful countenance, even if they were of low birth.

When riding past someone dressed in funeral garb, he would bow down and grasp the crossbar of his carriage.[99] He would do so even if the mourner was a lowly peddler.

When presented food with full ritual propriety, he would invariably assume a solemn expression and rise from his seat.

He would also assume a solemn expression upon hearing a sudden clap of thunder or observing a fierce wind.[100]

10.27 Startled by their arrival, a bird arose and circled several times before alighting upon a branch. [The Master] said, "This pheasant upon the mountain bridge—how timely it is! How timely it is!" Zilu saluted the bird, and it cried out three times before flying away.[101]

---

96. Being sick, he could not rise to greet his ruler or properly dress himself in court attire, but it would also be unseemly for him to receive his guest in civilian garb. He thus had himself arranged in bed so that he would be both ritually presentable and facing the door when the ruler entered.

97. A sign of respect and humbleness.

98. A gift of sacrificial meat carries with it a sort of ritual solemnity not possessed by a nonreligious gift, no matter how sumptuous it might be.

99. As a sign of respect.

100. As a sign of respect for Heaven's power.

101. While it is not entirely clear *why* the pheasant is being praised for timeliness (perhaps because it knows when to arise, when to alight, and when to fly off), it would seem that the ideal of timeliness—according perfectly with the demands of the situation at hand—sums up fairly well what is, in one interpretation, the

Book Eleven

11.4 The Master said, "Yan Hui is of no help to me—he is pleased with everything that I say."[102]

11.8 When Yan Hui died, Yan Lu, his father, requested the Master's carriage, so that it could be used for Yan Hui's coffin enclosure.

The Master replied, "Everyone recognizes his own son, whether he is talented or not. When Bo Yu, my own son, passed away, he had a coffin, but no enclosure. I did not go on foot in order to provide him with an enclosure. Having held rank below the ministers, it is not permissible for me to go on foot."

11.9 When Yan Hui passed away, the Master lamented, "Oh! Heaven has bereft me! Heaven has bereft me!"

11.12 Zilu asked about serving ghosts and spirits. The Master said, "You are not yet able to serve people—how could you be able to serve ghosts and spirits?"

"May I inquire about death?"

"You do not yet understand life—how could you possibly understand death?"

11.17 The Master said, "The head of the Ji Family is wealthier than even the Duke of Zhou ever was, and yet Ran Qiu collects taxes on his behalf to further increase his already excessive wealth. Ran Qiu is no disciple of mine. If you disciples were to sound the drums and attack him, I would not disapprove."

11.22 Zilu asked, "Upon learning of something that needs to be done, should one immediately take care of it?"

The Master replied, "As long as one's father and elder brothers are still alive, how could one possibly take care of it immediately?"[103]

[On a later occasion] Ran Qiu asked, "Upon learning of something that needs to be done, should one immediately take care of it?"

The Master replied, "Upon learning of it, you should immediately take care of it."

Zihua inquired, "When Zilu asked you whether or not one should immediately take care of something upon learning of it, you told him one should not, as

---

general theme of book 10: that the Master's actions accorded perfectly with the demands of ritual propriety, no matter what the circumstances.

102. The comment would seem to be meant ironically—cf. *Analects* 2.9.

103. That is, you should continue to defer to their judgment and not take the initiative.

long as one's father and elder brothers were still alive. When Ran Qiu asked the same question, however, you told him that one should immediately take care of it. I am confused, and humbly ask to have this explained to me."

The Master said, "Ran Qiu is overly cautious, and so I wished to urge him on. Zilu, on the other hand, is too impetuous, and so I sought to hold him back."[104]

11.26 Zilu, Zengxi, Ran Qiu, and Zihua were seated in attendance. The Master said to them, "I am older than any of you, but do not feel reluctant to speak your minds on that account. You are all in the habit of complaining, 'No one appreciates me.' Well, if someone were to appreciate you, what would you do?"

Zilu spoke up immediately. "If I were given charge of a state of a thousand chariots—even one hemmed in between powerful states, suffering from armed invasions and afflicted by famine—before three years were up I could infuse its people with courage and a sense of what is right."

The Master smiled at him.

He then turned to Ran Qiu. "You, Ran Qiu!" he said, "What would you do?"

Ran Qiu answered, "If I were given charge of a state sixty or seventy—or even fifty or sixty—square *li* in area, before three years were up, I could see that the people would have all that they needed. As for instructing its people in ritual practice and music, this is a task that would have to await the arrival of a gentleman."

The Master then turned to Zihua. "You, Zihua! What would you do?"

Zihua answered, "I am not saying that I would actually be able to do it, but my wish, at least, would be to learn it. I would like to serve as a minor functionary—properly clad in ceremonial cap and gown—in ceremonies at the ancestral temple, or at diplomatic gatherings."

The Master then turned to Zengxi. "You, Zengxi! What would you do?"

Zengxi stopped strumming his zither, and as the last notes faded away, he set the instrument aside and rose to his feet. "I would choose to do something quite different from any of the other three."

"What harm is there in that?" the Master said. "We are all just talking about our aspirations."

Zengxi then said, "In the third month of Spring, once the Spring garments have been completed, I should like to assemble a company of five or six young men

---

104. This is a paradigmatic example of how the Master's teachings were variously formulated depending upon the individual needs of his students—a Confucian version of the Buddhist practice of *upāya*, or "skillful means." On the distinctive characters of Ran Qiu and Zilu, compare *Analects* 6.12 and 9.12, respectively.

and six or seven boys to go bathe in the Yi River and enjoy the breeze upon the Rain Dance Altar, and then return singing to the Master's house."[105]

The Master sighed deeply, saying, "I am with Zengxi!"

The other three disciples left, but Master Zeng stayed behind. He asked, "What did you think of what the other disciples said?"

"Each of them was simply talking about their aspirations."

"Then why, Master, did you smile at Zilu?"

"One governs a state by means of ritual. His words failed to express the proper sense of deference, and that is why I smiled at him."

"Was Ran Qiu, then, not concerned with statecraft?"

"Since when did something sixty or seventy—even fifty or sixty—square *li* in area not constitute a state?"

"Was Zihua, then, not concerned with statecraft?"

"If ancestral temples and diplomatic gatherings are not the business of the feudal lords, what then are they? If Zihua's aspiration is a minor one, then what would be considered a major one?"[106]

Book Twelve

12.1 Yan Hui asked about Goodness.

The Master said, "Restraining yourself and returning to the rites constitutes Goodness. If for one day you managed to restrain yourself and return to the rites, in this way you could lead the entire world back to Goodness. The key to achieving Goodness lies within yourself—how could it come from others?"

Yan Hui asked, "May I inquire as to the specifics?"

The Master said, "Do not look unless it is in accordance with ritual; do not listen unless it is in accordance with ritual; do not speak unless it is in accordance with ritual; do not move unless it is in accordance with ritual."

---

105. According to traditional commentators, the Yi River was near Kongzi's home, and the Rain Dance Altar was located just above the river.

106. The Master is thus equally disapproving of Zilu's, Ran Qiu's, and Zihua's aspirations—all of which are overly focused upon statecraft techniques—although only Zilu's response is audacious enough to provoke a smile. The point is that true government is effected through the superior Virtue gained by ritual practice, and the task of the gentleman is thus to focus upon self-cultivation and attain a state of joyful harmony with the Way. Such harmony with the Way is exemplified by Zengxi's musical bent, his reluctance to speak about his aspirations, and the sense of spontaneous joy in the cultivated life conveyed by his answer. Zengxi is a disciple of Kongzi, but also the father of Master Zeng (see *Analects* 4.15, above).

Yan Hui replied, "Although I am not quick to understand, I ask permission to devote myself to this teaching."

12.2 Zhonggong[107] asked about Goodness.

The Master said, "'When in public, comport yourself as if you were receiving an important guest, and in your management of the common people, behave as if you were overseeing a great sacrifice.' Do not impose upon others what you yourself do not desire. In this way, you will encounter no resentment in your public or private life."[108]

Zhonggong replied, "Although I am not quick to understand, I ask permission to devote myself to this teaching."

12.5 Anxiously, Sima Niu remarked, "Everyone has brothers, I alone have none."[109]

Zixia replied, "I have heard it said, 'Life and death are governed by fate, wealth and honor are determined by Heaven.' A gentleman is respectful and free of errors. He is reverent and ritually proper in his dealings with others. In this way, everyone within the Four Seas is his brother.[110] How could a gentleman be concerned about not having brothers?"

12.7 Zigong asked about governing.

The Master said, "Simply make sure there is sufficient food, sufficient armaments, and that you have the confidence of the common people."

---

107. A disciple of Kongzi.

108. One interpretation is that the first set of advice concerns the virtue of *zhong*, "loyalty," the second that of *shu*, "sympathetic understanding." Cf. *Analects* 4.15 on these terms.

109. Sima Niu came from a prominent military family in Song and in fact left behind several elder brothers when he went abroad. One of his brothers, Huan Tui (*Analects* 7.23), planned and carried out an unsuccessful revolt against the rightful lord of Song in 483 BCE, and was forced to flee the state. Another of Sima Niu's brothers, Xiang Chao, was also a military official in Song; he was apparently a somewhat arrogant and self-aggrandizing man and was forced to flee the state after Huan Tui's attempted revolt, along with the remaining elder brothers. Sima Niu—apparently uninvolved in the revolt or its aftermath—resigned his official post in disgust and emigrated, ending up eventually in Lu, where he presumably had the conversation with Zixia recorded here. His comment that "he alone has no brothers" is thus not meant literally: the point is either that he has no brothers truly worthy of being considered brothers, or that all of his brothers are in exile or in constant danger of losing their lives and therefore as good as dead. Sima Niu is thus bemoaning the fate that has left him effectively without family, an exile from his home state.

110. "Within the Four Seas" means the entire world; China was viewed as being surrounded on all sides by oceans.

Zigong said, "If sacrificing one of these three things became unavoidable, which would you sacrifice first?"

The Master replied, "I would sacrifice the armaments."

Zigong said, "If sacrificing one of the two remaining things became unavoidable, which would you sacrifice next?"

The Master replied, "I would sacrifice the food. Death has always been with us, but a state cannot stand once it has lost the confidence of the people."

12.8 Ji Zicheng[111] said, "Being a gentleman is simply a matter of having the right native substance, and nothing else. Why must one engage in cultural refinement?"

Zigong replied, "It is regrettable, Sir, that you should speak of the gentleman in this way—as they say, 'a team of horses cannot overtake your tongue.' A gentleman's cultural refinement resembles his native substance, and his native substance resembles his cultural refinement. The skin of a tiger or leopard, shorn of its fur, is no different from the skin of a dog or sheep."[112]

12.9 Duke Ai said to Master You, "The harvest was poor and I cannot satisfy my needs. What should I do?"

Master You said, "Why do you not try taxing the people one part in ten?"[113]

"I am currently taxing them two parts in ten, and even so I cannot satisfy my needs. How could reducing the tax to one part in ten help?"

Master You answered, "If the common people's needs are satisfied, how could their lord be lacking? If the common people's needs are not satisfied, how can their lord be content?"

---

111. Ji Zicheng is described as a minister of Wei, but nothing else is known about him. Zigong served as an official in Wei for some time, and this is probably when this exchange took place.

112. Zigong's response invokes an interesting metaphor for the relationship of native substance and cultural refinement: although native substance is required (as an animal requires a hide), a gentleman possessing substance but unadorned by cultural refinement would be like a tiger or leopard shaved of its beautiful pelt—indistinguishable from any ordinary creature. Cf. *Analects* 6.18.

113. This was a traditional Zhou practice. According to the *Annals*, the traditional ten percent tithe on agricultural production was doubled by Duke Xuan of Lu in 593 BCE, and that higher rate was then continued as standard practice. It is possible that this exchange between Duke Ai and Master You took place during the Lu famine of 481 BCE (Year 14 of Duke Ai's reign), which occurred after back-to-back plagues of locusts in 484 and 483 BCE. Master You is thus suggesting a return to a taxation rate over one hundred years old—quite a radical cutback.

12.11 Duke Jing of Qi asked Kongzi about governing.

Kongzi responded, "Let the lord be a true lord, the ministers true ministers, the fathers true fathers, and the sons true sons."[114]

The Duke replied, "Well put! Certainly, if the lord is not a true lord, the ministers not true ministers, the fathers not true fathers, and the sons not true sons, even if there is sufficient grain, will I ever get to eat it?"

12.13 The Master said, "When it comes to hearing civil litigation, I am as good as anyone else. What is necessary, though, is to bring it about that there is no civil litigation at all."

12.17 Ji Kangzi[115] asked Kongzi about governing.

Kongzi responded, "To 'govern' [zhèng 政] means to be 'correct' [zhèng 正]. If you set an example by being correct yourself, who will dare to be incorrect?"

12.18 Ji Kangzi was concerned about the prevalence of robbers in Lu, and asked Kongzi about how to deal with this problem.

Kongzi said, "If you could just get rid of your own excessive desires, the people would not steal even if you rewarded them for it."

12.19 Ji Kangzi asked Kongzi about governing, saying, "If I were to execute those who lacked the Way in order to advance those who possessed the Way, how would that be?"

Kongzi responded, "In your governing, Sir, what need is there for executions? If you desire goodness, then the common people will be good. The Virtue of a gentleman is like the wind, and the Virtue of a petty person is like the grass—when the wind moves over the grass, the grass is sure to bend."

---

114. In 516 BCE, Kongzi arrived in Qi to find that Duke Jing, near the end of his reign, was in dire straits. His nominal minister, Chen Qi, had usurped control of the state, and the Duke's plan to pass over his eldest son for the succession had set off contention among his sons. Kongzi's advice is thus very topical. His point is that if everyone would simply concentrate on conscientiously fulfilling their role-specific duties, order would result naturally—there is no need for some special technique or theory of "governing" (cf. *Analects* 2.21). Many commentators have seen this passage as concerned with the theme of "rectifying names" (zhèng míng 正名) mentioned in *Analects* 13.3, whereby the actualities of one's behavior should be made to accord with the standard set by one's social role ("name").

115. A member of the Ji Family (cf. *Analects* 3.1), and senior minister in the state of Lu, who held power from 492 to 468 BCE.

12.22 Fan Chi asked about Goodness.

The Master replied, "Care for others."

He then asked about wisdom.

The Master replied, "Know others."

Fan Chi still did not understand, so the Master elaborated: "Raise up the straight and apply them to the crooked, and the crooked will be made straight."

Fan Chi retired from the Master's presence. Seeing Zixia, he said, "Just before I asked the Master about wisdom, and he replied, 'Raise up the straight and apply them to the crooked, and the crooked will be made straight.' What did he mean by that?"

Zixia answered, "What a wealth of instruction you have received! When Shun ruled the world, he selected from among the multitude, raising up Gao Yao, and those who were not Good then kept their distance. When Tang ruled the world, he selected from among the multitude, raising up Yi Yin, and those who were not Good then kept their distance."[116]

12.24 Master Zeng said, "The gentleman acquires friends by means of cultural refinement, and then relies upon his friends for support in becoming Good."

Book Thirteen

13.3 Zilu asked, "If the Duke of Wei[117] were to employ you to serve in the government of his state, what would be your first priority?"

The Master answered, "It would, of course, be the rectification of names."[118]

---

116. Gao Yao was Minister of Crime under Shun. See *Mengzi* 7A35 (in chapter 4 of this volume) for another reference to him. On Shun, Tang, and Yi Yin, see under *Important Figures* in the appendices.

117. This probably refers to Zhe, the grandson of Duke Ling of Wei (who appears in *Analects* 15.1 below), who took over the throne in 493 BCE.

118. On zhèng míng 正名, "rectification of names" or "correction of names," cf. *Analects* 6.25, 12.11, and 12.17 as well as Xunzi's "On Correct Naming" (*Xunzi* chapter 22, in chapter 9 of this volume). For a defense of the importance of this concept in the *Analects*, see Loy Hui-chieh, "*Analects* 13.3 and the Doctrine of 'Correcting Names,'" in Jones, *Confucius Now*, 37–48. Reading this passage in light of *Analects* 12.11 ("Let the lord be a true lord . . . the fathers true fathers, and the sons true sons."), it can be seen as a barb against the ruling family of Wei, whose disordered family relations eventually threw the state into chaos. The Duke doted upon his notorious wife, Nanzi (see *Analects* 6.28), whom his resentful son, Prince Kuai Kui, then attempted to kill. This attempt having failed, the son was forced to flee Wei, and the Duke's grandson, Zhe, subsequently took over the throne upon the Duke's death. Prince Kuai Kui then returned to Wei with the backing of a foreign army in an attempt to oust his son.

Zilu said, "Could you, Master, really be so far off the mark? Why worry about rectifying names?"

The Master replied, "How boorish you are, Zilu! When it comes to matters that he does not understand, the gentleman should remain silent. If names are not rectified, speech will not accord [with reality]; when speech does not accord [with reality], things will not be successfully accomplished. When things are not successfully accomplished, ritual practice and music will fail to flourish; when ritual and music fail to flourish, punishments and penalties will miss the mark. And when punishments and penalties miss the mark, the common people will be at a loss as to what to do with themselves. This is why the gentleman only applies names that can be properly spoken, and assures that what he says can be properly put into action. The gentleman simply guards against arbitrariness in his speech. That is all there is to it."

13.4 Fan Chi asked to learn about plowing and growing grain [from Kongzi].

The Master said, "When it comes to that, any old farmer would be a better teacher than I."

He asked to learn about growing fruits and vegetables.

The Master said, "When it comes to that, any old gardener would be a better teacher than I."

Fan Chi then left. The Master remarked, "What a common fellow that Fan Chi is! When a ruler loves ritual propriety, then none among his people will dare to be disrespectful. When a ruler loves rightness, then none among his people will dare to not obey. When a ruler loves trustworthiness, then none of his people will dare to not be honest. The mere existence of such a ruler would cause the common people throughout the world to bundle their children on their backs and seek him out. Of what use, then, is the study of agriculture?"

13.5 The Master said, "Imagine a person who can recite the three hundred *Odes* by heart but, when delegated a governmental task, is unable to carry it out, or when sent abroad as an envoy, is unable to engage in repartee. No matter how many odes he might have memorized, what good are they to him?"[119]

13.6 The Master said, "When the ruler is correct, his will is put into effect without the need for official orders. When the ruler's person is not correct, he will not be obeyed no matter how many orders he issues."

---

119. The point of learning is not mere scholastic knowledge, but rather the ability to apply this knowledge flexibly in a situation-specific manner. Cf. *Analects* 2.11.

13.12 The Master said, "If a true king were to arise, we would certainly see a return to Goodness after a single generation."[120]

13.16 The Duke of She asked about governing.

The Master said, "[Act so that] those near to you are pleased, and those who are far from you are drawn closer."

13.18 The Duke of She said to Kongzi, "Among my people there is one we call 'Upright Gong.' When his father stole a sheep, he reported him to the authorities."

Kongzi replied, "Among my people, those whom we consider 'upright' are different from this: fathers cover up for their sons, and sons cover up for their fathers. 'Uprightness' is to be found in this."[121]

13.20 Zigong asked, "What does a person have to be like before he could be called a true scholar-official?"

The Master said, "Conducting himself with a sense of shame, and not dishonoring his ruler's mandate when sent abroad as a diplomat—such a person could be called a scholar-official."

"May I ask what the next best type of person is like?"

"His lineage and clan consider him filial, and his fellow villagers consider him respectful to his elders."

"And the next best?"

"In his speech he insists on being trustworthy, and with regard to his actions, he insists that they bear fruit. What a narrow, rigid little man he is! And yet he might still be considered the next best."

"How about those who today are involved in government?"

The Master exclaimed, "Oh! Those petty functionaries are not even worth considering."

13.21 The Master said, "If you cannot manage to find a person of perfectly balanced conduct to associate with, I suppose you must settle for the wild or the fastidious. In their pursuit of the Way, the wild plunge right in, while the fastidious are always careful not to get their hands dirty."[122]

---

120. Because a true king rules through the gradual transformative power of Virtue rather than through harsh laws and punishments, which may achieve more immediate—but short-lived—results.

121. Cf. *Analects* 17.8, where the danger of an overly rigid or strict sense of honesty or uprightness is described as being "harmful"—the harm being, presumably, to such natural relationships as that between father and son. For a different account of this event, see *Han Feizi* chapter 49 (in chapter 10 of this volume).

122. Cf. *Mengzi* 7B37 (in chapter 4 of this volume).

13.24 Zigong asked, "What would you make of a person whom everyone in the village likes?"

The Master said, "I would not know what to make of him."

"What about someone whom everyone in the village hates?"

"I would still not know. Better this way: those in the village who are good like him, and those who are not good hate him."

Book Fourteen

14.1 Yuan Si asked about shame.

The Master said, "When the state has the Way, accept a salary; when the state is without the Way, to accept a salary is shameful."

"To refrain from competitiveness, boastfulness, envy, and greed—can this be considered Goodness?"

The Master said, "This can be considered difficult, but as for its being Good, that I do not know."

14.4 The Master said, "Those who possess Virtue will inevitably have something to say, whereas those who have something to say do not necessarily possess Virtue. Those who are Good will necessarily display courage, but those who display courage are not necessarily Good."

14.5 Nangong Kuo[123] said to Kongzi, "Yi was a skillful archer, and Ao was a powerful naval commander, and yet neither of them met a natural death. Yu and Hou Ji, on the other hand, did nothing but personally tend to the land, and yet they both ended up with possession of the world."[124]

The Master did not answer.

After Nangong Kuo left, the Master sighed, "What a gentlemanly person that man is! How he reveres Virtue!"[125]

---

123. Most commentators identify him as an official in the state of Lu.

124. Both Yi and Ao were legendary martial heroes of the Xia dynasty with questionable morals: Yi usurped the throne of one of the kings of the Xia dynasty, and Ao was the son of one of Yi's ministers. Ao himself subsequently murdered and dethroned Yi, and was in turn slain and overthrown by one of his own ministers. Yu and Hou Ji were moral worthies and heroes of civilized arts: Yu tamed the Yellow River and introduced irrigation, receiving the rulership of the world from Shun in return, while Hou Ji ("Lord Millet") is the mythical founder of agriculture and progenitor of the Zhou royal line.

125. The world is won, not through martial prowess, but through careful and patient cultivation. Commentators suggest that Nangong Kuo meant to compare Kongzi himself to Yu and Hou Ji, and that Kongzi thus remained silent out of modesty.

14.7 The Master said, "If you really care for others, can you then fail to put them to work? If you are really dutiful to someone, can you then fail to instruct him?"

14.12 Zilu asked about the complete person.

The Master said, "Take a person as wise as Zang Wuzhong, as free of desire as Gongchuo, as courageous as Zhuangzi of Bian, and as accomplished in the arts as Ran Qiu, and then acculturate them by means of ritual and music—such a man might be called a complete person."[126]

He then continued: "But must a complete person today be exactly like this? When seeing a chance for profit, he thinks of what is right; when confronting danger, he is ready to take his life into his own hands; when enduring an extended period of hardship, he does not forget what he had professed in more fortunate times—such a man might also be called a complete person."

14.13 The Master asked Gongming Jia about Gongshu Wenzi, saying, "Is it really true that your master did not speak, did not laugh, and did not take?"[127]

Gongming Jia answered, "Whoever told you that was exaggerating. My master only spoke when the time was right, and so people never grew impatient listening to him. He only laughed when he was genuinely full of joy, and so people never tired of hearing him laugh. He only took what was rightfully his, and so people never resented his taking of things."

The Master said, "Was he really that good? Could he really have been that good?"

14.24 The Master said, "In ancient times scholars learned for their own sake; these days they learn for the sake of others."

14.25 Qu Boyu[128] sent a messenger to Kongzi. Kongzi sat down beside him and asked, "How are things with your Master?"

The messenger replied, "My Master wishes to reduce his faults, but has not yet been able to do so."

After the messenger left, the Master said, "Now that is a messenger! That is a messenger!"[129]

---

126. Zang Wuzhong and Meng Gongchuo were both respected officials in Lu, and Zhuangzi was an official in the state of Bian who was legendary for his courage. (The latter is no relation to the Daoist philosopher whose work is included in chapter 8 of this volume.) On Ran Qiu, cf. *Analects* 5.8, 6.12, 11.17, 11.22, and 11.26.

127. Gongshu Wenzi was an official in the state of Wei, and Gongming Jia was presumably his disciple.

128. An official in the state of Wei.

129. Kongzi is praising Qu Boyu's noble intentions and realistic evaluation of himself as well as the modesty of his envoy's words. Cf. *Analects* 14.27.

14.27 The Master said, "The gentleman is ashamed to have his words exceed his actions."

14.29 Zigong was given to criticizing others.

The Master remarked sarcastically, "What a worthy man that Zigong must be! As for me, I hardly have the time for this."[130]

14.30 The Master said, "Do not worry that you are not recognized by others; worry rather that you yourself lack ability."

14.34 Someone asked, "What do you think of the saying, 'Requite injury with kindness'?"[131]

The Master replied, "With what, then, would one requite kindness? Requite injury with uprightness, and kindness with kindness."

14.35 The Master sighed, "No one understands me—do they?"

Zigong replied, "How can you say that no one understands you, Master?"

"I am not bitter toward Heaven, nor do I blame others. I study what is below in order to comprehend what is above. If there is anyone who could understand me, perhaps it is Heaven."

14.36 Gongbo Liao submitted an accusation against Zilu to the head of the Ji Family. Zifu Jingbo reported this to Kongzi, adding, "That master [i.e., Ji Kangzi] has certainly been led astray by Gongbo Liao, but my influence with him is still sufficient to see to it that Gongbo Liao's corpse is displayed at court or in the marketplace."[132]

The Master said, "Whether or not the Way is to be put into action is a matter of fate. Whether or not the Way is to be discarded is also a matter of fate. What power does Gongbo Liao have to affect fate!"

---

130. The Master's sarcastic response indicates that he is entirely focused upon cultivating and correcting himself; only someone who has mastered the Way has the luxury to begin evaluating others, and Zigong is hardly such a person.

131. "Kindness" here is Dé 德, which elsewhere is translated as "Virtue." The quoted phrase appears in *Daodejing* 63 (in chapter 6 of this volume)—and Kongzi's response to it is certainly anti-Laozian in flavor—but it was likely a traditional saying not necessarily identified with the *Daodejing* itself.

132. Zifu Jingbo, an official in the state of Lu, is claiming here that he has enough influence with his master, the de facto ruler of Lu, that he can both convince him of Zilu's innocence and see to it that his fellow minister, Gongbo Liao, is executed for his slander.

14.38 Zilu spent the night at Stone Gate. The next morning, the gatekeeper asked him, "Where have you come from?"

Zilu answered, "From the house of Kongzi."

"Isn't he the one who knows that what he does is impossible and yet persists anyway?"[133]

14.39 The Master was playing the stone chimes in the state of Wei.

A man with a wicker basket strapped to his back passed by the door of the Kong Family residence and remarked, "Whoever is playing the chimes like that certainly has something in his heart!" After listening for a moment, he added, "How despicable is this petty stubbornness! If no one understands you, just tend to yourself.

'If the river ford is deep, use the stepping-stones;
If it is shallow, simply raise your hem.'"[134]

The Master [hearing these comments] responded, "Such resoluteness! Who could take issue with that!"[135]

Book Fifteen

15.1 Duke Ling of Wei asked Kongzi about military formations.

Kongzi replied, "I know something about the arrangement of ceremonial stands and dishes for ritual offerings, but I have never learned about the arrangement of battalions and divisions."

He left the next day.

15.2 [When Kongzi was besieged] in the state of Chen, all of the provisions were exhausted, and his followers were so weak from hunger that they could not even

---

133. Cf. *Analects* 18.7. That is, Kongzi persists in his efforts to reform the world even though it appears hopeless. Later Confucians embraced this derisive comment with pride.

134. From the *Odes* (*Mao # 54*).

135. Kongzi's critic is wearing a wicker basket strapped to his back—the sign of a farmer or manual laborer—and yet has an ear for classical music and can quote from the *Odes*. No ordinary commoner, he is more likely a scholar who has gone into reclusion, whether for philosophical or political reasons. Like the gatekeeper in *Analects* 14.38, he is annoyed at Kongzi's persistence in the face of an indifferent world, and advises him to simply accord with the times—as he himself has presumably done. Kongzi's sarcastic response expresses contempt for such passivity and lack of resolution. Cf. *Analects* 8.7, 18.6, and 18.7.

stand. Upset, Zilu appeared before the Master and said, "Does even the gentleman encounter hardship?"

The Master said, "Of course the gentleman encounters hardship. The difference is that the petty man, encountering hardship, is overwhelmed by it."

15.3 The Master said, "Zigong, do you regard me as simply one who learns much and remembers it?"

Zigong said, "I do. Is that not the case?"

The Master said, "It is not. I string it together on a single thread."[136]

15.5 The Master said, "Is Shun not an example of someone who ruled by means of nonaction? What did he do? He made himself reverent and took his proper [ritual] position facing south, that is all."[137]

15.9 The Master said, "No scholar-official of noble intention or Good person would ever pursue life at the expense of Goodness, and in fact some may be called upon to give up their lives in order to fulfill Goodness."

15.11 Yan Hui asked about running a state.

The Master said, "Follow the calendar of the Xia, travel in the carriages of the Shang, and clothe yourself in the ceremonial caps of the Zhou.[138] As for music, listen only to the Shao and Wu.[139] Prohibit the tunes of Zheng, and keep glib people at a distance—for the tunes of Zheng are licentious, and glib people are dangerous."

15.16 The Master said, "I have never been able to do anything for a person who is not himself constantly asking, 'What should I do? What should I do?'"

---

136. Cf. *Analects* 4.15.

137. The ruler faces south, thus serving as the earthly correlate to the Pole Star (cf. *Analects* 2.1). On "nonaction" see the introduction to this chapter and *wuwei* under *Important Terms* in the appendices.

138. The calendar of the Xia—which was in fact something like a combination calendar and almanac, providing instructions for what to do at various points in the year—began the year in the spring and was apparently particularly well adapted to the cycles of the seasons and the needs of farmers. The state carriage of the Shang, according to commentators, was stately but relatively unadorned, while the ceremonial cap of the Zhou was elegant and practical; according to Bao Xian, it shielded both the eyes and the ears, making it easier to resist distractions and concentrate upon ritual.

139. The music of King Shun and King Wu, respectively.

15.18 The Master said, "The gentleman takes rightness as his substance, puts it into practice by means of ritual, gives it expression through modesty, and perfects it by being trustworthy. Now that is a gentleman!"

15.21 The Master said, "The gentleman seeks it in himself; the petty person seeks it in others."

15.24 Zigong asked, "Is there one teaching that can serve as a guide for one's entire life?"

The Master answered, "Is it not 'sympathetic understanding' (shù 恕)? Do not impose upon others what you yourself do not desire."

15.28 The Master said, "When the multitude hates a person, you must examine them and judge for yourself. The same holds true for someone whom the multitude loves."[140]

15.29 The Master said, "Human beings can broaden the Way—it is not the Way that broadens human beings."[141]

15.30 The Master said, "To make a mistake and yet to not change your ways—this is what is called truly making a mistake."

15.31 The Master said, "I once engaged in thought for an entire day without eating and an entire night without sleeping, but it did no good. It would have been better for me to have spent that time in learning."[142]

15.36 The Master said, "When it comes to being Good, defer to no one, not even your teacher."

15.37 The Master said, "The gentleman is true, but not rigidly trustworthy."[143]

---

140. Cf. *Analects* 13.24.

141. As Cài Mó 蔡謨 (Jin dynasty) explains, "The Way is silent and without action, and requires human beings to be put into practice. Human beings can harmonize with the Way—this is why the text reads: 'Human beings are able to broaden the Way.' The Way does not harmonize with humans—this is why the text reads: 'It is not the Way that broadens human beings.'"

142. Cf. *Analects* 2.15 and *Xunzi* chapter 1 (in chapter 9 of this volume).

143. Cf. *Analects* 19.11.

15.39 The Master said, "In education, there are no differences in kind."[144]

15.41 The Master said, "Words should convey their point, and leave it at that."

15.42 The [blind] Music Master Mian came to see Kongzi.

When they came to the steps, the Master said, "Here are the steps." When they reached his seat, the Master said, "Here is your seat." After everyone was seated, the Master informed him as to who was present, saying, "So-and-so is seated here, and So-and-so is seated over there."

When the Music Master left, Zizhang asked, "Is this the way to converse with a Music Master?"

The Master replied, "Yes, this is indeed the way to assist a Music Master."[145]

Book Sixteen

16.4 Kongzi said, "Beneficial types of friendship number three, as do harmful types of friendship. Befriending the upright, those who are true to their word, or those of broad learning—these are the beneficial types of friendship.[146] Befriending clever flatterers, skillful dissemblers, or the smoothly glib—these are the harmful types of friendship."

16.5 Kongzi said, "Beneficial types of joy number three, as do harmful types of joy. Taking joy in regulating yourself through the rites and music, in commending the excellence of others, or in possessing many worthy friends—these are the beneficial types of joy. Taking joy in arrogant behavior, idle amusements, or decadent licentiousness—these are the harmful types of joy."

---

144. This passage has traditionally been understood as a commentary on the basic educability of all people; cf. *Analects* 7.7, 17.2.

145. The post of Music Master was traditionally filled by blind persons in ancient China, both in order to give them a trade in which they could excel and because their sense of hearing was considered more acute than that of the sighted. Music Master Mian has presumably been brought to Kongzi's residence by an assistant, who then leaves him in Kongzi's care. The point of this passage seems to be the economy of expression of the Master, who puts aside the normal ritual behavior of a host in order to deftly and respectfully serve as a guide for the blind Music Master without being overly fussy or condescending.

146. "True to one's word" is liàng 諒, which had a negative connotation in previous passages (e.g., "rigidly trustworthy" in 15.37) but clearly has a positive sense here.

16.7 Kongzi said, "The gentleman guards against three things: when he is young, and his blood and *qi* are still unstable, he guards against the temptation of female beauty; when he reaches his prime, and his blood and *qi* have become unyielding, he guards against being contentious; when he reaches old age, and his blood and *qi* have begun to decline, he guards against being acquisitive."[147]

16.8 The Master said, "The gentleman stands in awe of three things: the Mandate of Heaven, great men, and the teachings of the sages. The petty person does not understand the Mandate of Heaven, and thus does not regard it with awe; he shows disrespect to great men, and ridicules the teachings of the sages."

16.9 Kongzi said, "Those who are born understanding it are the best; those who come to understand it through learning are second. Those who find it difficult to understand and yet persist in their studies come next. People who find it difficult to understand but do not even try to learn are the worst of all."

16.13 Ziqin asked Boyu, "Have you acquired any esoteric learning?"[148]

Boyu replied, "I have not. My father was once standing by himself in the courtyard and, as I hurried by with quickened steps, he asked, 'Have you learned the *Odes*?'[149] I replied, 'Not yet.' He said, 'If you do not learn the *Odes*, you will lack the means to speak.' I then retired and learned the *Odes*.

"On another day, my father was once again standing by himself in the courtyard and, as I hurried by with quickened steps, he asked, 'Have you learned ritual?'[150] I replied, 'Not yet.' He said, 'If you do not learn ritual, you will lack the means to take your place.' I then retired and learned ritual.

"These two things are what I have been taught."

Ziqin retired and, smiling to himself, remarked "I asked one question and got three answers: I learned about the *Odes*, I learned about ritual, and I learned how the gentleman keeps his son at a distance."

---

147. On qì 氣, see *Important Terms* in the appendices.

148. Boyu is Kongzi's son, and Ziqin is wondering whether or not—as the Master's own flesh and blood—Boyu received any special instruction withheld from the other disciples.

149. Boyu quickened his steps as a sign of respect; cf. 10.3.

150. Some commentators suggest that "ritual" (lǐ 禮) here meant the title of a text—such as the *Record of Ritual*. This, in turn, would be a sign of a quite late date for the composition of this passage.

Book Seventeen

17.2 The Master said, "By nature people are similar; they diverge as the result of practice."

17.8 The Master said, "Zilu! Have you heard about the six [virtuous] words and their six corresponding vices?"[151]

Zilu replied, "I have not."

"Sit! I will tell you about them.

"Loving Goodness without balancing it with a love for learning will result in the vice of foolishness. Loving wisdom without balancing it with a love for learning will result in the vice of deviance. Loving trustworthiness without balancing it with a love for learning will result in the vice of harmful rigidity. Loving uprightness without balancing it with a love for learning will result in the vice of intolerance. Loving courage without balancing it with a love for learning will result in the vice of unruliness. Loving resoluteness without balancing it with a love for learning will result in the vice of willfulness."

17.9 The Master said, "Little Ones, why do none of you learn the *Odes*? The *Odes* can be a source of inspiration and a basis for evaluation; they can help you to come together with others, as well as to properly express complaints. In the home, they teach you about how to serve your father, and in public life they teach you about how to serve your lord. They also broadly acquaint you with the names of various birds, beasts, plants, and trees."

17.10 The Master said to Boyu, "Have you mastered the *Odes* from the 'South of Zhou' and the 'South of Shao'?[152] A man who has not mastered the 'South of Zhou' and the 'South of Shao' is like someone standing with his face to the wall, is he not?"

17.11 The Master said, "When we say, 'the rites, the rites,' are we speaking merely of jade and silk? When we say, 'music, music,' are we speaking merely of bells and drums?"[153]

---

151. The literal meaning of bì 蔽—the word translated here as "vice"—is "to cover over" or "obscure." Mengzi uses it to describe how the heart can be "led astray" by things in *Mengzi* 6A15 (in chapter 4 of this volume); Xunzi uses it with the sense of "fixations" that can lead us to endorse inferior doctrines or ways of life (see *Xunzi* chapter 21, "Undoing Fixation," in chapter 9 of this volume).

152. These are the first two sections of the *Odes* and are used here to refer to the *Odes* as a whole. Cf. *Analects* 16.13.

153. Just as true music requires not merely instruments but sensitive musicians to play them, so true ritual requires not merely traditional paraphernalia but also emotionally committed, sensitive practitioners. Cf. *Analects* 2.7, 3.3, and 3.12.

17.13 The Master said, "The village worthy is the thief of virtue."[154]

17.18 The Master said, "I hate that purple has usurped the place of vermilion, that the tunes of Zheng have been confused with classical music, and that the clever of tongue have undermined both state and family."[155]

17.19 The Master sighed, "Would that I did not have to speak!"

Zigong said, "If the Master did not speak, then how would we little ones receive guidance from you?"

The Master replied, "What does Heaven ever say? Yet the four seasons are put in motion by it, and the myriad creatures receive their life from it. What does Heaven ever say?"

17.21 Zai Wo asked about the three-year mourning period, saying, "Surely one year is long enough. If the gentleman refrains from practicing ritual for three years, the rites will surely fall into ruin; if he refrains from music for three years, this will surely be disastrous for music. After the lapse of a year the old grain has been used up, while the new grain has ripened, and the four different types of tinder have all been drilled in order to rekindle the fire.[156] One year is surely long enough."

The Master asked, "Would you feel comfortable then eating your sweet rice and wearing your brocade gowns?"[157]

"I would."

The Master replied, "Well, if you would feel comfortable doing so, then by all means you should do it. When the gentleman is in mourning, he gets no pleasure from eating sweet foods, finds no joy in listening to music, and feels no comfort in his place of dwelling. This is why he gives up these things. But if you would feel comfortable doing them, then by all means you should!"

After Zai Wo left, the Master remarked, "This shows how lacking in Goodness this Zai Wo is! A child is completely dependent upon the care of his parents for the first three years of his life—this is why the three-year mourning period is the

---

154. See *Mengzi* 7B37 (in chapter 4 of this volume) for an elaboration of this passage.

155. Vermilion—the color of the Zhou—is the traditional and proper color for ceremonial clothing while purple is a more "modern" and increasingly popular variant. On the "tunes of Zheng," see *Analects* 15.11.

156. An annual ritual of renewal.

157. While mourning, one was restricted to a diet of plain rice and water and wearing rough hemp for clothing. One was to suspend most normal social activity, maintain particular demeanors, and refrain from familiar pleasures. A child was to maintain three years (often understood as into the beginning of the third year—i.e., approximately twenty-five months) of mourning for a deceased parent. These rigors were thought to express respect for the dead and serve as a spiritual exercise for the living.

common practice throughout the world. Did Zai Wo not receive three years of care from his parents?"

17.23 Zilu asked, "Does the gentleman admire courage?"

The Master said, "The gentleman admires rightness above all. A gentleman who possessed courage but lacked a sense of rightness would create political disorder, while a common person who possessed courage but lacked a sense of rightness would become a bandit."

17.25 The Master said, "Women and servants are particularly hard to manage: if you are too familiar with them, they grow insolent, but if you are too distant, they grow resentful."[158]

Book Eighteen

18.6 Kongzi passed Chang Ju and Jie Ni, who were yoked together pulling a plow through a field. He sent Zilu to ask them where the ford was to be found.[159]

Chang Ju inquired, "That fellow holding the reins there—who is he?"

Zilu answered, "That is Kongzi."

"Do you mean Kongzi of Lu?"

"The same."

"Then *he* should know where the ford is."[160]

Zilu then asked Jie Ni.

Jie Ni also replied with a question: "Who are you?"

"I am Zilu."

---

158. Some later commentators have tried—with little success—to soften this infamously misogynous passage. Its sense is probably that, considering their potentially dangerous sexual power and inability to control themselves, household women (i.e., wives and concubines), like servants, need to be managed firmly, but with respect, if they are to remain obedient and not overstep their proper roles.

159. Kongzi and his entourage were apparently attempting to cross a nearby river, but this passage is also to be read allegorically: the "ford" is the way out of the "great flood of chaos" mentioned below. The use of self-consciously primitive technology by these two figures (most plows were ox-drawn by this time), as well as their knowledge of Kongzi's identity revealed below, makes it clear that they are no ordinary commoners, but rather educated primitivist recluses who have deliberately rejected society and culture (cf. *Analects* 14.39). Like many of the figures in the *Zhuangzi* (in chapter 8 of this volume), their names appear to be allegorical ("Standing Tall in the Marsh" and "Prominent in the Mud," respectively); the appearance of this literary technique and the complex narrative quality of this passage mark it as quite late.

160. The comment is sarcastic. Kongzi should know, given that he is reputed to be so wise.

"The disciple of Kongzi of Lu?"

"Yes."

"The whole world is as if engulfed in a great flood, and who can change it? Given this, instead of following a scholar who merely avoids the bad people [of this age],[161] wouldn't it be better for you to follow scholars like us, who avoid the age itself?" He then proceeded to cover up his seeds with dirt and did not pause again.

Zilu returned and reported this conversation to Kongzi. The Master was lost in thought for a moment, and then remarked, "A person cannot flock together with the birds and the beasts. If I do not associate with the followers of men, then with whom would I associate? If the Way were realized in the world, then I would not need to change anything."[162]

18.7 Zilu was traveling with Kongzi, but had fallen behind. He encountered an old man carrying a wicker basket suspended from his staff. Zilu asked, "Have you seen my Master?"

The old man answered,

> "'Won't soil his dainty hands
> Can't tell millet from barley.'[163]

"Who, then, might your master be?" He then planted his staff in the ground and began weeding. [Not knowing how to reply,] Zilu simply remained standing with his hands clasped as a sign of respect.

The old man subsequently invited Zilu back to his house to stay the night. After killing a chicken and preparing some millet for Zilu to eat, he presented his two sons to him. On the next day Zilu caught up to Kongzi and told him what had happened.

"He must be a scholar recluse," the Master said. He sent Zilu back to the old farmer's house to meet with him again, but by the time Zilu got there the man had already disappeared. Zilu then remarked, "To avoid public service is to be without a sense of what is right. Proper relations between elders and juniors cannot be discarded—how, then, can one discard the rightness that obtains between ruler and

---

161. Referring to Kongzi's itinerant seeking after a ruler who would put his Way into practice.

162. Kongzi's compassion for the suffering of the world is such that he cannot take what he views as the easy way out—simply withdrawing from society and living the life of a noble, unsullied recluse (cf. *Analects* 18.8)—although his mission as a "wooden clapper" (*Analects* 3.24) is grueling and fraught with difficulties and frustrations.

163. This comment is a rhyming verse in the Chinese—an indication that again we are not dealing with an ordinary, illiterate farmer.

minister?[164] To do so is to wish to keep one's hands from getting dirty at the expense of throwing the great social order into chaos. The gentleman takes office in order to do what is right, even though he already knows that the Way will not be realized."[165]

18.8 Those men who went into seclusion include Bo Yi, Shu Qi, Yu Zhong, Yi Yi, Zhu Zhang, Liuxia Hui, and Shao Lian.[166]

The Master said, "Unwilling to lower their aspirations or bring disgrace upon their persons—such were Bo Yi and Shu Qi."

Of Liuxia Hui and Shao Lian he said, "Although they lowered their aspirations and brought disgrace upon their persons, at least their speech was in accord with their status and their actions were in accord with their thoughts."

Of Yu Zhong and Yi Yi he said, "Living in seclusion and freely speaking their minds, their persons remained pure and their resignations from office were well-considered."

He concluded, "I, however, am different from all of them in that I have no preconceived notions of what is permissible and what is not."[167]

Book Nineteen[168]

19.6 Zixia said, "Learning broadly and firmly retaining what one has learned, being incisive in one's questioning and able to reflect upon what is near at hand—Goodness is to be found in this."

19.7 Zixia said, "The various artisans dwell in their workshops in order to perfect their crafts, just as the gentleman learns in order to reach the end of his Way."

---

164. The point is that the old recluse recognizes the first set of relationships in requiting Zilu's expression of respect (of a younger man for an elder) with proper hospitality and in formally presenting his sons, but ignores the second by living in reclusion and avoiding any sort of official contact.

165. Cf. *Analects* 14.38.

166. These men were all famous recluses who withdrew from public service on moral grounds. For more on Bo Yi and Shu Qi, see *Important Figures* in the appendices.

167. Cf. *Analects* 4.10.

168. This book consists entirely of sayings from Kongzi's disciples. Many of these sayings are summaries or elaborations of themes already seen in earlier books.

19.11 Zixia said, "As long as one does not transgress the bounds when it comes to important Virtues, it is permissible to cross the line here and there when it comes to minor Virtues."[169]

19.12 Ziyou said, "Among the disciples of Zixia, the younger ones are fairly competent when it comes to tasks such as mopping and sweeping, answering summons, and entering and retiring from formal company, but these are all superficialities.[170] They are completely at a loss when it comes to mastering the basics. Why is this?"

When Zixia heard of this, he remarked, "Alas! Ziyou seems to have missed the point. Whose disciples will be the first to be taught the Way of the gentleman, and then in the end grow tired of it? It is like the grass and the trees: you make distinctions between them according to their kind.[171] The Way of the gentleman, how can it be slandered so? Starting at the beginning and working through to the end—surely this describes none other than the sage!"

19.14 Ziyou said, "Mourning should fully express grief and then stop at that."[172]

19.21 Zigong said, "A gentleman's errors are like an eclipse of the sun or the moon: when he errs, everyone notices it, but when he makes amends, everyone looks up to him."

Book Twenty

20.3 Kongzi said, "One who does not understand fate lacks the means to become a gentleman. One who does not understand ritual lacks the means to take his place.[173] One who does not understand words lacks the means to evaluate others."

---

169. Cf. *Analects* 15.37.

170. Literally, "the branches" (mò 末), contrasted with the "basics"—the "root" (běn 本)—below.

171. That is, the true potential gentleman can be recognized by how he handles the small matters taught at the beginning of the course of instruction.

172. Cf. *Analects* 15.41.

173. Cf. *Analects* 2.4.

SELECTIVE BIBLIOGRAPHY

Translations

Ames, Roger T., and Henry Rosemont, Jr., trans. *The Analects of Confucius: A Philosophical Translation*. New York: Ballantine Books, 1998. (Includes the Chinese text, extensive introduction, and bibliography, and notes upon recent archaeological finds related to the *Analects*.)

Brooks, E. Bruce, and A. Taeko Brooks, trans. *The Original Analects: Sayings of Confucius and His Successors*. New York: Columbia University Press, 1998. (Follows the Brookses' radical reorganization of the text and includes commentary on individual passages; the translation is at times awkward, but is perhaps the most precise and scholarly one available in English.)

Lau, D. C., trans. *Confucius: The Analects*. New York: Penguin Books, 1979. (The classic and most commonly read translation.)

Slingerland, Edward, trans. *Confucius: Analects: With Selections from Traditional Commentaries*. Indianapolis: Hackett Publishing Company, 2003. (Complete translation of the *Analects* with interlineal selections from traditional commentaries. For those who do not like the interlineal commentary format, there is also a version of this translation available with the commentary included as endnotes: *The Essential Analects: Selected Passages with Traditional Commentary* [Indianapolis: Hackett Publishing Company, 2006].)

Waley, Arthur, trans. *The Analects of Confucius*. Reprint, New York: Vintage Books, 1989. (Originally published in 1938, this is perhaps the smoothest and most literary of *Analects* translations.)

Secondary Works

Angle, Stephen, and Michael Slote, eds. *Virtue Ethics and Confucianism*. New York: Routledge, 2013. (Collection of essays on virtue ethics and the Confucian tradition.)

Fingarette, Herbert. *Confucius: The Secular as Sacred*. New York: Harper Torchbooks, 1972. (Emphasizes the communal and constitutive nature of the rites.)

Hall, David L., and Roger T. Ames. *Thinking Through Confucius*. Albany, NY: State University of New York Press, 1987. (Emphasizes the creative aspects of the Confucian tradition.)

Jones, David, ed. *Confucius Now: Contemporary Encounters with the* Analects. Peru, IL: Open Court, 2008. (Collection of essays from a wide variety of contemporary scholars of the *Analects*.)

Kupperman, Joel. "Confucius and the Problem of Naturalness." *Philosophy East & West* 18, no. 3 (1968): 175–85. (Discusses the question of how conscious, artificial practice can ever produce "natural," spontaneous behavior.)

Lin Yu-sheng. "The Evolution of the Pre-Confucian Meaning of *Jen* 仁 and the Confucian Concept of Moral Autonomy." *Monumenta Serica* 31 (1924): 172–204. (Classic discussion of the evolution of the term *ren*.)

Nivison, David S. *The Ways of Confucianism: Investigations in Chinese Philosophy*, edited by Bryan Van Norden. Chicago and La Salle, IL: Open Court Press, 1998. (A collection of essays on Confucianism.)

Olberding, Amy, ed. *Dao Companion to the "Analects."* New York: Springer, 2014. (An anthology of secondary essays.)

Roetz, Heiner. *Confucian Ethics of the Axial Age.* Albany, NY: State University of New York Press, 1993. (Argues for the convention-transcending nature of the Confucian project and the autonomy of the Confucian moral agent.)

Shun, Kwong-loi. "*Jen* and *Li* in the *Analects.*" *Philosophy East & West* 43, no. 3 (1993): 457–79. (On the relationship between the virtue of rén 仁 and lǐ 禮, "ritual practice.")

Slingerland, Edward. "The Situationist Critique and Early Confucian Virtue Ethics." *Ethics* 121, no. 2 (2011): 390–419. (Defense of virtue ethics against "situationist" critique, coupled with argument that the early Confucian form of virtue ethics is particularly robust from a modern psychological perspective.)

Taylor, Rodney. *The Religious Dimensions of Confucianism.* Albany, NY: State University of New York Press, 1990. (Emphasizes the oft-overlooked religious nature of the Confucian tradition.)

Van Norden, Bryan W., ed. *Confucius and the "Analects": New Essays.* New York: Oxford University Press, 2001. (Wide-ranging anthology on various aspects of the *Analects.*)

中国邮政 CHINA

80分

古代思想家——荀子

2000—20 (6—3)J

CHAPTER TWO

MOZI

Introduction

Mòzǐ 墨子, "Master Mo" (ca. 480–390 BCE), founded what came to be known as the Mòjiā 墨家 "Mohist School" of philosophy and is the figure around whom the text known as the *Mozi* was formed. His full name is Mò Dí 墨翟. Mozi is arguably the first true philosopher of China known to us. He developed systematic analyses and criticisms of his opponents' positions and presented an array of arguments in support of his own philosophical views. His interest and faith in argumentation led him and his later followers to study the forms and methods of philosophical debate, and their work contributed significantly to the development of early Chinese philosophy. Mozi himself was probably of quite humble origins. He may have been a member of the craft or artisan class, and his philosophy is distinctively anti-aristocratic. Early in life, he may have studied with followers of Kongzi. However, he went on to become a serious critic of the emerging Confucian tradition.[1]

Mozi was not just a philosopher. He led an organized utopian movement whose members engaged in direct social action, including the military defense of states and cities that he judged to be victims of wars of expansion. He was a strong and charismatic leader who inspired his followers to dedicate themselves to his unique view of social justice. This required them to lead austere and quite demanding lives under his direct control and command. Mozi could tax his followers, judge, and punish them; under certain circumstances he could even put them to death. The discipline that defined his movement is reflected in a number of his philosophical positions. His ideal state is highly centralized, orderly, and ideologically unified.

---

1. During Kongzi's life and after his death, people began to declare themselves followers of Kongzi and his Way. At this point, it makes sense to describe these people as constituting a "Confucian" tradition or "Confucianism."

Mozi saw ideological differences and the factionalism they spawned as the primary source of human suffering. Therefore, he sharply criticized the family-based ethical and political system of Kongzi for its inherent partiality and advocated a strict chain of command leading up through a monarch and resting in Heaven. In place of Kongzi's understanding of Rén 仁 as general "Goodness," Mozi interpreted *Ren* more specifically as "benevolence," and advocated a form of state consequentialism, which sought to maximize three basic goods: the wealth, order, and population of the state. As an alternative to Confucian familial love, he argued for jiān'ài 兼愛, which is often translated as "universal love" but is better understood as "impartial care." In Mozi's view, the central ethical problem was excessive *partiality*, not a lack of *compassion*. His primary goal was to change and shape behavior—in particular the way people are treated—and not to cultivate emotions, attitudes, or virtues. He showed little interest in what one would call moral psychology and embraced a simple and highly malleable view of human nature. This led him away from the widely observed Chinese concern with self-cultivation. His general lack of appreciation for psychological goods and the need to control desires and shape dispositions and attitudes also led him to reject categorically the characteristic Confucian concern with culture and ritual. These views are expressed in his arguments against elaborate funerals and musical performances, two mainstays of Confucianism.

While Mozi was not a self-cultivationist, he believed that human beings can change even apparently deeply held attitudes and dispositions quickly and easily. For a variety of reasons, he maintained that people could be induced to take up almost any form of behavior, even behavior that was suicidal. He shared a commonly held early Chinese belief in the psychological tendency to respond in kind to the treatment one receives. He further believed that in an effort to win the favor of their rulers, many people are inclined to act as their rulers desire. Those who do not respond to either of these influences can be motivated and controlled by a system of strict rewards and punishments, enforced by the state and guaranteed by the support of Heaven, ghosts, and spirits. Most important of all, Mozi believed that properly crafted rational arguments provide a strong if not entirely compelling motivation to act, for anyone who is able to understand them; presented with a superior argument, thinking people act accordingly.

Mozi's later following lasted until the time of the short-lived Qin dynasty (221–207 BCE), when the movement seems to have suddenly come to an end. The reasons for this are not well-documented, but it is most likely that a paramilitary group such as the Mohists would never have been tolerated by and could not survive during the centralized and militarized regime of the Qin. There is some irony in this, in that several prominent ideas in the Fǎjiā 法家 "Legalist" thought that served as the state ideology of the Qin find clear precedents in Mozi's philosophy. The later Mohists continued Mozi's early interests and developed sophisticated systems of logical analysis, mathematics, optics, physics, defensive warfare technology and strategy, and a formal ethics based upon calculations of benefit and harm. All of these philosophical concerns can be found in the early strata of the *Mozi* that are represented in the following selections.

Chapter Eight: Honoring the Worthy[2]

Our teacher Mozi[3] says, "The kings, dukes, and great officials who now rule the various states all want their states to be wealthy, their populations great, and their administrations orderly, and yet instead of wealth they get poverty, instead of great populations they get meager ones, and instead of order they get chaos. In this way they fundamentally miss what they desire and get what they dislike."

What is the reason for this?[4]

Our teacher Mozi says, "This is because the kings, dukes, and great officials who rule the various states are not able to honor the worthy and employ the capable in carrying out their rule. And so, in a state where there are many worthy men,

---

2. There are multiple versions of many of the central chapters of the *Mozi*; these probably reflect the views of the three different sects of Mohism, which appeared after Mozi's death. I have chosen what I consider to be the most interesting version of each chapter translated here. (In some cases, I have only translated what I regard as the most interesting sections within a given chapter.) Our chapter headings refer to the primary divisions in standard editions of the complete text.

3. The *Mozi* is unique among early Chinese philosophical texts in the manner in which it refers to its author. Most philosophers of the period were referred to as "Master so-and-so" by adding the honorific zǐ 子 after the person's surname (see *Important Terms* in the appendices). In the case of Mò Dí 墨翟 this would yield "Mozi." But the Mohists refer to their master as zǐmòzǐ 子墨子. This probably meant "Our teacher Master Mo." A similar prefixed use of *zi* is found in the *Gongyang* commentary on the *Spring and Autumn Annals*. (For the *Spring and Autumn Annals*, see *Important Texts* in the appendices.)

4. The *Mozi* often employs the literary device of an unnamed interlocutor to carry forth the dialogue.

good order will be secure, and in a state where there are few worthy men, good order will be tenuous. This is why it is the proper work of kings, dukes, and great officers to increase the number of worthy men in their states."

Since this is the case, what is the best way to go about increasing the number of worthy men?

Our teacher Mozi says, "It is analogous to the case of wanting to increase the number of good archers or charioteers in one's state. One must reward and esteem them, revere and praise them; then one can succeed in increasing the number of good archers or charioteers in one's state. How much more should this be done in the case of worthy men—those who are well versed in virtuous conduct, discrimination in discussion, and broadly knowledgeable! Such men are state treasures, guardians of the altars to the soil and grain.[5] They too must be rewarded and esteemed, revered and praised; then one can succeed in increasing the number of worthy men in one's state.

"This is why in ancient times, when the sage-kings ruled, they announced that:

> Those who are not righteous, I shall not enrich.
> Those who are not righteous, I shall not esteem.
> Those who are not righteous, I shall not regard as kin.
> Those who are not righteous, I shall not get close to.

"When the wealthy and eminent in the state heard this, they retired and thought to themselves, 'At first, we could rely on our wealth and eminence, but now the king promotes the righteous and does not turn away the poor and the humble. This being the case, we too must be righteous.' When the king's relatives heard this, they retired and thought to themselves, 'At first, we could rely on being royal kin, but now the king promotes the righteous and does not turn away the most distant relations. This being the case, we too must be righteous.' When those close to the king heard this, they retired and thought to themselves, 'At first, we could rely on being close to the king, but now the king promotes the righteous and does not turn away those far removed from him. This being the case, we too must be righteous.' When those far removed from the king heard this, they too retired and thought to themselves, 'At first, we thought that being far removed from the king meant we had nothing to rely upon, but now the king promotes the righteous and does not turn away those far removed from him. This being the case, we too must be righteous.' The word spread to those serving in distant cities and outlying regions, to the sons of nobles serving within the court, to all those within the capital, and on

---

5. The site of important state sacrifices and often used as a metaphor for the foundation and stability of the state. Cf. Mozi's various references to this and other sacrificial sites in "On Ghosts" (*Mozi* chapter 31, below).

out to the common people throughout the four corners of the kingdom. Hearing this, they all strove to be righteous."

What is the reason for such success?

Our teacher Mozi says, "Because those above employed those below for only one reason and those below served those above in only one way.[6] This state of affairs can be compared to the case of a rich man who builds a high wall around his house. Once the wall is complete, he has it cut through in one place and uses this for his door. If a thief should enter, the rich man can close the door and search for the thief, knowing that he has no way to escape. Why? Because the rich man has secured what is most vital.

"This is why in ancient times, when the sage-kings ruled, they promoted the virtuous and honored the worthy. Even someone who worked as a farmer, artisan, or merchant—if they had talent, they were promoted, given high rank and a handsome salary, entrusted with responsibility, and empowered to have their orders obeyed. The sage-kings said, 'If their rank is not high, the people will not revere them. If their salary is not substantial, the people will not put trust in them. If their orders are not empowered with authority, the people will not hold them in awe.' These three things were given to the worthy not as rewards but in order to help them complete their duties.

"And so, at that time, rank was awarded on the basis of virtue, work was assigned according to office, reward was distributed according to the amount of labor done, and salary allotted in proportion to the effort expended. And so, officials were not guaranteed constant nobility and people did not have to perpetually remain in a humble state. Those with ability were promoted, those without ability were demoted. This is what it means to 'promote public righteousness and prevent private resentment.'[7]

"And so, in ancient times, Yao promoted Shun from southern Fuyang,[8] entrusted him with the administration of his kingdom, and the world was at peace. Yu promoted Yi from central Yinfang, entrusted him with the administration of his kingdom, and the nine realms were brought to perfection.[9] Tang promoted Yi Yin from among the cooks in his kitchen, entrusted him with the administration

---

6. That is, people were evaluated and served only on the basis of their righteousness.

7. This seems to have been a recognizable political slogan of the time.

8. On Yao, Shun, and the other figures mentioned in this paragraph, see *Important Figures* in the appendices. Fuyang is a place of uncertain location.

9. Yi is Bó Yì 伯益 (not to be confused with the brother of Shu Qi—see *Important Figures* in the appendices). Bo Yi assisted Yu in his flood-control work and served him as an exemplary minister. Yinfang is a place of uncertain location. According to an ancient system of territorial division, China consisted of "nine realms."

of his kingdom, and his plans were all successful. King Wen promoted Hong Yao and Tai Yi from their work with rabbit snares, entrusted them with the administration of his kingdom, and the western territories submitted peacefully.[10] And so, at that time, even among those ministers with substantial salaries and prestigious positions, none failed to be reverent and cautious in carrying out their duties, and even among the farmers, craftsmen, and merchants, none failed to exert themselves in honoring virtue.

"And so good men should be employed as capable assistants and responsible agents. If a ruler is able to retain such men, then his plans will not be frustrated nor his body wearied with work. A ruler's fame shall be assured and his work successfully completed, his best tendencies will flourish and his worst shall not take form all because he retains the support of good men."

This is why our teacher Mozi says, "When things are going well, you must promote worthy men. When things are not going well, you must promote worthy men. And if you would reverently carry on the Way of Yao, Shun, Yu, and Tang, then you must honor the worthy. Honoring the worthy is the root and basis of good government."

Chapter Eleven: Obeying One's Superior

Our teacher Mozi says, "In ancient times, when people first came into being and before there were governments or laws, each person followed their own norm[11] for deciding what was right and wrong.[12] And so where there was one person there was one norm, where there were two people there were two norms, where there were ten people there were ten different norms. As many people as there were, that was how many norms were recognized. In this way people came to approve their own norms for what is right and wrong and thereby condemn the norms of others. And so, they

---

10. Hong Yao and Tai Yi were gamekeepers for King Wen. Technically, "rabbit snares" should be rendered "rabbit nets." See selection # 177 (*Mao* # 278) in Arthur Waley, *The Book of Songs* (London: Allen and Unwin, 1952) for a poem singing the praises of such a gamekeeper, describing him as a fitting companion and confidant for a king. (Note: *The Book of Songs* is Waley's translation of the classic otherwise referred to in this volume as the *Odes*; see *Odes* under *Important Texts* in the appendices.)

11. The character yì 義 that I here translate as "norm" (for deciding what is right and wrong) is often rendered as "right" or "righteousness" (see *Important Terms* in the appendices). The senses are clearly related, but the context here argues for "norm" as more appropriate.

12. "Right and wrong" is the translation of the Chinese terms shì/fēi 是非. Below, these terms are rendered verbally as "to approve" and "to condemn." Cf. *Mengzi* 2A6 and the accompanying note 28 (in chapter 4 of this volume).

mutually condemned each other's norms. For this reason, within families, there was resentment and hatred between fathers and sons and elder and younger brothers that caused them to separate and disperse and made it impossible for them to cooperate harmoniously with one another. Throughout the world, people used water, fire, and poison to harm and injure one another, to the point where if they had strength to spare, they would not use it to help each other; if they had excess goods, they would leave them to rot away rather than distribute them to one another; and if they had helpful teachings, they would hide them away rather than teach them to one another. The chaos that ruled in the world was like what one finds among the birds and beasts.

"Those who understood the nature of this chaos saw that it arose from a lack of rulers and leaders and so they chose the best person among the most worthy and capable in the world and established him as the Son of Heaven. The Son of Heaven was established, but because his strength was not sufficient for the task of ruling the entire world, they chose among the most worthy and capable in the world and installed the best among them as the three imperial ministers. The Son of Heaven and three imperial ministers were established, but because the world is so vast it was impossible for them to know and judge in each case what would be right or wrong, beneficial or harmful for the people of distant states and different regions. And so, they divided up the myriad states and established feudal lords and rulers. The feudal lords and rulers were established, but because their strength was not sufficient for the task before them, they chose among the most worthy and capable in the world and installed them as governors and local leaders.

"Once the governors and local leaders were in place, the Son of Heaven announced his rule to the people of the world saying, 'Whenever you hear of something good or bad, always inform your superior. Whenever your superior approves of something as right you too must approve of it. Whenever your superior condemns something as wrong you too must condemn it. Should a superior commit any transgression, one must offer proper remonstrance. Should your subordinates do anything good, one must widely recommend them. To obey one's superior and to avoid joining together with those in subordinate positions—such conduct will be rewarded by superiors and praised by subordinates. But if you hear of something good or bad and fail to inform your superior, if you are not able to approve of what your superior approves of and condemn what your superior rejects, if you do not offer proper remonstrance when a superior commits a transgression and do not widely recommend subordinates who do good, if you do not obey your superior and you join together with those in subordinate positions—such conduct will be punished by superiors and denounced by the people. This is how superiors shall determine rewards and punishments and they shall make careful examinations to ensure that their judgments are reliable.'

"And so, the leader of each village would be the most benevolent person in the village. When he announced his rule to the people of the village he would say, 'Whenever you hear of anything either good or bad, you must report it to the head of the district. Whenever the head of the district approves of something all of you must also approve of it. Whenever the head of the district condemns something all of you must also condemn it. Eliminate any bad teachings that you may have and study the good teachings of the head of the district. Eliminate any bad practices that you may have and study the good practices of the head of the district. If you do this then how could the district ever become disordered?'

"If we look into how good order was maintained in the district, what do we find? Was it not simply because the leader of the district was able to unify the norms followed within the district that he was able to maintain good order in it?

"The leader of each district would be the most benevolent person in the district. When he announced his rule to the people of the district he would say, 'Whenever you hear of anything either good or bad, you must report it to the ruler of the state. Whenever the ruler of the state approves of something all of you must also approve of it. Whenever the ruler of the state condemns something all of you must also condemn it. Eliminate any bad teachings that you may have and study the good teachings of the ruler of the state. Eliminate any bad practices that you may have and study the good practices of the ruler of the state. If you do this then how could the state ever become disordered?'

"If we look into how good order was maintained in the state, what do we find? Was it not simply because the ruler of the state was able to unify the norms followed within the state that he was able to maintain good order in it?

"The ruler of each state would be the most benevolent person in the state. When he announced his rule to the people of the state he would say, 'Whenever you hear of anything either good or bad, you must report it to the Son of Heaven. Whenever the Son of Heaven approves of something all of you must also approve of it. Whenever the Son of Heaven condemns something all of you must also condemn it. Eliminate any bad teachings that you may have and study the good teachings of the Son of Heaven. Eliminate any bad practices that you may have and study the good practices of the Son of Heaven. If you do this then how could the world ever become disordered?'

"If we look into how good order was maintained in the world, what do we find? Was it not simply because the Son of Heaven was able to unify the norms followed within the world that he was able to maintain good order in it?

"If the people of the world all obey their superiors on up to the Son of Heaven but do not obey Heaven, then Heavenly disasters still will not cease. Now, the hurricanes and torrential rains that regularly are visited upon the people is how Heaven punishes them for not obeying its will."

This is why our teacher Mozi says, "In ancient times, sage-kings created the Five Punishments[13] to facilitate good order among their people. These are like the main thread of a skein of silk or the drawstring of a net. They are how the sage-kings gathered in those in the world who refused to obey their superiors."

Chapter Sixteen: Impartial Caring

Our teacher Mozi says, "The business of a benevolent person is to promote what is beneficial to the world and eliminate what is harmful."

Granted that this is true, what are the greatest harms that are being done in the world today? Our teacher Mozi says, "It is things such as great states attacking small states, great families wreaking havoc on lesser families, the strong robbing the weak, the many doing violence to the few, the clever deceiving the ignorant, and the noble acting arrogantly toward the humble. These are some of the great harms being done in the world. In addition, there are rulers who are not kind, ministers who are not loyal, fathers who are not loving, and children who are not filial. These too are some of the great harms being done in the world. There are also those of low character who use weapons, poison, water, and fire to injure and steal from one another. These too are some of the great harms done in the world."

If we try to discover the origin of these different harms, where do we find they come from? Do they come from caring for and benefiting people? This clearly must be rejected as the origin of these harms. We must recognize that they come from hating and stealing from people. If we wish to distinguish those in the world who hate and steal from people, do we refer to them as impartial or partial? We clearly must call them partial. And so, it is those who are partial in their dealings with others who are the real cause of all the great harms in the world.

This is why our teacher Mozi says, "I condemn partiality."

Now those who condemn another's view must offer something in its place. If one condemns another's view without offering something in its place, this is like adding water to a flood or flame to a fire. Such appeals prove to have no merit.

This is why our teacher Mozi says, "Replace partiality with impartiality."

---

13. The Five Punishments are said to be tattooing the face, cutting off the nose, cutting off the feet, castration, and death.

Since this is what is correct, how then can we replace partiality with impartiality?

Our teacher Mozi says, "If people regarded other people's states in the same way that they regard their own, who then would incite their own state to attack that of another? For one would do for others as one would do for oneself. If people regarded other people's cities in the same way that they regard their own, who then would incite their own city to attack that of another? For one would do for others as one would do for oneself. If people regarded other people's families in the same way that they regard their own, who then would incite their own family to attack that of another? For one would do for others as one would do for oneself. And so, if states and cities do not attack one another and families do not wreak havoc upon and steal from one another, would this be a harm to the world or a benefit? Of course, one must say it is a benefit to the world."

If we try to discover the source of these different benefits, where do we find they come from? Do they come from hating and stealing from people? This clearly must be rejected as the source of these benefits. We must recognize that they come from caring for and benefiting people. If we wish to distinguish those in the world who care for and benefit people, do we refer to them as impartial or partial? We clearly must call them impartial. And so, it is those who are impartial in their dealings with others who are the real cause of all the great benefits in the world.

This is why our teacher Mozi says, "I approve of impartiality. Moreover, earlier I said that, 'The business of a benevolent person is to promote what is beneficial to the world and eliminate what is harmful.' And now I have shown that impartiality gives rise to all the great benefits in the world and that partiality gives rise to all the great harms in the world."

This is why our teacher Mozi says, "I condemn partiality and approve of impartiality for the reasons given above. If one takes impartiality as the correct standard and truly seeks to promote and procure what is beneficial to the world, then those with sharp ears and keen eyes will listen and look out for others. Those with stout legs and strong arms will work for others, and those who understand the Way will educate and instruct others. And so, men who reach old age without finding a wife and having children will get the support they need to live out their years. Young and helpless orphans, who are without father or mother, will find the support they need in order to reach maturity. Now such benefits can be attained only if impartiality is taken as the correct standard. And so, I don't see what reason any person in the world who has heard about impartiality can give for condemning it."

Though this is so, there are still people in the world who condemn impartiality, saying, "It is surely a fine thing. Nevertheless, how can it possibly be applied?"

Our teacher Mozi says, "If it could not be applied, even I would condemn it! But is there really anything that is fine that cannot be put to use? Let us consider both sides of the matter. Suppose there were two people: one who maintains partiality and one who maintains impartiality. And so, the person who maintains partiality would say, 'How can I possibly regard the well-being of my friends as I do my own well-being? How can I possibly regard the parents of my friends as I do my own parents?' And so, when his friends are hungry, the partial person does not feed them. When his friends are cold, he does not clothe them. When his friends are ill, he does not nurture them. And when his friends die, he does not bury them. This is what the partial person says and what he does. But this is not what the impartial person says nor is this how he acts. The impartial person says, 'I have heard that in order to be a superior person in the world, one must regard the well-being of one's friends as one regards one's own well-being; one must regard the parents of one's friends as one regards one's own parents. Only in this way can one be a superior person.' And so, when the impartial person's friends are hungry, he feeds them. When his friends are cold, he clothes them. When his friends are ill, he nurtures them. And when his friends die, he buries them. This is what the impartial person says and what he does.

"Now the words of the two people that we have considered contradict each other and their actions are diametrically opposed. Let us suppose, though, that both are trustworthy in what they say and reliable in what they do. And so, their words and deeds fit together like the two halves of a tally, and they always follow through and act on what they say. If we grant all of this, there is a further question I would like to ask. Suppose one must put on one's armor and helmet and go to war in a vast and open wilderness where life and death are uncertain; or suppose one was sent by one's ruler or high minister to the distant states of Ba, Yue, Qi, or Jing[14] and could not be sure of either reaching them or ever returning from one's mission. Under such conditions of uncertainty, to whom would one entrust the well-being of one's parents, wife, and children? Would one prefer that they be in the care of an impartial person or would one prefer that they be in the care of a partial person? I believe that under such circumstances, there are no fools in all the world. Even though one may not advocate impartiality, one would certainly want to entrust one's family to the person who is impartial. But this is to condemn impartiality in word but prefer it in deed, with the result that one's actions do not accord with what one says. And so, I don't see what reason any person in the world who has heard about impartiality can give for condemning it."

---

14. Ba, Yue, Qi, and Jing are four ancient states that were far removed from the center of Chinese civilization at the time.

Though this is so, there are still people in the world who condemn impartiality, saying, "It is an acceptable way for choosing reliable people but one can't use it to choose one's ruler."

Our teacher Mozi says, "Let us consider both sides of the matter. Suppose there were two rulers: one who maintains impartiality and one who maintains partiality. And so, the ruler who maintains partiality would say, 'How can I possibly regard the well-being of my myriad subjects as I do my own well-being? This is profoundly at odds with the way people in the world feel. How brief is the span of a person's life upon this earth! It rushes by like a galloping team of horses glimpsed through a crack!' And so, when his subjects are hungry, the partial ruler does not feed them. When his subjects are cold, he does not clothe them. When his subjects are ill, he does not nurture them. And when his subjects die, he does not bury them. This is what the partial ruler says and what he does. But this is not what the impartial ruler says nor is this how he acts. The impartial ruler says, 'I have heard that in order to be an enlightened ruler in the world, one must first worry about the well-being of one's people and then worry about oneself. Only in this way can one be an enlightened ruler.' And so, when the impartial ruler's people are hungry, he feeds them. When his people are cold, he clothes them. When his people are ill, he nurtures them. And when his people die, he buries them. This is what the impartial ruler says and what he does.

"Now the words of the two rulers that we have considered contradict each other and their actions are diametrically opposed. Let us suppose, though, that both are trustworthy in what they say and reliable in what they do. And so, their words and deeds fit together like the two halves of a tally, and they always follow through and act on what they say. If we grant all of this, there is a further question I would like to ask. Suppose there were a terrible epidemic in which most of the people suffered bitterly from hunger and cold and many lay dead and unburied in the ditches and gullies.[15] Between these two rulers, which one would the people then follow? I believe that under such circumstances, there are no fools in all the world. Even though one may not advocate impartiality, one would certainly want to follow the ruler who is impartial. But this is to condemn impartiality in word but prefer it in deed, with the result that one's actions do not accord with what one says. And so, I don't see what reason any person in the world who has heard about impartiality can give for condemning it."

Though this is so, there are still people in the world who condemn impartiality, saying, "Impartiality is benevolent and right but how can one practice it?

---

15. People lying unburied in the ditches and gullies was a common trope used to illustrate a state of profound misrule. Cf. for example, *Mengzi* 1B12, 2B4 (not in this volume).

The impossibility of practicing impartiality is like the impossibility of picking up Mount Tai and carrying it across the Chang Jiang or Huang He."[16] And so impartiality is something they want to do but feel is impossible to practice.

Our teacher Mozi says, "As for picking up Mount Tai and carrying it across the Chang Jiang or Huang He, this is something that no human being has ever done. But as for impartially caring for and benefiting one another, this is something that we know the four former sage-kings[17] themselves practiced."

How do we know that the four former sage-kings themselves followed these practices?

Our teacher Mozi says, "I am not of their age or time and so have not personally heard their voices or seen their faces, but I know this by what is written on bamboo and silk, etched on metal and stone, and inscribed on basins and bowls that have passed down to us through succeeding generations. For example, the *Great Oath*[18] says, 'The illumination of King Wen was like the sun and the moon. His brightness reached to the four directions and out to the western regions.' This describes the extensiveness of King Wen's impartial care for the world. It compares his impartiality to the way the sun and the moon impartially illuminate the entire world without showing any favoritism."

Though the impartiality that our teacher Mozi talks about here takes King Wen as its model, it is not just in the *Great Oath* that one finds such examples. The *Oath of Yu*[19] too offers such a model. Yu says,

> Come together, all my people, and heed my words! It is not that I, the little one,[20] dare to bring about such chaos; but the ruler of the Miao[21] is ever more unreasonable and deserves Heaven's punishment. This is why I now lead you, the rulers of the various states, on a campaign to rectify the ruler of the Miao.

---

16. Picking up Mount Tai and carrying it across a vast expanse of water is a common trope for an impossible task. Cf. *Mengzi* 1A7 (in chapter 4), where the vast expanse of water is the North Sea. The Chang Jiang, or Yangtze River, and the Huang He, or Yellow River, are the largest rivers in central China.

17. Kings Yu, Tang, Wen, and Wu (see *Important Figures* in the appendices).

18. The "Great Oath" was a speech purportedly given by King Wu. The original was said to be included in the *History* but was lost. A later forgery is included in the present edition of the *History* and part of it is quite similar to what Mozi quotes here. See James Legge, trans., *The Shoo King*, vol. 3 of *The Chinese Classics* (Oxford: Clarendon Press, 1871; Taipei: SMC Publishing 1991), 296–97.

19. The *Oath of Yu* is a lost section of the *History* that purportedly recorded the words of the sage-king Yu. Again, a passage that is quite similar to what Mozi quotes can be found in the present text. See Legge, *The Shoo King*, 64–65.

20. The "little one" (literally, "small child") is a self-deprecating term of self-reference used by virtuous kings.

21. The Miao are said to be a people who lived to the southeast in the area of present-day Hunan and Hubei.

This shows that the reason Yu launched a campaign to rectify the ruler of the Miao was not because he wanted to increase his wealth and honor, earn for himself additional favors and blessings, or because it pleased his eyes and ears, but rather because he wanted to contribute to the benefit of the world and eliminate what is harmful to it. Such was the impartiality of Yu.

Though the impartiality that our teacher Mozi talks about here takes Yu as its model, it is not just in the *Oath of Yu* that one finds such examples. The *Declaration of Tang*[22] too offers such a model. Tang says,

> I, the little one, Lü,[23] presume to use a dark-colored sacrifice to make my announcement to the Lord of Heaven above. I declare that Heaven's great drought is my responsibility. I do not know if I have committed some offense against those above or below. If there is any merit, I dare not conceal it. If there is any offense, I dare not excuse it. The judgment lies in your mind alone, Lord! If those within my domain have committed any offense, let the responsibility rest with me. If I have committed any offense, let the responsibility not fall upon those within my domain.

This shows that while Tang had the honor of being the Son of Heaven and possessed the wealth of the entire world, he still did not hesitate to present himself as an offering in his sacrificial declaration to the Lord on High, the ghosts, and the spirits. Such was the impartiality of Tang.

Though the impartiality that our teacher Mozi talks about here takes Tang as its model, it is not just in the *Oath of Yu* and the *Declaration of Tang* that one finds such examples. The *Odes of Zhou*[24] too offer such a model. The *Odes of Zhou* say,

> The King's Way is broad so broad;
> Without partiality or party.
> The King's Way is even so even;
> Without party or partiality.

---

22. The *Declaration of Tang* is another lost section of the *History*, one that purportedly recorded the words of the sage-king Tang. However, lines similar to what Mozi here quotes appear in *Analects* 20.1 (not in this volume). Similar lines can also be found scattered throughout the present *Announcement of Tang* section of the *History*. See Legge, *The Shoo King*, 184–90.

23. On the "little one," see note 20 above. Lü is the personal name of King Tang and in such a public context, this use of the personal name is another humble form of self-reference.

24. This leads us to look in the *Odes* (see *Important Texts* in the appendices). However, the present text has only the last four lines quoted here (*Mao* # 203) with slight variation. The first four lines, though, are found with slight variation in the present text of the *History* (see *Important Texts* in the appendices). For the last four lines, see James Legge, trans., *The She King*, vol. 4 of *The Chinese Classics* (Oxford: Clarendon Press, 1871; Hong Kong: Hong Kong University Press, 1970), 353; for the first four, see Legge, *The Shoo King*, 331.

Straight as an arrow;
As even as a whetstone.
It is what the noble man follows;
And the common man admires.

What I have been talking about here is not just some notion or theory. In ancient times, when Kings Wen and Wu ruled, they allocated everything equitably, rewarding the worthy and punishing the wicked without showing any partiality to their relatives or brothers. Such was the impartiality of Kings Wen and Wu. And the impartiality that our teacher Mozi talks about here takes Kings Wen and Wu as its models. So, I don't see what reason any person in the world who has heard about impartiality can give for condemning it.

Though this is so, there are still people in the world who condemn impartiality, saying, "It does not seek what is beneficial for one's parents, so does it not harm filial piety?"

Our teacher Mozi says, "Let us consider the case of a filial son who seeks what is beneficial for his parents. Does a filial son who seeks what is beneficial for his parents want other people to care for and benefit his parents or does he want other people to dislike and steal from his parents? According to the very meaning of filial piety, he must want other people to care for and benefit his parents. Given this, how should one act in order to bring about such a state of affairs? Should one first care for and benefit the parents of another, expecting that they in turn will respond by caring for and benefiting one's own parents? Or should one first dislike and steal from other people's parents, expecting that they in turn will respond by caring for and benefiting one's own parents? Clearly one must first care for and benefit the parents of others in order to expect that they in turn will respond by caring for and benefiting one's own parents. And so, for such mutually filial sons to realize unlimited good results, must they not first care for and benefit other people's parents? Or should they let it be the case that filial sons are the exception and not the rule among the people of the world?

"Let us consider what is said in the writings of the former kings. In the *Elegies*[25] it says,

There are no words that are left unanswered,
No virtue that is left without a response.
If you toss me a peach,
I respond with a plum.

25. The *Elegies* are a section in the *Odes*. Only the first two lines, with slight variation, appear in the present version of the text. See Legge, *The She King*, 514.

According to these lines, anyone who cares for others will receive care from them while anyone who dislikes others will in turn be disliked. And so, I don't see what reason any person in the world who has heard about impartiality can give for condemning it.

"Perhaps people will think that impartial care is too difficult to carry out. But things more difficult than this have been successfully carried out. In the past, King Ling of the state of Chu was fond of slender waists.[26] During his reign the people of Chu ate no more than one meal a day and became so weak that they could not raise themselves up without the support of a cane nor could they walk without leaning against a wall. Curtailing one's food is something very difficult to do, but masses of people did it in order to please King Ling. Within a single generation the people changed because they wanted to accord with the wishes of their superior.

"In the past, Gou Jian, King of the state of Yue, was fond of bravery. And so, he taught his soldiers and subjects to be brave. But since he was not sure if they were really brave, he had his ships set aflame and ordered that the drums signal an advance. His troops fell on top of one another in their forward charge and countless numbers of them perished in the water and flames. Even when they ceased drumming, still the troops did not retreat. We can say that the soldiers of Yue were resolute indeed! Charging into flames is something very difficult to do, but masses of people did it in order to please the King of Yue. Within a single generation the people changed because they wanted to accord with the wishes of their superior.

"In the past, Duke Wen of Jin was fond of rough and simple attire. During his reign the people of Jin wrapped themselves in sheets of cloth, wore sheepskin jackets, hats of raw silk, and hempen shoes. They would dress this way when they had an audience with the Duke and parade around in such attire at court. Getting people to wear rough and simple attire is something very difficult to do, but masses of people did it in order to please Duke Wen. Within a single generation the people changed because they wanted to accord with the wishes of their superior.

"Curtailing one's food, charging into flames, and wearing rough and simple attire are among the most difficult things in the world to get people to do, but masses of people did these things in order to please their superiors. Within a single generation the people changed. Why? Because they wanted to accord with the wishes of their superiors.

"Now as for impartially caring for and benefiting one another, such things are incalculably beneficial and easy to practice. The only problem is that there are no

---

26. This and the following story about the King of Yue are also cited by Han Feizi in "The Two Handles" (*Han Feizi* chapter 7, in chapter 10 of this volume).

superiors who take delight in them. If only there were superiors who delighted in them, who encouraged their practice through rewards and praise, and threatened those who violate them with penalties and punishments, I believe that the people would take to impartially caring for and benefiting one another just as naturally as fire rises up and water flows down. One could not stop these things from being practiced anywhere in the world.

"And so, impartiality is the way of the sage-kings. It offers security to kings, dukes, and great officials and provides ample food and clothing to the myriad people. So, for gentlemen there is nothing better than carefully inquiring into the nature of impartiality and working to carry it out. Those who do so are sure to be kind as rulers, loyal as ministers, loving as fathers, filial as sons, good companions as older brothers, and respectful as younger brothers. And so, any gentleman who wishes to be a kind ruler, loyal minister, loving father, filial son, a good companion as an elder brother, and respectful as a younger brother cannot but practice the kind of impartiality I have been describing. This is the way of the sage-kings and a great benefit to the myriad people."

Chapter Seventeen: A Condemnation of Aggressive War

[Our teacher Mozi says,] "Now suppose someone enters another's orchard and steals their peaches and plums. When the people hear about this, they will condemn such a person, and if those above who administer the government get hold of him, they will punish him. Why? Because he takes from others in order to benefit himself. Stealing another's dogs, hogs, chickens, and pigs is even more wrong than entering another's orchard and stealing their peaches and plums. Why? Because more is taken from others; it is even more inhumane and a more serious crime. Entering another person's stable and stealing their horses and cattle is even more wrong than stealing their dogs, hogs, chickens, and pigs. Why? Because more is taken from others. If more is taken from others, it is even more inhumane and a more serious crime. Killing an innocent person, stripping him of his clothes, and taking his spear and sword is even more wrong than entering his stable and stealing his horses and cattle. Why? Because more is taken from others. If more is taken from others, it is even more inhumane and a more serious crime. Up to this point, all the gentlemen of the world know well enough to condemn such actions and declare that they are wrong. But when it comes to the great wrong of attacking another state, they do not know enough to condemn it. Rather, they praise this and declare that it is the right thing to do. Can they be said to understand the difference between right and wrong?

"Killing someone is wrong and must be punished with execution. But if we extrapolate from this view, then killing ten people is ten times as bad and must be punished with ten executions, and killing one hundred people is one hundred times as bad and must be punished with one hundred executions. Up to this point, all the gentlemen of the world know well enough to condemn such actions and declare that they are wrong. But when it comes to the great wrong of attacking another state, they do not know enough to condemn it. Rather, they praise this and declare that it is the right thing to do. They really do not understand that this is wrong. That is why they record their praise of such activity and hand down these records to later generations. If they really understood that this is wrong, why would they record their wrongs and hand them down to later generations?

"Now suppose there is someone who does the following: when they see a little black, they say that it is black but when they see a lot of black, they say that it is white. We would just have to say that such a person cannot distinguish between black and white. Or suppose that when they taste a little bitterness, they say that it is bitter, but when they taste a lot of bitterness, they say that it is sweet. We would just have to say that such a person cannot distinguish between bitter and sweet. But now people see a small wrong and know enough to condemn it but see the great wrong of attacking another state and do not know enough to condemn it. Rather, they praise this and declare that it is the right thing to do. Can they be said to understand the difference between right and wrong? This is how we know that the gentlemen of the world are confused about the difference between right and wrong."

Chapter Twenty: For Moderation in Expenditures

[Our teacher Mozi says,] "When a sage rules a state, that state will be twice as well-off. When a sage rules the empire, the empire will be twice as well-off. But they are not made twice as well-off by adding territory from without. It is rather by eliminating wasteful expenditures within the state that such rulers are able to make them twice as well-off. When sage-kings rule, whenever they issue orders, undertake an enterprise, employ the people, or expend their resources, they never do anything that is not useful. And so, they never waste their resources or overburden their people yet are able to generate great benefits.

"What is the purpose of clothes? It is to protect us from the cold of winter and the heat of summer. The proper way to make clothes is such that they keep one warm in winter and cool in summer and that is all. Whatever does not contribute to these ends should be eliminated. What is the purpose of houses? It is to protect us from the wind and cold of winter, the heat and rain of summer, and to keep out robbers and thieves. Once these ends are secured that is all. Whatever does not contribute to these ends should be eliminated. What is the purpose of armor, shields, and weapons? It is to protect us from bandits, rebels, robbers, and thieves. Should there be bandits, rebels, robbers, and thieves, those who have armor, shields, and weapons will be victorious, while those without armor, shields, and weapons will not. And so, sages work to produce armor, shields, and weapons. Whenever they make armor, shields, and weapons they seek to make them as light, sharp, strong, and resilient as they can; that is all. Whatever does not contribute to these ends should be eliminated. What is the purpose of boats and vehicles? Vehicles are used to travel over land and boats are used to travel over water such that one can bring together and exchange what is beneficial throughout the world. The proper way to make boats and vehicles is such that they are as light and easy to use as possible and that is all. Whatever does not contribute to these ends should be eliminated. In making these various things, sage-kings never add anything that is not useful. And so, they never waste their resources or overburden their people yet are able to generate great benefits.

"If one could eliminate the fondness that kings, dukes, and great officials have for accumulating quantities of pearls and jades, birds and beasts, and dogs and horses, and use this revenue to increase the availability of clothes, houses, armor, shields, weapons, boats, and vehicles—could one double the numbers of these? Doubling the number of such things would not be hard. What then would it be hard to double? Only the number of people. And yet one can also double the number of people. In the past, the sage-kings established a law that said, "No man of twenty can be without a family. No woman of fifteen can be without a husband." Such was the law of the sage-kings. But since the sage-kings have passed away the people have grown remiss. Those who want to start a family at an early age do so at age twenty, while those who want to start a family late do so at age forty. If we combine these, it still means that men are starting families on average ten years later than the age decreed by the law of the sage-kings. If all of them have one child every three years, then two or three children should have been born during that ten-year period. And so, is it not only by getting people to start families early in life that one can double the population?

"This is the only way to double the population, but those who rule the world today actually work in many ways to lessen the population. They overwork and overtax their people to the point where many lack sufficient resources, with the result that those who die of hunger and cold are more than one can count. Moreover, the great officers encourage rulers to raise armies and attack neighboring states. The longer campaigns take up to a year while the shorter ones last several months.

This means that men and women don't see each other for long periods of time, and in this way the population is reduced. During these campaigns, some become ill and die because they lack a stable living arrangement with regular food and water; others die in ambushes, fiery assaults, sieges, and battles. Together, their numbers are beyond reckoning. This is because the rulers of today are finding more and more ways to lessen the population. Such things never occur when sages rule. Such is not the way sages rule. They find more and more ways to increase the population."

This is why our teacher Mozi says, "To eliminate everything that is not useful is to carry out the Way of the sage-kings and offer great benefit to the world."

Chapter Twenty-Five: For Moderation in Funerals

Our teacher Mozi says, "The way benevolent people plan on behalf of the world is just like the way filial children plan on behalf of their parents." Now how is it that filial children plan for their parents?

Our teacher Mozi says, "If their parents are poor, they do what they can to enrich them. If the members of their clan are few, they do what they can to increase their numbers. If the family is in chaos, they do what they can to make it well-ordered. In pursuing these ends they may find that their strength is insufficient, their resources inadequate, or their knowledge too limited, and that they fall short. But they would never hold back any of their strength or any scheme or advantage and not apply these in their efforts to realize their parents' well-being."

These are the three benefits that filial children plan for on behalf of their parents. And this is the way they work to realize these ends. This is also the way that benevolent people plan on behalf of the world.

Our teacher Mozi says, "If the world is poor, benevolent people do what they can to enrich it. If the people are few, benevolent people do what they can to increase their numbers. If the world is in chaos, benevolent people do what they can to make it well-ordered. In pursuing these ends benevolent people may find that their strength is insufficient, their resources inadequate, or their knowledge too limited, and that they fall short. But they would never hold back any of their strength or any scheme or advantage and not apply these in their efforts to realize the world's well-being."

These are the three benefits that benevolent people plan for on behalf of the world. And this is the way they work to realize these ends. But now the sage-kings of the three dynasties of old[27] have passed away and the world has lost sight of what

---

27. The Xia, Shang, and Zhou dynasties (see *Important Periods* in the appendices).

is right. The gentlemen of later ages are divided in their opinions. Some maintain that lavish funerals and prolonged mourning[28] are benevolent and right and the proper task of filial children. Others maintain that lavish funerals and prolonged mourning are neither benevolent nor right and are not the proper task of filial children.

Our teacher Mozi says, "These two groups contradict each other in word and oppose each other in deed. Both say, 'I am dutifully following the Way of Yao, Shun, Yu, Tang, Wen, and Wu,' and yet they contradict each other in word and oppose each other in deed. And so, people of later ages have become suspicious of the claims of both groups. If one doubts the claims of both groups then one should turn and consider them in regard to ruling the state and governing the people, to see whether or not lavish funerals and prolonged mourning promote the three benefits discussed earlier. If by following their words and implementing their plans concerning lavish funerals and prolonged mourning one really would enrich the poor, increase the population, and bring stability to precarious situations and order to chaos, then these things clearly are benevolent, right, and the proper task of filial children. Those who offer counsel could not but encourage them. Benevolent people would work to make such practices flourish throughout the world; they would seek to establish them and bring the people to praise them and to follow them, to the end of their days. However, if by following their words and implementing their plans concerning lavish funerals and prolonged mourning one really cannot enrich the poor, increase the population, or bring stability to precarious situations and order to chaos, then these things clearly are not benevolent and right or the proper task of filial children. Those who offer counsel could not but discourage them. Benevolent people would work to eradicate such practices throughout the world; they would seek to abolish them and bring the people to condemn them and to never follow them, to the end of their days. And so, from ancient times until the present, it has never been the case that bringing the world to a flourishing state and eliminating what is harmful to the world has led the state and the people to disorder."

Now there are many gentlemen in the world who are still in doubt as to whether or not lavish funerals and prolonged mourning are right or wrong, beneficial or harmful. And so, our teacher Mozi says, "Let us examine the case. Now if we were to implement the teachings of those who follow and uphold lavish funerals and prolonged mourning, then in mourning for a king, duke, or high official, they

---

28. Almost certainly, Mozi here has in mind the Confucians who maintained elaborate and prolonged rituals of mourning. See for example, *Analects* 17.21 (in chapter 1 of this volume), *Mengzi* 3A5 and 7A39 (in chapter 4 of this volume), and Xunzi chapter 19, "Discourse on Ritual" (in chapter 9 of this volume).

prescribe that there be several inner and outer coffins, a deep grave, many layers of burial clothes, elaborately and intricately embroidered funeral shrouds, and a massive burial mound. Among common men and women this would exhaust the resources of the entire family. And even a feudal lord would have to empty his entire state treasury before the appropriate amount of gold, jade, and pearls could adorn the body and the proper quantities of silk, carriages, and horses could fill up the tomb. In addition, since one is to see off the dead as if they were simply changing their abode, it is required that numerous draperies and canopies, offering vessels of various kinds, tables and chairs, pots and basins, spears and swords, feathered banners, and articles made of tooth and hide must be buried along with them. It is also said that when an emperor or feudal lord dies, as many as several hundred and no fewer than several tens of retainers are to be sacrificed in order to accompany the deceased.[29] When a general or great official dies, as many as several tens and no fewer than several are to be sacrificed."

What are the rules for one who is in mourning?

Our teacher Mozi says, "Mourners are to cry and wail irregularly, at all times of the day and night, and to sound as if their sobs are choked off. They are to dress in sackcloth, allow their tears to run down without wiping them away, and live in a mourning hut made of straw, sleeping upon a rush mat and using a lump of dirt as their pillow. Moreover, they are to encourage each other to refuse food and starve themselves and to wear thin clothing in order to suffer from the cold, so that they come to have sunken faces and eyes, a sallow and darkened complexion, poor hearing and sight, and limbs too weak to function. It is also said that the most noble of people uphold the rites of mourning to the point where they cannot rise up without assistance and cannot walk without a cane, and they follow these practices for three years. This is what would happen if the state took such teachings as its model and followed them as its Way. Should kings, dukes, and other great men follow such practices, they would not be able to come early to court and retire late in order to hear litigation and carry out the affairs of the government. Should officers and officials follow such practices, they would be unable to administer the Five Offices and Six Treasuries[30] in order to ensure that crops and timber are harvested and the

---

29. This refers to ritual sacrifice, most popular during the Shang but still practiced in Mozi's own time. Mengzi quotes Kongzi as definitively rejecting even the vestiges of such practices. See *Mengzi* 1A4 (not in this volume).

30. A list of these offices and their duties can be found in a later work called the *Liji* ("Book of Rites"). See the entry on the *Rites* under *Important Texts* in the appendices to this volume. For a translation, see James Legge, trans., *The Li Chi: Book of Rites*, vol. 1 (Oxford: Clarendon Press, 1885; New York: University Books, 1967), 109–10.

granaries kept full. Should farmers follow such practices, they would be unable to go out to the fields early and return home late in order to carry out the plowing, planting, and tending of crops. Should the various craftsmen follow such practices, they would be unable to work on boats and carts and fashion various vessels and utensils. Should women follow such practices, they would be unable to rise at dawn and retire at night in order to complete their work of spinning and weaving. And so lavish funerals entail burying a great deal of wealth, and prolonged mourning entails prohibiting people from pursuing their vocations for an extended period of time. The former takes wealth that has already been created and buries it, while the latter prohibits new members of society from being born for an extended period of time. To pursue wealth in this manner is like seeking a harvest while prohibiting plowing! Such practices have nothing to offer in regard to explaining how to become wealthy. And so, we now know that lavish funerals and prolonged mourning cannot enrich one's state."

But perhaps it has value for those who wish to increase the population of their states?

Our teacher Mozi says, "It has nothing to offer in this regard either. Now consider what would result if lavish funerals and prolonged mourning were adopted as official policy. When one's ruler died, one would mourn him for three years. When one's mother or father died, one would mourn them for three years. When one's wife or eldest son died, one would mourn them for three years. Whenever any of these five people died, one would mourn them for three years. Next, one would mourn for one's paternal uncles, brothers, and other sons, and one's various close relatives for five months. You are to mourn for several months for fraternal aunts, sisters, first cousins, and maternal uncles. And there are set standards describing the proper levels of emaciation mourners must attain. They are to have sunken faces and eyes, a sallow and darkened complexion, poor hearing and sight, and limbs too weak to function. It is also said that the most noble of people uphold the rites of mourning to the point where they cannot rise up without assistance and cannot walk without a cane, and follow these practices for three years.

"This is what would happen if the state took such teachings as its model and followed them as its Way. If the people starve themselves in this manner, then they will be unable to withstand the cold of winter or the heat of summer and countless numbers of them will grow ill and die. This greatly diminishes the chances for men and women to procreate. To seek to increase the population in this way is like seeking to increase people's longevity by getting them to fall upon their swords. Such practices have nothing to offer with regard to explaining how to increase the population. And so, we now know that lavish funerals and prolonged mourning cannot increase the number of people in one's state."

But perhaps it has value for those who wish to bring good order to the government?

Our teacher Mozi says, "It has nothing to offer in this regard either. Now consider what would result if lavish funerals and prolonged mourning were adopted as official policy. The state would be poor, the people few, and the government in chaos. This is what would happen if the state took such teachings as its model and followed them as its Way. If those above were to carry out these practices, they would be unable to attend to their affairs. If those below were to carry out these practices, they would be unable to pursue their various tasks. If those above are unable to attend to their affairs, then the government will be in chaos. If those below are unable to pursue their various tasks, then food and clothing will be in short supply. If these are in short supply, then a younger brother who seeks for such things from his elder brother will be refused and will come to feel unbrotherly. In time he will come to resent his elder brother. Children who seek for such things from their parents will be refused and will come to feel unfilial. In time they will come to resent their parents. Ministers who seek for such things from their rulers will be refused and will come to feel disloyal. In time they will rebel against their superiors. This will lead unruly and depraved people who lack proper clothing and sufficient food to build up resentment and indignation in their hearts and express it in wanton violence that cannot be stopped. And so, robbers and thieves will increase while decent and good people grow increasingly scarce. To seek to bring good order to one's state by increasing the number of thieves and robbers and decreasing the number of decent and good people is like asking someone who is standing in front of you to turn around three times without exposing his back to you. Such practices have nothing to offer in regard to explaining how to bring good order to the government. And so, we now know that lavish funerals and prolonged mourning cannot bring good order to one's state."

But perhaps it has value for those who wish to prevent large states from attacking small states?

Our teacher Mozi says, "It has nothing to offer in this regard either. Ever since the ancient sage-kings passed away and the world lost a sense of what is right, the feudal lords have relied upon force of arms to attack one another. To the south there are the kings of Chu and Yue and to the north there are the rulers of Qi and Jin.[31] They all mercilessly drill and train their troops with the aim of attacking and absorbing one another and thereby gaining control of all the world. And so, whenever a large state fails to attack a small one it is only because the small state has an abundant stock of provisions, well-maintained fortifications, and harmony

---

31. The rulers of these particular states were jousting for preeminence in Mozi's time.

between its rulers and subjects. This is why great states do not want to attack it. If its provisions were not abundant, its fortifications not well-maintained, or it lacked harmony between its rulers and subjects, then large states would want to attack it. Now consider what would result if lavish funerals and prolonged mourning were adopted as official policy. The state would be poor, the people few, and the government in chaos. If the state is poor, it lacks the means to accumulate abundant provisions. If its people are few, it lacks the labor needed to maintain its walls and moats. If it is in chaos, then it will not be victorious in attack nor secure in defense. And so, we now know that lavish funerals and prolonged mourning cannot prevent large states from attacking small ones."

But perhaps it has value for those who wish to win the blessings of the Lord on High, ghosts, and spirits?

Our teacher Mozi says, "It has nothing to offer in this regard either. Now consider what would result if lavish funerals and prolonged mourning were adopted as official policy. The state would be poor, the people few, and the government in chaos. If the state is poor its sacrificial offerings of millet and wine will not be clean and pure. If its people are few, there will not be enough of them to serve the Lord on High, ghosts, and spirits. And if its government is in chaos, then its sacrifices will not be offered regularly and at the proper times. Now suppose this reaches the point where serving the Lord on High, ghosts, and spirits is eventually prohibited and stopped. If such a policy is implemented, the Lord on High, ghosts, and spirits would discuss this among themselves up above saying, 'Which is better? To have or to not have such people? I suppose there is no difference to us whether they exist or not!' Then were the Lord on High, ghosts, and spirits to send down calamities and punishments and abandon such a people, would this not merely be fitting?[32]

"This is why the sages of old prescribed the following methods for burial. They said that a coffin of plain wood three inches thick is enough to house the body as it decays. There should be three layers of funeral clothes, enough to cover up the unpleasantness. As for the depth of the grave, it should not be so deep as to hit water but not so shallow as to allow a stench. The burial mound should rise no higher than three feet. If one followed these methods, the deceased was properly buried. The living must not engage in prolonged mourning but should quickly go

---

32. As can be clearly seen here and in the following two chapters (*Mozi* 26 and 31), Mozi was a religious conservative and a fundamentalist. He insisted that the belief in and worship of the Lord on High, ghosts, and spirits was necessary for a stable and flourishing society. He was very much opposed to the more naturalized, psychological interpretations of religious ceremony that were evolving among Confucian thinkers of the time. For more on the "Lord on High," see the Introduction to this volume. Cf. *Analects* 3.12, 6.22, 7.35, and 11.12 (in chapter 1 of this volume).

about their tasks, each person doing what they are best at in order to mutually benefit one another. These are the methods laid down by the sage-kings."

Now those who advocate lavish funerals and prolonged mourning say,
"Although lavish funerals and prolonged mourning cannot enrich the poor, increase
a sparse population, stabilize a precarious situation, or bring good order to chaos,
nevertheless, such is the Way of the sage-kings."

Our teacher Mozi says, "This is not the case. In ancient times, when Yao went
north to instruct the eight Di barbarian tribes,[33] he died en route and was buried on
the northern slopes of Mount Qiong.[34] His corpse was dressed in only three layers
of burial clothing and interred in a coffin of plain wood that was bound together
with common vines. Mourning began only after the coffin had been lowered into
the grave. The grave was then filled in and no burial mound was erected. Once the
burial was complete, oxen and horses freely crossed over the grave.[35] When Shun
went west to instruct the seven Rong barbarian tribes,[36] he died en route and was
buried in the marketplace of Nanji.[37] His corpse was dressed in only three layers
of burial clothing and interred in a coffin of plain wood that was bound together
with common vines. Once the burial was complete, the people in the market freely
crossed over the grave. When Yu went east to instruct the nine Yi barbarian tribes,[38]
he died en route and was buried on Mount Huiji.[39] His corpse was dressed in only
three layers of burial clothing and interred in a coffin of plain wood only three
inches thick. The coffin was bound with common vines; it was not fitted tightly
together nor was a ramp needed to lower it into the ground.[40] The grave was dug to
a depth that did not hit water but was not so shallow as to allow a stench to escape.
Once he was buried, the excess dirt was piled up as a burial mound. It came to no
more than three feet in height."

So, if we consider the case on the basis of these three sage-kings, lavish funerals
and prolonged mourning are not in fact the way of the sage-kings. These three kings

---

33. The name given to various non-Chinese people to the north of Chinese territory.

34. The location of this mountain is not clear, though it obviously was located somewhere to the north of
what was Chinese territory at the time.

35. Showing that it was not accorded any special status.

36. The name given to various non-Chinese people to the west of Chinese territory.

37. Scholars do not agree about the location of this town. It obviously was located somewhere to the west of
what was Chinese territory at the time.

38. The name given to various non-Chinese people to the east of Chinese territory. Thus, Mozi's narrative
purports to report on funeral practices throughout all of China and its three land borders.

39. A mountain located in Shanyin County, in the present-day Zhejiang Province.

40. This indicates that the grave was of very modest proportions for a king.

each were honored as the Son of Heaven and possessed all the wealth in the world. Is it plausible to suppose that they chose to be buried in the way in which they were buried because they were worried about having enough to spend?

But the way in which kings, dukes, and high officials are buried today is very different from this. There must be outer and inner coffins and a three-layered shroud of embroidered hide. Once the jade disks and stones are prepared, there must also be spears, swords, sacrificial vessels, pots and basins, embroidery, bolts of silk, and thousands of sets of bridles. The deceased must be provided with horses and carriages along with women entertainers and their instruments. There must be ramps leading down to and connecting with the tomb and the burial mound should resemble a hill or small mountain. The extent to which such practices interfere with the work of the people and dissipate their wealth is beyond calculation. But this is the degree to which people are willing to pursue useless endeavors.

This is why our teacher Mozi says, "Earlier, I began by saying that if by following the words and implementing the plans of those who advocate lavish funerals and prolonged mourning one really could enrich the poor, increase the population, and bring stability to precarious situations and order to chaos, then these things clearly are benevolent and right and the proper task of filial children. Those who offer counsel could not but encourage them. However, if by following the words and implementing the plans of those who advocate lavish funerals and prolonged mourning one really cannot enrich the poor, increase the population, and bring stability to precarious situations and order to chaos, then these things clearly are not benevolent and right or the proper task of filial children. Those who offer counsel could not but discourage them.

"But we have seen that those who seek to enrich their states through these practices will actually impoverish it. Those who seek to increase the population of their states through these practices will actually decrease it. Those who seek to bring good order to their states through these practices will simply throw it into chaos. Those who seek to stop large states from attacking small states through these practices will not succeed. And those who seek to gain the blessing of the Lord on High, ghosts, and spirits through these practices will receive only disaster. If we look up to the way of Yao, Shun, Yu, Tang, Wen, and Wu we find they were opposed to such practices. If we look down to the policies of Jie, Tyrant Zhou, You, and Li we find they accorded with such practices.[41] If we consider things on this basis, then clearly lavish funerals and prolonged mourning are not the way of the sage-kings."

---

41. Yao, Shun, Yu, Tang, Wen, and Wu are paradigmatically sagacious rulers, while Jie, Tyrant Zhou, You, and Li are paradigmatically vicious rulers. See *Important Figures* in the appendices.

Now those who support lavish funerals and prolonged periods of mourning say, "If lavish funerals and prolonged mourning really are not the way of the sage-kings, why is it that the gentlemen of the Middle Kingdom[42] continue these practices without interruption and follow them uncritically?"

Our teacher Mozi says, "This is just a case of people 'following what they are used to and approving of what is customary.'[43] In ancient times, east of the state of Yue was the state of Kaishu.[44] When a first son was born to the people of this state, they would carve him up and eat him, saying it was beneficial to his future younger brothers. When their father died, they would carry their mothers off to some distant place and abandon them there, saying, 'One cannot live with the wife of a ghost!' These practices were both official policy and the popular custom. They were continued without interruption and followed uncritically. But how can this be the way to realize what is benevolent and right? This is just a case of people 'following what they are used to and approving of what is customary.' South of the state of Chu was the state of the people of Yan.[45] When their parents died, they would remove and discard the flesh from their bones and then bury the bones.[46] This was the way to be a filial child. West of the state of Qin[47] was the state of Yiqu.[48] When their parents died, they would gather together kindling and firewood and burn the corpse. As the smoke would rise, they would say that their parents were 'ascending far off.' This was the way to be a filial child. These practices were both official policy and the popular custom. They were continued without interruption and followed uncritically. But how can this be the way to realize what is benevolent and right? This is just a case of people 'following what they are used to and approving of what is customary.'

"If we consider the funeral practices of these three states, then clearly they are deficient. If we consider the funeral practices of gentlemen in the Middle Kingdom,

---

42. That is, China.

43. This appears to have been a common saying of the times.

44. The precise location of this state is uncertain but its location, "east of the state of Yue," connotes a faraway and culturally primitive area.

45. The precise location of this state is uncertain but its location, "south of the state of Chu," connotes a faraway and culturally primitive area.

46. Such secondary reburial of bones, while never the dominant practice, is well attested in very early China. There is evidence for the practice in the Central Plains and Northwest as far back as the fifth millennium BCE. See David N. Keightley, "Early Civilization in China: Reflections on How It Became Chinese," in *Heritage of China,* ed. Paul S. Ropp (Berkeley, CA: University of California Press, 1990), 24.

47. Qin was the state farthest to the west and was considered culturally backward in Mozi's time.

48. In the basic annals section for the state of Qin in Sima Qian's *Shiji* ("Record of the Historian"), there is reference to a state by this name. Its exact location is still a matter of debate.

then clearly they are excessive. If one were to greatly increase the deficiency of the one and greatly diminish the excess of the latter, then there would be moderation in funerals. Even though it is good to give people clothing and food when they are alive, these things still must be given in moderation. When people die, it is good to give them funerals. But how could it be that in this alone we show no moderation?"

Our teacher Mozi says that this is the proper model for a funeral: "A coffin three inches thick is adequate for the decaying bones. Three layers of clothes are adequate for the decaying flesh. The grave should be dug to a depth that does not strike water but that also does not allow fumes to escape to the surface. The burial mound should only be high enough to clearly mark the spot. There should be crying as one sees the departed off and as one comes back from the grave. But as soon as people have returned to their homes, they should resume their individual livelihoods. There should be regular sacrificial offerings made to extend filiality to one's parents."

And so, I say that in this way our teacher Mozi's model neglects the good neither of the living nor of the dead. This is why our teacher Mozi says, "If gentlemen today sincerely wish to be benevolent and right and desire to become superior men, if they want to follow the way of the sage-kings of old, and work for the benefit of the people of the Middle Kingdom today, then they should make moderation in mourning their official policy and must not fail to examine this matter carefully."

Chapter Twenty-Six: Heaven's Will[49]

Our teacher Mozi says, "Gentlemen in the world today understand small matters but not those that are great. How do I know this? I know this from how they conduct themselves within their families. If one is living at home[50] and commits some offense against the head of the clan, there are always the homes of neighbors to which one might flee. And yet, one's parents, brothers, and friends will unite and caution one, saying, 'You must be careful! You must be circumspect! How can you live at home and offend against the head of the clan?' This is not only how things are in the case of living at home, it is also so in the case of living in a given state. If one is living in a state and commits some offense against the ruler of the state, there are always neighboring states to which one might flee. And yet, one's parents,

---

49. The word translated here as "will" is zhì 志, which means the settled and persisting intention of an agent. For Mozi, Heaven was less a personality with a capricious or unknowable will and more one with an established, observable, and predictable set of inclinations.

50. Mozi has in mind here the practice of living in a family compound, where several generations share a common courtyard but each have their separate quarters.

brothers, and friends will unite and caution one, saying, 'You must be careful! You must be circumspect! Who can live in a state and offend against its ruler?'

"Since people offer each other such strong admonitions in these cases, where there is still some place to which one might flee, should they not think it appropriate to offer even stronger warnings in a case where there is no place to which one might flee? For there is the saying, 'Committing offense in broad daylight, where can one flee to?'[51] The answer of course is that there is nowhere to flee. For Heaven will clearly see you even if you run to the forests, valleys, or hidden places where none lives. But for some reason the gentlemen of the world don't know enough to warn each other about offending Heaven. This is how I know that the gentlemen of the world understand small matters but not those that are great.

"This being the case, what is it that Heaven desires and what does it dislike? Heaven desires what is right and dislikes what is not right. This being so, if I lead the people of the world to act in accordance with what is right, then I will be doing what Heaven desires. And if I do what Heaven desires, then Heaven will do what I desire. Such being the case, what is it that I desire and what do I dislike? I desire good fortune and a substantial salary, and dislike calamities and disasters. If I do not do what Heaven desires but rather what it does not desire, then I will lead people to act in ways that lead them into disaster and calamity. But how do I know that Heaven desires what is right and dislikes what is not right? I say this is so because, throughout the world, wherever there is right there is life, and wherever there is an absence of right there is death. Wherever there is right there is wealth, wherever there is an absence of right there is poverty. Wherever there is right there is good order, wherever there is an absence of right there is disorder. Heaven desires to have life and dislikes death, desires to have wealth and dislikes poverty, desires to have good order and dislikes disorder. This is how I know that Heaven desires what is right and dislikes what is not right.

"Moreover, what is right is what offers a standard of governing. Such a standard is not given by subordinates to govern their superiors but rather must come from superiors to govern subordinates. This is why the people devote themselves to carrying out their various tasks but do not make up their own standard. There are ministers and officials to govern them. Ministers and officials devote themselves to carrying out their various tasks but do not make up their own standard. There are the three high counselors and feudal lords to govern them. The three high counselors and feudal lords devote themselves to administering the government but they do not make up their own standard. There is the Son of Heaven to govern them. The Son of Heaven does not make up his own standard. There is Heaven to govern

---

51. This seems to have been a common saying of the time but its source is unknown.

him. The gentlemen of the world clearly understand that the Son of Heaven governs the three high counselors and feudal lords, the ministers and officials and the people. But that Heaven governs the Son of Heaven is something that people do not yet clearly understand.

"This is why in ancient times the sage-kings of the three dynasties,[52] Yu, Tang, Wen, and Wu, wanted to make clear to the people of the world that Heaven governs the Son of Heaven. And so, each of them fattened up oxen and sheep, dogs and swine, and prepared pure offerings of millet and wine as sacrifices to the Lord on High, the ghosts, and spirits and prayed for Heaven's blessings. I have never heard of a case where Heaven prayed for blessings from the Son of Heaven and this is how I know that Heaven governs the Son of Heaven."

The Son of Heaven is the most honored person in the world and the richest person in the world. And so those who desire riches and honors cannot but accord with the will of Heaven. Those who accord with Heaven's will, caring for one another impartially, and benefiting one another in their interactions, will surely be rewarded. Those who oppose Heaven's will, disliking one another out of partiality and stealing from one another in their interactions, will surely be punished. This being so, who has accorded with Heaven's will and been rewarded? Who has opposed Heaven's will and been punished?

Our teacher Mozi says, "In ancient times the sage-kings of the three dynasties, Yu, Tang, Wen, and Wu, were among those who accorded with Heaven's will and were rewarded. In ancient times the vicious kings of the three dynasties, Jie, Tyrant Zhou, You, and Li, were among those who opposed Heaven's will and were punished."

That being so, how were Yu, Tang, Wen, and Wu rewarded?

Our teacher Mozi says, "On high they honored Heaven, in the middle realm they served the ghosts and spirits, and below they cared for human beings. And so, Heaven's will proclaimed, 'These men impartially care for those I care for and impartially benefit those I benefit. Their care for the people is extensive and the benefit they bring is substantial.' And so, Heaven made it come to pass that they each became the Son of Heaven and were given the wealth of all the world. Their descendants have continued for a myriad of generations; their goodness has been proclaimed throughout succeeding generations and spread throughout the world. They are praised down to the present day and are known as 'sage-kings.'"

That being so, how were Jie, Tyrant Zhou, You, and Li punished?

Our teacher Mozi says, "On high they maligned Heaven, in the middle realm they insulted the ghosts and spirits, and below they harmed human beings. And

---

52. The Xia, Shang, and Zhou dynasties (see *Important Periods* in the appendices).

so, Heaven's will proclaimed, 'These men through their partiality dislike those I care for and in their interactions harm those I benefit. Their dislike for the people is extensive and the harm they bring substantial.' And so, Heaven made it come to pass that they did not finish out their natural span of life and their line did not even span a single full generation. They are reviled down to the present day and are known as 'vicious kings.'"

That being so, how do we know that Heaven cares for the people of the world?

Our teacher Mozi says, "Because it sheds light upon all impartially."

How do we know that Heaven sheds light upon all equally?

Our teacher Mozi says, "Because it lays claim to all impartially."

How do we know that it lays claim to all impartially?

Our teacher Mozi says, "Because it accepts sacrificial offerings from all impartially."

How do we know that it accepts sacrificial offerings from all impartially?

Our teacher Mozi says, "Within the Four Seas, all those who live on cultivated grain[53] fatten up oxen and sheep, dogs, and swine, and prepare pure offerings of millet and wine as sacrifices to the Lord on High, the ghosts, and spirits. Since Heaven lays claim to all people, why would it not care for them? Moreover, as I teach, 'Those who kill one innocent person will suffer one misfortune.'[54] Who is it that kills an innocent person? It is a human being. Who is it that bestows misfortune? It is Heaven. If Heaven did not care for the people of the world, then why would it send down misfortunes when human beings kill one another? This is how I know that Heaven cares for the people of the world."

To accord with Heaven's will is to take right as the governing standard. To oppose Heaven's will is to take force as the governing standard. But what does one do who takes right as the governing standard?

Our teacher Mozi says, "Those who control great states will not attack small states. Those who control great families will not plunder lesser families. The strong will not rob the weak. The noble will not act arrogantly toward the humble. The clever will not deceive the foolish. Such things are beneficial to Heaven above, to ghosts and spirits in the middle realm, and to human beings below. Benefiting these three, there is none that is not benefited, and so the best of names will be accorded to such men and they will be called 'sage-kings.' Those who take force as the governing standard differ from this. They contradict this in word and oppose it in deed, like two men galloping away from one another on horseback. Those who

---

53. The settled, civilized Chinese as opposed to nomadic, uncivilized "barbarians."

54. In addition to occurring in all three versions of "Heaven's Will," this line is also found in *Mozi* chapter 4 (not in this volume).

control great states will thus attack small ones. Those who control great families will plunder lesser families. The strong will rob the weak. The noble will act arrogantly toward the humble. The clever will deceive the foolish. Such things are not beneficial to Heaven above, to ghosts and spirits in the middle realm, or to human beings below. Not benefiting these three, there is none that is benefited, and so the worst of names will be accorded to such men and they will be called 'vicious kings.'"

Our teacher Mozi says, "I hold to the will of Heaven as a wheelwright holds to his compass and a carpenter his square. Wheelwrights and carpenters hold fast to their compasses and squares in order to gauge what is round and square throughout the world, saying, 'What is plumb with this is true, what is not is false!' The books of all the gentlemen in the world today are so numerous that they cannot be exhaustively catalogued and their teachings and maxims are more than can be counted. Above they offer their opinions to the feudal lords and below they expound them to various men of worth. But they are far from what is benevolent and right! How do I know this? I say, 'I measure them with the clearest standard in all the world.'"

Chapter Thirty-One: On Ghosts

Our teacher Mozi says, "In the present age, since the sage-kings who ruled during the ancient three dynasties have passed away and the world has lost sight of what is right, the feudal lords all take force as their guiding standard.[55] As a result, rulers and other superiors are not kind, while ministers and other subordinates are not loyal. Fathers are not loving and sons are not filial, elder brothers are not good to their younger brothers, younger brothers are not respectful of their elders, and proper conduct in general is not observed. Those in charge of the government do not exert themselves in their administrative duties, while the common people do not exert themselves in the pursuit of their various tasks. This is also why people abandon themselves to licentiousness, violence, piracy, rebellion, thievery, and robbery, and use weapons, poisons, water, and fire to stop travelers on the roads and byways and rob their carriages, horses, coats, and furs in order to profit themselves. As a result, the world is in great disorder.

"If we ask how this came about, we will see that it is all because people have developed doubts concerning the existence of ghosts and spirits and do not understand that ghosts and spirits can reward the worthy and punish the wicked. Now if we could just persuade the people of the world to believe that ghosts and spirits can

---

55. The word translated as "guiding standard" is zhèng 正, which often means "what is correct" and is related to the word zhèng 政, which means "to rule." Mozi here is playing on these related senses. (Cf. *Analects* 12.17 in chapter 1 of this volume.)

reward the worthy and punish the wicked, then how could the world ever become disordered?"

Now those who maintain that there are no ghosts or spirits say, "Ghosts and spirits certainly do not exist!" Day and night they preach such ideas throughout the world and sow suspicion among the masses. They cause the people of the world to develop doubts concerning the existence of ghosts and spirits and as a result the world is thrown into disorder.

This is why our teacher Mozi says, "If the kings, dukes, great officials, and gentlemen of the world today really seek to promote what is beneficial to the world and eliminate what is harmful, they must inquire carefully into the issue of whether or not ghosts and spirits exist."

I accept that one must inquire carefully into the issue of whether or not ghosts and spirits exist. Granted this, what is the proper method for pursuing an inquiry into this issue?[56]

Our teacher Mozi says, "You proceed in the same way as in any other case of determining whether anything exists or does not exist; you must take as your standard the evidence provided by the eyes and ears of the people. If there really are people who have heard and seen something, then you must accept that such things exist. If no one has heard or seen anything, then you must accept that such things do not exist. If you intend to proceed in this way, why not try going into a district or village and ask the people there? If, in the course of human history, from ancient times up to the present, there really are people who have seen ghostly or spiritual entities or heard the sounds of ghosts or spirits, then how could one say that ghosts and spirits do not exist? If no one has ever heard or seen them, then how could one say that ghosts and spirits exist?"

Now those who maintain that ghosts and spirits do not exist say, "Throughout the world there are innumerable reports about hearing and seeing ghostly or spiritual entities, but who really can offer testimony about having heard or seen ghostly or spiritual entities?"[57]

Our teacher Mozi says, "If we are looking for a case where many people have seen and heard [about ghosts and spirits], then in ancient times Du Bo is a good example. King Xuan of Zhou[58] killed his minister Du Bo even though he

---

56. Notice that in what follows, Mozi appeals to what are called the "three gauges" in *Mozi* chapter 35, "A Condemnation of Fatalism" (below).

57. Mozi wants to distinguish mere hearsay and vague claims about spiritual beings from firm and clear testimony of their existence. In the examples he cites as evidence, the testimony is firsthand, detailed, and corroborated by multiple witnesses.

58. A king who ruled during the tenth generation of the Zhou dynasty. His reign dates are 827–782 BCE.

was completely innocent. Before he died, Du Bo said, 'My lord is killing me even though I am completely innocent. If the dead are indeed unconscious, then that will be the end of it. But if the dead are conscious, within three years' time my lord shall know of this!' Three years later King Xuan and various feudal lords were off hunting in the wilds. There were several hundred chariots and several thousand men on foot; the hunting party filled the entire field. At high noon, Du Bo appeared in a plain chariot pulled by white horses. He was wearing vermilion clothes and a hat, holding a vermilion bow, and clasping vermilion arrows under his arm. He pursued King Xuan of Zhou and shot him as he rode in his chariot; the arrow pierced the king's heart and splintered his spine. King Xuan collapsed in his chariot and, draped over his own bow case, he died. None of the men from Zhou who were there at the time failed to witness this and none even in remote places failed to hear about it. The event was recorded in the court chronicle of Zhou. Rulers referred to it when instructing their ministers, and fathers referred to it as a warning to their sons, saying, 'Be cautious! Be watchful! Misfortune will surely befall all those who kill the innocent, and they will suffer the punishments of ghosts and spirits in this swift fashion!' And so, if we look at things in terms of what is written in the court chronicle of Zhou, then how can we doubt that ghosts and spirits exist?

"But it is not just the court chronicle of Zhou that attests to such things; in ancient times, Duke Mu of Qin[59] was once in his ancestral temple at high noon when a spirit entered through the door. It had the face of a man and the body of a bird, wore a plain white robe with dark edging, and displayed a serious and dignified expression. When Duke Mu saw it, he was frightened and started to run away, but the spirit spoke to him saying, 'Do not fear! The Lord is pleased with your shining Virtue[60] and has dispatched me to extend your life by nineteen years.[61] He

---

59. Ruler of the state of Qin from 659 to 621 BCE.

60. In very early Chinese texts, spirits savored the míngdé 明德, "shining Virtue," of pious worshippers in the same visceral way they were thought to enjoy the smells and flavors of the sacrifice, and the pageantry and music of the ceremony. True Virtue would elicit spontaneous feelings of approval and joy while character or behavior that was è 惡, "vile," would give rise to disapproval and disgust. Such ideas can be seen in the later tradition. For example, in chapter 6 of the *Great Learning*, a cultivated person is said to be attracted to the good "like loving a lovely sight" and repelled by the bad "like hating a hateful smell" (in chapter 11 of this volume).

61. A span of nineteen years marked a specific astronomical and calendrical period called a zhāng 章. Unaware of the precession of the equinoxes, ancient Chinese astronomers believed that every nineteen years the winter solstice was the first day of the first month of the year and that on that day the sun would appear at exactly the same place in the zodiac. Hence nineteen years were thought to define a significant period of time, something akin to a generation. Compare the story of the butcher in *Zhuangzi* chapter 3 (in chapter 8 of this volume), whose knife remained keen for a period of nineteen years.

shall ensure that your state prospers and that your descendants flourish and hold on
to the state of Qin.' Clasping his hands together, Duke Mu saluted the spirit several times and, bowing his head, asked, 'May I inquire as to your name?' The spirit
replied, 'I am Gou Mang.' And so, if we accept what Duke Mu of Qin saw with his
own eyes, then how can we doubt that ghosts and spirits exist?

"But it is not just this record that attests to such things. In ancient times, Duke
Jian of Yan[62] killed his minister Zhuang Ziyi, who was completely innocent. Before
he died, Zhuang Ziyi said, 'My lord is killing me even though I am completely
innocent. If the dead are indeed unconscious, then that will be the end of it. But if
the dead are conscious, within three years' time my lord shall know of this!' After
one year had passed, Duke Jian was about to set off in his chariot to perform the
great sacrifice at Zu.[63] At high noon, as Duke Jian of Yan was setting off in his
chariot on the road to Zu, Zhuang Ziyi appeared, bearing a vermilion-colored staff,
and beat the Duke to death with it. There were none among the people of Yan
accompanying the Duke at the time who failed to witness this and none even in
remote places failed to hear about it. The event was recorded in the court chronicle
of Yan. Feudal lords passed it on to succeeding generations, saying, 'Misfortune will
surely befall all those who kill the innocent, and they will suffer the punishments
of ghosts and spirits in this swift fashion!' And so, if we look at things in terms of
what is written in the court chronicle of Yan, then how can we doubt that ghosts
and spirits exist?

"But it is not just the court chronicle of Yan that attests to such things. In
ancient times, in the time of Bao,[64] Lord Wen of Song, there was a minister, Guan
Gu, who served as Chief of Sacrifice. Once, while he was carrying out his duties
in the temple, a shaman appeared before him holding a staff and said, 'Guan Gu!
Why is it that the sacrificial jades are not of the proper size, the offerings of wine
and millet not clean and pure, the animals offered not without blemish and fully
fattened, and the sacrifices of each season not performed at the proper time? Is this
your doing or is Bao responsible?' Guan Gu replied, 'Bao is still a babe in swaddling

---

62. Ruler of the state of Yan. His reign dates are 504–493 BCE.

63. The name of a specific sacrificial site in the state of Yan. This adds an ironic cast to the story, for it was
commonly held that a state is maintained through the spiritual power of its state sacrifices. The following
lines, which are clearly a later note that became incorporated into the text, describe the locations of the
state sacrifices of other contemporary states and the fact that many people witnessed these events (and
hence the spiritual sighting noted in Mozi's story): "The state of Yan performed its great sacrifice at Zu, while
the state of Qi offered its sacrifice at Sheji, Song at Sanglin, and Chu at Yunmeng. Large numbers of men and
women would gather to observe these rituals."

64. Bao is the personal name of the ruler whose posthumous name was Lord Wen. He ruled the state of Song
from 610 to 589 BCE. He was also known as Duke Wen.

clothes. How could he be responsible? I, Guan Gu, the minister in charge, am the one who sees to this.' The shaman then raised his staff and clubbed him to death, and Guan Gu died upon the offering platform. There were none among the people of Song who were there at the time who failed to witness this and none even in remote places failed to hear about it. The event was recorded in the court chronicle of Song. Feudal lords passed it on to succeeding generations, saying, 'All those who fail to offer sacrifices with reverence and care will suffer the punishments of ghosts and spirits in this swift fashion!' And so, if we look at things in terms of what is written in the court chronicle of Song, then how can we doubt that ghosts and spirits exist?

"But it is not just the court chronicle of Song that attests to such things. In ancient times, among the ministers of Lord Zhuang of Qi[65] there were two named Wang Liguo and Zhong Lijiao. For three years, these two had been engaged in litigation against one another, but no definitive judgment could be reached in the matter. The Lord of Qi thought of putting them both to death, but feared killing an innocent man. He thought of acquitting them both, but feared letting a guilty man go free. And so, he arranged for them to provide a sheep for sacrifice and to use its blood to swear an oath of innocence upon Qi's sacred altar. The two men agreed to swear the oath, and so the ground was prepared, the sheep's throat was cut, and its blood was sprinkled about to consecrate the sacrifice. Wang Liguo's oath was read through without incident, but before they were even halfway done with Zhong Lijiao's oath, the sheep that had been sacrificed rose up and butted him, breaking his leg. Then the spirit of the altar appeared and struck Zhong Lijiao, killing him on the very place where he had sworn his oath. There were none among the people of Qi who were there at the time who failed to witness this and none even in remote places failed to hear about it. The event was recorded in the court chronicle of Qi. Feudal lords passed it on to succeeding generations, saying, 'All those who fail to be sincere when they swear an oath will suffer the punishments of ghosts and spirits in this swift fashion!' And so, if we look at things in terms of what is written in the court chronicle of Qi, then how can we doubt that ghosts and spirits exist?"

This is why our teacher Mozi says, "Even in the deepest valleys or vast forests, in those hidden places where no one lives, you must always act properly. For the ghosts and spirits will see what you do!"

Now those who maintain that there are no ghosts say, "How can what the multitude claim to have seen and heard be considered adequate for settling doubts about this issue? How can one who aspires to be known as a person of high status

---

65. Ruler of the state of Qi. His reign dates are 553–548 BCE.

or a gentleman throughout the world turn to and trust what the multitude claim to have seen and heard?"

Our teacher Mozi says, "If what the multitude claim to have seen and heard is not enough to win your trust and settle your doubts about this issue, then I am not sure whether you will consider the sage-kings of the three dynasties, or even them together with Yao and Shun, as adequate models.[66] In this regard, from the average person to nobles alike, all say that the sage-kings of the three dynasties [or even they together with Yao and Shun,] are adequate models of conduct. And so, if we assume that the three sage-kings of ancient times, or they together with Yao and Shun, are adequate models, then why don't we consider the actions of the former sage-kings?

"In ancient times, when King Wu had attacked the Yin and executed Tyrant Zhou, he had the various feudal lords divide up the sacrifices of Yin. He entrusted the interior sacrifices to those who were closely related and the exterior sacrifices to those who were distantly related.[67] Since he did this, King Wu must have believed in the existence of ghosts and spirits. This is why, when he had attacked the Yin and executed Tyrant Zhou, he had the various feudal lords divide up the sacrifices of Yin. If there were no ghosts and spirits, why would King Wu have bothered to divide up the sacrifices of Yin?

"It is not only the activities of King Wu that bear this out. Whenever the sage-kings of old rewarded anyone, they always did so at the ancestral shrine, and whenever they punished anyone, they always did so at the altar of soil. Why did they reward at the ancestral shrine? In order to announce to the spirits there that rewards were fairly apportioned. Why did they punish at the altar of soil? In order to announce to the spirits there that the cases were decided properly.

"But it is not just what can be found in books that bears this out. In the time of Emperor Shun and in the time of the sage-kings of the three dynasties Xia, Shang, and Zhou, on the very first day that they established their states and set up their capitals, they always selected the most perfectly aligned altar in the capital to serve as their ancestral shrine.[68] Also, they always chose the place where the trees grew most finely and luxuriantly and established it as the altar of soil. They also chose

---

66. The text is slightly garbled at this point. But the sense is something like "the sage-kings of the three dynasties (i.e., Yu, Tang, Wen, and Wu) *plus* Yao and Shun."

67. The interior sacrifices were to the Yin royal ancestors and hence needed to be carried out by their direct descendants. Mozi's point is that if there were no ghosts and spirits who received these sacrifices and were aware of who was sacrificing to them, there would have been no point in dividing up these religious duties.

68. Mozi's point here is that the conscious effort to properly align cities to harmonize with spiritual forces also reflects a belief in the existence of ghosts and spirits. For the seminal study of this aspect of Chinese culture, see Paul Wheatley, *The Pivot of the Four Corners: A Preliminary Enquiry into the Origins and Character of the Ancient Chinese City* (Chicago, IL: Aldine Publishing Company, 1971).

the most kind, filial, upright, and good from among the elders of their states to oversee and perform their sacrifices. They always chose the most plump, physically perfect, and properly colored of the six domesticated animals as their sacrificial offerings and ensured that the proper type, quality, and number of jade tablets and insignia were used. They always chose the most fragrant and perfectly ripened of the five grains in order to make their sacrificial wine and cakes, and this is why there was seasonal variation in these offerings. In these various ways, the ancient sage-kings ruled the world by putting the ghosts and spirits ahead of the people. This is why they declared that before any of the civil officials were appointed, the sacrificial implements and robes must first be stored away in the royal treasury, those in charge of overseeing and performing the sacrifices must all be presented and invested at court, and those animals to be used as sacrifices must be separated from the rest of their flocks and herds. This is how the sage-kings of ancient times carried out their rule. In ancient times, sage-kings always showed their devotion to the ghosts and spirits in these ways and their devotion was generous and substantial. But they worried that their descendants would not understand this and so they recorded their activities in books of bamboo and silk and passed these down to succeeding generations. Still, they worried that these bamboo and silk books would decay over time and become lost and that their descendants in succeeding ages would have no way to learn of this. And so, they repeated this knowledge by etching it on basins and bowls and inscribing it in metal and stone. There was still some concern that their descendants in later generations would not be reverent enough to receive blessings and so in the books of the former kings and among the teachings of the sages, within each length of silk text and every book's chapter, one finds numerous and repeated references to the existence of ghosts and spirits. Why is this the case? Because the sage-kings were devoted to the ghosts and spirits. Now when those who maintain that there are no ghosts and spirits say, 'There certainly are no ghosts and spirits!' this opposes what the sage-kings were devoted to. And whatever opposes what the sage-kings were devoted to is not the way one becomes a gentleman."

Now those who maintain that there are no ghosts say, "Exactly what textual sources are there to support your claims that in the books of the former kings and among the teachings of the sages, within each length of silk text and every book's chapter, one finds numerous and repeated references to the existence of ghosts and spirits?"

Our teacher Mozi says, "Among Zhou dynasty writings, such evidence is found within the *Elegies*.[69] The *Elegies* says,

---

69. The quotation is from the ode "King Wen" in the *Elegies* section of the *Odes* (*Mao* # 235). For a complete translation, see Legge, *The She King*, 427–31.

King Wen is on high,
How he shines in Heaven!
Though Zhou is an ancient land,
Its mandate was just recently granted.
Is not Zhou illustrious!
Is the Lord's mandate not timely!
King Wen ascends and descends,
He moves to the left and the right of the Lord.
How fine, how fine is King Wen!
His fame shall last forever!

If ghosts and spirits do not exist, then after he had died, how could King Wen move to the left and the right of the Lord? This is how I know that there are records of ghosts in the books of the Zhou.

"However, if only the books of the Zhou contained references to ghosts and one found no such references in the books of the Shang, then one could not take such stories as reliable models. But when we examine works from the Shang, we find passages such as the following,

> Oh, in the Xia of ancient times, before it was visited by misfortune, the various beasts and bugs below and even the soaring birds above—not one behaved in an irregular manner. How much less would one who had a human face have ventured to have a deviant heart! Even among the ghosts and spirits of the mountains and streams, none dared to be unruly.[70]

We see that by being respectful and sincere, the rulers of the Xia united Heaven and earth and protected the earth below. And if we consider why none of the ghosts and spirits of the mountains and streams dared to be unruly, we see that it was in order to assist Yu in his work. This is how I know that there are records of ghosts in the books of the Shang.

"However, if only the books of the Shang contained references to ghosts and one found no such references in the books of the Xia, then one could not take such stories as reliable models. So let us examine works from the Xia. The 'Declaration of Yu'[71] says,

---

70. The quoted passage is similar in content to parts of the "Instructions of Yi" section of the *History.* Cf. Legge, *The Shoo King,* 193–94.

71. In the present version of the *History* there is a passage that shares some of the language and general thrust of the text Mozi quotes. This passage is called the "Declaration at Gan," with Gan being the place named in the *Mozi* passage. For the present version, see Legge, *The Shoo King,* 152–55.

A great battle was being waged at Gan and in its midst the king called for his six commanders of the left and right flanks to gather around him. He then declared to the assembled army below, 'This ruler of Hu[72] has destroyed and reviled the Five Phases[73] and has been remiss and abandoned the Three Spheres.[74] Heaven shall cut off his mandate.'

Continuing, he said, 'This very afternoon I shall fight the ruler of Hu to decide what this day holds for us. You ministers, high officials, and common men, know that I do this not because I desire his fields and treasures but only to respectfully carry out the punishment decreed by Heaven. If those on the left do not respectfully carry out the duties of the left and those on the right do not respectfully carry out the duties of the right, you will not be respectfully carrying out Heaven's mandate. If you charioteers do not drive your chariots straight, you will not be respectfully carrying out Heaven's mandate. [Today you are carrying out Heaven's mandate.] That is why the rewards for proper performance on this day will be conferred at the ancestral shrine and the punishments for failure will be meted out at the altar of soil.'

"Why were the rewards for proper performance conferred at the ancestral shrine? In order to show the ghosts and spirits that they are fairly apportioned. Why were the punishments for failure meted out at the altar of soil? In order to show the ghosts and spirits that the cases were decided properly. And so, we see that the ancient sage-kings clearly believed that ghosts and spirits could reward the worthy and punish the wicked. This is why rewards were conferred at the ancestral shrine and punishments meted out at the altar of soil. This is how I know that there are records of ghosts in the books of the Xia."

And so, in former times, in the records of the Xia and in the following works of the Shang and the Zhou, there are numerous and repeated references to ghosts and spirits. Why is this the case? Because the sage-kings were devoted to them. How can anyone who considers what these books say still doubt the existence of ghosts and spirits? . . .

This is why our teacher Mozi says, "If the ability of ghosts and spirits to reward the worthy and punish the wicked could be firmly established as fact throughout the empire and among the common people, it would surely bring order to the state and great benefit to the people. If state officials are dishonest or corrupt in

---

72. A state ruled by relatives who shared the same surname as the Xia royal line. It was located in the present-day Shanxi Province.

73. These are the basic phases that the natural and human realms are supposed to pass through in orderly succession. They are wood, fire, earth, metal, and water. While a given phase is in "ascendance," the activities and phenomena associated with that phase are thought to guide the major course of events.

74. The realms of Heaven, earth, and human beings.

carrying out their duties or men and women engage in illicit relationships, the ghosts and spirits will see them! If the people turn to licentiousness, violence, rebellion, theft, or robbery and use weapons, poisons, water, or fire to attack travelers on the roads and byways and rob their carriages, horses, coats, and furs in order to profit themselves—there are ghosts and spirits who will see them![75] And so, state officials will not dare to be dishonest or corrupt. When they see good, they will not dare to not reward it and when they see wickedness, they will not dare to withhold punishment.[76] Thereupon, there will be an end to the common people turning to licentiousness, violence, rebellion, theft, or robbery and using weapons, poisons, water, or fire to attack travelers on the roads and byways and rob their carriages, horses, coats, and furs in order to profit themselves. And so, the world will be well-ordered." . . .

Our teacher Mozi says, ". . . If it were the case that ghosts and spirits do not really exist, then in offering sacrifices, all we would be doing is expending resources of wine and millet. But though we would be expending these resources, we would not simply be pouring the wine into a ditch or gully or throwing the millet away. Primary clan members[77] and people living out in the villages and towns all have a chance to drink the sacrificial wine and partake of the offerings. And so, even if the ghosts and spirits did not exist, these offerings would still be a means for welcoming and bringing together close family and gathering together and increasing fellowship among people living out in the villages and towns."[78] . . .

Chapter Thirty-Two: A Condemnation of Musical Performances[79]

Our teacher Mozi says, "The benevolent surely are those who devote themselves to finding ways to promote what is beneficial to the world while eliminating what

---

75. This line also occurs at the very beginning of the chapter.

76. Cf. "Honoring the Worthy." See *Mozi* chapter 8 (above).

77. That is, those who share the father's surname and are in line to continue his family's ancestral sacrifices.

78. Mozi shows no evidence of doubting the existence of ghosts and spirits, but the more sociological explanation for ritual sacrifice he offers here anticipates Xunzi's rich and wholly secular defense of ritual. See *Xunzi* chapter 19, "Discourse on Ritual" (in chapter 9 of this volume).

79. Mozi criticizes the elaborate musical performances that were sponsored by many states in early China. These events included complex and expensive orchestras and elaborate dancing and were often accompanied by lavish feasts. He argues that these waste vast resources of time, material, and effort without producing any tangible results. He is not directly criticizing music per se. On the other hand, he shows no sense that music serves any useful purpose in life. For a meticulous and incisive study of the production, performance, ritual, and beliefs surrounding ancient Chinese chime bells, see Lothar von Falkenhausen, *Suspended Music: Chime Bells in the Culture of Bronze Age China* (Berkeley, CA: University of California Press, 1993).

is harmful; this is why they are proper models for human conduct throughout the world. If something benefits the world then they will do it. If it does not benefit the world then they will stop doing it. Moreover, when the benevolent think about the people of the world, if there is something that attracts their eyes, delights their ears, pleases their palates, and gives comfort to their bodies but this thing can only be gotten by sacrificing the people's stock of food and clothing, they will not engage in it."

And so, our teacher Mozi does not condemn music because he thinks that the sounds of bells, drums, zithers, and pipes are not pleasing, nor because he thinks that inlaid and carved patterns and designs are not fine, nor because he thinks that roasts of grain- and grass-fed meat are not delicious, nor because he thinks that high towers, lofty halls, and secluded pavilions are not comfortable. Though his body knows the comfort of such places, his mouth the relish of such food, his eye the fineness of such patterns, and his ears the pleasure of such sounds, nevertheless, he sees that these do not accord with the practices of the sage-kings of old and do not promote the benefit of the people in the world today. And so, our teacher Mozi says, "Musical performances are wrong!"

Our teacher Mozi says, "These days, when kings, dukes, and other persons of high rank engage in the manufacture of musical instruments as a function of state, it is no simple matter like slicing through water or breaking apart a piece of sod. Rather, they must heavily tax the people in order to enjoy the sounds of bells, drums, zithers, and pipes. If the production of these instruments were truly analogous to the sage-kings' production of boats and carts, then I would not dare to condemn it. In ancient times, the sage-kings did indeed heavily tax the people in order to make boats and carts. But once these were completed and the people asked what they could be used for, they were told that the boats could be used for traveling over water while the carts could be used for traveling over land. By using these conveyances, gentlemen could rest their feet while common people could rest their shoulders and backs. And so, why did the people give over their resources in order to produce boats and carts without considering it a burden or an imposition? Because they knew they would get something in return that benefited them. Now if musical instruments produced a similar return that benefited the people, then I would not dare to condemn them.

"However, the present use of musical instruments imposes three hardships upon the people. Because of the expenditures involved in producing such instruments, those who are hungry are unable to get food, those who are cold are unable to obtain clothing, and those who toil are not afforded a chance to rest. These are the three greatest hardships upon the people. But what if we play the great bells, strike up the drums, sound the zithers, blow the pipes, and dance with shields and battle axes? Will this enable the people to procure food or clothing? I believe that such performances will not produce such results. But let us set aside such concerns for the moment. For, now, great states attack lesser states and great families assault lesser families, the strong rob the weak, the many do violence to the few, the clever deceive the simple, those of noble rank act arrogantly toward those of humble rank, and rebels and bandits flourish and cannot be stopped. But what if we play the great bells, strike up the drums, sound the zithers, blow the pipes, and dance with shields and battle axes? Will this bring order to the chaos that presently reigns in the world? I believe that such performances will not produce such results."

This is why our teacher Mozi says, "If we look to see whether heavily taxing the people to produce the sounds of great bells, drums, zithers, and pipes promotes the benefit of the people of the world and eliminates what is harmful to them, we see that it offers no such help."

This is why our teacher Mozi says, "Musical performances are wrong!"

Our teacher Mozi says, "These days, when kings, dukes, and great men sit up in their raised halls and broad pavilions and look down upon the great bells, the bells look like nothing more than inverted cauldrons. If there is no one to strike the great bells, how could they take delight in them? The bells must be struck in order to be enjoyed. But they cannot employ the very old or the very young to strike the bells. For the ears and eyes of such people are not sharp and clear, their limbs are not nimble and strong, the sounds they produce are not harmonious, and they cannot follow the complicated turns in the score. And so, kings, dukes, and great men must employ people in their prime, for their ears and eyes are sharp and clear, their limbs are nimble and strong, the sounds they produce are harmonious, and they can follow the complicated turns in the performance. If they employ men to make music, then these men must abandon their work of plowing, planting, and cultivation. If they employ women to make music, then these women must abandon their work of spinning, weaving, and sewing. These days, when kings, dukes, and great men put on musical performances, they divert such vast resources that could be used to produce food and clothing for the people."

This is why our teacher Mozi says, "Musical performances are wrong!"

Our teacher Mozi says, "Now let us suppose that the great bells, drums, zithers, and lutes have all been properly prepared. What pleasure would kings, dukes, and great men find in reverently listening to them all by themselves? Their enjoyment must come from listening to them in the company of common folk or gentlemen. But if they listen in the company of gentlemen, then those gentlemen must neglect the business of governing. And if they listen in the company of common folk, then those folk must abandon their proper work. These days, when kings, dukes, and great men put on musical performances, they divert such vast resources that could be used to produce food and clothing for the people."

This is why our teacher Mozi says, "Musical performances are wrong!"

Our teacher Mozi says, "In ancient times, Duke Kang of Qi[80] found excitement and delight in the performance of the Dance of Wan.[81] The performers of the dance were not permitted to wear coarse and simple clothing nor could they eat plain or common food because it was said that 'if their food and drink is not fine, their faces and complexion will be unworthy to look at. If their clothing is not fine, their figures and movements will be unworthy of view.' And so, their food had to be only the finest grains and meats and their clothing had to be only embroidered silk. They never worked to produce their own food and clothing but were always supported by the work of others."

This is why our teacher Mozi says, "These days, when kings, dukes, and great men put on musical performances, they divert such vast resources that could be used to produce food and clothing for the people."

This is why our teacher Mozi says, "Musical performances are wrong!"

Our teacher Mozi says, "Now human beings certainly are different from the various kinds of birds, beasts, and bugs that one can find in the world today. The various birds, beasts, and bugs rely upon their feathers and fur for their clothing, their hoofs and claws for their leggings and shoes, and grass and water for their food and drink. And so even if the males do not plow and cultivate the land and even if the females do not spin and weave, these creatures are still assured of having food and clothing. Human beings differ in this respect. Those who labor upon the land survive, while those who do not, perish. If gentlemen do not exert themselves in pursuing their duties at court, then the laws and administration will fall into chaos. If common folk do not exert themselves in carrying out their work, there will not be enough material goods.

"Now if men of rank and gentlemen in the world today believe that what I say is not true, let us try enumerating the allotted tasks that are pursued throughout the world in order to see the harm done by musical performances.

"Kings, dukes, and high officials begin their work at court early in the day and retire late in the evening, listening to litigation and carrying out the administration of government—these are their allotted tasks. Men of rank and gentlemen exhaust the strength of their limbs and exert every ounce of their wisdom attending to their official duties at court and collecting taxes and levies out in the passes, markets, mountains, forests, lakes, and rivers in order to fill the state's granaries and treasuries—these are their allotted tasks. Farmers go out to the fields at dawn and

---

80. Ruler of the state of Qi. His reign dates are 404–379 BCE.

81. A choreographed performance with musical accompaniment. For a description, see Waley, *Book of Songs*, 338–40.

return at dusk, plowing, planting, cultivating, and reaping great harvests of grain and other produce—these are their allotted tasks. Women rise at dawn and retire in the evening, spinning and weaving to produce hemp, silk, linen, and other types of cloth—these are their allotted tasks.

"Now if those who serve as kings, dukes, and high officials delight in musical performances and spend their time listening to them, they will not be able to begin their work at court early in the day and retire late in the evening, listening to litigation and carrying out the administration of government. As a result, the state will fall into chaos and the altar of grain will be in jeopardy. If men of rank and gentlemen delight in musical performances and spend their time listening to them, they will not be able to exhaust the strength of their limbs and exert every ounce of their wisdom attending to their official duties at court and collecting taxes and levies out in the passes, markets, mountains, forests, lakes, and rivers in order to fill the state's granaries and treasuries. As a result, the granaries and treasuries will not be full. If farmers delight in musical performances and spend their time listening to them, they will not be able to go out to the fields at dawn and return at dusk, plowing, planting, cultivating, and reaping great harvests of grain and other produce. As a result, the supply of food will be insufficient. If women delight in musical performances and spend their time listening to them, they will not be able to rise at dawn and retire in the evening, spinning and weaving to produce hemp, silk, linen, and other types of cloth. As a result, there will not be an adequate supply of cloth. What is the cause of great men abandoning the administration of the government and the common people neglecting their work? It is music!"

This is why our teacher Mozi says, "Musical performances are wrong!" Our teacher Mozi says, "How do I know that this is so? Among the works of the former kings, there is the following in Tang's *Official Punishments*:[82]

> To allow constant dancing in one's hall is called *Shamen's Fancy.* If gentlemen commit this offense, they are to be fined two bolts of silk. If it is a commoner, the fine is two hundred measures of yellow thread.[83]

The text goes on to say,

> Alas! The dancing goes on and on! The sound of the pipes is loud and clear! The Lord on High no longer supports him. He will lose the nine realms.[84] The Lord

---

82. There is no such section in the present *History* but in the chapter called "Instructions of Yin," there is a passage that shares much of the language and general thrust of Mozi's quotation. See Legge, *The Shoo King,* 196.

83. The text of the last line is garbled and the translation is tentative.

84. "He" refers to the tyrant Jie. The point of the passage is that Jie's personal debauchery testifies to his low character, which makes him offensive to Heaven and unfit to rule. Thus, it justifies sage Tang's attack on him. See *Important Figures* in the appendices.

on High no longer accommodates him and will send down a hundred calamities. His family will be ruined and annihilated.

"If we look into why he lost the nine realms, we see it is simply because he promoted musical performances. The *Wu Guan*[85] says,

> Qi[86] then abandoned himself to lust and music; he drank and ate in the wilds. Qiang! Qiang! The flutes and chimes sounded vigorously! He sank, besotted with wine! He ate gluttonously in the wilds! The Dance of Wan was elegant and fine and its performance was heard in Heaven. But Heaven did not approve.

"And so, above, Heaven and the ghosts did not approve and, below, the people were not benefited."

This is why our teacher Mozi says, "If men of rank and the gentlemen of the world really want to promote what is beneficial to the world and eliminate what is harmful to it, then they will prohibit and put an end to this thing called music!"

Chapter Thirty-Five: A Condemnation of Fatalism

Our teacher Mozi says, "The kings, dukes, and great officials who now rule the various states all want their states to be wealthy, their populations great, and their administrations orderly, and yet instead of wealth they get poverty, instead of great populations they get meager ones, and instead of order they get chaos. In this way they fundamentally miss what they desire and get what they dislike."[87]

What is the reason for this?

Our teacher Mozi says, "This is because, among the people, there are so many who maintain a belief in fatalism. Those who believe in fatalism say, 'If the state is fated to be rich, then it will be rich; if it is fated to be poor, then it will be poor. If the state is fated to have a large population, then the population will be large; if it is fated to have a meager population, then the population will be meager. If the state is fated to be well-ordered, then it will be well-ordered; if it is fated to be in chaos, then it will be in chaos. If one is fated to live a long time, then one will live a long time; if one is fated to die young, then one will die young. If something is fated to occur, then no matter how hard one tries to change this, what good will it do?' Above they use this doctrine to persuade the kings, dukes, and great officials, and

---

85. An unknown text.

86. Qi is the son of Yu, founder of the Xia dynasty. He succeeded his father to the throne. The point of the passage is to illustrate his bad moral character, which made him offensive to Heaven and unfit to rule.

87. These same lines occur as the opening of *Mozi* chapter 8, "Honoring the Worthy" (above).

below they deploy it to interfere with the work of the people. Therefore, those who maintain a belief in fatalism are not benevolent and their claims must be carefully examined."

Since this is the case, how are we to go about carefully examining their claims?

Our teacher Mozi says, "When one advances claims, one must first establish a standard of assessment. To make claims in the absence of such a standard is like trying to establish on the surface of a spinning potter's wheel where the sun will rise and set.[88] Without a fixed standard, one cannot clearly ascertain what is right and wrong or what is beneficial and harmful. And so, in assessing claims, one must use the three gauges."[89]

What are the "three gauges?"

Our teacher Mozi says, "The gauges of precedent, evidence, and application."

How does one assess a claim's precedents?

Our teacher Mozi says, "One looks up for precedents among the affairs and actions of the ancient sage-kings."

How does one assess a claim's evidence?

Our teacher Mozi says, "One looks down to examine evidence of what the people have heard and seen."

How does one assess a claim's application?

Our teacher Mozi says, "One implements it as state policy and sees whether or not it produces benefit for the state, families, and people. These are what are called the three gauges for assessing claims." . . .

Chapter Thirty-Nine: Against Confucianism

1. Confucians say, "In loving kin there are different degrees; in honoring the worthy there are different grades." This describes differences based on nearness or distance

---

88. This describes the practice of determining how far from true east and west the sun would rise and set. It consisted of aligning a set of gnomons (see the following note) with the rising and setting sun and using these to triangulate true east and west. It would be impossible to carry out this procedure on the surface of a spinning potter's wheel, just as it would be impossible to use such a wheel as a sundial. For a description and discussion of this procedure and other uses of such gnomons, see A. C. Graham, *Later Mohist Logic, Ethics and Science* (Hong Kong: The Chinese University of Hong Kong, 1978), 370–71, and Joseph Needham, *Mathematics and the Sciences of the Heavens and the Earth,* vol. 3 of Needham, ed., *Science and Civilisation in China* (London: Cambridge University Press, 1959), 284–302.

89. The word I have translated as "gauge" (biǎo 表) is a gnomon used to "gauge" the direction and movement of the sun's shadow. For an illustration, see the Title Support Page for this volume at www.hackettpublishing .com/rccp-support.

and who is honored or humble. Their rituals say that "One mourns one's father
and mother for three years.[90] One mourns one's wife and eldest son for three years.
One mourns for uncles, brothers, and other sons for one year and mourns other
close relatives for five months." Now, the length of mourning is supposed to reflect
whether the deceased is near or distant, and so near relatives should be mourned for
longer periods and more distant relatives for shorter periods. But [their rituals prescribe that one's] wife, eldest son, and father are treated as equally [near]. The length
of mourning is supposed to reflect whether the deceased is honored or humble, but
[their rituals prescribe that] one's wife, eldest son, and father are treated as equally
[honorable], while one's uncles and brothers are treated as humbly as the other sons.
What is more perverse than this!

When the parent of a Confucian dies, he lays out their corpse without dressing it
for burial, climbs up on the roof and looks down into the well, pokes into rat holes,
and inspects every wash basin searching for the person. Now, if the person really
still exists, then this behavior is the height of stupidity. If the person really is gone
and they insist on looking for them, this is the height of hypocrisy!

2. Confucians strongly uphold the existence of fate and explain this belief by saying, "Long life or early death, poverty or wealth, safety or danger, order or disorder
surely are fated by Heaven; one cannot alter them one way or another. Failure
or success, reward or punishment, good or bad fortune are determined; neither
human knowledge nor effort is capable of doing anything about this." If the various
officials believe this, they will be remiss in performing their assigned duties; if the
common people believe this, they will be remiss in carrying out their particular
work. If government is not well-ordered, there will be chaos; if farming is done in
a lax manner, there will be poverty. [Working to prevent] poverty and disorder are
the root of [good] governance and yet Confucians take [the existence of fate] to be
a central teaching of their Way. This is a great harm to the people of the world.[91]

3. Moreover, [Confucians] deploy ornately embellished rituals and music in order
to seduce people, and prolonged mourning and hypocritical grief in order to
deceive their parents. They work to establish [their doctrine of] fate, ignore poverty [in the state], and reside in arrogance and haughtiness. They act against what
is most fundamental, abandon work, and rest in indolence and pride. They show

90. See *Analects* 17.21 (in chapter 1 of this volume), and the second note to that passage.

91. For Confucian discussions of fate, see *Analects* 6.10, 12.5, 14.36, and 20.3 (in chapter 1 of this volume),
and *Mengzi* 7A1, 7A2, and 7A3 (in chapter 4 of this volume).

voracious desire for food and drink but are lazy when it comes to doing their work. They often suffer from hunger and cold and are in danger of freezing or starving [to death] but lack the ability to avoid these. This is how they behave: they stuff their cheeks like a hamster, glare like a billy goat, and rear up like a wild boar. When a gentleman laughs at them, they reply, "How could such a useless individual understand the good Confucian?" In summer, they beg for grain; when the crops have been harvested, they follow after grand funerals with all their sons and grandsons tagging along behind them, eating and drinking their fill. If they manage to supervise only a few funerals, they will get all that they need. They rely upon the treasure of other families to carry out their business and depend upon the fields of other men to assure their honor. When a rich person holds a funeral, they are delighted and gleefully proclaim, "This is an opportunity for clothing and food!"

5. Confucians say, "Gentlemen must follow the ancient style of dress and speech in order to be humane." I reply, "The so-called ancient style of dress and speech was once new, and so when ancient people used such speech and wore such clothes, they must not have been gentlemen. This being the case, must one wear clothes that are not the clothes of a gentlemen and use speech that is not the speech of a gentlemen in order to be humane?"

6. Confucians also say, "Gentlemen follow [the old] and do not innovate."[92] I reply, "In ancient times, Yi created the bow, Yu invented armor, Xi Zhong invented chariots, artisan Qiu invented boats; this being the case, are the tanners, armorers, and carpenters of today all cultivated people but Yi, Yu, Xi Zhong, and artisan Qiu all petty people? Moreover, what Confucians follow must have been invented by someone. This being the case, is what they follow in every respect the Way of a petty person?"

7. Confucians also say, "In victory, gentlemen do not pursue the fleeing [enemy] and do not shoot from behind cover. When the enemy scatters in retreat they help by pushing their carts along." I reply, "If all involved are humane people, then without saying a word they will get along. Humane people instruct one another in what to accept and what to reject, what is right and what is wrong. Those who lack a good reason follow those who have one; those who do not know follow those who do. If one has nothing more to say, one must submit; if one sees what is good, one must accept it. Why would one stand in opposition? But if two violent forces are locked in struggle, even if the victorious side desires not to pursue the fleeing [enemy] or shoot from behind cover, and when their enemy scatters in retreat they

92. Cf. *Analects* 7.1 and 9.3 (in chapter 1 of this volume).

help by pushing their carts along, though they devote themselves completely to these tasks, still, they will never become gentlemen. Suppose there is a violent and cruel state and a sage seeks to eliminate the harm it does from the world by leading an army on a punitive expedition. If in victory he accepts and follows the Confucian method and commands his troops not to pursue the fleeing [enemy] or shoot from behind cover, and when their enemy scatters in retreat they help by pushing their carts along, then these violent and rebellious men will escape with their lives and the harm to the world will not be eliminated. This is to inflict cruelty upon all mothers and fathers and bring profound ruin to the world. Nothing is more contrary to right than this!"

8. Confucians also say, "Gentlemen are like bells; they make a sound when struck; if not struck, they do not make a sound." I reply, "Humane people are thoroughly conscientious in service to their superiors and filial in service to their parents. If their superiors work for the good, they praise them; if their superiors make a mistake, they admonish them. This is the Way to serve another as minister. Now, if they 'make a sound when struck but do not make a sound if not struck' then they conceal knowledge and withhold effort, remain silent and wait to be asked before responding. Even though they have something of great benefit to their ruler or parents, they will not mention it unless asked. If some enemy from abroad was about to create chaos [within the state] or some insurrection was afoot [within], and before these were launched no one but themselves had knowledge of these things, then even though their ruler and parents all were standing before them, they would not mention any of this unless asked. This is to be a traitor of epic proportions. If this is how they serve as ministers, they are not conscientious; if this is how they serve their parents, they are not filial; if this is how they serve their elder brothers, they are not respectful; if this is how they treat others, they are neither upright nor good."

9. Every method and teaching concerned with humaneness and right should be used on a grand scale to bring good order to the people and on a small scale to carry out the duties of one's office. Such things should be applied afar to confer broad benefit and nearby to cultivate oneself. One should not dwell in what is contrary to the right; one should not implement what contradicts good order. One should work directly and indirectly at encouraging the benefit of all-under-Heaven and cease doing anything that does not bring benefit. This is the Way of the gentleman. What I have heard of the conduct of [this fellow] Kong Qiu[93] is fundamentally and diametrically opposed to this.

---

93. Referring to Kongzi by his full name instead of as "Master Kong" (Kongzi) is an intentional act of disrespect; hence the addition of "this fellow" in the English translation.

14. Once [this fellow] Kong Qiu was in heightened straights between Cai and Chen,[94] having nothing to eat but soup made from wild plants, without even any rice to mix with it. After ten days, Zilu offered him some cooked pork; Kong Qiu did not ask where the meat came from and simply ate it. [Zilu] then commandeered someone's clothing and bartered it for some wine. Kong Qiu did not ask where the wine came from and simply drank it. And yet, when Duke Ai invited Kongzi to join him, he would not sit unless the mat was straight and would not eat unless his meat was cut properly.[95] Zilu approached him and asked, "Why did you behave in a contrary way when in Chen and Cai?" [This fellow] Kong replied, "Come! I will explain it to you. Earlier, you and I were trying however we could to stay alive; now, we are trying however we can to act righteously." When hunger-stricken, he did not decline taking whatever came his way in order to maintain his life; when fully fed, he acted hypocritically in order to aggrandize himself. What foulness, perversity, deceit, and hypocrisy is there greater than this!

---

94. Cf. *Analects* 15.2 (in chapter 1 of this volume).

95. Cf. *Analects* 10.12 (in chapter 1 of this volume) and *Analects* 10.8 (not in this volume).

SELECTIVE BIBLIOGRAPHY

Translations

Johnston, Ian, trans. *The Mozi: A Complete Translation*. New York: Columbia University Press, 2010. (The first complete English translation of Mozi's works.)

Mei, Yi-pao, trans. The *Ethical and Political Works of Motse*. London: Arthur Probsthain, 1929. (An early but still valuable translation of some of Mozi's works.)

Watson, Burton, trans. *Mo Tzu: Basic Writings*. New York: Columbia University Press, 1963. (A readable, selected English translation of the Mozi. Contains selections from each set of synoptic chapters, plus one of the "Against Confucians" chapters.)

Secondary Works

Fraser, Chris. *The Philosophy of the Mòzi: The First Consequentialists*. New York, Columbia University Press, 2016. (A sustained though controversial interpretation of Mozi's philosophy.)

Graham, Angus C. *Divisions in Early Mohism Reflected in the Core Chapters of Mo-tzu*. Singapore: National University of Singapore, Institute of East Asian Philosophies, 1985. (An intriguing though speculative study that argues that the synoptic chapters can be rearranged to reveal three schools of later Mohist thought, each with a distinct political agenda and philosophical position.)

———. *Later Mohist Logic, Ethics and Science*. Hong Kong: The Chinese University Press, 1978. (A brilliant reconstruction, translation, and analysis of later Mohist philosophy and science.)

Ivanhoe, Philip J. "Mohist Philosophy." In vol. 6 of *The Routledge Encyclopedia of Philosophy*, 451–55. London: Routledge Press, 1998. (An introduction to the philosophy of Mozi and his followers.)

Lowe, Scott. *Mo Tzu's Religious Blueprint for a Chinese Utopia*. Lewiston: The Edwin Mellon Press, Ltd, 1992. (A general study of early Mohist religious thought. Offers brief though incisive criticisms of much of the contemporary scholarship available in English.)

Nivison, David S. "Two Roots or One?" In *The Ways of Confucianism: Investigations in Chinese Philosophy*, edited by Bryan W. Van Norden, 133–48. La Salle, IL: Open Court Press, 1996. (A philosophically sophisticated discussion of the ethical thought and theory of moral action of the later Mohist, Yi Zhi.)

Yates, Robin D. S. "The Mohists on Warfare: Technology, Technique, and Justification." *Journal of the American Academy of Religion* 47, no. 3 (Thematic Issue S, 1980): 549–603.

CHAPTER THREE

YANGIST WRITINGS

Introduction

The term for human "nature" (xìng 性) occurs only twice in the *Analects* (5.13 and 17.2; see chapter 1 of this volume), and in one of those passages we are told that Kongzi did not discuss it. The term is never mentioned in the writings of the early Mohists. It was Yáng Zhū 楊朱, in the early fourth century BCE, who made human nature a central topic in Chinese thought.

No writings reliably attributed to Yang Zhu himself have survived, and every claim about him is disputed. (It has even been argued that he is a mythical figure.) However, a plausible case can be made that he offered something like the following line of reasoning. Human nature is implanted in us by Heaven. Since Heaven favors the Way, to follow our nature is to follow the Way.[1] For all their differences, Mohists and Confucians seem to agree in advocating self-sacrifice in the name of the Way. But nothing seems more "natural" for humans than to preserve their own lives and satisfy their own desires. On this basis, Yang Zhu argued that both the Mohist and Confucian Ways are distortions of our natures. We are misled into distorting our natures only because of foolish desires for fame and misconceptions about what is really profitable.

Yang Zhu's own Way has been described as psychological egoism (the claim that humans are motivated only by self-interest), ethical egoism (the claim that humans *should* do only what is in their self-interest), or "privatism" (the claim that humans should do what is in the interest of themselves and their immediate family).[2] The "Yang Zhu" chapter of the *Liezi*

---

1. Similar teleological foundations for ethics are found in many premodern civilizations, although the detailed understandings of the higher power, human nature, and the "Way" of following the nature differ substantially among traditions. For more on the concept of "nature" (*xing*) see the *Mean*, chapter 1 (in chapter 11 of this volume) and *Nature Comes from the Mandate* (in chapter 12 of this volume).

2. Mengzi briefly describes Yang Zhu's position in 3B9 and 7A26 (in chapter 4 of this volume), but what he says is consistent with any of these interpretations.

attributes unrestrained hedonism to him, but this work is now recognized as being largely unrelated to the historical Yang Zhu. It is more likely that Yang Zhu advocated a moderate satisfaction of physical desires, consistent with living a long life. (He is somewhat comparable to Epicurus in this respect.) He may also have advocated caring not just for oneself, but also for one's immediate family members.

Although we have no certain source for Yang Zhu's views, some scholars think that "Robber Zhi," in the following mythical dialogue, represents Yangist views.[3] He is used as a spokesman in this dialogue because he rejects conventional morality and the social structure it has created. The historical Yang Zhu probably did not advocate thievery and violence.

"Robber Zhi"

Kongzi was friends with Liuxia Ji, whose younger brother was known as "Robber Zhi." Robber Zhi and his nine thousand henchmen crisscrossed the world terrorizing the feudal lords. He tunneled under walls and unhinged doors, rustled people's cattle and horses, and made off with their wives and daughters. He was so greedy for gain he forgot his own relatives, ignoring his parents and siblings and neglecting his ancestors. When he came around, great states manned the barricades and small ones retreated to their strongholds.

Kongzi said to Liuxia Ji, "A father must be able to rule his son and an older brother instruct a younger or else there is no point in having those relationships. Now you are one of the ablest men of your generation, but your brother is Robber Zhi, a menace to the whole world, and you can't set him right. Excuse me for saying it, but I'm ashamed for you. May I go talk to him?"

Liuxia Ji said, "You say a father must be able to rule his son and an older brother instruct a younger. But if he already won't follow his father's rules or listen to his brother's instructions, what good will it do for you to debate with him? His mind rushes like a river and his thoughts roar like the wind. He is strong enough to

---

3. This dialogue is *not* by Yang Zhu himself. It is from *Zhuangzi* chapter 29. This is one of the "Miscellaneous Chapters," which are not by the same author as the "Inner Chapters" that we emphasize in our *Zhuangzi* selections (in chapter 8 of this volume). For a complete translation of "Robber Zhi" as well as other possibly Yangist writings, see A. C. Graham, *Chuang-Tzu: The Inner Chapters* (London; Boston: Allen & Unwin, 1981; Indianapolis: Hackett Publishing Company, 2001), 224–58 (pagination follows the reprint).

resist any enemy and clever enough to glorify any wrong. If you go along with him he is happy, but if you resist he gets angry and verbally abusive. You mustn't go."

But Kongzi wouldn't listen. So, with Yan Hui as his driver and Zigong as his attendant, he went to see Robber Zhi. Robber Zhi was just at that moment resting his henchmen on the south slope of Mount Tai, mincing and munching on human livers.[4] Kongzi dismounted from his carriage and stepped forward to present himself to Robber Zhi's attendant. "I am Kong Qiu from Lu.[5] I hear your general has the most exalted righteousness," he said, bowing twice respectfully.

The attendant went inside. Robber Zhi was furious when he heard. His eyes blazed like stars and his hair bristled until it raised his cap. "Isn't this that clever and artificial fellow Kong Qiu from Lu?[6] Tell him this for me: 'You talk and prattle, blindly praising Wen and Wu, capped with a tree branch cap and belted with the ribs of cows. Crafting misleading theories, you eat without farming and dress without weaving. With your flapping lips and clucking tongue, you dare to create rights and wrongs to bewilder the rulers of the world and keep the scholars from returning to their root. You blindly fabricate filial piety and brotherly love in an effort to insinuate yourself with the wealthy and propertied. The weight of your crimes is enormous. Hurry home! Otherwise, I'll add your liver to my afternoon snack."

Kongzi again sent word, "I have the good fortune to know your brother, Ji, and want only to pay my respects."

The attendant relayed the message and Robber Zhi said, "Bring him in!" Kongzi shuffled forward. Politely declining the offered mat, he retreated a few steps and bowed twice to Robber Zhi. Robber Zhi was furious. He leaned on his sword with both legs sprawled, glaring, and growled like a nursing tigress, "Qiu, come forward! If what you say pleases me, you live. Otherwise, you die!"[7]

"I have heard that there are three Virtues in the world," said Kongzi. "To grow big and tall, with matchless good looks, so that young and old, rich and poor alike adore you—this is the highest Virtue. To have knowledge that encompasses Heaven and earth and the ability to argue anything—this is intermediate Virtue. To be brave and determined and to gather a band of followers—this is the lowest Virtue.

---

4. This is not *quite* as grotesque as it sounds. Eating the liver of one's enemy has traditionally been thought of as a way to capture his courage for oneself.

5. Qiu is Kongzi's personal name.

6. The word "artificial" here and below is wěi 偽. Xunzi uses the same term to refer to the "deliberate effort" required to transform a person into a sage. (See the introduction to *Xunzi* in chapter 9 in this volume.) So Xunzi exalts precisely what "Robber Zhi" (and Yang Zhu) condemned.

7. It is extremely rude of Robber Zhi to address Kongzi by his personal name, Qiu. One uses a personal name only to address a subordinate or a very close friend.

Someone with even one of these Virtues is worthy to face south and call himself king. And you, General, combine all three! You are six foot four, with glowing face and eyes, lips like cinnabar, teeth like a row of seashells, voice like a bell. Yet you are known as 'Robber' Zhi! Excuse me for saying so, General, but I'm ashamed for you on this account. If you would be willing to listen to me, General, I would ask to travel as your envoy south to Wu and Yue, north to Qi and Lu, east to Song and Wei, and west to Jin and Chu, and have them build you a great walled state hundreds of *li* in size, with a town of hundreds of thousands of households. They will honor you, General, as a feudal lord. You can start over in the world, disbanding your troops, laying down your arms, gathering your family, and sacrificing to your ancestors. It will be the act of a sage and the wish of the world!"

Robber Zhi was furious. "Qiu, come forward! People who can be leashed by profit or whipped by words are called fools! Simpletons! Dolts! That I am so tall and handsome that people like me is a gift I owe to my parents. Don't you think I'd know it without your flatteries? And I've heard that those who flatter people to their faces slander them behind their backs. All your talk of a walled state and a multitude of people is meant to leash me with profit and distract me like a dolt. Even if I had such a state, how could I hold on to it? There is no walled state bigger than the world. Yao and Shun held the world, but their heirs lack the territory to stick an awl into. Tang and Wu stood as emperors, but their offspring were exterminated.[8] Isn't that the result of their great profit?

"I've heard that in olden times there were so many beasts and so few people that they lived in nests for safety. They gathered acorns and chestnuts by day, and by night they roosted in trees. So, they were called The People Who Nest.[9] In olden times they didn't know to wear clothes but gathered a lot of wood in the summer and burned it in the winter. So, they were called The People Who Know How To Live. In Shen Nong's time they lay down dead tired and got up wide awake.[10] They knew their mothers but not their fathers and lived together with the deer. They farmed their own food and wove their own clothes and had no idea of hurting each other. *This* was the high point Virtue achieved!

"But the Yellow Emperor could not sustain it. He fought with Chi You in Zhuolu field until the blood flowed a hundred *li*.[11] Yao and Shun arose and established a

---

8. On Yao, Shun, Tang, and Wu, see *Important Figures* in the appendices.

9. Cf. *Mengzi* 3B9 (in chapter 4 of this volume).

10. On Shen Nong, see *Important Figures* in the appendices.

11. On the Yellow Emperor, see Huang Di in *Important Figures* in the appendices. For more on his battle with Chi You, see Mark E. Lewis, *Sanctioned Violence in Ancient China* (Albany, NY: State University of New York Press, 1990) and Michael Puett, *The Ambivalence of Creation* (Palo Alto, CA: Stanford University Press, 2001).

mob of underlings. Tang exiled his lord, Wu killed Tyrant Zhou, and ever since the strong oppress the weak and the many tyrannize the few. The rest are just the descendants of these rebels. Now you cultivate the Way of Wen and Wu, monopolizing the world's debate to instruct posterity. In your flowing robes and cinched belt, you lie and trick to fool the world's rulers. In your lust for eminence, there is no robber greater than you. If they call me 'Robber Zhi,' why don't they call you 'Robber Qiu'?

"With your sweet talk you turned Zilu into a follower and got him to doff his jaunty cap, unbuckle his long sword, and accept your instruction so that the whole world said Kong Qiu knows how to stop violence and right wrongs. In the end, Zilu tried to kill the lord of Wei. But he failed, and they hung his pickled corpse on the east gate. This is the failure of your teachings.

"You call yourself a man of ability or a sage? You were evicted from Lu twice, had to cover your tracks out of Wei, got in trouble in Qi, and were surrounded between Chen and Cai. No place in the world can tolerate you. You taught Zilu how to get pickled and brought him disaster. If you can't take care of yourself and can't take care of anyone else, what's this Way of yours worth?[12] . . .

"[The Yellow Emperor, Yao, Shun, Yu, Tang, and Wu] are those whom the world exalts. But if we categorize them, they all forcefully went against their essence and nature because profit confused them about their true self. So their actions were extremely shameful. . . . Among those called 'loyal ministers' in their era, none could compare to Prince Bi Gan and Wu Zixu. Zixu sank in the Yangtze River, and Bi Gan got his heart cut out.[13] Although these two men were called the 'loyal ministers' of their era, in the end the world laughs at them. From the preceding, we can see that neither Zixu nor Bi Gan is worth honoring. In trying to persuade me, Qiu, if you tell me about the affairs of ghosts, then I am incapable of knowing anything about that. But if you tell me about the affairs of humans, then it does not go beyond the preceding. This is all that I have heard and know.

"Now let me tell *you* something about the human essence. The eyes want to see colors. The ears want to hear sounds. The mouth wants to taste flavors. And

---

12. On Kongzi's problems in Wei and Chen, see *Analects* 15.1 and 15.2 (in chapter 1 of this volume). Kongzi predicted a violent end for Zilu (in *Analects* 11.13, not in this volume), and he did in fact die in combat. Different versions and explanations for these events occur in the Confucian literature (for instance, *Mengzi* 5A8, 5B1, 6B6, and 7B18, not in this volume).

13. Wu Zixu, the loyal prime minister to the king of Wu, repeatedly warned the king to govern more responsibly. When the king grew tired of his advice, he ordered him to commit suicide. Bi Gan continually implored Tyrant Zhou to be a more benevolent ruler. Eventually Zhou said, "I have heard that sages have seven chambers in their hearts. Bi Gan has the voice of a sage. Let us see if he has the heart of a sage!" Zhou then cut Bi Gan's heart out of his chest. (Bi Gan's supposed tomb is still preserved as a memorial in Henan Province.)

the emotions want fulfillment. People live at most a hundred years, usually eighty, sometimes sixty. Subtracting time spent recovering from illness, mourning death, and fretting over worries, there are only four or five days a month people can open their mouth and laugh. Heaven and earth go on forever, but people die when their time comes. Put this perishable good in that eternal space and its time flashes by like a galloping horse past a crack in the wall. If you're not gratifying your wishes and cherishing your days, then you do not understand the Way. I reject everything you say. Go home right now, without another word! This Way of yours is a crazy, fraudulent, vain, empty, and artificial business. It is no way to fulfill your true self. Why even talk about it?"

Kongzi bowed twice and shuffled off. He exited the gate, mounted his chariot, and fumbled three times reaching for the reins. His eyes were dull, as though he couldn't see, and his complexion was like dead ashes. Leaning on the rail with his head drooping, he could barely breathe. Returning to Lu, he ran into Liuxia Ji outside the east gate. Liuxia Ji said, "I've missed you for the last few days. Your horse and carriage look like you've been traveling. You didn't go see Zhi, did you?"

Kongzi looked up at the heavens and sighed. "Yes."

Liuxia Ji said, "And didn't he resist your ideas as I predicted?"

"Yes. As they say, I have taken some painful medicine when I wasn't sick. I ran off to pat the tiger's head and braid its whiskers, and I barely escaped its jaws."[14]

---

14. The concluding paragraph is ambiguous. Is Kongzi simply stating that his meeting with Robber Zhi was unpleasant and dangerous? Or has Kongzi learned from Robber Zhi that the Way of the sage-kings (the "painful medicine") is something that humans do not need in their natural state (because they are not "sick" originally), and that following this Way leads to risking one's life needlessly (like braiding a tiger's whiskers)?

SELECTIVE BIBLIOGRAPHY

Emerson, John J. "Yang Chu's Discovery of the Body." *Philosophy East & West* 46, no. 4 (1996): 533–66. (Argues that Yang Zhu did not defend either egoism or individualism as it is understood in the modern West but simply valorized private and family life over public and court life.)

Graham, Angus C. "The Background of the Mencian Theory of Human Nature." In *Studies in Chinese Philosophy and Philosophical Literature*, 7–66. Singapore: Institute for East Asian Philosophies, 1986. Reprint, Albany, NY: State University of New York Press, 1990. (Detailed, scholarly discussion of the development of the notion of human nature in ancient China.)

———. *Disputers of the Tao*. Chicago: Open Court Press, 1989. (Discussion of Yang Zhu on pp. 53–64.)

Kushner, Thomasine. "Yang Chu: Ethical Egoist in Ancient China." *Journal of Chinese Philosophy* 7, no. 5 (1980): 319–25. (Interprets Yang Zhu as similar to a Western individualist.)

鄒國亞聖公 孟軻

CHAPTER FOUR

MENGZI (MENCIUS)

Introduction

Mèngzǐ 孟子 was a Chinese Confucian philosopher who lived in the fourth century BCE. He was born after Kongzi died, so he never studied under Kongzi, or even met him. However, Mengzi tried to teach, practice, and defend the Way of Kongzi as he understood it. Although he is not nearly as well known in the West as Kongzi, Mengzi has long been regarded in China (and throughout East Asia) as second only to Kongzi himself in importance as a Confucian thinker.

The collection of Mengzi's sayings, dialogues, and debates with others is known simply as the *Mengzi* (or, following the Jesuit Latinization of his name, the *Mencius*). It is divided into seven "books," each of which is subdivided into two parts (called the "A" and "B" parts in English), which are then further divided into "chapters." So, for example, *Mengzi* 1B3 is book 1, second part, chapter 3.

Mengzi sees the main intellectual opponents of the Way of Kongzi as being the teachings of Yang Zhu and Mozi (*Mengzi* 3B9, 7A26). Mozi, as we saw in chapter 2 of this volume, advocated a kind of universalistic consequentialism. There are few, if any, texts that have survived to the present day that we can confidently identify as presenting the teachings of Yang Zhu, so we do not know exactly what his philosophy was. However, it seems clear that Yang Zhu emphasized following one's xìng 性, "nature" (see *Important Terms* in the appendices), and claimed that the teachings of both Mohism and Confucianism ask us to act contrary to our natures by making what Yang Zhu saw as excessive sacrifices for others. (For a text that may be influenced by Yang Zhu's ideas, see "Robber Zhi" in chapter 3 of this volume.) On this basis, Mengzi accuses Yang Zhu of being a sort of ethical egoist.

Mengzi agrees with Yang Zhu that humans have a nature, which they should follow. Indeed, he criticizes a rival philosopher, Gaozi, for suggesting that ethical cultivation must involve violating one's nature (*Mengzi* 6A1). However, Mengzi argues against Yang Zhu that there are incipient virtuous inclinations in one's nature (*Mengzi* 6A6). He frequently describes these inclinations using the metaphor of "sprouts," comparing ethical cultivation to tending these sprouts (*Mengzi* 2A2, 2A6, 6A7–8). Mengzi presents various kinds of evidence for the existence of ethical "sprouts" in humans, including the "giveaway" actions of adults who spontaneously manifest these inclinations (such as King Xuan, whose sympathy for an ox being led to slaughter shows his nascent compassion [*Mengzi* 1A7]), and "thought experiments" (such as asking us what our intuitions are about how a normal human would react to the sight of a child about to fall into a well [*Mengzi* 2A6], or to the sight of the corpses of loved ones rotting by the roadside [*Mengzi* 3A5]).

It is important to understand that, although the presence of the sprouts guarantees the goodness of *human nature,* this does not entail that most *humans* are actually good. Mengzi stresses that a bad environment (and failure to cultivate oneself) can almost destroy one's original nature (*Mengzi* 6A8). Furthermore, our compassion for others and disdain for doing what is wrong are innate, but only incipient. Thus, the task of moral cultivation is to "extend" or "fill out" the reactions from the paradigmatic cases where we already have them to the relevantly similar cases where we do not yet have them, but ought to (*Mengzi* 7A15, 7A17, 7B31).

Mengzi thinks that most people will be unable to develop their nature without having their basic needs met for things such as food (*Mengzi* 7A27). Indeed, Mengzi provides specific advice about proper farm management (*Mengzi* 3A3), showing his concern with the practicalities of governing. Once people's fundamental needs are met, basic—but universal—ethical education is crucial (*Mengzi* 1A7, 3A4). However, Mengzi recognizes that, while everyone has the capacity to become a sage, not everyone will realize that ability.

Advanced ethical cultivation requires education under a wise teacher. Mengzi's students pose him questions, often involving conundrums from two works that were already quite old and almost canonical by Mengzi's time: the *History* and the *Odes* (*Mengzi* 5A2, 7B3; see *Important Texts* in the appendices). It is significant that much of Mengzi's teaching is based on concrete cases, rather than abstract principles. Although he clearly thinks that there is a best Way to live, and a best choice in every situation (*Mengzi* 4B29), his approach is "particularistic" in emphasizing the context-sensitivity of virtue (*Mengzi* 4A17). Thus, he tries to cultivate in his students a skill that goes beyond any simple tool or technique (*Mengzi* 7B5).

This is perhaps part of his reason for suggesting that you should "seek for in your heart" what "you do not get from doctrines" (*Mengzi* 2A2).

Mengzi uses his particular conception of human nature to provide a response to both Mohism and Yangism. As we have seen, Mengzi agrees with the Yangists that humans have a nature that they should follow, but argues that the Yangists have supplied an impoverished account of the contents of that nature. Against the Mohists, Mengzi argues that there is a natural order of development of human compassion, and that, as a matter of psychological fact, humans must learn to love members of their own family before they can learn to love strangers (*Mengzi* 7A15, 7A45). Some Mohists in Mengzi's era seem to have conceded this point, but argued that the feeling of compassion cultivated in the family should be extended outward to love everyone equally. However, Mengzi claims that, given the way in which our compassion develops out of love of kin, any effort to love everyone equally violates our naturally greater compassion for family members (*Mengzi* 3A5). Finally, Mengzi argues that the effort to base one's actions on lì 利, "benefit" or "profit," even if it is the profit of one's kingdom as a whole, will be self-defeating (*Mengzi* 1A1).

Book One

1A1 Mengzi had an audience with King Hui of Liang. The King said, "Sir, you have come, not regarding one thousand *li* as too far. Surely you will have something to profit my state?"

Mengzi said in response, "Why must Your Majesty say 'profit'? Let there be benevolence and righteousness and that is all. Your Majesty says, 'How can my state be profited?' The Counselors say, 'How can my family be profited?' The scholars and commoners say, 'How can I be profited?' Those above and those below mutually compete for profit and the state is endangered.

"In a case where the ruler of a state that can field ten thousand chariots is murdered, it must be by a family that can field a thousand chariots. In a case where the ruler of a state that can field a thousand chariots is murdered, it must be by a family that can field a hundred chariots. One thousand out of ten thousand, or one hundred out of a thousand, cannot be considered to not be a lot. But if righteousness is put behind and profit is put ahead, one will not be satisfied without grasping from others.

"There have never been those who were benevolent who abandoned their parents. There have never been those who were righteous who put their ruler last. Let Your Majesty say, 'Benevolence and righteousness,' and that is all. Why must you say 'profit'?"

1A3 King Hui of Liang said, "In relation to the state, We exert our heart to the utmost. When there is a famine in the region inside the river, then We move people to the region east of the river, and move grain to the region inside the river. When there is a famine in the region east of the river, We do the converse. When We examine the government of neighboring states, there is none that exerts itself as We do. Yet the people of neighboring states do not grow fewer, and Our people do not grow more numerous. How is this?"

Mengzi responded, "Your Majesty is fond of war. Allow me to use an illustration from warfare: Thunderingly, the drums beat the soldiers forward; their swords have already clashed; casting aside their armor and trailing their weapons they run away. Some run a hundred paces and then stop; others run fifty paces and then stop. How would it be if those who ran fifty paces laughed at those who ran a hundred paces?"

He responded, "That is unacceptable. They simply did not run a hundred paces. But what they did is running away too."

Mengzi said, "If Your Majesty understands this, then you will not expect your people to be more numerous than those of neighboring states." . . .

1A7 King Xuan of Qi asked, "May I hear from you of the actions of the Lord Protectors Huan of Qi and Wen of Jin?"

Mengzi said in response, "The disciples of Kongzi did not give accounts of the actions of Huan and Wen. Because of this, they were not passed on to later generations, and I, your servant, have not heard of them.[1] But, if you insist, then may we talk about being a genuine king?"[2]

Xuan said, "What must one's Virtue be like so that one can become a king?"

Mengzi said, "One cares for the people and becomes a king. This is something no one can stop."

Xuan said, "Can one such as I care for the people?"

---

1. Mengzi is not being truthful here. In *Mengzi* 4B21 (not in this volume) Mengzi says there *are* historical records of Huan and Wen. See also *Mengzi* 4B11 (below) on honesty.

2. Xuan is a king in name only. See wáng 王 ("king") under *Important Terms* in the appendices.

Mengzi said, "He can."

Xuan said, "How do you know that I can?"

Mengzi said, "I heard your attendant Hu He say,

> The King was sitting up in his hall.[3] There was an ox being led past below. The King saw it and said, 'Where is the ox going?' Someone responded, 'We are about to consecrate a bell with its blood.' The King said, 'Spare it. I cannot bear its frightened appearance, like an innocent going to the execution ground.' Someone responded, 'So should we abandon the consecrating of the bell?' The King said, 'How can that be abandoned? Exchange it for a sheep.'"

Mengzi continued, "I do not know if this happened."

Xuan said, "It happened."

Mengzi said, "This feeling is sufficient to be a king.[4] The commoners all thought Your Majesty was being stingy. But I knew that Your Majesty could not bear the frightened appearance of the ox."

The King said, "That is so. There really were commoners like that. Although Qi is a small state, how could I be stingy about one ox? It was just that I could not bear its frightened appearance, like an innocent going to the execution ground. Hence, I exchanged it for a sheep."

Mengzi said, "Let Your Majesty not be surprised at the commoners' taking you to be stingy. You took a small thing and exchanged it for a big thing. How could they understand? If Your Majesty were pained at its being innocent and going to the execution ground, then what is there to choose between an ox and a sheep?"

The King laughed and said, "What was this feeling really?! It's not the case that I begrudged its value and exchanged it for a sheep. But it makes sense that the commoners would say I was stingy."

Mengzi said, "There is no harm. This is just the way benevolence works. You saw the ox but had not seen the sheep. As for the relation of gentlemen to birds and beasts, if they see them living, they cannot bear to see them die. If they hear their cries, they cannot bear to eat their flesh. Hence, gentlemen keep their distance from the kitchen."

The King was pleased and said, "The *Odes* say,

> Another person had the heart,
> But I measured it.[5]

---

3. Since ancient times in China, royal palaces have included halls raised above the ground, often looking out onto the courtyard below. See the Title Support Page for this volume at www.hackettpublishing.com /rccp-support for an image of such a hall. Cf. *Zhuangzi* chapter 13 (in chapter 8 of this volume).

4. "Feeling," here and below, is literally "heart," xīn, 心. See *Important Terms* in the appendices.

5. *Mao* # 198 (see *Odes* under *Important Texts* in the appendices).

This describes you. I was the one who did it. I reflected and sought it out, but did not understand my heart. You spoke, and in my heart there was a feeling of compassion. In what way does this heart accord with being a king?"

Mengzi said, "Suppose there were someone who reported to Your Majesty, saying, 'My strength is sufficient to lift five hundred pounds, but not sufficient to lift one feather. My eyesight is sufficient to examine the tip of an autumn hair,[6] but I cannot see a wagon of firewood.' Would Your Majesty accept that?"

Xuan said, "No."

Mengzi said, "In the present case, your kindness is sufficient to reach birds and beasts, but the benefits do not reach the commoners. Why is this case alone different? Hence, not lifting one feather is due to not using one's strength. Not seeing a wagon of firewood is due to not using one's eyesight. The commoners not receiving care is due to not using one's kindness. Hence, Your Majesty's not being a genuine king is due to not acting; it is not due to not being able."

Xuan said, "What is the difference between concrete cases of not doing and not being able?"

Mengzi said, "'Pick up Mount Tai and leap over the North Sea.' If you say, 'I cannot,' this is truly not being able. 'Massage the stiff joints of an elderly person.' If you say, 'I cannot,' this is not acting; it is not a case of not being able. So, Your Majesty's not being a king is not in the category of picking up Mount Tai and leaping over the North Sea. Your Majesty's not being a king is in the category of massaging the stiff joints of an elderly person.

"Treat your elders as elders, and extend it to the elders of others; treat your young ones as young ones,[7] and extend it to the young ones of others; then you can turn the whole world in the palm of your hand. The *Odes* say,

> He set an example for his wife,
> It extended to his brothers,
> And so, he controlled his family and state.[8]

This means that he simply took this feeling and applied it to that. Hence, if one extends one's kindness, it will be sufficient to care for all within the Four Seas. If one does not extend one's kindness, one will lack the wherewithal to care for one's wife and children. That in which the ancients greatly exceeded others was no other than this. They were simply good at extending what they did. In the present case your kindness is sufficient to reach birds and beasts, but the benefits do not

---

6. An animal's hair is finest (and hence thinnest) during the autumn.

7. That is, "Treat your elders and young ones as elders and young ones *should* be treated."

8. *Mao # 240.*

reach the commoners. Why is this case alone different? Weigh, and then you will distinguish the light and the heavy. Measure, and then you will distinguish the long and the short. Things are all like this, the heart most of all. Let Your Majesty measure it.

"Perhaps Your Majesty can only be happy in his heart by rallying soldiers, endangering his scholars and ministers, and incurring the resentment of the other lords?"

Xuan said, "No. How could I be happy about these things?"

Mengzi said, "Could I hear Your Majesty's greatest desire?" The King smiled and did not speak.

Mengzi said, "Is it because your hearty and sweet foods are insufficient for your mouth? Are your light and warm clothes insufficient for your body? Or yet because there are insufficient beautiful and charming sights for your eyes to look at? Are there insufficient melodies for your ears to listen to? Are your servants insufficient to order about in front of you? Your Majesty's various ministers *are* sufficient to serve you. Does Your Majesty actually do what you do for these things?!"

Xuan said, "No. It is not for the sake of these things."

Mengzi said, "Then Your Majesty's greatest desire can be known. You desire to govern the land, bring to your court the states of Qin and Chu, oversee the Central States, and dominate the barbarians. By means of such things as you do, to seek such things as you desire, is like climbing a tree in search of a fish."

The King said, "Is it as extreme as that?"

Mengzi said, "The danger is greater than that! If one climbs a tree in search of a fish, although one will not get a fish, there will not be any disaster afterward. By means of such things as you do, to seek such things as you desire, if one exhausts the strength of one's heart in doing it, afterward there must be disaster."

Xuan said, "Could I hear of this?"

Mengzi said, "If the people of Zou and the people of Chu fought, who does Your Majesty think would win?"

Xuan said, "The people of Chu would win."

Mengzi said, "So the small definitely cannot match the big, the few definitely cannot match the many, the weak definitely cannot match the strong. The region within the seas is nine thousand square *li*. Qi amounts to one thousand. To take on eight with one, how is this different from Zou matching Chu?!

"Simply return to the fundamentals. Suppose Your Majesty were to bestow benevolence in governing. This would cause all under Heaven who serve others to want to take their place in Your Majesty's court, all those who plow to want to plow in Your Majesty's uncultivated fields, all merchants to want to place their goods in Your Majesty's markets, all those who travel to wish to use Your Majesty's roads. All under Heaven who wish to complain of their rulers would desire to report to Your Majesty. If it were like this, who could stop it?"[9]

The King said, "I am ignorant and unable to undertake this. But I am willing for you, Master, to redirect my resolution, enlighten, and instruct me. Although I am not clever, please let me try."

Mengzi said, "To lack a constant livelihood, yet to have a constant heart—only a scholar is capable of this. As for the people, if they lack a constant livelihood, it follows that they will lack a constant heart. And if one simply fails to have a constant heart, dissipation and evil will not be avoided. When they thereupon sink into crime, to go and punish them is to trap the people. When there are benevolent people in positions of authority, how is it possible to trap the people? For this reason, an enlightened ruler, in regulating the people's livelihood, must ensure that it is sufficient, on the one hand, to serve one's father and mother, and on the other hand, to nurture wife and children. In good years, one is always full. In years of famine, one escapes death. Only when the people have a regulated livelihood do they rush toward the good, and thus the people follow the ruler easily.

"Nowadays, in regulating the people's livelihood, on the one hand it is insufficient to serve one's father and mother, on the other it is insufficient to nurture wife and children. In good years, one is always bitter. In years of famine, one cannot escape death. This is a case in which one fears not having the means to save people from death. How could one have leisure for teaching ritual and righteousness?

"If Your Majesty wishes to put benevolent government into effect, then simply return to the fundamentals. Plant every household of five *mu* with mulberry trees, and fifty-year-olds can wear silk. Let the nurturing of chickens, pigs, and dogs not be neglected, and seventy-year-olds can eat meat. If you do not disturb the seasonal work in each field of one hundred *mu*, a household with eight mouths to feed need not go hungry. If you are careful about the teachings of the schools, explaining the righteousness of filial piety and fraternal respect, then those with gray hair will not be carrying loads on the roads. For the old to wear silk and eat meat, and the black-haired people[10] to be neither hungry nor cold, yet for their ruler not to become a king—such a thing has never happened."

1B5 . . . King Xuan of Qi said, "Your teachings are excellent!"

Mengzi responded, "If Your Majesty regards them as excellent, then why do you not put them into practice?"

---

9. That is, who could stop such a ruler from eventually becoming king of all the world?

10. That is, the Chinese people.

The King said, "We have a weakness. We are fond of wealth."

He responded, "In former times, Duke Liu was fond of wealth.[11] The *Odes* say,

> He stacked, he stored,
> He bundled up dried meat and grain,
> In bags, in sacks,
> Thinking to gather together and bring glory.
> His bows and arrows were displayed,
> With shields, spears, and battle-axes,
> He commenced his march.[12]

Hence, those who stayed at home had loaded granaries, and those who marched had full provisions. Only then could he 'commence his march.' If Your Majesty is fond of wealth but allows the common folk to possess wealth, what difficulty is there in being a genuine king?"

The King responded, "We have a weakness. We are fond of sex."

Mengzi responded, "In former times, King Tai was fond of sex, and loved his wife. The *Odes* say,

> The Ancient Duke Danfu
> Came in the morning, riding his horse,
> Following the banks of the Western waters,
> He came to the foot of Mount Qi,
> With his Lady Jiang.
> They came and both settled there.[13]

At that time, there were no dissatisfied women in private, or any unmarried men in public. If Your Majesty is fond of sex but accords the common folk the same privileges, what difficulty is there in being a genuine king?"

1B6 Mengzi spoke to King Xuan of Qi, saying, "If, among Your Majesty's ministers, there were one who entrusted his wife and children to his friend, and traveled to the state of Chu, and when he returned, he discovered that his friend had let his wife and children become cold and hungry—how should one deal with this?"

The King said, "Abandon him."

Mengzi said, "If the sergeant-at-arms is not able to keep order among the scholars, how should one deal with this?"

---

11. Duke Liu and King Tai (referred to below as Duke Danfu) are ancestors of the Zhou royal family and considered paradigms of virtuous rulers.

12. *Mao # 250.*

13. *Mao # 237.*

The King said, "Discharge him."

Mengzi said, "If the region within the four borders is not well-ordered, then how should one deal with this?" The King turned toward his attendants and changed the topic.

1B8 King Xuan of Qi asked, "Is it the case that Tang banished Tyrant Jie, and that Wu struck down Tyrant Zhou?"

Mengzi responded, saying, "There are such accounts in the historical records."

The King said, "Is it acceptable for subjects to kill their rulers?"

Mengzi said, "One who violates benevolence should be called a 'thief.' One who violates righteousness is called a 'mutilator.' A mutilator and thief is called a mere 'fellow.' I have heard of the execution of a mere fellow 'Zhou,' but I have not heard of the killing of one's ruler."

Book Two

2A2 Gongsun Chou asked, "Suppose that you, Master, were to be appointed to the position of high noble or prime minister in Qi and were able to put the Way into practice there. If it were so, it would not be surprising at all if the ruler of Qi were to become a lord protector or a genuine king. If it were like this, would it perturb your heart or not?"

Mengzi said, "It would not. My heart has been unperturbed since I was forty."

Gongsun Chou said, "In that case, you, Master, have far surpassed Meng Ben."[14]

Mengzi said, "This is not difficult. Gaozi had an unperturbed heart before I."[15]

Gongsun Chou said, "Is there a way of cultivating an unperturbed heart?"

Mengzi said, "There is. As for Bogong You's cultivation of courage, his body would not shrink, his eyes would not blink. He regarded the least slight from someone like being beaten in the marketplace. Insults he would not tolerate from a common fellow coarsely clad[16] he also would not tolerate from a ruler who could field

---

14. The Qing dynasty commentator Jiao Xun reports that "Meng Ben, when traveling by water, did not avoid serpents, and, when traveling by land, did not avoid rhinoceroses and tigers."

15. Gaozi is a rival philosopher whom Mengzi debates in *Mengzi* 6A1 ff. (below). For a discussion of Mengzi's critique of Gaozi, see David S. Nivison, "Philosophical Voluntarism in Fourth-Century China," in *The Ways of Confucianism* (Chicago: Open Court Publishing, 1996), 121–32. For a discussion of the different accounts of courage presented in this passage, see Bryan W. Van Norden, "Mengzi on Courage," in *The Philosophy of Religion,* edited by Peter A. French, Theodore E. Uehling, and Howard K. Wettstein, *Midwest Studies in Philosophy,* vol. 21 (Notre Dame, IN: University of Notre Dame Press, 1997), 237–56.

16. I borrow this well-turned phrase from D. C. Lau, trans., *Mencius* (New York: Penguin Books, 1970), 76.

ten thousand chariots. He looked upon running a sword through a ruler who could field ten thousand chariots as like running through a common fellow. He did not treat the various lords with deference. If an insult came his way, he had to return it.

"As for Meng Shishe's cultivation of courage, he said, 'I look upon defeat the same as victory. To advance only after sizing up one's enemy, to ponder whether one will achieve victory and only then join battle, this is to be in awe of the opposing armies. How can I be certain of victory? I can only be without fear.'

"Meng Shishe resembled Master Zeng. Bogong You resembled Zixia.[17] Now, as for the courage of the two, I do not really know which was better. Nonetheless, Meng Shishe preserved something important.

"Formerly, Master Zeng speaking to Zixiang said, 'Are you fond of courage? I once heard about great courage from the Master:[18]

> If I examine myself and am not upright, although I am opposed by a common fellow coarsely clad, would I not be in fear? If I examine myself and am upright, although I am opposed by thousands and tens of thousands, I shall go forward.'

Meng Shishe's preservation of his *qi* was still not as good as Master Zeng's preservation of what is important."

Gongsun Chou said, "I venture to ask whether I could hear about your unperturbed heart, Master, and Gaozi's unperturbed heart?"

Mengzi answered, "Gaozi said, 'What you do not get from doctrines, do not seek for in your heart. What you do not get from your heart, do not seek for in the *qi*.' 'What you do not get from your heart, do not seek for in the *qi*,' is acceptable. 'What you do not get from doctrines, do not seek for in your heart,' is unacceptable.

"Your resolution is the commander of the *qi*. *Qi* is that which fills up the body. When your resolution is fixed somewhere, the *qi* sets up camp there. Hence, it is said, 'Maintain your resolution. Do not injure the *qi*.'"[19]

Gongsun Chou asked, "Since you have already said, 'When your resolution is fixed somewhere, the *qi* sets up camp there,' why do you add, 'Maintain your resolution. Do not injure the *qi*'?"

---

17. On Master Zeng, see *Analects* 8.7. On Zixia, see *Analects* 3.8, 6.13, and 19.12 (in chapter 1 of this volume).

18. By "the Master" he means Kongzi. What follows may be intended as a direct quotation from Kongzi, but it may also be Master Zeng paraphrasing the Master's teaching.

19. Recall that, according to Mengzi, the heart (xīn 心, see *Important Terms* in the appendices) is the seat of our ethical inclinations (*Mengzi* 2A6 and 6A6). The "resolution" (zhì 志) is not a separate faculty, but is simply the heart directed toward a certain goal or object. Contrast what Zhuangzi suggests about the relationship between what one hears, one's heart, and the *qi* in *Zhuangzi* chapter 4, "The Human Realm" (in chapter 8 of this volume). On *qi*, see *Important Terms* in the appendices.

Mengzi said, "When your resolution is unified it moves the *qi*. When the *qi* is unified it moves your resolution. Now, stumbling and running have to do with the *qi*, but nonetheless they perturb one's heart."

Gongsun Chou said, "I venture to ask wherein you excel, Master."

Mengzi said, "I understand words. I am good at cultivating my floodlike *qi*."

Gongsun Chou said, "I venture to ask what is meant by 'floodlike *qi*.'"

Mengzi said, "It is difficult to put into words. It is a *qi* that is supremely great and supremely unyielding. If one cultivates it with uprightness and does not harm it, it will fill up the space between Heaven and earth. It is a *qi* that unites righteousness with the Way. Without these, it starves. It is produced by accumulated righteousness. It cannot be obtained by a seizure of righteousness. If some of one's actions leave one's heart unsatisfied, it will starve. Consequently, I say that Gaozi never understood righteousness, because he regarded it as external.[20]

"One must work at it, but do not aim at it directly. Let the heart not forget, but do not 'help' it grow. Do not be like the man from Song.[21] Among the people of the state of Song there was one who, concerned lest his seedlings not grow, pulled on them. Wearily, he returned home, and said to his family, 'Today I am worn out. I helped the seedlings to grow.' His son rushed out and looked at it. The seedlings were withered. Those in the world who do not 'help' their seedlings to grow are few. Those who abandon them, thinking it will not help, are those who do not weed their seedlings. Those who 'help' them grow are those who pull on the seedlings. Not only does this not help, but it even harms them."

Gongsun Chou said, "What is meant by 'understanding words'?"[22]

Mengzi said, "If someone's expressions are one-sided, I know that by which they are deluded.[23] If someone's expressions are excessive, I know that by which they are entangled. If someone's expressions are heretical, I know that by which they are separated from the Way. If someone's expressions are evasive, I know that by which they are exhausted. When these states grow in the heart, they are harmful in governing. When they are manifested in governing, they are harmful in one's activities. When sages arise again, they will surely follow what I have said."

---

20. On the externality of righteousness, see *Mengzi* 6A4–5 (below).

21. The people of Song were the butt of many jokes. Cf. *Zhuangzi* chapter 1 (in chapter 8 of this volume) and *Han Feizi* chapter 49 (in chapter 10 of this volume).

22. Cf. *Analects* 20.3 (in chapter 1 of this volume).

23. The notion that people can be deluded (or "fixated") by seeing only part of the Way also appears in *Analects* 17.8 (in chapter 1 of this volume), and is a central notion in *Xunzi* chapter 21, "Undoing Fixation" (in chapter 9 of this volume).

Gongsun Chou said, "Zai Wo and Zigong were good at rhetoric. Ran Niu, Minzi, and Yan Yuan were good at discussing virtuous actions.[24] Kongzi combined all these excellences, but said, 'When it comes to rhetoric, I am incapable.' In that case, are you, Master, already a sage?!"

Mengzi said, "Oh, what kind of talk is that?! Long ago, Zigong asked Kongzi, 'Are you, Master, really a sage?' Kongzi replied, 'As for being a sage, I am incapable of that. I study without tiring and teach without wearying.'[25] Zigong said, 'To study without tiring is wisdom; to teach without wearying is benevolence. Being benevolent and wise, the Master is certainly already a sage!' So, to be a sage is not something Kongzi was comfortable with. So how could you ask *me* that?!"

Gongsun Chou said, "Formerly, I heard the following: Zigong, Ziyou, and Zizhang all had one aspect of a sage. Ran Niu, Minzi, and Yan Yuan had all aspects of a sage, but in miniature. I venture to ask in which group you would be comfortable?"

Mengzi said, "Leave this topic for now."

Gongsun Chou said, "What about Bo Yi and Yi Yin?"[26]

Mengzi said, "Their Ways were different. If he was not his ruler, he would not serve him; if they were not his subjects, he would not direct them; if things were orderly, he would advance; if they were chaotic, he would retreat. This was Bo Yi. Whom do I serve who is not my ruler? Whom do I direct who are not my subjects? If things were orderly, he would advance, and if they were chaotic, he would also advance. This was Yi Yin. When one should take office, he would take office; when one should stop, he would stop; when one should take a long time, he would take a long time; when one should hurry, he would hurry. This was Kongzi. All were sages of ancient times. I have never been able to act like them, but my wish is to learn from Kongzi."

Gongsun Chou asked, "Were Bo Yi and Yi Yin at the same level as Kongzi?"

Mengzi said, "No. Since humans were first born there has never been another Kongzi."

Gongsun Chou said, "In that case, were there any similarities?"

Mengzi said, "There were. If any became ruler of a territory of a hundred *li*, he would be able to possess all under Heaven by bringing the various lords to his court. And if any could obtain all under Heaven by performing one unrighteous deed, or killing one innocent person, he would not do it. In these things they are the same."

Gongsun Chou asked, "I venture to ask wherein they differed?"

---

24. These people were disciples of Kongzi, as were the additional people in the next list below.

25. Similar comments are attributed to Kongzi in *Analects* 7.2 and 7.34 (in chapter 1 of this volume).

26. For Bo Yi and Yi Yin, see *Important Figures* in the appendices.

Mengzi said, "Zai Wo, Zigong, and You Ruo had wisdom sufficient to recognize a sage. Even if they exaggerated, they would not have done so to the extent of flattering someone they were fond of. Zai Wo said, 'In my view of Kongzi, he is far more noble than Yao and Shun!' Zigong said, 'He sees their rituals and appreciates their government; he hears their music and appreciates their Virtue; from a hundred generations later, through the succession of a hundred kings, nothing gets away from him. Since humans were first born, there has never been another like the Master.' You Ruo said, 'Is it only true of people? The unicorn among beasts, the phoenix among birds, Mount Tai among hills, and rivers and seas among flowing waters, are all of a kind. The sage among people is also of the same kind. Some stand out from this kind; some stick up from the row; since humans were first born, there has never been one who stands out more than Kongzi.'"

2A6 Mengzi said, "Humans all have hearts that are not unfeeling toward others. The former kings[27] had hearts that were not unfeeling toward others, so they had governments that were not unfeeling toward others. If one puts into practice a government that is not unfeeling toward others by means of a heart that is not unfeeling toward others, bringing order to the whole world is in the palm of your hand.

"The reason why I say that humans all have hearts that are not unfeeling toward others is this. Suppose someone suddenly saw a child about to fall into a well: everyone in such a situation would have a feeling of alarm and compassion—not because one sought to get in good with the child's parents, not because one wanted fame among their neighbors and friends, and not because one would dislike the sound of the child's cries.

"From this we can see that if one is without the heart of compassion, one is not a human. If one is without the heart of disdain, one is not a human. If one is without the heart of deference, one is not a human. If one is without the heart of approval and disapproval,[28] one is not a human. The heart of compassion is the sprout of benevolence. The heart of disdain is the sprout of righteousness. The heart of deference is the sprout of propriety. The heart of approval and disapproval is the sprout of wisdom.[29]

---

27. That is, the sage-kings of antiquity, such as Yao and Shun. See *Important Figures* in the appendices.

28. The words here rendered "approval" and "disapproval" are shì 是 and fēi 非, respectively. A common meaning of these terms is "right" and "wrong" but in this context Mengzi intends not only knowledge but approval of what is right and disapproval of what is wrong.

29. Mengzi also discusses these four cardinal virtues in *Mengzi* 4A27 and 6A6. For more on rén 仁, "benevolence," see *Mengzi* 1A7. For more on yì 義, "righteousness," see *Mengzi* 6A10. For more on zhì 智, "wisdom," see *Mengzi* 5A9. On Mengzi's general view of self-cultivation, see *Mengzi* 7A17 and 7B31. "Propriety" here is lǐ 禮, the character for "ritual" elsewhere. Mengzi is suggesting that an inclination toward ritual activity is innate in us. See *Mengzi* 3A5 for a possible illustration of this.

"People having these four sprouts is like their having four limbs. To have these four sprouts but to say of oneself that one is unable to be virtuous is to steal from oneself. To say that one's ruler is unable to be virtuous is to steal from one's ruler. In general, having these four sprouts within oneself, if one knows to fill them all out, it will be like a fire starting up, a spring breaking through! If one can merely fill them out, they will be sufficient to care for all within the Four Seas. If one merely fails to fill them out, they will be insufficient to serve one's parents."

2B13 Mengzi left the state of Qi.[30] While on the road, Chongyu asked, "It seems that you, Master, have an unhappy countenance. The other day, I heard it from you, Master, that [Kongzi said], 'The gentleman does not resent Heaven for his troubles, nor does he cast aspersions upon other people.'"[31]

Mengzi said, "That time [in which Kongzi spoke] is the same as this time. Every five hundred years, there must arise a sage-king. Between them, there must be those whose names are known to a generation for their accomplishments. From the founding of the Zhou dynasty, it has already been more than seven hundred years. Numerically, this is excessive. And if one examines it in terms of the conditions of the world, then it is possible that a new sage-king will arise. Now, Heaven does not yet desire to pacify the world. If it desired to pacify the world, who besides me in the present time is there to help do it? Why would I be unhappy?!"[32]

Book Three

3A3 . . . Mengzi said, "The well-field system takes a one-*li*-square piece of land, amounting to 900 *mu*.[33] At its center is the public field. Eight families each keep privately 100 *mu*, and jointly cultivate the public field. Only after the public work is completed do they dare do their private work. This is the distinctive role of the rural people." . . .

---

30. Mengzi left the state of Qi because his efforts to persuade the ruler to implement the "benevolent government" policies he advocated had failed. See *Mengzi* 1A7, 1B5, 1B6, and 1B8 (all found in this chapter).

31. Cf. *Analects* 14.35 (in chapter 1 of this volume).

32. For a discussion of interpretations of this passage, see Philip J. Ivanhoe, "A Question of Faith: A New Interpretation of *Mencius* 2B.13," *Early China* 13 (January 1988): 153–65.

33. The "well-field system" begins with the idea of taking a square region of land and subdividing it into nine equal fields. The boundaries between these regions would then look something like this: 井. Pronounced jǐng, this happens to be the character for "well" in Chinese, hence the expression "well-field."

3A4 There was a certain Xu Xing who, on account of the doctrines of Shen Nong,[34] went from the state of Chu to Teng, and, going in person to his gate, told Duke Wen, "People from distant parts have heard that you, My Lord, practice benevolent government. I wish to receive a homestead and become one of your subjects." Duke Wen gave him a place. His followers were a few dozen people, all of whom wore coarse clothing and made sandals and mats for a living.

Chen Liang's disciple Chen Xiang and his younger brother Xin carried their plows on their backs and went from Song to Teng, saying, "We have heard that you, My Lord, practice the government of a sage. This is to be a sage. I wish to become the subject of a sage."

Chen Xiang met Xu Xing and was delighted. He completely abandoned his former studies and studied with him instead. Chen Xiang met Mengzi and discoursed on the doctrines of Xu Xing, saying, "The ruler of Teng is truly a worthy ruler. Nonetheless, he has not yet heard the Way. The worthy plow with their subjects and then eat, eating breakfast and dinner with them and then governing. In the present case, Teng has granaries and treasuries; this is to harm the people in order to nurture oneself. How can this be worthy?"

Mengzi said, "Xuzi must plant his grain first and only then eat?"

Chen said, "That is so."

Mengzi said, "Xuzi must weave his cloth and only then wear clothes?"

Chen said, "No. Xuzi wears hemp."

Mengzi said, "Does Xuzi wear a cap?"

Chen said, "He does."

Mengzi said, "What sort does he wear?"

Chen said, "He wears plain silk."

Mengzi said, "Does he weave it himself?"

Chen said, "No. He exchanges millet for it."

Mengzi said, "Why does Xuzi not weave it himself?"

Chen said, "That would interfere with farming."

Mengzi said, "Does Xuzi use clay pots for cooking, and an iron plow?"

Chen said, "That is so."

Mengzi said, "Does he make them himself?"

Chen said, "No. He exchanges millet for them."

Mengzi said, "Exchanging millet for tools does not harm the blacksmith. And when the blacksmith exchanges tools for millet, does this really hurt the farmer?! Why does Xuzi not become a blacksmith, and only get everything from his own

---

34. For Shen Nong, Yao, and Shun (the latter two are mentioned later in this passage), see *Important Figures* in the appendices.

household to use? Why does he exchange things in such confusion with the various artisans? Why does Xuzi not avoid all this trouble?"

Chen said, "The activities of the various artisans inherently cannot be done along with farming."

Mengzi said, "In that case, can governing the world alone be done along with farming? There are the affairs of great people, and the affairs of lesser people. Furthermore, the products of the various artisans are available to each person. If one can make use of them only after one has made them oneself, this will lead the whole world to exhaustion. Hence it is said, 'Some labor with their hearts; some labor with their physical strength.' Those who labor with their hearts govern others; those who labor with their physical strength are governed by others. Those who are governed by others feed those others; those who govern others are fed by those others. This is righteousness throughout the world.[35] . . .

"It is the way of people that if they are full of food, have warm clothes, and live in comfort, but are without instruction, then they come close to being animals. Sage-king Shun was anxious about this too, so he instructed Xie to be Minister of Instruction, and instruct them about human relations: the relation of father and children is one of love, ruler and minister is one of righteousness, husband and wife is one of distinction, elder and younger is one of precedence, and that between friends is one of trust. Yao said, 'Encourage them, draw them forward, straighten them, rectify them, help them, make them practice, assist them, make them get it themselves, and then benefit them.' Since the sage's anxiousness for his subjects was like this, could he have the free time to farm?" . . .

[Chen said,] "If we follow the Way of Xuzi, market prices will never vary, and there will be no artifice in the state. Even if one sends a child to go to the market, no one will cheat him. Cotton cloth or silk cloth of the same length will be of equal price. Bundles of hemp or silk of the same weight will be of equal price. The same amount of any of the five grains will be the same price. Shoes of the same size will be of equal price."

Mengzi said, "It is the essence of things to be unequal.[36] One thing is twice or five times more than another, another ten or a hundred times more, another a thousand or ten thousand times more. If you line them up and identify them, this will bring chaos to the world. If a great shoe and a shoddy shoe are the same price,

---

35. What follows in the original text is a historical narrative (similar to that in *Mengzi* 3B9) that explains the achievements of the sage-rulers of old in making civilization possible.

36. Zhuangzi may be implicitly criticizing this passage in *Zhuangzi* chapter 2, "On Equalizing Things" (in chapter 8 of this volume).

will anyone make the former? If we follow the Way of Xuzi, we will lead each other into artifice. How can this bring order to the state?"

3A5 The Mohist Yi Zhi sought to see Mengzi through the help of Xu Bi.[37] Mengzi said, "I am definitely willing to see him, but today I am still ill. When my illness improves, I will go and see him. Yi Zhi does not have to come." The next day, he again sought to see Mengzi. Mengzi said, "Today I [still] can [not] see him. [But] if one is not upright, the Way will not be manifest. I will make him upright.[38]

"I have heard that Yi Zhi is a Mohist. Mohists, in regulating mourning, take frugality as their Way. Yi Zhi longs to change the world to the Mohist Way. Surely, he honors the Mohist practice because he regards it as right? Nonetheless, Yi Zhi buried his parents lavishly, so he served his parents by means of what he demeans."

Xu Bi told Yi Zhi this. Yi Zhi said, "As for the Way of the Confucians, the ancients tended the people 'like caring for children.'[39] What does this saying mean? I take it to mean that love is without distinctions, but it is bestowed beginning with one's parents."

Xu Bi told Mengzi this. Mengzi said, "Does Yi Zhi truly hold that one's affection for one's elder brother's son is like one's affection for one's neighbor's child? There is only one thing to be gleaned from that saying: when a crawling child is about to fall into a well, it is not the child's fault. Furthermore, Heaven, in producing the things in the world, causes them to have one source, but Yi Zhi gives them two sources.[40]

"Now, in past ages, there were those who did not bury their parents. When their parents died, they took them and abandoned them in a ditch. The next day they passed by them, and foxes were eating them, bugs were sucking on them. Sweat broke out on the survivors' foreheads. They turned away and did not look. Now, it was not for the sake of others that they sweated. What was inside their hearts broke through to their countenances. So, they went home and, returning

---

37. For more on Mohism, see *Mengzi* 3B9 and 7A26, as well as chapter 2 of this volume.

38. Notice that the conversation between Mengzi and Yi Zhi is conducted using Xu Bi as an intermediary (presumably because Mengzi is ill). Cf. *Analects* 10.19 (in chapter 1 of this volume).

39. This is a line from the *History*. See James Legge, trans., *The Shoo King*, vol. 3 of *The Chinese Classics* (Oxford: Clarendon Press, 1871; Taibei: SMC Publishing, 1991), 389.

40. David S. Nivison argues ("Two Roots or One?" in Nivison, *The Ways of Confucianism* [La Salle, IL: Open Court Press, 1996], 133–48) that the two sources (běn 本, literally "roots") Yi Zhi accepts are (1) our innate sense of benevolence, which is first directed toward our parents (cf. *Mengzi* 7A15), and (2) a doctrine of universalization that instructs us to extend this innate feeling so that it applies to everyone equally.

with baskets and shovels, covered them. If covering them was really right, then when filial children and benevolent people cover their parents, it must also be part of the Way."

Xu Bi told Yi Zhi this. Yi Zhi looked thoughtful for a moment and said, "He has taught me."

3B2 . . . Mengzi said, "When a daughter marries, her mother instructs her. Sending her off at the gate, she cautions her, saying, 'When you go to your family, you must be respectful, and you must be cautious. Do not disobey your husband.' To regard obedience as proper is the Way of a wife or concubine."[41] . . .

3B9 Gongduzi said, "Outsiders all say that you are fond of disputation, Master. I venture to ask why?"

Mengzi said, "How could I be fond of disputation? I simply have no choice. The people of the world were born long ago, and have alternated between being orderly and chaotic. In the time of Yao, the waters overflowed their courses, inundating the central states. Serpents occupied the land, and the people were unsettled. In low-lying regions, they made nests in trees. On the high ground, they lived in caves. The *History* says, 'The deluge warned us.'[42] 'The deluge' refers to the flooding water. Yu was directed to regulate the waters. Yu dredged out the earth and guided the water into the sea, chasing the reptiles into the marshes. The waters flowed out through the channels, and these became the Jiang, Huai, He, and Han rivers. The dangers to people having been eliminated, birds and beasts harmful to humans were destroyed, and only then were humans able to live on the plains.

"After Yao and Shun passed away, the Way of the sages decayed. Cruel rulers arose one after another, destroying homes to make ponds, so that the people had nowhere they could rest.[43] They made people abandon the fields so that they could be made into parks, so that the people could not get clothes and food. Evil doctrines and cruel practices also arose. As parks, ponds, and marshes became more numerous, the birds and beasts returned. By the time of Tyrant Zhou, the world was again in great disorder. The Duke of Zhou assisted King Wu in punishing Tyrant Zhou; he attacked the state of Yan, and after three years executed its ruler; he

---

41. On the ethical status of women, see also *Mengzi* 4B33.

42. See Legge, *The Shoo King*, 60. On the *History* and *The Spring and Autumn Annals* (mentioned below), see under *Important Texts* in the appendices. On Yao, Shun, Yu and the other figures mentioned in this and the following paragraph, see under *Important Figures* in the appendices.

43. The ponds referred to in this line, and the parks referred to in the next, were for the use of the ruler only, and not for the benefit of the people.

drove Feilian to a corner by the sea and terminated him; he eliminated fifty states; he drove tigers, leopards, rhinoceroses, and elephants far off, and the whole world rejoiced. The *History* says, 'Splendid indeed were the plans of King Wen! Great indeed were the achievements of King Wu! They assist and instruct us descendants. In all things they are correct, and lack nothing.'[44]

"With the decay of the Way, evil doctrines and cruel actions again arose. Ministers murdering their rulers—this happened. Sons murdering their fathers—this happened. Kongzi was afraid, and composed the *Spring and Autumn Annals*. The *Spring and Autumn Annals* is the activity of the Son of Heaven.[45] For this reason, Kongzi said, 'Those who appreciate me, will it not be because of the *Spring and Autumn Annals*? Those who blame me, will it not be because of the *Spring and Autumn Annals*?'

"Once again, a sage-king has not arisen; the various lords are dissipated; pundits engage in contrary wrangling; the doctrines of Yang Zhu and Mozi fill the world.[46] If a doctrine does not lean toward Yang, then it leans toward Mo. Yang is 'for ourselves.' This is to not have a ruler. Mo is 'impartial caring.' This is to not have a father. To not have a father and to not have a ruler is to be an animal. Gongming Yi said, 'In your kitchens there is fat meat, and in your stables there are fat horses. Your people look gaunt, and in the wilds are the bodies of those dead of starvation. This is to lead animals to devour people.'

"If the Ways of Yang and Mo do not cease, and the Way of Kongzi is not made evident, then evil doctrines will dupe the people, and obstruct benevolence and righteousness. If benevolence and righteousness are obstructed, that leads animals to devour people. I am afraid that people will begin to devour one another! If we defend the Way of the former sages, fend off Yang Zhu and Mozi, and get rid of specious words, then evil doctrines will be unable to arise. If they arise in one's heart, they are harmful in one's activities. If they arise in one's activities, they are harmful in governing. When sages arise again, they will certainly not differ with what I have said.

"Formerly, Yu suppressed the flood, and the world was settled. The Duke of Zhou incorporated the barbarians, drove away ferocious animals, and the common people were at peace. Kongzi completed the *Spring and Autumn Annals*, and disorderly ministers and brutal sons were afraid. The *Odes* say,

---

44. See Legge, *The Shoo King,* 581.

45. The Chinese line here is ambiguous. It could mean that the *Spring and Autumn Annals* contains accounts of the activities of the ruler, or that composing it is the prerogative of the ruler.

46. On the philosophy of Mozi, see also *Mengzi* 3A5 and 7A26, as well as the *Mozi* (in chapter 2 of this volume). On the philosophy of Yang Zhu, see *Mengzi* 7A26 and "Robber Zhi" (in chapter 3 of this volume).

The barbarians of the west and north, these he chastised.
Jing and Shu, these he punished.
Thus no one dared to take us on.[47]

Those who [act as if they] have no father and no ruler, these the Duke of Zhou chastised. I, too, desire to rectify people's hearts, to bring to an end evil doctrines, to fend off bad conduct, to get rid of specious words, so as to carry on the work of these three sages. How could I be fond of disputation? I simply have no choice. Anyone who can with words fend off Yang Zhu and Mozi is a disciple of the sages."

3B10 Kuang Zhang said, "Wasn't Cheng Zhongzi an incorruptible scholar?![48] While living in Wuling, he did not eat for three days, until his ears did not hear, and his eyes did not see. Above a well there was a plum tree whose fruit had been half-eaten by worms. Crawling, he went over to eat from it, and only after three bites could his ears hear and his eyes see."

Mengzi said, "Among the scholars of the state of Qi, Zhongzi stands out like a thumb among the fingers. Nonetheless, how could Zhongzi be incorruptible? To fill out what Zhongzi attempts, one would have to be an earthworm.[49] Now, an earthworm eats dry earth above and drinks muddy water below. The house in which Zhongzi lives, was it built by Bo Yi, or was it in fact built by Robber Zhi? Was the millet that he eats planted by Bo Yi, or was it in fact planted by Robber Zhi? This cannot be known."[50]

Kuang said, "Why is that a problem? He himself weaves sandals of hemp, his wife spinning the hemp, in exchange for these other things."

Mengzi said, "Zhongzi comes from a great family of Qi. His elder brother Dai received a salary of ten thousand bushels of grain from estates at Ge. He regarded his brother's salary as an unrighteous salary, and would not live off of it. He regarded his brothers' dwelling as an unrighteous dwelling, and would not live in it. He left his elder brother, distancing himself from his mother, and lived in Wuling. On a later day, he visited home, and someone had given a live goose to his elder brother as a gift. He knitted his brow and said, 'What will you use this cackling thing for?!' After that, his mother killed the goose, and gave it to him to eat. His elder brother came home and said, 'This is the meat of that "cackling thing."' Zhongzi went out and threw it up. If it comes from his mother, he doesn't eat it, but if it comes from

---

47. *Mao # 300.* Jing is another name for the state of Chu. Shu was a small state located in what is now Anhui Province.

48. Cheng Zhongzi may be another follower of Xu Xing (see *Mengzi 3A4*).

49. Compare the notion of "filling out" the sprouts in *Mengzi 2A6*.

50. On Bo Yi and Robber Zhi, see *Important Figures* in the appendices.

his wife, then he eats it. If it's his elder brother's dwelling, then he won't live in it; if it's in Wuling, then he lives in it. Is this really being able to fill out the category of action that he considers righteous?! Someone like Zhongzi must be an earthworm in order to fill out what he attempts."

Book Four

4A10 Mengzi said, "One cannot have a discussion with those who are destroying themselves. One cannot act with those who throw themselves away. Those whose words are opposed to propriety and righteousness are who I mean by 'those who are destroying themselves.' Those who say, 'I myself am unable to dwell in benevolence and follow righteousness' are who I mean by 'those who throw themselves away.' Benevolence is people's peaceful abode. Righteousness is people's proper path. For one to vacate one's peaceful abode and not dwell in it, or for one to set aside one's proper path and not follow it—how sad!"

4A11 Mengzi said, "The Way lies in what is near, but people seek it in what is distant; one's task lies in what is easy, but people seek it in what is difficult. If everyone would treat their kin as kin, and their elders as elders, the world would be at peace."

4A15 Mengzi said, "Of what is present within a person, nothing is more ingenuous than the pupils of the eyes. The pupils cannot hide one's evil. If, in one's bosom, one is upright, the pupils will be bright. If, in one's bosom, one is not upright, the pupils will be shady. If one listens to people's words and looks at their pupils, how can they hide?!"

4A17 Chunyu Kun said, "That men and women should not touch in handing something to one another—is this the ritual?"[51]
　　Mengzi said, "It is the ritual."
　　Chunyu Kun said, "If your sister-in-law were drowning, would you pull her out with your hand?"
　　Mengzi said, "To not pull your sister-in-law out when she is drowning is to be a beast. That men and women should not touch in handing something to one another is the ritual, but if your sister-in-law is drowning, to pull her out with your hand is discretion."[52]
　　Chunyu Kun said, "Currently, the world is drowning! Why is it that you, sir, do not pull it out?"

---

51. Chunyu Kun was a rival philosopher.

52. Quán 權, "discretion," literally means "weighing," as on a balance. On "discretion," see also *Mengzi* 7A26.

Mengzi said, "When the world is drowning, one pulls it out with the Way; when one's sister-in-law is drowning, one pulls her out with one's hand. Do you want me to save the world with a pull of my hand?"

4A27 Mengzi said, "The core of benevolence is serving one's parents. The core of righteousness is obeying one's elder brother. The core of wisdom is knowing these two and not abandoning them. The core of ritual is to regulate and adorn these two. The core of music is to delight in these two.

"If one delights in them then they grow. If they grow then how can they be stopped? If they cannot be stopped, then without realizing it one's feet begin to step in time to them and one's hands dance according to their rhythms."[53]

4B2 When Zichan was in charge of the government of the state of Zheng, he used his own carriage to carry people across the Zhen and the Wei rivers. Mengzi said, "He was kind, but did not understand how to govern. By September, the foot bridges are to be repaired, and by October, the carriage bridges are to be repaired, so the people no longer face the difficulty of wading across the rivers.[54] If gentlemen are equitable in governing, it is acceptable even to order people out of their way while they travel. How can they carry every single person across? Hence, there will simply not be enough days if, in governing, one tries to make everyone happy."

4B6 Mengzi said, "The propriety that is not propriety, the righteousness that is not righteousness—the great person will not practice these."[55]

4B8 Mengzi said, "People must have some things that they do not do, and only then can they really do anything."

4B11 Mengzi said, "As for great people, their words do not have to be trustworthy,[56] and their actions do not have to bear fruit. They rest only in righteousness."

---

53. I owe the translation of these last lines to Philip J. Ivanhoe.

54. The rivers have fords that are shallow enough to wade across on foot, or drive through in a carriage. The bridges are damaged each year by the heavy rains in the spring and summer. Consequently, they must be repaired in the autumn.

55. Cf. *Mengzi* 7B37.

56. To illustrate a case in which a great person's words do not have to be trustworthy, the Han dynasty commentator Zhao Qi refers to *Analects* 13.18 (in chapter 1 of this volume) in which upright "sons cover up for their fathers." Compare also *Mengzi* 1A7, above, note 1, and *Analects* 13.20 (in chapter 1 of this volume).

4B12 Mengzi said, "Great people are those who do not lose the hearts of their 'children.'"[57]

4B18 Xuzi said, "Kongzi several times spoke of water, saying, 'Ah water! Ah water!'[58] What did he find so worthy about water?" Mengzi said, "It gushes from the spring, not letting up day or night, only advancing after filling up the hollows, and going on to the Four Seas. Things that have a source are like this.[59] It was simply this that he found so worthy. If it merely fails to have a source, the rain collects during the spring months, and the drainage ditches are all full. However, you can just stand and wait and it will become dry. Hence, gentlemen are ashamed to have their reputation exceed what they genuinely are."

4B19 Mengzi said, "That by which humans differ from birds and beasts is slight. The people abandon it. The gentleman preserves it. The sage-king Shun was insightful about things. He was perceptive about human relationships. He acted out of benevolence and righteousness. He did not act out benevolence and righteousness."

4B24 . . . Mengzi said, "The people of the state of Zheng sent Zizhuo Ruzi to invade the state of Wei. Wei sent Si of Yugong to pursue him. Zizhuo Ruzi said, 'Today my illness is acting up. I am unable to hold my bow. I suppose I shall die.' He asked his chariot driver, 'Who is it that chases me?' His driver said, 'It is Si of Yugong.' He said, 'I shall live!' His driver said, 'Si of Yugong is the best archer of the state of Wei. What do you mean, Master, when you say, "I shall live"?' He said, 'Si of Yugong studied archery under Tuo of Yingong. Tuo of Yingong studied archery under me. Now, Tuo of Yingong is an upright person. Those whom he chooses for friends must be upright.'

"Si of Yugong arrived and said, 'Why do you not hold your bow, Master?' He said, 'Today my illness is acting up. I am unable to hold my bow.' He replied, 'I, petty person that I am, studied archery under Tuo of Yingong. Tuo of Yingong studied archery under you, Master. I cannot bear to take your Way and turn it against you, Master. Nonetheless, what I do today is my ruler's business. I dare not cast it aside.' He pulled out some arrows and hit them against the wheel of his chariot, breaking off their tips. He then shot off a set of four arrows and only then returned."

---

57. I translate this line according to the interpretation of the Han dynasty commentator Zhao Qi, where "children" is a metaphor for the ruler's subjects. (Cf. 3A5, in which Mengzi says that good rulers treat their subjects like "children," using the same term as in this passage.) However, many interpreters follow the reading of the Song dynasty commentator Zhu Xi: "Great people are those who do not lose their heart of a child," where "heart of a child" refers to one's innate good nature.

58. Cf. *Analects* 6.23 and 9.17 (in chapter 1 of this volume).

59. On the notion of one's běn 本 ("source," or what is "fundamental"), see also *Mengzi* 3A5 and 6A10.

4B28 Mengzi said, "That by means of which gentlemen differ from others is that they preserve their hearts. Gentlemen preserve their hearts through benevolence and through propriety. The benevolent love others, and those who have propriety respect others. Those who love others are generally loved by others. Those who respect others are generally respected by others.

"Here is a person who is harsh to me. A gentleman in this situation will invariably examine himself, saying, 'I must not be benevolent. I must be lacking in propriety. How else could this situation have come upon me?!' If he examines himself and *is* benevolent, and if he examines himself and *has* propriety, yet the other person is still harsh, a gentleman will invariably examine himself, saying, 'I must not be loyal.' If he examines himself and *is* loyal, yet the other person is still harsh, a gentleman says, 'This person is simply incorrigible! What difference is there between a person like this and an animal?! What point is there in rebuking an animal?'" . . .

4B29 Yu and Houji were in a peaceful era, yet they were so busy governing that they passed the doors of their homes three times without entering. Kongzi deemed them worthy. Yan Hui was in a chaotic era, lived in a narrow alleyway, subsisting upon meager bits of rice and water—other people could not have borne such hardship, and yet it never spoiled Yan Hui's joy. Kongzi deemed him worthy.[60]

Mengzi said, "Yu, Houji, and Yan Hui had the same Way. Yu thought that, if there were anyone in the world who drowned, it was as if he had drowned them himself. Houji thought that, if there were anyone in the world who was starving, it was as if he had starved them himself. Hence, their urgency was like this. If Yu, Houji, and Yan Hui had exchanged places, they all would have done as the others.

"Now, suppose there is someone from your household involved in an altercation outside. It is acceptable to go and help even though you are disheveled and not fully dressed. But if there is someone from your village involved in an altercation outside, it is foolish to go and help when you are disheveled and not fully dressed. Even bolting your door is acceptable in this case."

4B33 There was a man of the state of Qi who lived in a home with his wife and concubine. When the husband went out, he would always return full of wine and meat. His wife asked whom he ate with, and they were those of the highest wealth and rank. His wife told his concubine, "When our husband goes out, he always returns full of wine and meat. When I ask whom he ate with, it is always those of the highest wealth and rank. Yet no one noteworthy ever comes here. I shall go and spy on where our husband goes."

---

60. On Yan Hui, see *Analects* 6.11 (in chapter 1 of this volume). For more on Yu and Houji, see *Important Figures* in the appendices.

Arising early, she discreetly followed where her husband went. Throughout the city, there was no one who stopped to chat with him. In the end, he approached those performing sacrifices among the graves beyond the East Wall of the city, and begged for their leftovers. If this was not enough, he would then look around and approach others. This was his way of getting his fill.

His wife returned home and told his concubine, saying, "A husband is someone whom we look toward till the ends of our lives. And he's like this!" And with the concubine she cursed her husband, and they cried together in the middle of the courtyard. But their husband did not know this, and came happily home, strutting before his wife and concubine.

From the perspective of a gentleman, it is rare indeed that the means by which people seek wealth, rank, profit, and success would not make their wives and concubines cry together in shame![61]

Book Five

5A2 Wan Zhang asked, "The *Odes* say,

> How should one proceed in taking a wife?
> One must inform one's parents.[62]

If this saying is trustworthy, it seems that no one would follow it more than the sage Shun. How is it that Shun took a wife without informing them?"

Mengzi said, "If he had informed them, he would have been unable to take a wife. For a man and a woman to dwell together in one home is the greatest of human relations.[63] If he had informed them, he would be abandoning the greatest of human relations, which would have caused resentment toward his parents. Because of this he did not inform them."

Wan Zhang said, "I have now received your instruction regarding Shun's taking a wife without informing his parents. But how is it that the Emperor gave his daughter to Shun as a wife and did not inform them?"

Mengzi said, "The Emperor knew too that if he informed them, he would not be able to give his daughter to him as a wife."

Wan Zhang said, "His parents made Shun repair the grain silo, and then they took the ladder away and his father set fire to the silo, but Shun escaped. Then they

---

61. A sense of shame is related to the "sprout of disdain" (see *Mengzi* 2A6; cf. *Mengzi* 7A7). Consequently, this passage suggests that women, too, have the sprouts or hearts of virtue (see *Mengzi* 2A6). On the ethical status of women, see also *Mengzi* 3B2.

62. *Mao* # 101. On Shun (discussed later in this passage), see *Important Figures* in the appendices.

63. On the "human relations," see also *Mengzi* 3A4 and 4B19.

made him dig a well. He left the well, but, not knowing this, they covered up the well. His brother Xiang said, 'The credit for the plot to kill this ruler is all mine! His oxen and sheep, his granaries and silos shall be my parents', but his spear and shield, his lute, and his bow are mine! And I shall make my two sisters-in-law service me in bed!' So, Xiang went into Shun's room, but Shun was on his bed playing his zither. Xiang, looking embarrassed, said, 'I was worried and thinking of you!' Shun said, 'The various ministers of mine—help me to direct them.' But surely Shun did not fail to understand that Xiang planned to murder him?"

Mengzi said, "How could he not understand? But when Xiang was anxious, he was also anxious; when Xiang was happy, he was also happy."

Wan Zhang asked, "In that case, did Shun feign happiness?"

Mengzi said, "No. Formerly, someone made a gift of a live fish to Zichan of the state of Zheng. Zichan had the pond keeper take care of it in the pond. But the pond keeper cooked it, and reported back to Zichan, 'When I first let it go, it seemed sickly, but in a little while it perked up, and went off happily.' Zichan said, 'It's where it should be! It's where it should be!' The pond keeper left and said, 'Whoever said that Zichan was wise! I have already cooked and eaten it, and he says, "It's where it should be! It's where it should be!"' Hence, gentlemen can be tricked by what is in accordance with their practices, but it is hard to ensnare them with what is not the Way. Xiang came in accordance with the Way of one who loves his elder brother. Hence, Shun genuinely trusted him and was happy about him. How could he have feigned it?"

5A9 Wan Zhang asked, "Someone said that the sage Boli Xi sold himself to a herder in the state of Qin for five ram skins, and fed cattle, because he sought to meet Duke Mu of Qin. Is this story trustworthy?"

Mengzi said, "It is not. That is not the case. This was fabricated by those obsessed with taking office. Boli Xi was a person of the state of Yu.[64] The people of the state of Jin, in exchange for jade from Chui Ji and a team of horses from Qu, gained rite of passage through Yu to attack the state of Guo.[65] Qi of Gong remonstrated against this, but Boli Xi did not remonstrate against it. He knew that the Duke of Yu could not be remonstrated with, so he left and went to Qin. He was already seventy years old. If he did not yet know that it would be base to feed oxen in order to seek to meet Duke Mu of Qin, could he have been called wise? He knew that the Duke of Yu could not be remonstrated with so he did not

---

64. A small state in which the ancestors of Shun were said to be enfeoffed. It was located in what is now the northeast part of Pinglu county in modern Shanxi Province.

65. A small state ruled by the descendants of King Wen's younger brother. It was located in what is now Pinglu county in modern Shanxi Province.

remonstrate with him. Can this be called unwise? He knew that the Duke of Yu was about to perish, so he abandoned him first. This cannot be called unwise. When he was, in good time, raised to prominence in Qin, he knew that Duke Mu was someone with whom he could work, so he became his minister. Can this be called unwise? He was a minister in Qin and made his ruler distinguished throughout the world, so that he is an example for later ages. Is this something he would be capable of if he were not a worthy person? To sell oneself so as to accomplish things for one's lord—even a villager who cared for himself would not do this. Can one say that a worthy person would do it?"

Book Six

6A1 Gaozi said, "Human nature is like a willow tree; righteousness is like cups and bowls. To make human nature benevolent and righteous is like making a willow tree into cups and bowls."[66]

Mengzi said, "Can you, sir, following the nature of the willow tree, make it into cups and bowls? You must violate and rob the willow tree, and only then can you make it into cups and bowls. If you must violate and rob the willow tree in order to make it into cups and bowls, must you also violate and rob people in order to make them benevolent and righteous? If there is something that leads people to regard benevolence and righteousness as misfortunes for them, it will surely be your doctrine, will it not?"

6A2 Gaozi said, "Human nature is like swirling water. Make an opening for it on the eastern side, then it flows east. Make an opening for it on the western side, then it flows west. Human nature's not distinguishing between good and not good is like water's not distinguishing between eastern and western."

Mengzi said, "Water surely does not distinguish between east and west. But does it not distinguish between upward and downward? Human nature's being good is like water's tending downward. There is no human who does not tend toward goodness. There is no water that does not tend downward.

"Now, by striking water and making it leap up, you can cause it to go past your forehead. If you guide it by damming it, you can cause it to remain on a mountaintop. But is this the nature of water?! It is that way because of the circumstances. That humans can be caused to not be good is due to their natures also being like this."

---

66. Gaozi was a rival philosopher (see also *Mengzi* 2A2). Compare his comment here (as well as his statement in 6A4 below that the desires for food and sex are nature) with Xunzi's comments in *Xunzi* chapter 1, "An Exhortation to Learning" and *Xunzi* chapter 23, "Human Nature Is Bad" (in this volume, chapter 9).

6A3 Gaozi said, "Life is what is meant by 'nature.'"[67]

Mengzi said, "Is *life is what is meant by 'nature'* the same as *white is what is meant by 'white'*?"[68]

Gaozi said, "It is."

Mengzi said, "Is the white of a white feather the same as the white of white snow, and is the white of white snow the same as the white of white jade?"

Gaozi said, "It is."

Mengzi said, "Then is the nature of a dog the same as the nature of an ox, and is the nature of an ox the same as the nature of a human?"

6A4 Gaozi said, "The desires for food and sex are nature. Benevolence is internal; it is not external. Righteousness is external; it is not internal."[69]

Mengzi said, "Why do you say that benevolence is internal and righteousness is external?"

Gaozi said, "They are elderly, and we treat them as elderly. It is not that they are elderly because of us. Similarly, that is white, and we treat it as white, according to its being white externally to us. Hence, I say it is external."

Mengzi said, "[Elderliness] is different from whiteness. The whiteness of a [white] horse is no different from the whiteness of a gray-haired person. But surely we do not regard the elderliness of an old horse as being no different from the elderliness of an old person?[70] Furthermore, do you say that the one who is elderly is righteous, or that the one who treats another as elderly is righteous?"

Gaozi said, "My younger brother I love; the younger brother of a person from Qin I do not love. In this case, it is I who feel happy [because of my love for my brother]. Hence, I say that it is internal. I treat as elderly an elderly person from Chu, and I also treat as elderly my own elderly. In this case, it is the elderly person who feels happy. Hence, I say that it is external."[71]

---

67. The Song dynasty commentator Zhu Xi remarks, "'Life' refers to that by means of which humans and animals perceive and move." The Han dynasty commentator Zhao Qi suggests that Gaozi's comment means that, "In general, things that are the same in being alive will all have the same nature."

68. In ancient Chinese dialectic, "white" was the stock example of a term that functions the same way regardless of the context of its occurrence. See Angus C. Graham, *Disputers of the Tao* (La Salle, IL: Open Court Press, 1989), 150–55, and also chapter 5 of this volume.

69. Cf. Gongduzi's explanation in *Mengzi* 6A5 of what it means for a virtue to be "internal."

70. Because an elderly person deserves to be treated with deference and respect, while an elderly horse is, in Mengzi or Gaozi's view, almost worthless.

71. The Song dynasty commentator Zhu Xi explains, "He means that the love is determined by me, hence benevolence is internal; respect is determined by elderliness, hence righteousness is external."

Mengzi said, "Savoring the roast of a person from Qin is no different from savoring my roast. So, what you describe is also the case with objects. Is savoring a roast, then, also external?"

6A5 Meng Jizi asked Gongduzi, "Why do you say that righteousness is internal?"[72]

Gongduzi said, "I act out of my respect, hence I say that it is internal."

Meng Jizi said, "If a fellow villager is older than your eldest brother by a year, then whom do you respect?"

Gongduzi said, "I respect my brother."

Meng Jizi said, "When you are pouring wine, then whom do you serve first?"

Gongduzi said, "I first pour wine for the fellow villager."[73]

Meng Jizi said, "The one whom you respect is the former, but the one whom you treat as elder is the latter. Hence, it really is external. It does not come from [how you feel] internally."

Gongduzi was not able to answer. He told Mengzi about it. Mengzi said, "Next time, ask him, 'Do you respect your uncle? or do you respect your younger brother?' He will say, 'I respect my uncle.' Then you say, 'When your younger brother is playing the part of the deceased in the sacrifice, then whom do you respect?' He will say, 'I respect my younger brother.' Then you say, 'What happened to the respect for your uncle?' He will say, 'The reason [why my respect changes] has to do with the role my younger brother occupies.' Then you also say, 'In the case you asked about in our previous discussion, the reason why my respect changes has to do with the role the fellow villager occupies. Ordinary respect is directed toward my brother, but temporary respect is directed toward the fellow villager.'"

Meng Jizi, upon hearing all this, said, "If you respect your uncle, then it is respect. If you respect your younger brother, then it is respect. So, it really is external. It does not come from [how you feel] internally."

Gongduzi said, "On a winter day, one drinks broth. On a summer day, one drinks water. Are drinking and eating also, then, external?"

6A6 Gongduzi said, "Gaozi says, 'Human nature is neither good nor not good.' Some say, 'Human nature can become good, and it can become not good.' Therefore, when the sages Wen and Wu arose, the people were fond of goodness. When the tyrants You and Li arose, the people were fond of destructiveness. Some say, 'There are natures that are good, and there are natures that are not good.' Therefore, with Yao as ruler, there was Xiang. With the Blind Man as a father, there was

---

72. Meng Jizi is a follower of Gaozi. Gongduzi is a follower of Mengzi.

73. Because ritual dictates that the elder person be served first.

Shun.[74] And with Tyrant Zhou as their nephew, and as their ruler besides, there were Viscount Qi of Wei and Prince Bi Gan.[75] Now, you say that human nature is good. Are all those others, then, wrong?"

Mengzi said, "As for their essence, they can become good. This is what I mean by calling their natures good. As for their becoming not good, this is not the fault of their potential. Humans all have the heart of compassion. Humans all have the heart of disdain. Humans all have the heart of respect. Humans all have the heart of approval and disapproval. The heart of compassion is benevolence. The heart of disdain is righteousness. The heart of respect is propriety. The heart of approval and disapproval is wisdom. Benevolence, righteousness, propriety, and wisdom are not welded to us externally. We inherently have them. It is simply that we do not reflect upon them.[76] Hence, it is said, 'Seek it and you will get it. Abandon it and you will lose it.' Some differ from others by two, five, or countless times—this is because they cannot exhaust their potentials. The *Odes* say,

Heaven gives birth to the teeming people.
If there is a thing, there is a norm.
This is the constant people cleave to.
They are fond of this beautiful Virtue.[77]

Kongzi said, 'The one who composed this ode understood the Way!'[78] Hence, if there is a thing, there must be a norm. It is this that is the constant people cleave to. Hence, they are fond of this beautiful Virtue."

6A7 Mengzi said, "In years of plenty, most young men are gentle; in years of poverty, most young men are cruel. It is not that the potential that Heaven confers on them varies like this. They are like this because of that by which their hearts are sunk and drowned.

"Consider barley. Sow the seeds and cover them. The soil is the same and the time of planting is also the same. They grow rapidly, and by the time of the summer

---

74. See *Mengzi* 5A2 for a story illustrative of the evil of Shun's brother Xiang and his father, the so-called "Blind Man." See under *Important Figures* in the appendices for other people mentioned in this passage.

75. On Bi Gan, see chapter 3, note 13 in this volume.

76. Mengzi also discusses these virtues in *Mengzi* 2A6 and 4A27. For more on rén 仁, "benevolence," see *Mengzi* 1A7. For more on yì 義, "righteousness," see *Mengzi* 6A10. For more on zhì 智, "wisdom," see *Mengzi* 5A9. For more on sī 思, "reflection" or "concentration," see *Mengzi* 6A15. For all four terms, also consult the appropriate entries under *Important Terms* in the appendices. On Mengzi's general view of self-cultivation, see *Mengzi* 7A17 and 7B31.

77. *Mao* # 260.

78. No quotation such as this is found in the received text of the *Analects*.

solstice they have all ripened. Although there are some differences, these are due to the richness of the soil, and to unevenness in the rain and in human effort. Hence, in general, things of the same kind are all similar. Why would one have any doubt about this when it comes to humans alone? We and the sage are of the same kind. Hence, Longzi said, 'When one makes a shoe for a foot one has not seen, we know that one will not make a basket.' The similarity of all the shoes in the world is due to the fact that the feet of the world are the same.

"Mouths have the same preferences in flavors. The master chef Yi Ya was the first to discover that which our mouths prefer. If it were the case that the natures of mouths regarding flavors varied among people—just as dogs and horses are different species from us—then why is it that throughout the world all preferences follow Yi Ya in flavors? The fact that, when it comes to flavors, the whole world looks to Yi Ya is due to the fact that mouths throughout the world are similar.

"Ears are like this too. When it comes to sounds, the whole world looks to music master Shi Kuang. This is due to the fact that ears throughout the world are similar. Eyes are like this too. When it comes to a handsome man like Zidu, no one in the world does not appreciate his beauty. Anyone who does not appreciate the beauty of Zidu has no eyes. Hence, I say that mouths have the same preferences in flavors, ears have the same preferences in sounds, eyes have the same preferences in attractiveness. When it comes to hearts, are they alone without preferences in common?

"What is it that hearts prefer in common? I say that it is fine patterns and righteousness. The sages first discovered what our hearts prefer in common. Hence, fine patterns and righteousness delight our hearts like meat delights our mouths."

6A8 Mengzi said, "The trees of Ox Mountain were once beautiful. But because it bordered on a large state, hatchets and axes besieged it. Could it remain verdant? Due to the rest it got during the day or night, and the moisture of rain and dew, it was not that there were no sprouts or shoots growing there. But oxen and sheep then came and grazed on them. Hence, it was as if it were barren. People, seeing it barren, believed that there had never been any timber there. Could this be the nature of the mountain?!

"When we consider what is present in people, could they truly lack the hearts of benevolence and righteousness?![79] That by which they discard their good heart is simply like the hatchets and axes in relation to the trees.[80] With them besieging it day by day, can it remain beautiful? With the rest it gets during the day or night, and the restorative effects of the morning *qi*, their likes and dislikes are sometimes close to those of others. But then what they do during the day again fetters and

---

79. On "the hearts of benevolence and righteousness," see *Mengzi* 2A6 and 6A6.

80. The phrase liáng xīn 良心, "good heart," is reminiscent of the liáng zhì 良知, "best knowledge," and liáng néng 良能, "best capability," mentioned in *Mengzi* 7A15.

destroys it. If the fettering is repeated, then the evening *qi* is insufficient to preserve it. If the evening *qi* is insufficient to preserve it, then one is not far from a bird or beast. Others see that he is a bird or beast, and think that there was never any capacity there. Is this what a human truly is?!

"Hence, if it merely gets nourishment, there is nothing that will not grow. If it merely loses its nourishment, there is nothing that will not vanish. Kongzi said, 'Grasped then preserved; abandoned then lost. Its goings and comings have no fixed time. No one knows its home.'[81] Was it not the heart of which he spoke?"

6A10 Mengzi said, "Fish is something I desire; bear's paw[82] is also something I desire. If I cannot have both, I will forsake fish and select bear's paw. Life is something I desire; righteousness is also something I desire. If I cannot have both, I will forsake life and select righteousness. Life is something I desire, but there is something I desire more than life. Hence, I will not do just anything to obtain it. Death is something I hate, but there is something I hate more than death. Hence, there are calamities I do not avoid. If it were the case that someone desired nothing more than life, then what means that could obtain life would that person not use? If it were the case that someone hated nothing more than death, then what would that person not do that would avoid calamity? From this we can see that there are means of obtaining life that one will not employ. From this we can also see that there are things that would avoid calamity that one will not do. Therefore, there are things one desires more than life and there are also things one hates more than death. It is not the case that only the worthy person has this heart. All humans have it. The worthy person simply never loses it.[83]

"A basket of food and a bowl of soup—if one gets them then one will live; if one doesn't get them then one will die. But if they're given with contempt, then even a homeless person will not accept them. If they're trampled upon, then even a beggar won't take them. However, when it comes to a salary of ten thousand bushels of grain, then one doesn't notice propriety and righteousness and accepts them. What do ten thousand bushels add to me? Do I accept them for the sake of a beautiful mansion? for the obedience of a wife and concubines? to have poor acquaintances be indebted to me? In the previous case, for the sake of one's own life one did not accept what was offered. In the current case, for the sake of a beautiful mansion one does it. In the previous case, for the sake of one's own life one did not accept what was offered. In the current case, for the obedience of a wife and concubine one does it. In the previous case, for the sake of one's own life one did not

---

81. No quotation like this is found in the received text of the *Analects*.

82. A culinary delicacy.

83. Xunzi seems to challenge this conception of the role of desire in *Xunzi* chapter 22, "On Correct Naming" (in chapter 9 of this volume).

accept what was offered. In the current case, in order to have poor acquaintances be indebted to oneself one does it. Is this indeed something that one can't stop doing? This is what is called losing one's fundamental heart."[84]

6A12 Mengzi said, "Suppose someone has a ring finger that is bent and will not straighten, and it is not the case that it hurts or that it interferes with one's activities. But if there is something that can straighten it, one will not consider the road from one end of the world to the other too far, because one's finger is not as good as other people's. If one's finger is not as good as other people's, one knows to dislike it. But if one's heart is not as good as other people's, one does not know to dislike it. This is what is called not appreciating the categories of importance."

6A15 Gongduzi asked, "We are the same in being humans. Yet some become great humans and some become petty humans. Why?"

Mengzi said, "Those who follow their greater part become great humans. Those who follow their petty part become petty humans."

Gongduzi said, "We are the same in being humans. Why is it that some follow their greater part and some follow their petty part?"

Mengzi said, "It is not the office of the ears and eyes to reflect, and they are misled by things. Things interact with things and simply lead them along. But the office of the heart is to reflect. If it reflects, then it will get [Virtue]. If it does not reflect, then it will not get it.[85] This is what Heaven has given us. If one first takes one's stand on what is greater, then what is lesser will not be able to snatch it away. This is how to become a great human."

Book Seven

7A1 Mengzi said, "To fully apply one's heart is to understand one's nature.[86] If one understands one's nature, then one understands Heaven. To preserve one's mind and nourish one's nature is the means to serve Heaven. To not become conflicted over the length of one's life, and to cultivate oneself to await it, is the means to stand and await one's fate."

7A2 Mengzi said, "Everything is fate. But one only accepts one's proper fate. For this reason, someone who understands fate does not stand beneath a crumbling

---

84. "Fundamental" is literally běn 本, "root." Cf. *Mengzi* 3A5.

85. On sī 思, "reflection" or "concentration," see also *Mengzi* 6A6 above and *Important Terms* in the appendices.

86. This should be read in the light of *Mengzi* 6A6.

wall. To die through fully following the Way is one's proper fate. To die as a criminal is not one's proper fate."

7A3 Mengzi said, "'If one seeks it, one will get it; if one abandons it, one will lose it.'[87] In this case, seeking helps in getting, because the seeking is in oneself. 'There is a way to seek it, and getting it depends on fate.' In this case, seeking does not help in getting, because the seeking is external."[88]

7A4 Mengzi said, "The ten thousand things are all brought to completion by us.[89] To turn toward oneself and discover Sincerity—there is no greater delight than this. To firmly act out of sympathetic understanding[90]—there is nothing closer to benevolence than this."

7A7 Mengzi said, "A sense of shame is indeed important for people! Those who are crafty in their contrivances and schemes have no use for shame. If one is not ashamed of not being as good as others, how will one ever be as good as others?"[91]

7A15 Mengzi said, "That which people are capable of without studying is their best capability. That which they know without pondering is their best knowledge.

"Among babes in arms there is none that does not know to love its parents. When they grow older, there is none that does not know to respect its elder brother. Treating one's parents as parents[92] is benevolence. Respecting one's elders is righteousness. There is nothing else to do but extend these to the world."[93]

7A17 Mengzi said, "Do not do that which you would not do; do not desire that which you would not desire. Simply be like this."[94]

---

87. Cf. *Mengzi* 6A6.

88. The Song dynasty commentator Zhu Xi says, "'In oneself' means that benevolence, righteousness, propriety, and wisdom are all things that my nature has. . . . 'Is external' means that riches, honor, profit, and success are all external things."

89. Many other translators follow the reading of the Song dynasty commentator Zhu Xi, according to which the sentence means, "The ten thousand things are all complete within us."

90. See the *Great Learning* and the *Mean* (in chapter 11 of this volume) on "Sincerity." See *Analects* 15.24 (in chapter 1 of this volume) on "sympathetic understanding."

91. The Song dynasty commentator Zhu Xi says, "A sense of shame is the heart of disdain that we have inherently" (cf. *Mengzi* 2A6 and 6A6).

92. That is, as parents should be treated (including having the proper feelings toward them).

93. Cf. *Mengzi* 7A17 and 7B31.

94. This passage should be read in the light of *Mengzi* 7B31.

7A26 Mengzi said, "Yang Zhu favored being 'for ourselves.' If plucking out one hair from his body would have benefited the whole world, he would not do it. Mozi favored 'impartial caring.' If scraping himself bare from head to heels would benefit the whole world, he would do it. Zimo held to the middle.[95] Holding to the middle is close to it. But if one holds to the middle without discretion,[96] that is the same as holding to one extreme. What I dislike about those who hold to one extreme is that they detract from the Way. They elevate one thing and leave aside a hundred others."

7A27 Mengzi said, "Those who are starving find their food delicious; those who are parched find their drink delicious. They have no standard for food and drink because their hunger and thirst injure it. Is it only the mouth and belly that hunger and thirst injure?! Human hearts too are subject to injury. If one can prevent the injury of hunger and thirst from being an injury to one's heart, then there will be no concern about not being as good as other people."

7A35 Tao Ying asked, "When Shun was Son of Heaven, and Gao Yao was his Minister of Crime, if 'the Blind Man' had murdered someone, what would they have done?"[97]

Mengzi said, "Gao Yao would simply have arrested him!"

Tao Ying asked, "So, Shun would not have forbidden it?"

Mengzi said, "How could Shun have forbidden it? Gao Yao had a sanction for his actions."

Tao Ying asked, "So, what would Shun have done?"

Mengzi said, "Shun looked at casting aside the whole world like casting aside a worn sandal. He would have secretly carried him on his back and fled, to live in the coastland, happy to the end of his days, joyfully forgetting the world."

7A39 King Xuan of Qi wanted to shorten the period of mourning. Gongsun Chou said, "Isn't mourning for a year better than stopping completely?"

Mengzi said, "This is like if someone were twisting his elder brother's arm, and you simply said to him, 'How about doing it more gently?' Simply instruct him in filial piety and brotherly respect."

---

95. On Mozi, see *Mengzi* 3A5 and 3B9, as well as the *Mozi* (in chapter 2 of this volume). On Yang Zhu, see *Mengzi* 3B9 and "Robber Zhi" (in chapter 3 of this volume). We know nothing about Zimo beyond what this passage tells us.

96. On "discretion," see *Mengzi* 4A17 and note 52 above.

97. Tao Ying is a follower of Mengzi. On Shun, see under *Important Figures* in the appendices. On Shun's father, the "Blind Man," see *Mengzi* 5A2.

One of the imperial sons had a mother who died. His tutor asked on his behalf to let him mourn for a few months.[98] Gongsun Chou said, "How about this case?"

Mengzi said, "In this case, he desires to mourn the full period but he cannot. Even doing it one extra day would be better than stopping completely. What I had been talking about before was a case in which he did not do it, even though nothing prevented it."

7A45 Mengzi said, "Gentlemen, in relation to animals, are sparing of them, but are not benevolent toward them. In relation to the people, they are benevolent toward them, but do not treat them as kin. They treat their kin as kin, and then are benevolent toward the people. They are benevolent toward the people, and then are sparing of animals."[99]

7B3 Mengzi said, "It would be better to not have the *History* than to completely believe it. I accept only two or three passages in the 'Completion of the War' chapter. A benevolent person has no enemies in the world. When the one who was supremely benevolent [King Wu] attacked the one who was supremely unbenevolent [Tyrant Zhou], how could the blood have flowed till it floated the grain-pounding sticks?"[100]

7B5 Mengzi said, "A carpenter or a wheelwright can give another his compass or T-square, but he cannot make another skillful."

7B11 Mengzi said, "If one is fond of making a name for oneself, one may be able to relinquish a state that can field a thousand chariots. But if one is just not that kind of person, relinquishing a basket of rice or a bowl of soup would show in one's face."

7B16 Mengzi said, "Benevolence is being a human. To bring them into harmony and put it into words is the Way."[101]

7B24 Mengzi said, "The mouth in relation to flavors, the eyes in relation to sights, the ears in relation to tones, the nose in relation to odors, the four limbs in relation to comfort—these are matters of human nature, but they are mandated.[102]

---

98. Chinese commentators explain that the son's mother was a secondary wife of the king, and the king's primary wife opposed letting him mourn for the full three-year period. On the three-year mourning period, see *Analects* 17.21 (in chapter 1 of this volume).

99. Cf. *Mengzi* 1A7 and 3A5.

100. See Legge, *The Shoo King*, 315. For King Wu and Tyrant Zhou, see *Important Figures* in the appendices.

101. Alternative translation: "To bring them into harmony is called the Way."

102. That is, they are mandated (or required) by Heaven.

A gentleman does not refer to them as 'human nature.' Benevolence in relation to father and son, righteousness in relation to ruler and minister, propriety in relation to guest and host, wisdom in relation to value, the sage in relation to the Way of Heaven—these are mandated, but they involve human nature. A gentleman does not refer to them as 'mandated.'"

7B31 Mengzi said, "People all have things that they will not bear. To extend this reaction to that which they will bear is benevolence. People all have things that they will not do. To extend this reaction to that which they will do is righteousness. If people can fill out the heart that does not desire to harm others, their benevolence will be inexhaustible. If people can fill out the heart that will not trespass, their righteousness will be inexhaustible. If people can fill out the core reaction[103] of not accepting being addressed disrespectfully, there will be nowhere they go where they do not do what is righteous. If a scholar may not speak and speaks, this is flattering by speaking. If one should speak but does not speak, this is flattering by not speaking. These are both in the category of trespassing."

7B37 Wan Zhang asked, "When in the state of Chen, Kongzi said, 'Perhaps I should return home. The scholars of my school are wild and hasty, advancing and grasping, but do not forget their early behavior.'[104] When in Chen, why did Kongzi think of the wild scholars of his home state of Lu?"

Mengzi said, "Kongzi said, 'If I do not get to associate with those who attain the Way, then must it not be those who are wild or squeamish? Those who are wild advance and grasp. Those who are squeamish have some things that they will not do.'[105] Did Kongzi not want those who attained the Way?! He could not be sure of getting them. Hence, he thought of the next best."

Wan Zhang said, "I venture to ask what one must be like, such that one can be called 'wild.'"

Mengzi said, "Those like Qin Zhang, Zengxi, and Mu Pi are the ones Kongzi called 'wild.'"[106]

Wan Zhang said, "Why did he call them 'wild'?"

Mengzi said, "Their resolutions were grand. They said, 'The ancients! The ancients!' But if one calmly examines their conduct, it does not match their

---

103. Compare *Mengzi* 4A27 on the notion of a "core" reaction.

104. Compare *Analects* 5.22 (in chapter 1 of this volume).

105. Compare *Analects* 13.21 (in chapter 1 of this volume).

106. Unfortunately, we know almost nothing about these three individuals. However, there is an interesting and revealing anecdote involving Zengxi in *Analects* 11.26 (in chapter 1 of this volume).

resolutions and words. If he also failed to get those who are wild, he desired to get to associate with those who disdain to do what is not pure. These are the squeamish. They are the next best.

"Kongzi said, 'The only ones who pass by my door without entering my home whom I do not regret getting as associates are the village worthies. The village worthies are the thieves of virtue.'"[107]

Wan Zhang said, "What must one be like, such that one can be called a 'village worthy'?"

Mengzi said, "The village worthies are those who say,

> Why are [the resolutions of the wild scholars] so grand? Their words take no notice of their actions, and their actions take no notice of their words. Then they say, 'The ancients! The ancients!' And why are the actions [of the squeamish] so solitary and aloof? Born in this era, we should be for this era. To be good is enough.

Eunuch-like, pandering to their eras—these are the village worthies."

Wan Zhang said, "If the whole village declares them worthy people, there is nowhere they will go where they will not be worthy people. Why did Kongzi regard them as thieves of virtue?"

Mengzi said, "If you try to condemn them, there is nothing you can point to; if you try to censure them, there is nothing to censure. They are in agreement with the current customs; they are in harmony with the sordid era in which they live. That in which they dwell seems to be loyalty and trustworthiness; that which they do seems to be blameless and pure. The multitude delight in them; they regard themselves as right. But you cannot enter into the Way of Yao and Shun with them. Hence, Kongzi said they are 'thieves of virtue.'

"Kongzi said, 'I hate that which seems but is not. I hate weeds out of fear that they will be confused with seedlings.[108] I hate cleverness out of fear that it will be confused with righteousness. I hate glibness out of fear that it will be confused with trustworthiness. I hate the tunes of the state of Zheng out of fear that they will be confused with genuine music. I hate purple out of fear that it will be confused with vermilion.[109] I hate the village worthies, out of fear that they will be confused with those who have Virtue.'

"The gentleman simply returns to the standard. If the standard is correct, then the multitudinous people will be inspired. When the people are inspired, then there will be no evil or wickedness."

---

107. Cf. *Analects* 17.13 (in chapter 1 of this volume).

108. Note that "seedlings" is also used in *Mengzi* 2A2 as a metaphor for one's incipient, natural virtues. Compare also the use of "sprouts" in *Mengzi* 2A6.

109. Cf. *Analects* 15.11 and 17.18 (in chapter 1 of this volume).

SELECTIVE BIBLIOGRAPHY

Translations

Lau, D. C., trans. *Mencius*. New York: Penguin Books, 1970. (This is still an excellent complete English translation, and includes several helpful appendices. Lau also published a revised, two-volume translation with the accompanying Chinese text: *Mencius,* 2 vols. [Hong Kong: Chinese University Press, 1984].)

Legge, James, trans. *The Works of Mencius*. Reprint, New York: Dover Books, 1970. (This is a reprint of Legge's revised 1895 translation, which includes the Chinese text and extensive notes. It is still one of the best, although Legge's English is sometimes dated.)

Van Norden, Bryan W., trans. *Mengzi: With Selections from Traditional Commentaries*. Indianapolis: Hackett Publishing Company, 2008. (This is a complete translation with an interlineal commentary that frequently quotes the orthodox commentary of Zhu Xi. For those who do not like the interlineal commentary format, there is also a version of this translation available with the commentary included as endnotes: *The Essential Mengzi: Selected Passages with Traditional Commentary* [Indianapolis: Hackett Publishing Company, 2009].)

Secondary Works

Chan, Alan K. L., ed. *Mencius: Contexts and Interpretations*. Honolulu: University of Hawaii Press, 2002. (Good anthology of secondary essays.)

Graham, Angus C. "The Background of the Mencian Theory of Human Nature." In *Studies in Chinese Philosophy and Philosophical Literature*, 7–66. Albany, NY: State University of New York Press, 1990. (Originally published in 1967. This is an excellent overview of the context for Mengzi's use of xìng 性, "nature.")

Ihara, Craig. "David Wong on Emotions in Mencius." *Philosophy East & West* 41, no. 1 (1991): 45–54. (A critique of Wong, "Is There a Distinction?," listed below.)

Ivanhoe, Philip J. *Ethics in the Confucian Tradition: The Thought of Mencius and Wang Yangming*. Second edition. Indianapolis: Hackett, 2002. (A good examination of Mengzi and how he differs from one of his Neo-Confucian interpreters.)

Lau, D. C. "On Mencius' Use of the Method of Analogy in Argument." Appendix 5 of Lau, *Mencius* (listed above under *Translations*). (On *Mengzi* 6A1 ff.)

Liu, Xiusheng, and Philip J. Ivanhoe, eds. *Essays on the Moral Philosophy of Mengzi*. Indianapolis: Hackett Publishing Company, 2002.

Nivison, David S. *The Ways of Confucianism*. Chicago, IL: Open Court Press, 1996. (Essays on a variety of passages and topics relating to Mengzi. The essay "Motivation and Moral Action in Mencius" has been especially influential.)

Shun, Kwong-loi. *Mencius and Early Chinese Thought.* Stanford, CA: Stanford University Press, 1997. (Excellent discussion of many passages and problems in the *Mengzi.*)

Van Norden, Bryan W. "Mengzi on Courage." In *The Philosophy of Religion,* edited by Peter A. French, Theodore E. Uehling, and Howard K. Wettstein, 237–56. Midwest Studies in Philosophy, vol 21. Notre Dame, IN: University of Notre Dame Press, 1997. (On the virtue of courage in the *Mengzi,* particularly as dealt with in passage 2A2.)

———. *Virtue Ethics and Consequentialism in Early Chinese Philosophy.* New York: Cambridge University Press, 2007. (Discussion of Kongzi and Mengzi as virtue ethicians and Mozi as a consequentialist.)

Wong, David. "Is There a Distinction between Reason and Emotion in Mencius?" *Philosophy East & West* 41, no. 1 (1991): 31–44. (Discusses some of the issues raised by *Mengzi* 1A7. See also Ihara, "David Wong on Emotions," listed above.)

Yearley, Lee H. *Mencius and Aquinas: Theories of Virtue and Conceptions of Courage.* Albany, NY: State University of New York Press, 1990. (A comparative study with many insights into Mengzi's conception of the virtues.)

CHAPTER FIVE

THE SCHOOL OF NAMES

Introduction

In the late fourth century BCE, Chinese philosophy underwent a "language crisis" in which thinkers called into question the adequacy of language to consistently describe the world and guide behavior. In this chapter, we offer three selections that illustrate this trend in Chinese thought. The thinkers whose work is translated in this chapter were later grouped together under the label "The School of Names" (Míngjiā 名家); however, they were not a part of an organized movement, like the earlier Confucians and Mohists were. One of the leading figures in this crisis was Huì Shī 惠施 (or Master Hui, Huìzǐ 惠子, late fourth century BCE). He defended a series of paradoxes, which are our first selection below.[1] None of Huizi's arguments for these paradoxes survive. However, the first two seem to present paradoxes of space, arguing that (1) there must be a largest "thing" and a smallest "thing," and (2) all spatial lengths can be divided into dimensionless points (which would imply that the identification of spatial boundaries between things is arbitrary). The rest of the theses (3–9) seem to depend upon the fact that whether or not a claim is "acceptable" (kě 可) depends upon the perspective from which it is evaluated. Consider the seventh paradox: "I left for Yue today but arrived yesterday." If I left for the state of Yue on Monday and arrived on Tuesday, I might truthfully say on Monday "I left for Yue today" but truthfully say on Wednesday "I arrived yesterday." The first nine theses thus undermine the objectivity of both qualitative and spatial distinctions between things, while the final paradox draws an ethical conclusion: (10) because distinctions between things are merely conventional, we ought to love everyone equally. Thus, in Huizi's thought we find argumentation used to establish conclusions that are contrary to common sense but have ethical implications. (This is

---

1. Hui Shi's theses are preserved in *Zhuangzi* chapter 33, "The World" (not in this volume). For more about Hui Shi (Huizi), see also Zhuangzi's dialogues with and comments about Huizi in *Zhuangzi* chapters 1, 2, 5, 17, 18, and 24 (in chapter 8 of this volume).

reminiscent of much of Western philosophy, from the ancient Greek Plato up through Derek Parfit among recent English-speaking philosophers.)

Our second selection, "On the White Horse," by Gōngsūn Lóngzǐ 公孫龍子 (fl. 300 BCE), gives us a sense of what kind of arguments may have spurred the language crisis. "On the White Horse" is a debate over whether it could be true that "a white horse is not a horse" (or "white horses are not horses"). Here is a hint to one possible interpretation. The expression "X is not Y" (like the Chinese X 非 Y) is ambiguous. It could mean "X is not a member of the group Y" or it could mean that "X is not identical with Y."[2] The Objector in the dialogue interprets "a white horse is not a horse" as meaning that "things that are horses and are white are not horses" (which is false), but the Advocate in the dialogue interprets "a white horse is not a horse" as meaning that "things that are white and horses are not identical with things that are simply horses" (which is true).[3] "On the White Horse" may be a simple sophistry, but if it is making a serious philosophical point, perhaps it is similar to Huizi's paradoxes: to illustrate that the "acceptability" of language depends upon one's (arbitrarily adopted) perspective.

Our third selection in this chapter is another dialogue attributed to Gongsun Longzi, "On Referring to Things." One of the leading Western experts on the "School of Names," Angus C. Graham, remarked that "of all Chinese philosophical writings it is perhaps the one which most fascinates readers with the taste for solving difficult riddles, but no two commentators have ever agreed in interpreting it."[4] Graham produced several radically different translations of the text himself.[5] According to the

---

2. Contrast the uses of "is not" in "Batman is not a bat" and "Batman is not Clark Kent." We see both uses in the dialogue between Zhuangzi and Huizi at the bridge over the Hao River (*Zhuangzi* chapter 17, in chapter 8 of this volume), where we find both "You are not a fish" and "You are not me."

3. The two speakers in the dialogue are not named. Here they are labeled "Advocate," who defends the thesis that a white horse is not a horse, and "Objector," who argues against this thesis. The section headings ("A," "B," etc.) are also not in the original.

4. Angus C. Graham, *Later Mohist Logic, Ethics, and Science* (London: School of Oriental and African Studies, 1978), 457.

5. See Graham, *Later Mohist Logic*, 464–67; Graham, "Three Studies of Kung-sun Lung," in Graham, *Studies in Chinese Philosophy and Philosophical Literature*, edited by Angus C. Graham, (Singapore: Institute for East Asian Philosophies, 1986; Albany, NY: State University of New York Press, 1990), 213–15; Graham, *Disputers of the Tao* (La Salle, IL: Open Court, 1989), 92–94. Graham's interpretations differ from the one presented in this chapter in that Graham takes one of the key issues in the work to be the paradox of how to refer to "the world" (tiānxià 天下): "Since one uses names to point out things from each other, how can 'world' function as a name? . . . The name 'world' does not point anything out, yet no thing is not what it points out" (Graham, *Disputers,* 92). Graham's alternative interpretation is quite plausible.

translation offered below, "On Referring to Things" is about a paradox of reference. Clearly, one of the distinctive features of language is that words refer to things. (For example, "Diego" is a name I use to refer to my French Bulldog.) Anything in the world can be referred to. Indeed, we might be tempted to define "thing" (wù 物) as what we can use a "name" (or "word" míng 名) to "refer" to (zhǐ 指, literally "to point at"). Now, "reference" itself is not an additional "thing" in the world, so it seems that we cannot refer to reference. However, if we cannot refer to reference, how can we explain what reference is, or fix reference definitively?

Taken together, the theses of Huizi and the two brief works by Gongsun Longzi undermine our confidence in language. Meaningful language requires reference, but reference depends upon establishing an arbitrary perspective from which to refer. These paradoxes might seem quaint, but some of the greatest Western philosophers of the twentieth century wrestled with similar issues, and were forced into similar paradoxes, including Ludwig Wittgenstein, who distinguished between what can "be said" in language and what can only "be shown," arguing that "what expresses *itself* in language, *we* cannot express by means of language," and W. V. O. Quine, who concluded that reference is always "indeterminate," because there is no way to specify what we are referring to that does not already assume a background system of reference.[6] In ancient China, in response to the "language crisis," the later Mohists and the Confucian Xunzi tried to use careful reasoning to protect language from what they saw as the sophistries of thinkers like Gongsun Longzi.[7] On the other hand, "Daoist" texts often embrace paradox and evince much less confidence in the power of rational argumentation than Huizi apparently did. Thus, the *Daodejing* opens with a line that might be translated as "Ways can be put into words, but they are not constant Ways. / Names can be named, but they are not constant names."[8] And Zhuangzi exclaims, "Saying is not just blowing. Saying says something. But if what it says is not fixed, then does it really say anything? Or does it say nothing?"[9]

---

6. See Ludwig Wittgenstein, *Tractatus Logico-Philosophicus,* translated by D. F. Pears and B. F. McGuinness (New York: Routledge, 1975), 4.121 (emphasis in original), and W. V. O. Quine, "Ontological Relativity," *The Journal of Philosophy* 65, no. 7 (4 April 1968): 185–212.

7. *Xunzi* chapter 22, "On Correct Naming" (in chapter 9 of this volume) is in part a reaction to the language crisis.

8. *Daodejing* chapter 1 (for a slightly different translation, see chapter 6 of this volume).

9. *Zhuangzi* chapter 2 (in chapter 8 of this volume). Zhuangzi also debated Huizi on several occasions (see *Zhuangzi* chapters 1, 5, 17, and 18 [in chapter 8 of this volume]), and refers to Gongsun Longzi (see *Zhuangzi* chapter 2 [also in chapter 8 of this volume]).

1. Hui Shi (Huizi), Theses

1. There is nothing outside what is supremely large. Call it the "great one." There is nothing inside what is supremely small. Call it the "small one."

2. That which has no thickness cannot be accumulated, yet it can be a thousand leagues large.

3. Heaven and Earth are equally low. Mountains and marshes are on the same level.

4. At the moment that the Sun is at its highest, it is setting. At the moment that something is born, it is dying.

5. When things that are very similar are differentiated from things that are less similar, this is called "small comparison." When the myriad things are all similar and are all different, this is called "great comparison."

6. The South is inexhaustible yet exhaustible.

7. I left for Yue today but arrived yesterday.

8. Linked rings can be separated.

9. I know the center of the world: it is north of Yan and south of Yue.[10]

10. Indiscriminately care for the myriad things. Heaven and Earth are one whole.

2. Gongsun Longzi, "On the White Horse"

A

Can it be that a white horse is not a horse?[11]
Advocate: It can.

Objector: How?

---

10. Yan was a state in the far north, while Yue was a state in the far south.

11. An alternative possible translation, here and below, is "white horses are not horses." In addition, it is possible that the issue is not whether the statement "a white horse is not a horse" is *always* true, but whether it is *possible* for it to be true.

Advocate: "Horse" is that by means of which one names the shape. "White" is that by means of which one names the color. What names the color is not what names the shape. Hence, I say that a white horse is not a horse.

B

Objector: If there are white horses, one cannot say that there are no horses. If one cannot say that there are no horses, doesn't that mean that there are horses? For there to be white horses is for there to be horses. How could it be that the white ones are not horses?

Advocate: If one wants a horse, that extends to a yellow or black horse. But if one wants a white horse, that does not extend to a yellow or black horse. Suppose that a white horse were a horse. Then what one wants [in the two cases] would be the same. If what one wants were the same, then a white [horse] would not differ from a horse. If what one wants does not differ, then how is it that a yellow or black horse is sometimes acceptable and sometimes unacceptable? It is clear that acceptable and unacceptable are mutually contrary. Hence, yellow and black horses are the same [in that, if there are yellow or black horses], one can respond that there are horses, but one cannot respond that there are white horses. Thus, it is evident that a white horse is not a horse.

C

Objector: You think that horses that are colored are not horses. In the world, it is not the case that there are horses with no color. Can it be that there are no horses in the world?

Advocate: Horses certainly have color. Hence, there are white horses. If it were the case that horses had no color, there would simply be horses, and then how could one select a white horse?[12] A white horse is a horse and white. A horse and a white horse [are different]. Hence, I say that a white horse is not a horse.

D

Objector: "Horse" not yet combined with "white" is horse. "White" not yet combined with "horse" is white. If one combines "horse" and "white," one uses the

---

12. Following this sentence in the original Chinese, there is a sentence that reads, "Hence, white is not horse." This does not seem to make any sense in context, so it has been omitted.

compound phrase "white horse." This is to take what is not combined and combine them as a phrase.[13] Hence, I say that it cannot be that a white horse is not a horse.[14]

Advocate: You think that there being white horses is there being horses. Is it acceptable to say that there being white horses is there being yellow horses?

Objector: It is not acceptable.

Advocate: If you think that there being horses is different from there being yellow horses, this is for yellow horses to be different from horses. If you differentiate yellow horses from horses, this is to think that yellow horses are not horses. To think that yellow horses are not horses, yet to think that white horses are horses—this is to turn things upside down and inside out![15] This is the most incoherent doctrine and confused discourse in the world!

E

Objector: If there are white horses, one cannot say that there are no horses, because of what is called "the separability of white."[16] Only according to those people who do not separate can having a white horse not be said to be having a horse.[17] Hence, the reason we think there are horses is only that we think that "horse" is "there are horses." It is not that we think "there are white horses" is "there are horses." Hence,

---

13. This sentence is a *defense* of saying that "a white horse is a horse." (See the next note for an interpretation.) However, following this sentence in the original Chinese, there is a sentence that reads, "That is not acceptable." This does not seem to make any sense in context, so that sentence has been omitted. However, many translators retain that sentence, which would mean that the sentence immediately prior to this note is an *objection* to saying that "a white horse is not a horse."

14. The argument may be that, since "horse" refers to horse when it is used as a simple expression, it must continue to refer to horse when it becomes part of a compound expression. Since we can obviously say that "a horse is a horse," we can also say that "a white horse is a horse."

15. Literally, "this is for flying things to enter the water, and for the inner and outer coffins to be in different places!"

16. "Separability" seems to have been a technical term in ancient Chinese philosophy of language. It apparently referred to the possibility of discussing separately two terms that were used in a compound expression. For example, one Chinese commentator observes that "There must be a shape corresponding to a name, and the best way to examine the shape is to distinguish the colour from it." (Translation from Graham, *Later Mohist Logic*, 175.)

17. Translation of this line follows the *Dao zang* version of the text.

because of the reason that there are horses, one cannot say that a [white] horse [is not] a horse.

Advocate: "White" does not fix that which is white. It ignores that. The expression "white horse" fixes that which is white. That which fixes what is white is not white. "Horse" is indifferent to color. Hence, [if you were only looking for a horse,] a yellow or black horse would each be appropriate. "White horse" does select for color. So [if you were looking for a white horse,] a yellow or black horse would be rejected on account of its color. Hence, only a white horse alone would be appropriate. That which does not reject is not what does reject. Hence, I say that a white horse is not a horse.

3. Gongsun Longzi, "On Referring to Things"

1. No thing is not a referent, but reference is not a referent.

2. In the world, without reference, no thing could be called a "thing." Nothing in the world is reference, so how can a thing be called a "referent"?

3. Reference is not what exists in the world. Things are what exists in the world. It is not acceptable to regard what exists in the world as what does not exist in the world.

4. In the world, there is no reference, and things cannot be called "reference." What cannot be called "reference" is not reference. As for what reference is not: no thing is ever reference.

5. That, in the world, there is no reference and things cannot be called "reference," is because it is not the case that there exists something that is not a referent. Since it is not the case that there exists something that is not a referent, no thing is ever not a referent. No thing is ever not a referent, yet reference is not a referent.

6. That reference does not exist in the world is generated by each thing's having a name without [itself] engaging in reference. To call "reference" what does not engage in reference is to combine what does not engage in reference [with what does]. To treat what does engage in reference as what does not engage in reference is unacceptable.

7. Moreover, reference is that in the world that combines. It is because reference does not exist in the world that no things can be said to not be a referent. Because they cannot be said to not be a referent, it is not the case that there exists something that is not a referent. Because it is not the case that

there exists something that is not a referent, no thing is ever not a referent. Yet reference is not not reference either. Reference and things [together] are not reference [either].

8. If in the world there existed no things that are referents, who precisely could say, "it is not a referent"? If no things existed in the world, who precisely could say, "it refers"? If in the world there were reference but no things referred to, who precisely could say, "it is not a referent" and who precisely could say, "there are no things that are not referents"?

9. Moreover, reference intrinsically does not refer to itself. So how is it that we must wait upon things and only then with them engage in reference?

SELECTIVE BIBLIOGRAPHY

Translations

Johnson, Ian, and Wang Ping, trans. *The Mingjia and Related Texts*. Hong Kong: Chinese University of Hong Kong Press, 2020. (Collection of translated texts with the original Chinese.)

Secondary Works

Fung, Yiu-ming, ed. *Dao Companion to Chinese Philosophy of Logic*. New York: Springer, 2020. (Anthology of secondary essays on issues related to ancient Chinese philosophy of language.)

Graham, Angus C. *Disputers of the Tao*. Chicago: Open Court Press, 1989. (Excellent non-technical discussion of Huizi, Gongsun Longzi, and their general intellectual context on pp. 75–95. However, note that Graham radically rearranges the received text of "On the White Horse," whereas the translation above follows the received text as closely as possible.)

————. *Studies in Chinese Philosophy and Philosophical Literature*. Singapore: Institute for East Asian Philosophies, 1986; reprint, Albany, NY: State University of New York Press, 1990. (Includes three important technical articles on the writings attributed to Gongsun Longzi, including "On the White Horse.")

Harbsmeier, Christoph. *Language and Logic*. Volume 7, part I of *Science and Civilisation in China*, edited by Joseph Needham. New York: Cambridge University Press, 1998. (A magisterial overview.)

Suter, Rafael, Lisa Indraccolo, and Wolfgang Behr, eds. *The "Gongsun Longzi" and Other Neglected Texts: Aligning Philosophical and Philological Perspectives*. De Gruyter, 2020. (Anthology of secondary essays, focusing on the works attributed to Gongsun Longzi.)

Van Norden, Bryan W. "Language and Paradox in the 'School of Names.'" Chapter 7 of *Introduction to Classical Chinese Philosophy*. Indianapolis: Hackett Publishing, 2011. (Nontechnical introduction to the issues and explanations of some of the paradoxes.)

CHAPTER SIX

LAOZI

Daodejing

Introduction

Traditionally, Lǎozǐ 老子 is said to have been an older contemporary of Kongzi (Confucius), and the author of the *Laozi* or *Dàodéjīng* 道德經. But most contemporary scholars regard Laozi (literally "Old Master") as a mythical character and the *Laozi* as a composite work. The present version of the text consists of short passages, from a variety of sources, over half of which are rhymed. These were collected together into a single volume of eighty-one chapters, which were then divided into two books. Book I consists of chapters 1 through 37, the Dào 道, "Way," half of the text; Book II consists of chapters 38 through 81, the Dé 德, "Virtue," half. On the basis of this organization, this version of the text came to be known as the *Daodejing*, which means simply "The Classic of *Dao* and *De*." This division in no way reflects the contents of the chapters themselves, except that the first chapter begins with the word *Dao* and the thirty-eighth chapter begins by describing the highest *De*. The text may have reached its present form some time during the third or perhaps second century BCE. Another version of the text, named after its place of discovery, Mǎwángduī 馬王堆, is similar in content and firmly dated to the middle of the second century BCE. But in the *Mawangdui* version, the order of the books is reversed, giving us the *Dedaojing*.

Though it was probably cobbled together from different sources, the *Laozi* may well have been assembled during a relatively short period of time and perhaps even by a single editor. When it was put together, China was near the end of a prolonged era of fierce interstate rivalry known as the Warring States Period (see *Important Periods* in the appendices). The text can be understood, at least in part, as a reaction to this troubled age. In it we hear the lament of a time tired of war and chaos, one yearning for a bygone age of innocence, security, and peace. The text denounces wars of expansion and government corruption, tracing both complaints to the unbounded greed and ambition of those in power. These ideas are connected to the view that excessive desire is bad per se and to the related belief that our "real" or "natural" desires are actually quite modest and limited. The text claims that it is unnatural to have excessive desires and that having them will not only not lead to a satisfying life but will lead, paradoxically, to destitution, want, alienation, and self-destruction.

The *Laozi* appeals to an earlier golden age in human history, before people made sharp distinctions among things. This was a time when values and qualities were not clearly distinguished, when things simply were as they were and people acted out of pre-reflective spontaneity. Chapter 38 describes the history of the decline of the Way from an earlier golden age to its present debased state. The *Dao* declined as civilization and human self-consciousness arose. The *Laozi* urges us to return to the earlier, natural state when the Way was fully realized in the world. We are to "untangle," "blunt," and "round off" the sharp corners of our present life and let our "wheels move only along old [and presumably more comfortable] ruts."

According to the *Laozi*, the *Dao* is the source, sustenance, and ideal state of all things in the world. It is "hidden" and it contains within it the patterns of all that we see, but it is not ontologically transcendent. In the apt metaphor of the text, it is the "root" of all things. The *Dao* is zìrán 自然, "so of itself" or "spontaneous," and its unencumbered activity brings about various natural states of affairs through wúwéi 無為, "nonaction" (see *Important Terms* in the appendices). Human beings have a place in the *Dao* but are not particularly exalted. They are simply things among things (a view well-represented by the marvelous landscape paintings inspired by Daoism). Because of their unbridled desires and their unique capacity to think, act intentionally, and alter their nature—thus acting contrary to *wuwei* and bringing about states that are not *ziran*—humans tend to forsake their proper place and upset the natural harmony of the Way. The *Laozi* seeks to undo the consequences of such misguided human views and practices and lead us to "return" to the earlier ideal. The text is more a form of philosophical therapy than the presentation of a theory. We are to be challenged by its paradoxes and moved by its images and poetic cadence more than by any arguments it presents.

Book One

Chapter One

A Way that can be followed is not a constant Way.[1]
A name that can be named is not a constant name.
Nameless, it is the beginning of Heaven and earth;[2]
Named, it is the mother of the myriad creatures.
And so,
> Always eliminate desires in order to observe its mysteries;
> Always have desires in order to observe its manifestations.
These two come forth in unity but diverge in name.
Their unity is known as an enigma.[3]
Within this enigma is yet a deeper enigma.
The gate of all mysteries!

Chapter Two

Everyone in the world knows that when the beautiful strives to be beautiful, it is repulsive.
Everyone knows that when the good strives to be good, it is no good.[4]
And so,
> To have and to lack generate each other.[5]
> Difficult and easy give form to each other.

---

1. Unlike the case of the following line, which has a similar basic structure, there is no way to reproduce in English the alternating nominal and verbal uses of the word dào 道, "Way." More literally, the first line reads, dào 道 [a] "Way," "path," or "teaching," kě dào 可道, [which] "can be talked about" or "followed," fēi cháng dào 非常道, "is not a constant Way." Cf. the grammar and sense of the poem "The Thorny Bush Upon the Wall" in the *Odes* (*Mao # 46*) (see *Important Texts* in the appendices). Compare the second sentence of section seven and the last line of section twenty of *Nature Comes from the Mandate* (in chapter 12 of this volume). For other passages that discuss the Way and names, see chapters 32, 34.

2. On the idea of being "nameless," see chapters 32, 37, and 41.

3. Cf. the reference to xuán tóng 玄同, "Enigmatic Unity," in chapter 56.

4. The point is the common theme that self-conscious effort to be excellent in any way fatally undermines itself. Cf. for example, chapters 38, 81.

5. Cf. chapter 40.

Long and short offset each other.

High and low incline into each other.

Note and rhythm harmonize with each other.

Before and after follow each other.

This is why sages abide in the business of nonaction,[6] and practice the teaching that is without words.[7]

They work with the myriad creatures and turn none away.[8]

They produce without possessing.[9]

They act with no expectation of reward.[10]

When their work is done, they do not linger.[11]

And, by not lingering, merit never deserts them.

Chapter Three

Not paying honor to the worthy leads the people to avoid contention.

Not showing reverence for precious goods[12] leads them to not steal.

Not making a display of what is desirable leads their hearts away from chaos.[13]

This is why sages bring things to order by opening people's hearts[14] and filling their bellies.

They weaken the people's commitments and strengthen their bones;

They make sure that the people are without "knowledge,"[15] or desires;

And that those with knowledge do not dare to act.

Sages enact nonaction and everything becomes well ordered.

---

6. For wúwéi 無為, "nonaction," see *Important Terms* in the appendices. A study of this idea, which explores the notion across different schools of early Chinese philosophy, is Edward G. Slingerland's *Effortless Action: Wuwei as Conceptual Metaphor and Spiritual Ideal in Early China* (New York: Oxford University Press, 2003).

7. Cf. a similar line in chapter 43.

8. Cf. chapter 34.

9. This line also occurs in chapters 10 and 51.

10. This line also appears in chapters 10, 51, and 77.

11. Recognizing that the credit for their success lies with the Way and not with themselves is a characteristic attitude of Daoist sages. For similar ideas, see chapters 9, 17, 34, and 77. This and the previous line occur together in chapter 77.

12. For other passages discussing "precious goods," see chapters 12 and 64.

13. Cf. *Analects* 12.18 (in chapter 1 of this volume).

14. See xīn 心, "heart," under *Important Terms* in the appendices.

15. "Knowledge" here is zhì 知 (meaning 智, "wisdom"). See this under *Important Terms* in the appendices.

Chapter Four

The Way is like an empty vessel;
No use could ever fill it up.
Vast and deep!
It seems to be the ancestor of the myriad creatures.
It blunts their sharpness;[16]
Untangles their tangles;
Softens their glare;
Merges with their dust.
Deep and clear!
It seems to be there.
I do not know whose child it is;
It is the image of what was before the Lord himself![17]

Chapter Five

Heaven and earth are not benevolent;
They treat the myriad creatures as straw dogs.[18]
Sages are not benevolent;
They treat the people as straw dogs.
Is not the space between Heaven and earth like a bellows?
Empty yet inexhaustible!
Work it and more will come forth.
An excess of speech will lead to exhaustion,[19]
It is better to hold on to the mean.

Chapter Six

The spirit of the valley never dies;
She is called the "Enigmatic Female."

---

16. This line and the next three, preceded by two lines from chapter 52, appear in chapter 56.

17. This is the only occurrence in the text of the character dì 帝, "Lord," a name for the high god or supreme ancestral spirit of ancient China. For other passages concerning xiàng 象, "image," see chapters 14, 21, 35, and 41.

18. "Straw dogs" were used as ceremonial offerings. Before and during the ceremony, they were protected and cherished, but as soon as the ceremony ended, they were discarded and defiled. Others interpret the characters in this expression as "straw and dogs." The point is the same.

19. Cf. the opening lines of chapter 23.

The portal of the Enigmatic Female
Is called the root of Heaven and earth.
An unbroken, gossamer thread;
It seems to be there.
But use will not unsettle it.

Chapter Seven

Heaven is long-lasting;
Earth endures.
Heaven is able to be long-lasting and earth is able to endure, because they do not
    live for themselves.
And so, they are able to be long-lasting and to endure.
This is why sages put themselves last and yet come first;
Treat themselves as unimportant and yet are preserved.
Is it not because they have no thought of themselves, that they are able to perfect
    themselves?

Chapter Eight

The highest good is like water.
Water is good at benefiting the myriad creatures, while not contending with
    them.
It resides in the places that people find repellent, and so comes close to the
    Way.
In a residence, the good lies in location.
In hearts, the good lies in depth.
In interactions with others, the good lies in benevolence.
In words, the good lies in trustworthiness.
In government, the good lies in orderliness.
In carrying out one's business, the good lies in ability.
In actions, the good lies in timeliness.
Only by avoiding contention can one avoid blame.

Chapter Nine

To hold the vessel upright in order to fill it[20] is not as good as to stop in time.
If you make your blade too keen, it will not hold its edge.
When gold and jade fill the hall, none can hold on to them.

---

20. The reference is to a "tilting vessel" that would fall over and pour out its contents if filled to the top.

To be haughty when wealth and honor come your way is to bring disaster upon
 yourself.
To withdraw when the work is done is the Way of Heaven.[21]

Chapter Ten

Embracing your soul and holding on to the One, can you keep them from departing?[22]
Concentrating your *qi*, "vital energies,"[23] and attaining the utmost suppleness, can
 you be a child?
Cleaning and purifying your enigmatic mirror, can you erase every flaw?
Caring for the people and ordering the state, can you eliminate all knowledge?
When the portal of Heaven opens and closes, can you play the part of the feminine?
Comprehending all within the four directions, can you reside in nonaction?
To produce them!
To nurture them!
To produce without possessing;[24]
To act with no expectation of reward;[25]
To lead without lording over;
Such is Enigmatic Virtue![26]

Chapter Eleven

Thirty spokes are joined in the hub of a wheel.
But only by relying on what is not there[27] do we have the use of the carriage.
By adding and removing clay we form a vessel.
But only by relying on what is not there do we have use of the vessel.
By carving out doors and windows we make a room.
But only by relying on what is not there do we have use of the room.
And so,
> What is there is the basis for profit;
> What is not there is the basis for use.

---

21. For similar lines, see chapters 2, 17, 34, and 77.

22. For other examples of "the One," see chapters 22, 39, and 42.

23. See qì 氣 under *Important Terms* in the appendices.

24. This line also appears in chapters 2 and 51.

25. This line also appears in chapters 2, 51, and 77.

26. Chapter 51 concludes with the same four lines. For another passage concerning xuándé 玄德, "Enigmatic
Virtue," see chapter 65.

27. Literally, only by relying on "nothing" (i.e., the empty space of the hub) can the wheel turn and the
carriage roll.

Chapter Twelve

The five colors blind our eyes.[28]
The five notes deafen our ears.
The five flavors deaden our palates.
The chase and the hunt madden our hearts.
Precious goods impede our activities.
This is why sages are for the belly and not for the eye;
And so, they cast off the one and take up the other.[29]

Chapter Thirteen

Be apprehensive about favor or disgrace.
Revere calamity as you revere your own body.
What does it mean to be apprehensive about favor and disgrace?
To receive favor is to be in the position of a subordinate.
When you get it be apprehensive;
When you lose it be apprehensive.
This is what it means to be apprehensive about favor and disgrace.
What does it mean to revere calamity as you revere your own body?
I can suffer calamity only because I have a body.
When I no longer have a body, what calamity could I possibly have?
And so,

> Those who revere their bodies as if they were the entire world can be given
> custody of the world.

> Those who care for their bodies as if they were the entire world can be entrusted
> with the world.

Chapter Fourteen

Looked for but not seen, its name is "minute."
Listened for but not heard, its name is "rarefied."
Grabbed for but not gotten, its name is "subtle."[30]

---

28. These sets of five refer to conventional standards of evaluation in regard to the different sensory faculties.
The passage is not a rejection of the pleasures of the senses, nor does it express skepticism regarding the senses
per se. Rather, like the view one finds in *Zhuangzi* chapter 2 (in chapter 8 of this volume), it expresses a profound distrust of conventional categories and values and advocates moderation of sensual pleasures.

29. This line also appears in chapters 38 and 72.

30. Cf. the thought expressed in these lines to what one finds in chapter 35.

These three cannot be perfectly explained, and so are confused and regarded as
    one.
Its top is not clear or bright,
Its bottom is not obscure or dark.
Trailing off without end, it cannot be named.
It returns to its home, back before there were things.[31]
This is called the formless form, the image of no thing.[32]
This is called the confused and indistinct.
Greet it and you will not see its head;
Follow it and you will not see its tail.
Hold fast to the Way of old, in order to control what is here today.
The ability to know the ancient beginnings, this is called the thread of the Way.

Chapter Fifteen

In ancient times, the best and most accomplished scholars
Were subtle, mysterious, enigmatic, and far-reaching.
Their profundity was beyond understanding.
Because they were beyond understanding, only with difficulty can we try to describe
    them:
    Poised, like one who must ford a stream in winter.
    Cautious, like one who fears his neighbors on every side.
    Reserved, like a visitor.
    Opening up, like ice about to break.
    Honest, like unhewn wood.[33]
    Broad, like a valley.
    Turbid, like muddy water.
Who can, through stillness, gradually make muddied water clear?
Who can, through movement, gradually stir to life what has long been still?
Those who preserve this Way do not desire fullness.
And, because they are not full, they have no need for renewal.

---

31. Returning to an ideal past state is a common theme in the text. For other examples see chapters 16, 25,
28, 30, and 52.

32. For other passages that concern *xiang*, "image," see chapters 4, 21, 35, and 41.

33. Pǔ 朴, "unhewn wood," is a symbol for anything in its unadulterated natural state. In other contexts, I
will translate it as "simplicity," but here and in certain later passages the metaphor is an important part of the
passage's sense. For other examples, see chapters 19, 28, 32, 37, and 57.

Chapter Sixteen

Attain extreme tenuousness;
Preserve quiet integrity.
The myriad creatures are all in motion!
I watch as they turn back.
The teeming multitude of things, each returns home to its root;
And returning to one's root is called stillness.
This is known as returning to one's destiny;
And returning to one's destiny is known as constancy.
To know constancy is called "enlightenment."
Those who do not know constancy wantonly produce misfortune.
To know constancy is to be accommodating.
To be accommodating is to work for the good of all.
To work for the good of all is to be a true king.
To be a true king is to be Heavenly.
To be Heavenly is to embody the Way.
To embody the Way is to be long-lived,
And one will avoid danger to the end of one's days.[34]

Chapter Seventeen

The greatest of rulers is but a shadowy presence;
Next is the ruler who is loved and praised;
Next is the one who is feared;
Next is the one who is reviled.
Those lacking in trust are not trusted.[35]
But [the greatest rulers] are cautious and honor words.[36]
When their task is done and work complete,[37]
Their people all say, "This is just how we are."[38]

---

34. This line also appears in chapter 52.

35. This line appears again in chapter 23. I interpret it as an expression of the *Daodejing's* characteristic view on Dé 德, "Virtue." For a discussion of the idea of "Virtue" in the *Daodejing* and how it differs from related Confucian conceptions of "Virtue" or "moral charisma," see my "The Concept of *de* ('Virtue') in the *Laozi*," in Mark Csikszentmihalyi and Philip J. Ivanhoe, eds., *Essays on Religious and Philosophical Aspects of the "Laozi"* (Albany, NY: State University of New York Press, 1999), 239–57. For other passages concerning the concept of trust, see chapters 49 and 63.

36. Sages are reluctant and slow to speak, but their words are worthy of complete trust.

37. Cf. chapters 2, 9, 34, and 77.

38. Literally, "We are this way zìrán 自然." See *ziran* under *Important Terms* in the appendices. For other examples, see chapters 23, 25, 51, and 64.

Chapter Eighteen

When the great Way is abandoned, there are benevolence and righteousness.
When wisdom and intelligence come forth, there is great hypocrisy.
When the six familial relationships are out of balance, there are kind parents and
    filial children.
When the state is in turmoil and chaos, there are loyal ministers.[39]

Chapter Nineteen

Cut off sageliness, abandon wisdom, and the people will benefit one-hundred-fold.
Cut off benevolence, abandon righteousness, and the people will return to being
    filial and kind.
Cut off cleverness, abandon profit, and robbers and thieves will be no more.
This might leave the people lacking in culture;
So, give them something with which to identify:
    Manifest plainness.
    Embrace simplicity.[40]
Do not think just of yourself.
Make few your desires.

Chapter Twenty

Cut off learning and be without worry!
How much distance is there really between agreement and flattery?
How much difference is there between the fair and the foul?
What other people fear one cannot but fear.
    Immense!
    Yet still not at its limit!
The multitude are bright and merry;
As if enjoying a grand festival;
As if ascending a terrace in springtime.
I alone am still and inactive, revealing no sign;[41]
Like a child who has not yet learned to smile.
Weak and weary, I seem to have nowhere to go.
The multitude all have more than enough.

---

39. The idea that more can lead to less and its implication that less can yield more is a theme that appears in several places in the text. For examples see chapters 19 and 38.

40. Literally, "unhewn wood." See note 33 above.

41. In this passage, the author enters into an autobiographical mode. See also chapters 69 and 70.

I alone seem to be at a loss.
> I have the mind of a fool!
> Listless and blank!

The common folk are bright and brilliant.
I alone am muddled and confused.
The common folk are careful and discriminating.
I alone am dull and inattentive.
> Vast!
> Like the ocean!
> Blown about!
> As if it would never end!

The multitude all have something to do.
I alone remain obstinate and immobile, like some old rustic.
I alone differ from others, and value being nourished by mother.

Chapter Twenty-One

The outward appearance of great Virtue comes forth from the Way alone.
As for the Way, it is vague and elusive.
Vague and elusive!
Within is an image.[42]
Vague and elusive!
Within is a thing.
Withdrawn and dark!
Within is an essence.
This essence is genuine and authentic.
Within there is trust.
From ancient times until the present day, its name has never left it.
It is how we know the origin of all things.
How do I know what the origin of all things is like?
Through this!

Chapter Twenty-Two

Those who are crooked will be perfected.
Those who are bent will be straight.
Those who are empty will be full.
Those who are worn will be renewed.

---

42. For other passages concerning *xiang*, "image," see chapters 4, 14, 35, and 41.

Those who have little will gain.

Those who have plenty will be confounded.

This is why sages embrace the One and serve as models for the whole world.[43]

They do not make a display of themselves and so are illustrious.

They do not affirm their own views and so are well known.

They do not brag about themselves and so are accorded merit.

They do not boast about themselves and so are heard of for a long time.[44]

Because they do not contend, no one in the world can contend with them.[45]

The ancient saying "Those who are crooked will be perfected" is not without substance![46]

Truly the sages are and remain perfect.

Chapter Twenty-Three

To be sparing with words is what comes naturally.

And so,

A blustery wind does not last all morning;

A heavy downpour does not last all day.

Who produces these?

Heaven and earth!

If not even Heaven and earth can keep things going for a long time,

How much less can human beings?

This is why one should follow the Way in all that one does.

One who follows the Way identifies with the Way.

One who follows Virtue identifies with Virtue.

One who follows loss identifies with loss.

The Way is pleased to have those who identify with the Way.

Virtue is pleased to have those who identify with Virtue.

Loss is pleased to have those who identify with loss.

Those lacking in trust are not trusted.[47]

---

43. For other examples of "the One," see chapters 10, 39, and 42.

44. See chapter 24 for a set of lines similar to the preceding four.

45. The same line appears in chapter 66.

46. While the *Daodejing* does not cite ancient sages or texts by name, here and elsewhere it clearly does quote ancient sources. For other examples see chapters 42, 62, and 69.

47. The same line appears in chapter 17. See note 35 above.

Chapter Twenty-Four

Those who stand on tiptoe cannot stand firm.

Those who stride cannot go far.

Those who make a display of themselves are not illustrious.

Those who affirm their own views are not well known.

Those who brag about themselves are not accorded merit.

Those who boast about themselves are not heard of for long.[48]

From the point of view of the Way, such things are known as "excess provisions and
   pointless activities."

All creatures find these repulsive;

And so, one who has the Way does not abide in them.[49]

Chapter Twenty-Five

There is a thing confused yet perfect, which arose before Heaven and earth.

Still and indistinct, it stands alone and unchanging.

It goes everywhere, yet is never at a loss.

One can regard it as the mother of Heaven and earth.

I do not know its proper name;

I have given it the style "the Way."[50]

Forced to give it a proper name, I would call it "Great."

The Great passes on;

What passes on extends into the distance;

What extends into the distance returns to its source.[51]

And so,

> The Way is great;
>
> Heaven is great;
>
> Earth is great;
>
> And a true king too is great.

In the universe are four things that are great and the true king is first among them.

People model themselves on the earth.

The earth models itself on Heaven.

---

48. See chapter 22 for a set of lines similar to the preceding four.

49. This line appears again in chapter 31.

50. There is a play here on the difference between one's míng 名, "proper name," and one's zì 字, "style." In traditional Chinese society one does not use the former, personal name in public. And so, the author can be understood as saying he is not intimately familiar with the Dao and so knows only its style, or perhaps that it would be unseemly to speak its true and proper name to unfamiliars.

51. Cf. the description of the Way found in *Zhuangzi* chapter 6 (in chapter 8 of this volume).

Heaven models itself on the Way.

The Way models itself on what is natural.[52]

Chapter Twenty-Six

The heavy is the root of the light.

The still rules over the agitated.[53]

This is why sages travel all day without leaving their baggage wagons.

No matter how magnificent the view or lovely the place, they remain aloof and unaffected.

How can a lord who can field ten thousand chariots take lightly his role in the world?

If he is light, he loses the root;

If he is agitated, he loses his rule.

Chapter Twenty-Seven

One who is good at traveling leaves no tracks or traces.

One who is good at speaking is free of slips or flaws.

One who is good at numbers need not count or reckon.

One who is good at closing up needs no bolts or locks, yet what they have secured cannot be opened.

One who is good at binding needs no rope or string, yet what they have tied cannot be undone.

This is why sages are good at saving people and so never abandon people,[54]

Are good at saving things and so never abandon things.

This is called inheriting enlightenment.[55]

And so,

> The good person is teacher of the bad;
>
> The bad person is material for the good.

Those who do not honor their teachers or who fail to care for their material, though knowledgeable are profoundly deluded.

This is a fundamental mystery.

---

52. "Natural" is *ziran*.

53. Cf. chapter 45.

54. Cf. chapter 62.

55. The expression xí míng 襲明, "inheriting enlightenment," is open to numerous interpretations. I take it as describing the good that bad people inherit from those who already are enlightened.

Chapter Twenty-Eight

Know the male but preserve the female, and be a canyon for all the world.

If you are a canyon for all the world, constant Virtue will never leave you, and you
can return home to be a child.

Know the white but preserve the black, and be a model for all the world.

If you are a model for all the world, constant Virtue will never err, and you can
return home to the infinite.

Know glory but preserve disgrace, and be a valley for all the world.

If you are a valley for all the world, constant Virtue will always be sufficient, and
you can return to being unhewn wood.[56]

When unhewn wood is broken up, it becomes vessels.[57]

Sages put these to use and become leaders of the officials.

And so, the greatest carving cuts nothing off.

Chapter Twenty-Nine

Those who would gain the world and do something with it, I see that they will
fail.[58]

For the world is a spiritual vessel and one cannot put it to use.

    Those who use it ruin it.

    Those who grab hold of it lose it.[59]

And so,

    Sometimes things lead and sometimes they follow;

    Sometimes they breathe gently and sometimes they pant;

    Sometimes they are strong and sometimes they are weak;

    Sometimes they fight and sometimes they fall;

This is why sages cast off whatever is extreme, extravagant, or excessive.

Chapter Thirty

One who serves a ruler with the Way will never take the world by force of arms.

For such actions tend to come back in kind.

Wherever an army resides, thorns and thistles grow.

---

56. Or "simplicity." See note 33 above.

57. Qì 器, "vessel" or "implement," is a common metaphor for a government official. Playing on this image,
it carries the slightly negative connotation of someone with limited "capacity." Cf. *Analects* 2.12 (in chapter 1
of this volume; see also the note to that passage).

58. For qǔ tiānxià 取天下, "gaining the world," see chapters 48 and 57.

59. These two lines also appear in chapter 64.

In the wake of a large campaign, bad harvests are sure to follow.
Those who are good at military action achieve their goal and then stop.
They do not dare to rely on force of arms.
They achieve their goal but do not brag.
They achieve their goal but do not boast.
They achieve their goal but are not arrogant.
They achieve their goal but only because they have no other choice.
They achieve their goal but do not force the issue.
For after a period of vigor, there is old age.
To rely on such practices is said to be contrary to the Way.
And what is contrary to the Way will come to an early end.[60]

Chapter Thirty-One

Fine weapons are inauspicious instruments;
All creatures find them repulsive.
And so, one who has the Way does not rely upon them.
At home, a cultivated person gives precedence to the left;
At war, a cultivated person gives precedence to the right.[61]
Weapons are inauspicious instruments, not the instruments of a cultivated
person.
But if given no other choice, the cultivated person will use them.
Peace and quiet are the highest ideals;
A military victory is not a thing of beauty.
To beautify victory is to delight in the slaughter of human beings.
One who delights in the slaughter of human beings will not realize his ambitions
in the world.
On auspicious occasions, precedence is given to the left;
On inauspicious occasions, precedence is given to the right.
The lieutenant commander is stationed on the left;
The supreme commander is stationed on the right.
This shows that the supreme commander is associated with the rites of mourning.
When great numbers of people have been killed, one weeps for them in grief and
sorrow.
Military victory is associated with the rites of mourning.

---

60. The final three lines also appear at the end of chapter 55.

61. The left side being associated with happy and auspicious events and the right side with sad and inauspicious events.

Chapter Thirty-Two

The Way is forever nameless.[62]
Unhewn wood[63] is insignificant, yet no one in the world can master it.
If barons and kings could preserve it, the myriad creatures would all defer to them
    of their own accord;
Heaven and earth would unite and sweet dew would fall;
And the people would be peaceful and just, though no one so decrees.
When unhewn wood is carved up, then there are names.
Now that there are names, know enough to stop!
To know when to stop is how to stay out of danger.[64]
Streams and torrents flow into rivers and oceans,
Just as the world flows into the Way.

Chapter Thirty-Three

Those who know others are knowledgeable;
Those who know themselves are enlightened.
Those who conquer others have power;
Those who conquer themselves are strong;
Those who know contentment are rich.[65]
Those who persevere have firm commitments.
Those who do not lose their place will endure.
Those who die a natural death are long-lived.[66]

Chapter Thirty-Four

How expansive is the great Way!
Flowing to the left and to the right.
The myriad creatures rely upon it for life, and it turns none of them away.[67]
When its work is done, it claims no merit.[68]
It clothes and nourishes the myriad creatures, but does not lord it over them.

---

62. On the idea of being "nameless," see chapters 1, 37, and 41.

63. Or "simplicity." See note 33 above.

64. Cf. the similar line in chapter 44.

65. For the value of zú 足, "contentment," see chapters 44 and 46.

66. Cf. the teaching quoted in chapter 42.

67. Cf. chapter 2.

68. Cf. chapters 2, 9, 17, and 77.

Because it is always without desires, one could consider it insignificant.[69]
Because the myriad creatures all turn to it and yet it does not lord it over them, one
    could consider it great.
Because it never considers itself great, it is able to perfect its greatness.

Chapter Thirty-Five

Hold on to the great image and the whole world will come to you.[70]
They will come and suffer no harm;
They will be peaceful, secure, and prosperous.
Music and fine food will induce the passerby to stop.
But talk about the Way—how insipid and without relish it is!
Look for it and it cannot be seen;
Listen for it and it cannot be heard;
But use it and it will never run dry!

Chapter Thirty-Six

What you intend to shrink, you first must stretch.
What you intend to weaken, you first must strengthen.
What you intend to abandon, you first must make flourish.
What you intend to steal from, you first must provide for.
This is called subtle enlightenment.
The supple and weak overcome the hard and the strong.
Fish should not be taken out of the deep pools.
The sharp implements of the state should not be shown to the people.[71]

Chapter Thirty-Seven

The Way does nothing yet nothing is left undone.[72]
Should barons and kings be able to preserve it, the myriad creatures will transform
    themselves.[73]

---

69. Literally, one could míng 名, "name," it or classify it among the small.

70. For other passages that concern *xiang*, "image," see chapters 4, 14, 21, and 41.

71. The proper sense of lì qì 利器, "sharp implements," is a matter of considerable controversy. Whether it
refers to the weapons of the state, its ministers, labor-saving tools, the Daoist sage, or something else is hard
to say, so I have left it ambiguous. Cf. the use in chapter 57.

72. Cf. the similar line in chapter 48.

73. For zì huà 自化, "transform themselves," see chapter 57.

After they are transformed, should some still desire to act,
I shall press them down with the weight of nameless unhewn wood.[74]
Nameless unhewn wood is but freedom from desire.
Without desire and still, the world will settle itself.

Book Two

Chapter Thirty-Eight

Those of highest Virtue do not strive for Virtue, and so they have it.
Those of lowest Virtue never stray from Virtue, and so they lack it.
Those of highest Virtue practice nonaction and never act for ulterior motives.
Those of lowest Virtue act and always have some ulterior motive.
Those of highest benevolence act but without ulterior motives.
Those of highest righteousness act but with ulterior motives.
Those who are ritually correct[75] act, but if others do not respond, they roll up their
    sleeves and resort to force.
And so,
    When the Way was lost there was Virtue;
    When Virtue was lost there was benevolence;
    When benevolence was lost there was righteousness;
    When righteousness was lost there were the rites.
The rites are the wearing thin of loyalty and trust and the beginning of chaos.
The ability to predict what is to come is an embellishment of the Way and the
    beginning of ignorance.
This is why the most accomplished reside in what is thick, not in what is thin.
They reside in what is most substantial, not in mere embellishment.
And so, they cast off the one and take up the other.[76]

Chapter Thirty-Nine

In the past, among those who attained the One were these:[77]
    Heaven attained the One and became pure;
    Earth attained the One and became settled;
    The spirits attained the One and became numinous;

---

74. Or "nameless simplicity." See note 33 above. On the idea of being "nameless," see chapters 1, 32, and 41.

75. The word rendered here as "ritually correct" is lǐ 禮, which in other contexts is translated as "having propriety."

76. This line also appears in chapters 12 and 72.

77. For other examples of "the One," see chapters 10, 22, and 42.

The valley attained the One and became full;

The myriad creatures attained the One and flourished;

Barons and kings attained the One and became mainstays of the state.

All of this came about through the One.

If Heaven lacked what made it pure, it might rip apart.

If earth lacked what made it settled, it might open up.

If the spirits lacked what made them numinous, they might cease their activity.

If the valley lacked what made it full, it might run dry.

If the myriad creatures lacked what made them flourish, they might become extinct.

If barons and kings lacked what made them honored and eminent, they might fall.

And so,

What is honored has its root in what is base;

What is lofty has its foundation in what is lowly.

This is why barons and kings refer to themselves as,

"The Orphan," "The Desolate," or "The Forlorn."[78]

Is this not a case where what is base serves as the foundation?

Is it not?!

And so, the greatest of praise is without praise.

Do not desire what jingles like jade; desire what rumbles like rock!

Chapter Forty

Turning back is how the Way moves.

Weakness is how the Way operates.

The world and all its creatures arise from what is there;

What is there arises from what is not there.

Chapter Forty-One

When the best scholars hear about the Way,

They assiduously put it into practice.

When average scholars hear about the Way,

They sometimes uphold it and sometimes forsake it.

When the worst scholars hear about the Way,

They laugh at it!

If they did not laugh at it, it would not really be the Way.

And so, the common saying has it:

The clearest Way seems obscure;

The Way ahead seems to lead backward;

---

78. The same expressions occur in chapter 42.

The most level Way seems uneven;
Highest Virtue seems like a valley;
Great purity seems sullied,
Ample Virtue seems insufficient;
Solid Virtue seems unstable;
The simple and genuine seems fickle;
The great square has no corners;
The great vessel takes long to perfect;
The great note sounds faint;
The great image is without shape;[79]
The Way is hidden and without name.[80]
Only the Way is good at providing and completing.

Chapter Forty-Two

The Way produces the One.
The One produces two.
Two produces three.
Three produces the myriad creatures.[81]
The myriad creatures shoulder *yin* and embrace *yang;*
By blending these *qi,* "vital energies," they attain harmony.
People most despise being orphaned, desolate, or forlorn;
And yet, barons and kings take these as their personal appellations.[82]
And so,

> Sometimes diminishing a thing adds to it;
> Sometimes adding to a thing diminishes it.

---

79. For other passages that concern xiàng 象, "image," see chapters 4, 14, 21, and 35.

80. On the idea of being "nameless," see chapters 1, 32, and 37.

81. The precise referents of these terms are hard to determine. I take the Way to be the most inclusive term designating the hidden, underlying source of things. The "one" would then be its xiàng 象, "image," the closest thing we can have to a picture or representation of the Way. (For other examples, see chapters 10, 22, and 39.) The "two" would then be the fundamental qì 氣, "vital energies," *yin* and *yang* (see *qi* and *yin* and *yang* under *Important Terms* in the appendices). These, together with our image of the Way as a unified whole, give rise to everything in the world. A similar scheme is described in the "Great Appendix" to the *Changes* (see Justin Tiwald and Bryan W. Van Norden, eds., *Readings in Later Chinese Philosophy: Han Dynasty to the Twentieth Century* [Indianapolis: Hackett Publishing Company, 2014], 49). This process, whatever its particulars, was understood as a natural progression. There was no creator, and the "nothing" out of which things arose is a primal state of undifferentiated vital energy, the state of no things but not absolute Nothingness. See Slingerland's comments on these passages in *Effortless Action.*

82. See chapter 39.

What others teach, I too teach: "The violent and overbearing will not die a natural death."
I shall take this as the father of all my teachings.

Chapter Forty-Three

The most supple things in the world ride roughshod over the most rigid.
That which is not there can enter even where there is no space.
This is how I know the advantages of nonaction!
The teaching that is without words,[83]
The advantages of nonaction,
Few in the world attain these.

Chapter Forty-Four

Your name or your body, which do you hold more dear?
Your body or your property, which is of greater value?
Gain or loss, which is the greater calamity?
And so, deep affections give rise to great expenditures.
Excessive hoarding results in great loss.
Know contentment and avoid disgrace;[84]
Know when to stop and avoid danger;[85]
And you will long endure.

Chapter Forty-Five

Great perfection seems wanting, but use will not wear it out.
Great fullness seems empty, but use will not drain it.
Great straightness seems crooked;
Great skillfulness seems clumsy;
Great speech seems to stammer.
Agitation overcomes cold.
Stillness overcomes heat.
Purity and stillness rectify Heaven and earth.

---

83. Cf. the similar line in chapter 2.

84. For the value of "contentment," see chapters 33 and 46.

85. Cf. the similar line in chapter 32.

Chapter Forty-Six

When the world has the Way, fleet-footed horses are used to haul dung.
When the world is without the Way, war horses are raised in the suburbs.[86]
The greatest misfortune is not to know contentment.[87]
The worst calamity is the desire to acquire.
And so, those who know the contentment of contentment are always content.

Chapter Forty-Seven

Without going out the door, one can know the whole world.
Without looking out the window, one can see the Way of Heaven.
The further one goes, the less one knows.
This is why sages
Know without going abroad,
Name without having to see,
Perfect through nonaction.

Chapter Forty-Eight

In the pursuit of learning, one does more each day;
In the pursuit of the Way, one does less each day;
One does less and less until one does nothing;[88]
One does nothing yet nothing is left undone.[89]
Gaining the world always is accomplished by following no activity.[90]
As soon as one actively tries, one will fall short of gaining the world.

Chapter Forty-Nine

Sages do not have constant hearts of their own;
They take the people's hearts as their hearts.
I am good to those who are good;
I also am good to those who are not good;

---

86. Very close to the city, thus showing a heightened state of mobilization.

87. For the value of "contentment," see chapters 33 and 44.

88. Until one reaches the state of *wuwei*, "nonaction."

89. Cf. the similar lines in chapter 37.

90. For wúshì 無事, "no activity," see chapters 57 and 63. For *qu tianxia*, "gaining the world," see chapters 29 and 57.

This is to be good out of Virtue.[91]
I trust the trustworthy;
I also trust the untrustworthy.
This is to trust out of Virtue.
Sages blend into the world and accord with the people's hearts.
The people all pay attention to their eyes and ears;
The sages regard them as children.

Chapter Fifty

Between life and death,
Three out of ten are the disciples of life;[92]
Three out of ten are the disciples of death;
Three out of ten create a place for death.[93]
Why is this?
Because of their profound desire to live.[94]
I have heard that those good at nurturing life,
On land do not meet with rhinoceroses or tigers,
And in battle do not encounter armored warriors.
Rhinoceroses find no place to thrust their horns;
Tigers find no place to sink their claws;
Soldiers find no place to drive in their blades.
Why is this?
Because such people have no place for death.

Chapter Fifty-One

The Way produces them;
Virtue rears them;

---

91. I read this line, and the three lines below it, as playing on the etymological and semantic relationship between Dé 德, "virtue," and dé 得, "to get." Since those with virtue naturally are good to and trust others, they accrue ("get") Virtue; this enables them to gain ("get") the support of others and realize ("get") their greater ends. Cf. chapters 17, 23, 27, and 38.

92. Cf. chapter 76.

93. This passage has been interpreted in a wide variety of ways. I take its general theme to be the preservation of one's natural span of life, here connected to the idea that wanting something too badly often leads to its opposite. Some are fated to live long and others to die young. But about one in three bring misfortune on themselves. The missing person in ten is of course the sage. By not doing, sages avoid creating a place for death to enter.

94. Cf. chapter 75.

Things shape them;

Circumstances perfect them.

This is why the myriad creatures all revere the Way and honor Virtue.

The Way is revered and Virtue honored not because this is decreed, but because it
is natural.

And so, the Way produces them and Virtue rears them;

Raises and nurtures them;

Settles and confirms them;

Nourishes and shelters them.

To produce without possessing;[95]

To act with no expectation of reward;[96]

To lead without lording over;

Such is Enigmatic Virtue![97]

Chapter Fifty-Two

The world had a beginning;

This can be considered the mother of the world.

Knowing the mother, return and know her children;

Knowing her children, return and preserve their mother;

And you will avoid danger to the end of your days.[98]

Stop up the openings;

Close the gates;[99]

To the end of your life you will remain unperturbed.

Unstop the openings;

Multiply your activities;

And to the end of your life you will be beyond salvation.

To discern the minute is called "enlightenment."

To preserve the weak is called "strength."

Use this light and return home to this enlightenment.

Do not bring disaster upon yourself.

This is called "practicing the constant."

---

95. This line also appears in chapters 2 and 10.

96. This line also appears in chapters 2, 10, and 77.

97. Chapter 10 concludes with these same four lines. For xuán dé 玄德, "Enigmatic Virtue," see chapter 65.

98. This line also appears in chapter 16.

99. This and the preceding line also appear in chapter 56.

Chapter Fifty-Three

If I know anything at all, I know that in following the great Way, there is but one
    concern:
The great Way is smooth and easy;
Yet people love to take shortcuts![100]
The court is resplendent;
Yet the fields are overgrown.
The granaries are empty;
Yet some wear elegant clothes;
Fine swords dangle at their sides;
They are stuffed with food and drink;
And possess wealth in gross abundance.
This is known as taking pride in robbery.
Far is this from the Way!

Chapter Fifty-Four

What is firmly grounded will not be pulled out.
What is firmly embraced will not be lost.
Through the sacrifices of one's descendants, it will never cease.
Cultivate it in oneself and its Virtue will be genuine.[101]
Cultivate it in one's family and its Virtue will be more than enough.
Cultivate it in one's village and its Virtue will be long-lasting.
Cultivate it in one's state and its Virtue will be abundant.
Cultivate it throughout the world and its Virtue will be everywhere.[102]
And so,
    Take stock of the self by looking at the self;
    Take stock of the family by looking at the family;
    Take stock of the village by looking at the village;
    Take stock of the state by looking at the state;
    Take stock of the world by looking at the world;

---

100. See *Analects* 6.14 (not in this volume) for a related use of the word jìng 徑, "shortcut."

101. "It" refers to the Way. Note that in this and the following lines the word translated as "Virtue" also clearly has the sense of a kind of "power."

102. The progression from cultivating the Way in oneself to cultivating it throughout the empire is reminiscent of the progression one sees in the Classic section of the *Great Learning* (in chapter 11 of this volume). Wing-tsit Chan points out that Mencius identifies this basic idea as a "common saying" in *Mengzi* 4A5 (not in this volume). (See Wing-tsit Chan, trans., *The Way of Lao Tzu [Tao te ching]* [Chicago, IL: University of Chicago Press, 1963], 196.)

How do I know that the world is this way?
Through this!

Chapter Fifty-Five

Those who are steeped in Virtue are like newborn children;[103]
Venomous creatures will not strike them;
Fierce beasts will not seize them;
Birds of prey will not snatch them away.
Their bones are weak and sinews yielding and yet their grip is firm.
They do not yet know the union of male and female, but their potency is at its
    height.
This is because they are perfectly pure;
They can wail all day without growing hoarse.
This is because they are perfectly balanced.
Knowing balance is called "constancy."
Knowing constancy is called "enlightenment."
What helps life along is called "inauspicious."[104]
When the heart is used to guide the *qi*, "vital energies," this is called "forcing
    things."[105]
For after a period of vigor there is old age.
To rely on such practices is said to be contrary to the Way.
And what is contrary to the Way will come to an early end.[106]

Chapter Fifty-Six

Those who know do not talk about it;
Those who talk about it do not know.
Stop up the openings;

---

103. The early Confucian Mengzi also uses the newborn as an image for his ideal state of mind. See his discussion of the chìzǐ zhī xīn 赤子之心, "child's heart," in *Mengzi* 4B12 (in chapter 4 of this volume).

104. Cf. the closing lines of *Zhuangzi* chapter 5 (in chapter 8 of this volume), where Zhuangzi says, "Follow the natural and do not help life along" (yì shēng 益生).

105. Early Daoists tended to advocate allowing one's *qi* to find its natural course. For example, see the "fasting of the heart" passage in *Zhuangzi* chapter 4 (in chapter 8 of this volume). They were opposed to those such as the early Confucian Mengzi, who argued that the heart should guide the vital energies. See Mengzi's discussion of nourishing the "floodlike *qi*" in *Mengzi* 2A2 (in chapter 4 of this volume).

106. The final three lines also appear at the end of chapter 30.

Close the gates;[107]
Blunt the sharpness;
Untangle the tangles;
Soften the glare;
Merge with the dust.[108]
This is known as Enigmatic Unity.[109]
And so,
> One can neither be too familiar with nor too distant from them;
> One can neither benefit nor harm them;
> One can neither honor nor demean them.
And so, they are honored by the whole world.[110]

Chapter Fifty-Seven

Follow what is correct and regular in ordering your state;
Follow what is strange and perverse in deploying your troops;
Follow no activity and gain the world.[111]
How do I know that things are this way?
Through this!
The more taboos and prohibitions there are in the world, the poorer the people.
The more sharp implements the people have, the more benighted the state.[112]
The more clever and skillful the people, the more strange and perverse things arise.
The more clear the laws and edicts, the more thieves and robbers.
And so, sages say,
> "I do nothing and the people transform themselves;
> I prefer stillness and the people correct and regulate themselves;
> I engage in no activity and the people prosper on their own;
> I am without desires and the people simplify[113] their own lives."

---

107. This and the preceding line also appear together in chapter 52.

108. This and the preceding three lines also appear together in chapter 4.

109. Cf. chapter 1, "Their unity is known as an enigma."

110. This line also appears in chapter 62.

111. For *wushi*, "no activity," see chapters 48 and 63. For *qu tianxia*, "gaining the world," see chapters 29 and 48.

112. For the expression "sharp implements," see chapter 36 and note 71.

113. Literally, "unhewn wood." See note 33 above.

Chapter Fifty-Eight

The more dull and depressed the government, the more honest and agreeable the people.

The more active and searching the government, the more deformed and deficient the people.

Good fortune rests upon disaster;

Disaster lies hidden within good fortune.

Who knows the highest standards?

Perhaps there is nothing that is truly correct and regular!

What is correct and regular turns strange and perverse;

What is good turns monstrous.

Long indeed have the people been deluded.

And so, sages are

Square but do not cut,

Cornered but do not clip,

Upright but not imposing,

Shining but not dazzling.

Chapter Fifty-Nine

In bringing order to the people or in serving Heaven, nothing is as good as frugality.

To be frugal is called submitting early on.

Submitting early on is known as deeply accumulating Virtue.

If you deeply accumulate Virtue, nothing can stand in your way.

If nothing can stand in your way, no one will know your limits.

If no one knows your limits, you can possess the state.

If you possess the mother of the state, you can long endure.

This is known as deep roots and strong stems.

This is the Way of long life and far-reaching vision.

Chapter Sixty

Ruling a great state is like cooking a small fish.[114]

When one manages the world through the Way, ghosts lose their numinous qualities.

It's not that ghosts really lose their numinous qualities, but that their numinous qualities do not injure human beings.[115]

---

114. The idea is that too much attention and meddling will make either fall apart.

115. Laozi seems here to be arguing against the idea, seen in thinkers like Mozi et al., that the ideal state requires the active participation of ghosts and other spirits in meting out rewards or punishments. Laozi does

Not only do their numinous qualities not injure human beings, sages too do not
  injure human beings.[116]
Since neither of these two injures human beings, Virtue gathers and accrues to both.

Chapter Sixty-One

A great state is like the delta of a mighty river;[117]
It is where the whole world gathers.
It is the female of the whole world.[118]
The female always gets the better of the male through stillness.
Through stillness, she places herself below the male.
And so, a great state, by placing itself below a lesser state, can take the lesser state.
A lesser state, by placing itself below a great state, can be taken by the greater state.
And so, one places itself below in order to take;
The other places itself below in order to be taken.
The great state wants no more than to provide for all people alike.
The lesser state wants no more than to find someone to serve.
Since both can get what they want, it is fitting that the great state places itself in
  the lower position.

Chapter Sixty-Two

The Way is the inner sanctum of the myriad creatures.[119]
It is the treasure of the good man and the savior of the bad.
Fine words can sell things;[120]
Noble deeds can promote someone;

---

not deny the existence of such beings but, like Kongzi, sees a direct appeal to them as inappropriate. Cf.
Kongzi's advice concerning ghosts and spirits in *Analects* 6.22 (in chapter 1 of this volume).

116. They do not disturb the people through too much attention and meddling.

117. Literally, xià liú 下流, "low flow." Cf. the use of the same term in *Analects* 19.20 (not in this volume):
"The gentleman dislikes living in low places (*xia liu*) where all the foul things of the world collect." The Daoist
of course inverts Confucian values, esteeming what the world regards as lowly.

118. In the sense that the ideal great state places itself below and attracts the whole world. Also, like a valley
or the delta of a river, the great state is like a woman in being fertile and having the ability to feed the whole
world. Consider the common metaphor of the Tigris and Euphrates rivers as the "cradle of civilization." Cf.
chapter 66.

119. "Inner sanctum" is the translation of ào 奧, the southwest corner of one's house where the household
gods are lodged and worshipped.

120. Cf. chapter 81.

But can one cast away the bad in people?[121]

And so, when setting up the Son of Heaven or appointing the Three Ministers,[122]

Those who offer up precious jades and present fine steeds are not as good as those who stay in their seats and promote this Way.

Why was this Way so honored in ancient times?

Did they not say that through it,

"One could get what one seeks and escape punishment for one's crimes?"

And so, this is why it is honored by the whole world.[123]

Chapter Sixty-Three

Act, but through nonaction.

Be active, but have no activities.[124]

Taste, but have no tastes.[125]

No matter how great or small, many or few,

Repay resentment with Virtue.[126]

Plan for what is difficult while it is easy.

Work at what is great while it is small.

The difficult undertakings in the world all start with what is easy.

The great undertakings in the world all begin with what is small.

This is why sages never work at great things and are able to achieve greatness.

Those who easily enter into promises always prove unworthy of trust.

Those who often think that things are easy regularly encounter difficulties.

And so, sages consider things difficult and in the end are without difficulties.

---

121. Cf. chapter 27.

122. Cf. Mozi's discussion of how the Son of Heaven and Three Ministers are to be appointed, in *Mozi* chapter 11, "Obeying One's Superior" (in chapter 2 of this volume).

123. This line also appears in chapter 56.

124. For *wushi*, "no activities," see chapters 48 and 57.

125. The idea in each case is that one should do what one does in unpremeditated and spontaneous response to the situation at hand. One should do away with set schemes, categories, standards, and plans, and follow one's natural inclinations and tendencies. And so, for example, one should taste and savor what one finds pleasing, not what others might enjoy or what accords with some socially sanctioned view about good taste. Cf. chapter 12.

126. Here we see a clear contrast with the view of early Confucians. See *Analects* 14.34 (in chapter 1 of this volume). Cf. chapter 49.

Chapter Sixty-Four

What is at peace is easy to secure.
What has yet to begin is easy to plan for.
What is brittle is easy to scatter.
What is faint is easy to disperse.
Work at things before they come to be;
Regulate things before they become disordered.
A tree whose girth fills one's embrace sprang from a downy sprout;
A terrace nine stories high arose from a layer of dirt;
A journey of a thousand leagues began with a single step.
 Those who use it ruin it.
 Those who grab hold of it lose it.[127]
This is why sages practice nonaction and so do not ruin;
They do not lay hold and so do not lose.
People often ruin things just when they are on the verge of success.
Be as careful at the end as you are at the beginning, and you will not ruin things.
This is why sages desire to be without desires and show no regard for precious goods.[128]
They study what is not studied and return to what the multitude pass by.[129]
They work to support the myriad creatures in their natural condition and never
 dare to act.

Chapter Sixty-Five

In ancient times, those good at practicing the Way did not use it to
enlighten the people, but rather to keep them in the dark.[130]

---

127. These two lines also appear in chapter 29.

128. Cf. *Mengzi* 7B35 (not in this volume), "For cultivating the heart and mind nothing is better than to make few one's desires."

129. Daoist sages take nature as their model. In philosophical discussions of the time, there was a debate about whether the proper content of learning is part of or opposed to what is naturally so. This debate in turn was a reflection of a larger debate about the character of human nature. Mengzi endorses only particular natural tendencies—those that incline us toward morality—and on this basis claims that human nature is good. Xunzi argues that our untutored nature inclines us toward bad states of affairs. On this basis he concludes that our nature is bad and must be reformed through protracted study and practice. We can see Laozi, Mengzi, and Xunzi as representing a spectrum of views about the proper content of learning that reflects their different views about the goodness of our pre-reflective nature, running from greatest to least confidence in our raw natural state.

130. The idea that the best of actions flow forth without reflection or knowledge was not uncommon in early China. In his note on this line, Wing-tsit Chan cites a passage from the *Odes* in which the Lord on High commends King Wen for his behavior: "Without reflection or knowledge, you comply with my principles" (*Mao # 241*). (See Chan, *The Way of Lao Tzu*, 216.) Cf. *Analects* 15.5 (in chapter 1 of this volume).

The people are hard to govern because they know too much.
And so,

To rule a state with knowledge is to be a detriment to the state.

Not to rule a state through knowledge is to be a blessing to the state.

Know that these two provide the standard.
Always to know this standard is called Enigmatic Virtue.[131]
How profound and far-reaching is Enigmatic Virtue!
It turns back with things;
And only then is there the Great Compliance.[132]

Chapter Sixty-Six

The rivers and ocean are able to rule over a hundred valleys, because they are good
at placing themselves in the lower position.[133]
And so, they are able to rule over a hundred valleys.
This is why if you want to be above the people, you must proclaim that you are
below them.
If you want to lead the people, you must put yourself behind them.
This is how sages are able to reside above the people without being considered a burden,
How they are able to be out in front of the people without being regarded as a harm.
This is why the whole world delights in supporting them and never wearies.
Because they do not contend, no one in the world can contend with them.[134]

Chapter Sixty-Seven

The whole world agrees in saying that my Way is great but appears unworthy.
It is only because it is great that it appears to be unworthy.
If it appeared worthy, would it not have become small long ago?
I have three treasures that I hold on to and preserve:

The first I call loving kindness;

The second I call frugality;

The third I call never daring to put oneself first in the world.

---

131. For *xuan de*, "Enigmatic Virtue," see chapters 10 and 51.

132. This is the only occurrence of the expression dà shùn 大順, "Great Compliance," in the text. However, as
Arthur Waley points out in his note to this chapter, it does occur in *Zhuangzi* chapter 12 (not in this volume).
(See Arthur Waley, trans., *The Way and Its Power* [New York: Grove Press, 1963], 223.) Note too that the same
word *shun* appears in *Mao* # 241, quoted in note 130 above.

133. Cf. chapter 61.

134. The same line appears in chapter 22.

The kind can be courageous;

The frugal can be generous;

Those who never dare to put themselves first in the world can become leaders of
the various officials.

Now, to be courageous without loving kindness,

To be generous without frugality,

To put oneself first without putting oneself behind others,

These will lead to death.[135]

If one has loving kindness, in attack one will be victorious,

In defense one will be secure.

For Heaven will save you and protect you with loving kindness.

Chapter Sixty-Eight

Those good at fighting are never warlike.[136]

Those good at attack are never enraged.

Those good at conquering their enemies never confront them.

Those good at using others put themselves in a lower position.

This is called the Virtue of non-contention;

This is called the power of using others;

This is called matching up with Heaven, the highest achievement of the ancients.

Chapter Sixty-Nine

Military strategists have a saying,

"I never dare to play host but prefer to play guest.[137]

I never dare to advance an inch but retreat a foot."

This is called a formation without form,

Rolling up one's sleeve but having no arm,

Forcing the issue but lacking an enemy.[138]

Who can avoid misfortune in war?

But there is none greater than underestimating the enemy!

Underestimating the enemy almost cost me my three treasures.[139]

And so, when swords are crossed and troops clash, the side that grieves shall be victorious.

---

135. The idea that true virtue lies in a harmony within a tension, that it requires a balance between extremes,
is seen in many traditions. Early Confucians, too, held a version of this view. For example, see *Analects* 8.2
(in chapter 1 of this volume).

136. That is, they are not overly aggressive or pugnacious.

137. They avoid initiating the action, the first move being the prerogative of the host.

138. Cf. the last two lines with a similar line in chapter 38.

139. See chapter 67 for a possible reference.

Chapter Seventy

My teachings are easy to understand and easy to implement;
But no one in the whole world has been able to understand or implement them.
My teachings have an ancestor and my activities have a lord;
But people fail to understand these, and so I am not understood.
Those who understand me are rare;[140]
Those who take me as a model are honored.
This is why sages wear coarse cloth while cherishing precious jade.[141]

Chapter Seventy-One

To know that one does not know is best;
Not to know but to believe that one knows is a disease.[142]
Only by seeing this disease as a disease can one be free of it.
Sages are free of this disease;
Because they see this disease as a disease, they are free of it.

Chapter Seventy-Two

When the people do not fear what warrants awe,
Something truly awful will come to them.
Do not constrain their homes or villages.
Do not oppress their lives.
Because you do not oppress them, you will not be oppressed.
This is why sages know themselves but do not make a display of themselves;
They care for themselves but do not revere themselves.
And so, they cast off the one and take up the other.[143]

Chapter Seventy-Three

To be courageous in daring leads to death;
To be courageous in not daring leads to life.

---

140. Cf. this complaint with Kongzi's remark in *Analects* 14.35 (in chapter 1 of this volume).

141. They appear common and unworthy on the outside but possess a secret treasure within. In *Analects* 17.1 (not in this volume), a man named Yang Huo criticizes Kongzi's reluctance to take office by asking him, "Can one who cherishes his treasure within and allows his state to go astray be considered benevolent?" Cf. *Analects* 9.13 (in chapter 1 of this volume).

142. This passage is similar in thought to *Analects* 2.17 (in chapter 1 of this volume).

143. This line also appears in chapters 12 and 38.

These two bring benefit to some and loss to others.
Who knows why Heaven dislikes what it does?
Even sages regard this as a difficult question.
The Way does not contend but is good at victory;
Does not speak but is good at responding;
Does not call but things come of their own accord;
Is not anxious but is good at laying plans.
Heaven's net is vast;
Its mesh is loose but misses nothing.

Chapter Seventy-Four

If the people are not afraid of death, why threaten them with death?
"But what if I could keep the people always afraid of death and seize and put to
    death those who dare to act in strange or perverse ways?
Who then would dare to act in such a manner?"[144]
There is always the killing done by the Chief Executioner.[145]
The Chief Executioner is the greatest carver among carpenters.
Those who would do the work of the greatest carver among carpenters, rarely avoid
    wounding their own hands.

Chapter Seventy-Five

The people are hungry because those above eat up too much in taxes;
This is why the people are hungry.
The people are difficult to govern because those above engage in action;
This is why the people are difficult to govern.
People look upon death lightly because those above are obsessed with their own
    lives;[146]
This is why the people look upon death lightly.
Those who do not strive to live are more worthy than those who cherish life.

Chapter Seventy-Six

When alive human beings are supple and weak;
When dead they are stiff and strong.

---

144. These two lines introduce a question and mark a dialogue within the text. Cf. *Analects* 12.19 (in chapter
1 of this volume).

145. The death that Heaven brings to each person.

146. Cf. chapter 50.

When alive the myriad creatures, plants, and trees are supple and weak;
When dead they are withered and dry.
And so,
> The stiff and the strong are the disciples of death;[147]
> The supple and weak are the disciples of life.
This is why,
> A weapon that is too strong will not prove victorious;
> A tree that is too strong will break.
The strong and the mighty reside down below;
The soft and the supple reside on top.[148]

Chapter Seventy-Seven

The Way of Heaven, is it not like the stretching of a bow?
What is high it presses down;
What is low it lifts up.
It takes from what has excess;
It augments what is deficient.
The Way of Heaven takes from what has excess and augments what is deficient.
The Way of human beings is not like this.
It takes from the deficient and offers it up to those with excess.
Who is able to offer what they have in excess to the world?
Only one who has the Way!
This is why sages act with no expectation of reward.[149]
When their work is done, they do not linger.[150]
They do not desire to make a display of their worthiness.

Chapter Seventy-Eight

In all the world, nothing is more supple or weak than water;
Yet nothing can surpass it for attacking what is stiff and strong.
And so, nothing can take its place.
That the weak overcomes the strong and the supple overcomes the hard,
These are things everyone in the world knows but none can practice.
This is why sages say,

---

147. Cf. chapter 50.

148. The Han dynasty commentator Wang Bi illustrates the point of these last two lines with the examples of the roots of a tree and its twigs.

149. This line also appears in chapters 2, 10, and 51.

150. Cf. chapters 2, 9, 17, and 34. This and the previous line also appear together in chapter 2.

Those who can take on the disgrace of the state
Are called lords of the altar to the soil and grain.[151]
Those who can take on the misfortune of the state,
Are called kings of all the world.[152]
Straightforward words seem paradoxical.

Chapter Seventy-Nine

In cases of great resentment, even when resolution is reached, some resentment
  remains.
How can this be considered good?
This is why sages maintain the left-hand portion of the tally,[153]
But do not hold people accountable.
Those with Virtue oversee the tally;
Those without Virtue oversee collection.[154]
The Way of Heaven plays no favorites;
It is always on the side of the good.

Chapter Eighty

Reduce the size of the state;
Lessen the population.
Make sure that even though there are labor-saving tools, they are never used.
Make sure that the people look upon death as a weighty matter and never move to
  distant places.
Even though they have ships and carts, they will have no use for them.
Even though they have armor and weapons, they will have no reason to deploy
  them.

---

151. These were the main altars of the state and a common metaphor for its independence and well-being.

152. The idea that the worthiest rulers are willing to offer themselves to Heaven as surrogates on behalf of the people and in the name of the state is a motif seen in writings of this period and earlier. See King Tang's pronouncement to the spirits in *Analects* 20.1 (not in this volume) and Davis S. Nivison, "'Virtue' in Bone and Bronze," in *The Ways of Confucianism* (Chicago, IL: Open Court Press, 1996), especially 20–24.

153. The left-hand portion of a contract of obligation, the part that was held by the creditor.

154. The central idea of this chapter, which is seen throughout the text, is that one cannot force others to be good. If one resorts to force, one's actions will eventually rebound in kind upon oneself. The only way to affect others and turn them to the good is through the power of one's *De*, "Virtue."

Make sure that the people return to the use of the knotted cord.[155]
Make their food savory,
Their clothes fine,
Their houses comfortable,
Their lives happy.
Then even though neighboring states are within sight of each other,
Even though they can hear the sounds of each other's dogs and chickens,
Their people will grow old and die without ever having visited one another.

Chapter Eighty-One

Words worthy of trust are not refined;
Refined words are not worthy of trust.[156]
The good do not engage in disputation;
Those who engage in disputation are not good.[157]
Those who know are not full of knowledge;
Those full of knowledge do not know.
Sages do not accumulate.
The more they do for others, they more they have;
The more they give to others, the more they possess.
The Way of Heaven is to benefit and not harm.
The Way of the sage is to act but not contend.

---

155. That is, let them abandon writing. The use of the knotted cord to keep track of records is mentioned in the "Great Appendix," Part 2, to the *Changes*, and *Zhuangzi* chapter 10 (not in this volume), as well as elsewhere in the early literature. The details are unclear but the practice probably entailed making a knot in a cord for every ten or twenty units counted. Thus, it resembles the Western practice of notching or "scoring" a piece of wood for every twenty units counted, each notch representing a "score" or twenty.

156. In *Analects* 14.4 (in chapter 1 of this volume), Kongzi says, "Those who possess Virtue will inevitably have something to say, whereas those who have something to say do not necessarily possess Virtue." Cf. chapter 62.

157. Confucians too had a general mistrust of glib talkers and disputation. This reflects their similar, though distinct, beliefs about the power of a good person's *De*, "Virtue," to sway others. For examples, see *Analects* 1.3 (in chapter 1 of this volume) and Mengzi's explanation of why he must engage in disputation, though not being fond of it, found in *Mengzi* 3B9 (in chapter 4 of this volume).

SELECTIVE BIBLIOGRAPHY

Translations

Chan, Alan K. L., trans. *Two Visions of the Way: A Study of the Wang Pi ad the Ho-shang Kung Commentaries on the "Lao-Tzu."* Albany, NY: State University of New York Press, 1991. (A translation and study of the two most influential commentaries on the *Laozi*.)

Chan, Wing-tsit, trans. *The Way of Lao Tzu (Tao-te ching).* Chicago, IL: University of Chicago Press, 1963. (An accurate and scholarly translation that makes revealing use of the commentarial tradition.)

Hendricks, Robert G., trans. *Lao-Tzu Te-Tao Ching.* New York: Ballantine, 1989. (A fine translation and introduction to the *Mawangdui* version of the text.)

Lau, D. C., trans. *Tao Te Ching.* Baltimore: Penguin Books, 1963. (An elegantly terse translation with informative introduction and appendices.)

Lynn, Richard John, trans. *The Classic of the Way and Virtue: A New Translation of the "Tao-te ching" as Interpreted by Wang Pi.* New York: Columbia University Press, 1999. (A translation that includes the historically influential "Outline Introduction to the *Laozi*" and textual commentary by Wang Bi.)

Waley, Arthur, trans. *The Way and Its Power.* New York: Grove Press, 1963. (A thoughtful translation with a substantial introduction.)

Secondary Works

Creel, Herrlee G. *What Is Taoism? And Other Studies in Chinese Cultural History.* Chicago, IL: The University of Chicago Press, 1970. (Contains several seminal essays on the thought and history of the text.)

Csikszentmihalyi, Mark, and Philip J. Ivanhoe, eds. *Essays on Religious and Philosophical Aspects of the "Laozi."* Albany, NY: SUNY Press, 1999. (An anthology of essays on the thought of the text.)

Kohn, Livia, and Michael LaFargue, eds. *Lao-tzu and the "Tao-te-ching."* Albany, NY: SUNY Press, 1998. (A broad range of essays on the text, its reception, and its interpretation.)

Lau, D. C. "The Treatment of Opposites in Lao Tzu 老子." *Bulletin of the School of Oriental and African Studies* 21 (1958): 344–60. (An intriguing exploration of one of the more paradoxical aspects of the text.)

Liu, Xiaogan, ed. *Dao Companion to Daoist Philosophy.* New York: Springer, 2015. (An anthology of secondary essays with sections on "The *Laozi* and the Bamboo Texts," "The *Zhuangzi*," and later religious and philosophical Daoism.)

CHAPTER SEVEN

SHEN DAO

Introduction

Very little is known about Shèn Dào 慎到, the purported author of the *Shenzi Fragments*. He seems to have been active in the latter half of the fourth century BCE and the first part of the third but does not seem to have held any significant political position. While often classified as a Legalist thinker, in no small part because of how extensively he is quoted in chapter 40 of the *Han Feizi*, the following fragments should make clear that he is influenced by a range of thinkers, including Laozi.

When reading the *Shenzi Fragments*, it is important to keep in mind that they are just that—fragments. No complete edition of the work attributed to Shen Dao has existed since at least the tenth century CE. What remains, and what is presented in part here, are fragments of varying lengths, collected from a range of other texts throughout Chinese history that have cited Shen Dao. However, this is a very incomplete record of Shen Dao's ideas and makes coming to a comprehensive understanding of his views quite difficult. Furthermore, we must always keep in mind that any interpretation of these fragments must remain tentative, for there is the possibility that the fuller context within which the received fragments were recorded—a context now lost to us—might necessitate a different interpretation.

These caveats aside, we do find within the existing fragments a surprisingly coherent political vision. Like many of his time, Shen Dao is interested in human psychology and the patterns of the natural world around us, and he takes an understanding of these to be essential to developing a viable social and political organization. Unlike many early Chinese thinkers, however, Shen Dao wishes to separate ethics from political philosophy, in part because he is quite skeptical about the possibility of altering or developing the dispositions that human beings are born with and changing their motivations. Instead, in Shen Dao's account, people always act in their own interests, and any social system that wishes to sustain itself must take this into account and set up a system of rules and regulations to restrict self-interested actions detrimental to social organization. Furthermore, and this is among the most important contributions of these fragments, Shen Dao emphasizes that feelings of resentment and expectation arise not merely when we do not get what we desire, but specifically when we believe that there is a chance of achieving our desires, but that chance is frustrated by some identifiable agent. In order to avoid such feelings, which ultimately undermine the power and efficacy of the state, Shen Dao sought to design a political system that not only would mirror critical features of the natural world but would also come to be regarded as being as inevitable and disinterested as nature itself.

Shenzi Fragments (selections)

Section 1: Awe-Inspiring Potency[1]

While Heaven is bright, it does not worry that the people are in the dark. While the earth is bountiful, it does not worry that there is insufficiency among the people. While the sage is potent, he does not worry that the people are endangered. Even though Heaven does not worry that the people are in the dark, those who open up doors and windows certainly can take from [Heaven] in order to obtain their own illumination, though Heaven does nothing. Even though the earth does not worry that there is insufficiency among the people, those who chop down trees and cut grasses can certainly draw from [the earth] in order to obtain their own bounty, though the earth does nothing. Even though the sage does not worry that people are endangered, those of the hundred surnames who take the sage as their standard from above and harmonize with those below can certainly draw from [the sage] in order to attain their own security, though the sage does nothing.[2] Thus, while the sage is able to avoid harming the people when occupying a position

---

1. "Potency" is Dé 德, which is translated elsewhere in this volume as "Virtue." However, in the *Shenzi Fragments*, as in the *Han Feizi*, it does not connote a *moral* power. Rather, it refers to a potency that need not have moral characteristics.

2. "Those of the hundred surnames" refers to a particular class of individuals—those with status sufficiently high to have a surname. They are differentiated from the lower classes, and will typically have some degree of education and wealth, in contrast with those referred to as "the people" or "the masses."

above, he is not able to keep the people from harming themselves. However, those of the hundred surnames are able to stop the people from harming themselves. The manner in which the sage possesses all under Heaven is that he accepts it; he does not take it. The relationship between those of the hundred surnames and the sage is that they nourish him; they do not make him nourish them. And so, the sage does nothing. . . .

Today, the state lacks a constant Way, and offices lack constant models. Because of this, the state is deteriorating day by day. Even if they have been well-educated, [competent] officials will be insufficient [in number]. When officials are insufficient, then the patterns of the Way will languish. When the patterns of the Way languish, there will be a yearning for the worthy and the wise. When there is a yearning for the worthy and the wise, the most crucial elements for governing the entire state will depend on the mind of a single person.

In ancient times, setting up the emperor and honoring him was not for the benefit of that single person. It is said, "If the world lacks a foremost object of honor, then patterns will lack what connects them to one another; the connection of these patterns is for the sake of the empire." So, the [position of] emperor was established in order to serve the empire; the empire was not established in order to serve the emperor. The [position of] lord was established in order to serve the state; the state was not established in order to serve the lord. The [position of] prime minister was established in order to serve the officials; the officials were not established in order to serve the prime minister.

Even if the law is not good, it is still better than having no law at all. Casting coins to divide property and drawing lots to apportion horses is not done because casting coins and drawing lots lead to equal distribution. Rather, they are methods that cause those who do well not to know toward whom to feel grateful and cause those who do badly not to know toward whom to feel resentful. These are the means by which resentment and expectation are blocked.

An enlightened ruler, when assigning tasks and offices, does so on the basis of discernment; when deciding punishments and distributing wealth, he does so on the basis of the law; when exercising potency and regulating what is within [his household], he does so on the basis of ritual. Therefore, desires will not lead to interference in the cycle of the seasons, affection will not lead to violations of the law, honors accorded will not go beyond protocol, salaries will not exceed rank, officials will not hold more than one post, and artisans will not pursue more than one craft. Use ability as the basis for awarding tasks. Use the tasks performed as the basis for awarding benefits. If things are done in this manner, then above there will not be an excess of rewards, and below there will not be an excess of wealth.

Section 2: Following

The Way of Heaven is such that if you "follow" then you will be great, while if you alter then you will be insignificant. To "follow" means to follow the dispositions of people. Among people, no one fails to act for himself. If you try to alter them and cause them to act for you, then there will be none whom you can secure and employ. Therefore, the former kings did not use as ministers those who would not accept a salary, and they did not take as partners in difficult endeavors those whose salary was not large. In circumstances where people are not able to act for themselves, those above will not get any use out of them. Therefore, if you make use of people who act for their own benefit rather than those who act for your benefit, then there are none whom you cannot secure and employ. This is what is called following [their dispositions].

Section 3: The People Are Mixed

. . . The wisdom of the lord is not necessarily the greatest among the people. If his wisdom is not the greatest and yet he wants to use his goodness to completely shelter those below, he will be incapable of succeeding. Even if we were to suppose that the lord's wisdom was the greatest, if as a single lord he were to completely provide for those below, then he would have to toil laboriously. If he were to toil laboriously, then he would be wearied. If wearied, then he would be enfeebled. If enfeebled, then he would again return to the Way of being incapable of taking care of [those below]. Therefore, if the lord takes on responsibility himself and personally carries out tasks, then his subjects will not pursue their affairs. This is to change the position of lord and minister and is called inversion and perversity. If there is inversion and perversity, then there will be chaos. If the lord of men delegates responsibility to his ministers and does not personally take on their tasks, then his ministers will all pursue their affairs. This is the proper arrangement between lord and minister, and the difference between order and chaos, and it is essential that this be examined.

Section 4: Understanding Loyalty

. . . Thus, that which caused Tyrant Jie's downfall is not something that the sage Yao could have survived, and yet Yao had unsurpassable goodness, while every bad action was attributed to Jie. So, [what really matters is whether one] secures or loses the right people. Hence, the timber for the imperial court does not all come from the branches of a single tree, and a white fur coat does not come from the pelt of a single fox. The conferring of order or disorder, security or danger, survival or destruction, glory or dishonor is not due to the strength of a single person.

Section 6: The Lord and His People

When the lord of the people abandons the law and relies on himself to govern, then punishments and rewards as well as firings and hirings will arise out of the lord's heart. If this is the case, then those who receive rewards, even if appropriate, will always expect more, and those who receive punishments, even if appropriate, will ceaselessly expect leniency. When the lord abandons the law and relies on his heart to make judgments about severity, then the same accomplishments will have different rewards while the same crimes will receive different punishments. It is from this that resentment arises. Thus, those who apportion horses draw lots, while those who apportion fields cast coins. It is not because coins or lots are wiser than men, but rather they are the means by which to get rid of private interests and block resentment. Therefore, it is said,

> Since a great lord employs the laws and does not personally act, affairs are decided by the law.

That which the law confers is such that each by means of its divisions receives his rewards and punishments and none expects [anything different] from his lord. Therefore, resentment does not arise and there is harmony between superior and subjects.

Section 7: The Lord and His Ministers

One who is lord of the people does not listen to the voices of many. He depends on the law and relies upon quantitative techniques in order to assess success and failure. As for words that are not in accordance with the law, he does not open his ears to them. As for labors that are not in accordance with the law, he does not reckon them as accomplishments. As for relatives who do not labor hard, he does not employ them in office. In regard to offices, he shows no preference to relatives. In regard to the law, he grants no favor to those he cares for. There is nothing done by those above or below that is not in accordance with the law.

Section 8: Fragments

68. Those who work to control water build up dikes and undo blockages. Even among the Yi and Mo, the methods are similar. [These methods] are learned from water; they are not learned from the sage Yu.

73. Therefore, milfoil and tortoiseshell divination are how decisions are recorded publicly. Balance weights and beams are how true weight is established publicly. Documents and contracts are how trust is established publicly. Standardized measurements are how length and volume are determined publicly. Laws, institutions, rituals, and documents are how norms are set up publicly. In all these cases, establishing public standards is the means by which private interests are eliminated.

75–77. Among the achievements of the law, none is greater than causing private interests to not be pursued. Among the achievements of the lord, none is greater than causing the people to not quarrel. Now, establishing the law and yet still pursuing private interests leads to conflict between the private and the law, and the chaos of this is greater than if there were no laws at all. Establishing a lord and yet still revering the worthies leads to conflict between worthies and lords, and the chaos of this is greater than if there were no lord at all. Therefore, in states that have the Way, when the law is established, then private goodness will not be pursued. When a lord is established, then worthies will not be revered. People are united under the lord and affairs are decided by the law—this is the great Way of the state.

78–79. Thus, if in ordering a state, one were to do away with its laws, then there would be chaos; if its laws were to be preserved and not modified, then it would decline; if it were to have its laws but allow private interests to manifest themselves, then this is called not abiding by the law. Those who are willing to exert themselves to serve the law are those of the hundred surnames. Those who are willing to lay down their lives in service of the law are the officials. Those who change the laws in accordance with the Way are the lords and chiefs.

82. If a rabbit runs through the streets, a hundred people will pursue it. This is not because a single rabbit is sufficient to be divided among a hundred people but rather because its allotment has not yet been determined. When allotments have not yet been determined, even Yao would exhaust his strength [to attain it], and even the more so for the masses. If piles of rabbits fill the market, and people pass by without turning their heads, it is not because they do not desire rabbits [but rather because] the allotment has already been decided. When allotment has already been decided,

then people, even if they are base, will not contend with one another. Therefore, governing all under Heaven and the state rests in making allotments and that is all.

102. When a balance weight and beam are employed, cheating with respect to weight is impossible. When rulers are employed, discrepancies with respect to length are impossible. When laws and standards are employed, swindling by deception and fraud is impossible.

103. When a craftsman completes a coffin, he does not dislike the fact that people die; where there is profit, odiousness is forgotten.

107. If one discards the Way and [its proper] techniques and gives up standards and measurements, seeking to understand all under Heaven through the understanding of one man, whose understanding could be sufficient for this?

120. If you are dealing with something weighing several tens of pounds and ask Yu if you are off by a fraction of an ounce, even he would not be able to tell. But if you suspend it by means of balance weight and beam, then you will not be off by so much as a hair. Thus, one does not need to rely upon the intelligence of a Yu. Rather, the intelligence of average people is sufficient to know this.

SELECTIVE BIBLIOGRAPHY

Translations

Harris, Eirik Lang. *The Shenzi Fragments: A Philosophical Analysis and Translation*. New York: Columbia University Press, 2016. (Includes a complete translation of the fragments. Attempts to situate the fragments in the historical milieu of the times as well as laying out the core tenets of Shen Dao's political philosophy.)

Secondary Works

Harris, Eirik Lang. "Developing Political Realism: Some Ideas from Classical China." In *Pluralizing Philosophy's Past—New Reflections in the History of Philosophy*, edited by Amber Griffioen and Marius Backmann. New York: Palgrave, forthcoming.

Rubin, Vitali. "Shen Tao and Fa-Chia." *Journal of the American Oriental Society* 94, no. 3 (1974): 337–46.

Thompson, P. M. *The "Shen Tzu" Fragments*. Oxford: Oxford University Press, 1979. (Primarily a textual analysis of the fragments attributed to Shen Dao, this text provides a wealth of historical information.)

Yang, Soon-ja. "Shen Dao's Own Voice in the *Shenzi* Fragments." *Dao: A Journal of Comparative Philosophy* 10, no. 2 (2011): 187–207.

CHAPTER EIGHT

ZHUANGZI

Introduction

Little is known of Zhuāngzǐ 莊子 beyond what we can gather from the book named after him. Much of the book, however, is unapologetically fictional, so the stories it tells about him provide us more insight into his persona than into the historical facts of his life. We know from external sources that his friend Huizi served in the court of King Hui of Liang (370–319 BCE), which places Zhuangzi at the end of the fourth century BCE. However, the version of the *Zhuangzi* we have was assembled around 300 CE, and although some passages seem to have been written by Zhuangzi, the book must initially have been compiled by his followers and then supplemented by later contributors and editors. The following selections are drawn primarily from the first seven chapters of the *Zhuangzi,* which scholars generally recognize as the earliest portions of the text and which may have been written by Zhuangzi himself.

Zhuangzi has a huge vocabulary, draws freely from history and mythology, and is equally at home writing poetry, logical analyses, dialogue, and narrative. His references to Kongzi, Laozi, and the Mohists demonstrate that he was familiar with their ideas, though the absence of quotations leaves uncertain whether he had access to the same texts we do. He debates Huizi in several passages, and the influence of the "School of Names" on his philosophy of language is clear.[1] Zhuangzi was a younger contemporary of Mengzi, and although he never mentions him by name, several passages seem to be implicit critiques of his views.

Zhuangzi does not present his ideas systematically or define his central terms. But he regularly speaks of Tiān 天, "Heaven," as the highest ideal for all things. He contrasts *Tian,* which could also be translated as "nature," to rén 人, "people" or "humanity." The human, for Zhuangzi, includes everything from concrete activities that interfere with nature, such as the

---

1. For more on Huizi (also known as Hui Shi) and "The School of Names," see chapter 5 in this volume.

mutilation of criminals, to abstract ideas, such as shì/fēi 是非, "right and wrong," that people project onto the world. Zhuangzi also speaks of Dào 道, "the Way," which encompasses both the Way the world is and the way for people to live in it. Though he believes there is a Way, he is skeptical of our ability to learn much about it through words or thinking. In fact, he attacks thinking in order to make room, instead, for experience and intuition. Sometimes his attacks are direct, with arguments illustrating the limitations of language, and sometimes indirect, with strange stories having no obvious moral or hero. Rather than delivering a message of its own, the *Zhuangzi* seems to go out of its way to defy understanding. In this sense, though the stories are often fantastic, the book is meant to offer a realistic lesson in the uselessness of trying to figure out life. Thinking and talking do have a place, though: Zhuangzi does a lot of both of them. The challenge is to harmonize thinking and talking with the other, incomprehensible aspects life.

In the Han dynasty, the historian Sima Qian classified Zhuangzi as a member of the Daoist school (along with Laozi), rather than as a Confucian or a Mohist. This is an oversimplification. There was no "Daoist school" in his time, and, as readers will soon see, he would have resisted any classification of this sort. He knew and thought a lot about the other philosophers presented in this book, particularly Kongzi. But his relationships to them were too complex to be summarized as simple agreement or disagreement. The influence of these other thinkers on Zhuangzi and the implications of his arguments for their ideas are complex and difficult questions that readers will have to sort out for themselves, with the help of some of the secondary literature that is listed following the translation.

Chapter One: Wandering Round and About

In the northern darkness there is a fish named Minnow. No one knows how many thousand *li* around he is. He changes into a bird named Breeze.[2] No one knows

---

2. The exact meaning of the bird's name is unclear, but it was pronounced similarly to the word for wind. For a photograph of a Chinese statue depicting Minnow turning into Breeze, see the Title Support Page for this volume at www.hackettpublishing.com/rccp-support.

how many thousand *li* across she is. She ruffles and flies, and her wings are like clouds hanging from Heaven. As the seas turn, she thinks to migrate to the southern darkness. The southern darkness is Heaven's pool.[3]

The *Tales of Qi*[4] records wonders. It says, "In her migration to the southern darkness, Breeze flaps along the water for three thousand *li*, spirals up on a whirlwind to ninety thousand *li*, and goes six months at a stretch."

Horse-shaped clouds, motes of dust, living things blowing breath at each other—is the blue-green of Heaven its proper color or just its being so endlessly far away? It looks just the same to her gazing down from above.

If water isn't deep, it can't support big boats. Spill a cup of water on the floor and crumbs will be its boats. But put the cup there and it will stick— because the water is too shallow and the boat too big. If wind isn't deep, it can't support big wings. This is why Breeze rises ninety thousand *li* with the wind there beneath her. Only then can she rest on the wind, carrying blue Heaven on her back, and nothing can stop her. Only then does she set her sights to the south.

The cicada and the student-dove laugh at her, saying, "When we start up and fly, we struggle for the elm or the sandalwood. Sometimes we don't even make it but just plunk to the ground. What is she doing rising ninety thousand *li* and heading south?" People going to the green meadows can bring three meals and return with their bellies still full. People going a hundred *li* need to grind grain for an overnight. People going a thousand *li* need to gather grain for three months. What do these two little bugs know?

Little knowledge does not measure up to big knowledge, or few years to many. How do I know this is so? The morning mushroom does not know the waxing and waning of the moon, and the Hui-cricket does not know spring and fall. This is because they are short-lived. South of Chu there is a turtle called Dark Genius, which counts five hundred years as a single spring and five hundred years as a single fall. In high antiquity there was a tree called Big Spring, which counted eight thousand years as a single spring and eight thousand years as a single fall. Nowadays, only eight-hundred-year-old Pengzu is famous, and everyone compares themselves to him. Isn't it sad?[5]

---

3. The word translated as "Heaven" also means both sky and Nature. See under *Important Terms* in the appendices.

4. We have no knowledge of this text and, judging from its name, it appears to be fictitious. Here and elsewhere, Zhuangzi may be parodying appeals to textual authority by appealing to fanciful "classics."

5. On Pengzu, see *Analects* 7.1 (in chapter 1 of this volume; see also the accompanying note).

This was the subject of King Tang's questions to his teacher, Cramped:[6]

> In the bald north there is a dark sea, Heaven's pool. There is a fish there whose breadth is several tens of thousands of *li*. No one knows his length. His name is Minnow. There is a bird there, whose name is Breeze. Her back is as huge as Mount Tai, and her wings are like clouds hanging from Heaven. Circling on the whirlwind, she spirals upward ninety thousand *li*, bursts through the clouds and mist, carrying the blue sky. Afterward she heads south, traveling to the southern darkness.

The accusing quail laughs at her, saying, "Where is *she* going? I rear up and don't go more than a few yards before coming down, soaring and roaming amid brambles and briars—this indeed is the perfection of flying! Where is she going?" This is the debate between little and big.

People who know how to do one job, handle a small town, or impress a ruler to get put in charge of a state see themselves like this. Songzi would still laugh at them. The whole world could praise him and he would not be encouraged. The whole world could condemn him and he would not be upset. He has fixed the difference between inner and outer and distinguished the limits of glory and disgrace. Yet he stops there. He is unconventional, but there is still something left unplanted.[7]

Liezi rides about on the wind. It's wonderful! He's gone two weeks at a time. His attitude toward wealth is unconventional. But, though he manages to avoid walking, he still relies on something.[8] If he could chariot the norms of Heaven and earth and ride the changes in the six mists[9] to wander the inexhaustible, then what would there be to rely on? Hence it is said that perfect people have no self, spiritual people have no accomplishment, and sagely people have no name.

The sage-king Yao offered his empire to the hermit Whence: "To keep the torches burning when the sun and moon are shining is troubling too much for light.

---

6. Tang's teacher is named "Jí 棘," which commentators explain means narrow, as opposed to "Tāng 湯," which means broad. *Liezi* chapter 5 is entitled "The Questions of Tang" and contains an expanded version of what might have been their conversation. For a translation, see A. C. Graham, trans., *The Book of Lieh-Tzu: A Classic of Tao* (London: John Murray, 1960; New York: Columbia University Press, 1990), 92–117. For more on King Tang, see Tang under *Important Figures* in the appendices.

7. For more on Songzi, see *Important Figures* in the appendices.

8. Little is known of Liezi. The book that bears his name (see above, note 6) contains scant biographical information. He may have been a practitioner of magic, or an ascetic who achieved freedom by withdrawing from the world. Either way, Zhuangzi's highly metaphoric criticism of him here suggests that he would have been better off accepting the world as it is.

9. "Mists," here and below, is qì 氣. See *Important Terms* in the appendices.

Irrigating the fields when the spring rains are falling is working too hard for water. You are here, my teacher, and the empire is in order. With me still presiding over it, I feel defective. Please take it."

Whence said, "With you ordering it, the empire is well-ordered. If I were to go ahead and replace you, would it be for the name? But name is only the guest of reality. Do I want to be the guest? The tailor bird nesting in the deep forest takes no more than a branch. The mole drinking at the river takes no more than a bellyful. Give it up, my lord. I have no use for the empire. Though the cook at the sacrifice fails to order the kitchen, the presiding priest does not leap over the goblets and platters to replace him."

Shoulder Dig said to Stepbrother,[10] "I heard what Jie Yu said.[11] It was big but didn't stand for anything. It went on and on without coming back. I was frightened by what he said. It was as endless as the Milky Way, full of inconsistencies, and didn't approach the human situation."

Stepbrother asked, "What did he say?"

"He said there are spiritual people living in the distant Maiden Mountains. Their skin is like frost, and they are gentle and restrained as virgins. They don't eat the five grains but sip wind and drink dew. They chariot the cloudy mists, ride the flying dragons, and wander beyond the Four Seas. By concentrating their spirit, they keep things from harm and ripen the harvests. I thought he was crazy and didn't believe him."

Stepbrother said, "Yes. The blind can't appreciate beautiful patterns or the deaf bells and drums. But are blindness and deafness confined to the physical form? Your knowledge has them, too. His talk is like a fertile woman.[12] Those people he describes, with that Virtue of theirs, will align with the ten thousand things and make them one. The world longs for chaos, but why should they fret and make the world their business? Nothing can harm these people. Though a great flood should knock against Heaven, they would not drown. Though a heat wave should melt stone and scorch the earth, they would not burn. From their dust and chaff you could mold the sages Yao and Shun. Why would they want to make things their

---

10. This character's name, Lian Shu, may also suggest a connection to the Shu clan, one of the Three Families that ruled Kongzi's native state of Lu for most of his lifetime.

11. In *Analects* 18.5 (not in this volume), Jie Yu, known as The Madman of Chu, criticizes Kongzi for wasting his efforts on a lost cause. When Kongzi tries to speak with him, he runs away.

12. Jie Yu's words are "like a fertile woman" in the sense that they await the right kind of person in order to bear offspring (that is, to be understood).

business? A man of Song[13] invested in ceremonial caps and took them to Yue. But the Yue people cut their hair and tattoo their bodies and had no use for them. Yao brought order to the people of the empire and stabilized the government within the seas. But when he went to see the four masters of the distant Maiden Mountains, north of the Fen River, he lost the world in a daze."[14]

Huizi said to Zhuangzi, "The king of Wei[15] left me the seeds of a big gourd. I planted them, and when they grew, the fruit was a yard across. I filled them with water but they weren't sturdy enough to hold it. I split them into ladles but they were too big to dip into anything. It wasn't that they weren't wonderfully big, but they were useless. So, I smashed them."[16]

Zhuangzi said, "You, sir, are certainly clumsy about using big things. There were some people in Song who were good at making ointment to prevent chapped hands. Year after year, they used it in their business bleaching silk. A traveler heard about it and asked to buy the formula for a hundred pieces of gold. The clan assembled and consulted, saying, 'For years we've bleached silk and never made more than a few pieces of gold. Today in a single morning we can sell the trick for a hundred pieces. Let's give it to him!'

"The traveler got it and recommended it to the king of Wu, who was having trouble with the state of Yue. The king of Wu put him in command, and that winter he met the men of Yue in a naval battle. Using the ointment to keep his soldiers' hands from chapping, he defeated Yue badly and was rewarded with a portion of the conquered territory. The ability to prevent chapped hands was the same in either case. But one gained territory while the others never escaped bleaching silk because what they used it for was different.[17] Now you had these gigantic gourds.

---

13. The people of Song were the butt of many jokes. Cf. *Mengzi* 2A2 (in chapter 4 of this volume) and *Han Feizi* chapter 49 (in chapter 10 of this volume).

14. Earlier in Chinese history, the Fen River had been the northwestern border separating the Chinese from the non-Chinese world (i.e., the "barbarians"). By Zhuangzi's time, however, military expansion and cultural assimilation had moved the boundary back, so the Fen was closer to the center.

15. Wei is another name for the state of Liang. Hence this is King Hui of Liang, the same ruler who employed Huizi in his administration. For more about Huizi (or Hui Shi), see chapter 5 of this volume.

16. It is clear from the beginning of the next anecdote that Huizi's story here is meant as a criticism of Zhuangzi.

17. Wu and Yue were two non-Chinese states to the south that were gradually incorporated into the Chinese world during the Spring and Autumn and Warring States periods. (See *Important Periods* in the appendices.) When hostilities broke out between them in 510 BCE, Wu dominated initially, which was presumably when Zhuangzi's story was meant to take place. Yue rallied its forces, however, and destroyed Wu in 473 BCE, which probably meant execution for the traveler or his descendants. The history of Wu, which would have been familiar to Zhuangzi's contemporary readers, makes the moral of the parable uncertain.

Why not lash them together like big buoys and go floating on the rivers and lakes instead of worrying that they were too big to dip into anything? Your heart is full of underbrush, my friend."[18]

Huizi said to Zhuangzi, "I have a big tree, the kind people call Spring. Its trunk is so gnarled it won't take a chalk line, and its branches are so twisted they won't fit a compass or square. It stands by the road but no builder looks twice at it. Your talk is similarly big and useless, and everyone alike rejects it."

Zhuangzi said, "Haven't you seen a weasel? It bends down then rises up. It springs east and west, not worrying about heights or depths—and lands in a snare or dies in a net. Now the yak is so big he looks like clouds hanging from Heaven. He sure can be big, but he can't catch mice. You have a big tree and are upset that you can't use it. Why not plant it by a nothing-at-all village in a wide empty waste? You could do nothing, dilly-dallying by its side, or nap, ho-hum, beneath it. It won't fall to any axe's chop and nothing will harm it. Since it isn't any use, what bad can happen to it?"

Chapter Two: On Equalizing Things

Master Dapple of the South Wall sat leaning on his armrest. He looked up and sighed, vacant, as though he'd lost his counterpart. Yancheng Ziyou[19] stood before him in attendance. "What's this?" he said. "Can the body really be turned into dried wood? Can the heart really be turned into dead ashes? The one leaning on the armrest now is not the one who leaned on it before!"

Master Dapple said, "My, isn't that a good question you've asked, Ziyou! Just now I lost myself. Do you know? You've heard the pipes of people, but not the pipes of earth. Or if you've heard the pipes of earth, you haven't heard the pipes of Heaven."

"May I ask what you mean?"

"The Big Lump belches breath and it's called wind. If only it wouldn't start! When it starts, the ten thousand holes begin to hiss. Don't you hear the *shsh-shsh*? In the mountain vales there are great trees a hundred spans around with knots

---

18. Xīn 心 can be translated as either "heart" or "mind," though the latter is usually more appropriate for Zhuangzi. The description of Huizi's mind as full of underbrush may be a reference to Mengzi's metaphor of moral sprouts (see, for example, *Mengzi* 2A6 and 6A6 in chapter 4 of this volume). See also *xin* under *Important Terms* in the appendices. See notes 36, 39, 49, and 70, below, regarding other possible implicit references to Mengzi

19. This is evidently Kongzi's disciple, Ziyou, who is described in *Analects* 17.4 (not in this volume) as using music to instruct people in the Way.

like noses, like mouths, like ears, like sockets, like rings, like mortars, like ditches, like gullies. Gurgling, humming, hooting, whistling, shouting, shrieking, moaning, gnashing! The leaders sing 'Eeeeeeh!' The followers sing 'Ooooooh!' In a light breeze it's a little chorus, but in a gusty wind it's a huge orchestra. And when the violent winds are over, the ten thousand holes are empty. Haven't you witnessed the brouhaha?"

Ziyou said, "So the pipes of earth are those holes, and the pipes of people are bamboo flutes. May I ask about the pipes of Heaven?"

Master Dapple said, "Blowing the ten thousand differences, making each be itself and all choose themselves—who provokes it? Does Heaven turn? Does earth stay still? Do the sun and moon vie for position? Who is in charge here? Who pulls the strings? Who sits with nothing to do, gives it a push and sets it in motion? Do you think it's locked in motion and can't be stopped? Or do you think it's spinning out of control and can't slow itself down? Do the clouds make the rain? Or does the rain make the clouds? Who rumbles all this out? Who sits there with nothing to do and takes perverse delight in egging it on? The wind rises in the north—now west, now east, now dilly-dallying up above. Who huffs and puffs it? Who sits with nothing to do and blows it? May I ask the cause?"[20]

> Big knowledge is boundless,[21]
> little knowledge is unbound.
> Big talk is unstoppable,
> little talk doesn't stop.
> In sound sleep, spirits mingle,
> on waking, bodies open out.
> They greet and grapple,
> and use their hearts all day to struggle.

The humble ones, the high ones, the hidden ones: the little fears panic, the big fears calm.

> They fly like an arrow from a bow

---

20. I follow Graham in importing the final lines of this passage, from "Does Heaven turn?" to the end, from a later chapter.

21. This next section seems to be a mixture of verse and self-commentary. The Chinese words for "boundless" and "unbound" sound similar; the difference in their meanings is a matter of dispute among commentators, and the argument equivocates on whether big is supposed to be better than little. Zhuangzi is perhaps intentionally trying to produce this confusion in his readers. (Zhuangzi frequently uses the rhetorical device of rhyming reduplicatives. Some studies suggest that it is a translinguistic phenomenon that such phrases, like "flim-flam" and "ooga-booga," convey a mixture of confusion and mystery.)

That's the way they guard their rights and wrongs.

They stick like they'd sworn an oath.

That's the way they hold to victory.

They die like fall and winter.

That describes their daily deterioration. They drown; and what makes it happen can't bring them back.

They're sated as though sealed.

That describes their stagnation. As the heart nears death, nothing can bring it back to vitality.

> Happiness, anger, despair, joy,
> planning, sighing, bending, freezing,
> elegance, ease, candor, posturing—
> They are music out of emptiness,
> mist condensing into mushrooms!

Day and night they alternate in front of us without our knowing where they sprout. Enough! Enough! Morning and evening we've got them, wherever they come from.

> Without them there would not be me,
> without me there would be nothing to choose.

This is close. But no one knows what makes it like this. It seems as though there is a true master, but you can't get a glimpse of it. In our actions we take the self on faith, but we can't see its form. There is essence but no form.[22]

The hundred bones, the nine orifices, the six organs all exist together. Which do I think of as closest to me? Do you like them all? Or do you have a favorite? If so, are the rest its servants and concubines? Can't servants and concubines rule among themselves? Can they take turns being lord and servant? But if there is a true lord among them, whether I find its essence or not makes no difference to its truth.

Once you take a complete form, you don't forget it until the end. Clashing with things and rubbing against them, the race is run at a gallop and nothing can stop it. Isn't it sad? Your whole life slaving away and never seeing the completion of your labors. Exhausted, you drudge and slave away without knowing where to turn for rest. Can you not mourn? People say they are not dead, but what difference does it make? Your form changes and your heart goes with it. Can you tell me that's not

---

22. On "essence" (qíng 情), see below, note 65, and *Important Terms* in the appendices.

mournful? Is everyone's life really this confused? Or am I the only one confused and not other people?

If a made-up heart counts as a teacher, then who doesn't have a teacher? Why should it just be the self-chosen experts on the order of things who have them? Stupid people would have them, too. But to have right and wrong before you've made up your heart—that's like leaving for Yue today and getting there yesterday![23] That's like saying what isn't is. What isn't is? Even the spiritual sage Yu couldn't make sense of that. How could I?

Saying is not just blowing. Saying says something. But if what it says is not fixed, then does it really say anything? Or does it say nothing? We think it is different from the peeping of fledglings. But is there really any difference or isn't there? How is the Way obscured that there are true and false? How are words obscured that there are "right" (shì 是) and "wrong" (fēi 非)? Where can you go that the Way does not exist? How can words exist and not be okay? The Way is obscured by small completions.[24] Words are obscured by glory and show. So, we have the rights and wrongs of the Confucians and the Mohists. Each calls right what the other calls wrong and each calls wrong what the other calls right. But if you want to right their wrongs and wrong their rights, it's better to throw them open to the light.

> There is nothing that cannot be looked at that way.
> There is nothing that cannot be looked at this way.
> But that is not the way I see things;
> Only as I know things myself do I know them.

Hence it is said, "'That' (bǐ 彼) comes from 'this' (shì 是) and this follows from that."[25] This is the doctrine of the parallel birth of "this" and "that." Even so, born together they die together. Dying together they are born together. If they are both okay, they are both not okay. If they are both not okay, they are both okay. If they are right in a way, they are wrong in a way. If they are wrong in a way, they are right in a way. For this reason, the sage does not follow this route but illuminates things with

---

23. This is a reference to one of the paradoxes of Huizi (see chapter 5 in this volume).

24. The phrase translated as "small completions" or "small accomplishments" also referred to small groupings of instruments in contrast to a complete orchestra. People lose sight of the whole because of their attention to a part.

25. In this section, Zhuangzi exploits a pun in Classical Chinese, where shì 是 can be a pronoun, "this" (contrasted with "that," bǐ 彼) or a verb, meaning "is right" (contrasted with "is wrong," fēi 非). Zhuangzi is suggesting that just as whether something is "this" or "that" depends upon your perspective, so it depends upon one's perspective whether something is "right" or "wrong."

Heaven's light.[26] He just goes along with things. What is this is also that, and what is that is also this. That is both right and wrong. This is also both right and wrong. So, is there really a this and a that? Or isn't there any this or that? The place where neither this nor that finds its counterpart is called the pivot of the Way. Once the pivot finds its socket it can respond endlessly. What's right is endless. And what's wrong is endless, too. This is why I say it's better to throw them open to the light.

Making a point to show that a point is not a point is not as good as making a nonpoint to show that a point is not a point. Using a horse to show that a horse is not a horse is not as good as using a nonhorse to show that a horse is not a horse.[27] Heaven and earth are one point, the ten thousand things are one horse.

Okay? Okay. Not okay? Not okay. A way is made by walking it. A thing is so by calling it. How is it so? In so-ing it, it is so. How is it not so? In not-so-ing it, it is not so. There is always a way in which things are so. There is always a way in which things are okay. There is nothing that is not so, nothing that is not okay. You can insist that it is a twig or a pillar, a freak or the beautiful Xi Shi.[28] No matter how diverse or strange, the Way comprehends them as one. Their division is their completion and their completion is their ruin. But nothing is completed or injured when they are again comprehended as one. Only the penetrating person knows to comprehend them as one. Don't insist but lodge in the usual. The usual is useful. You can use it to penetrate. When you penetrate, you get it. Get it and you're almost there. Just go along with things. Doing that without knowing how things are is what I call the Way.

But exhausting the spirit trying to illuminate the unity of things without knowing that they are all the same is called "three in the morning." What do I mean by "three in the morning"? When the monkey trainer was passing out nuts, he said, "You get three in the morning and four at night." The monkeys were all angry. "All right," he said, "you get four in the morning and three at night." The monkeys were all pleased. With no loss in name or substance, he made use of their joy and anger because he went along with them. So, the sage harmonizes people with right and wrong and rests them on Heaven's wheel. This is called walking two roads.

---

26. Translating the word for "Heaven" as "nature," this line could be read "lets them shine by their natural light."

27. A reference to the "School of Names" thinker Gongsun Longzi. See "On the White Horse" (in chapter 5 of this volume).

28. Xi Shi was a legendary beauty sent by the king of Yue to marry the king of Wu, spy on him, and help overthrow his kingdom.

In olden days, people's knowledge got somewhere. Where did it get? There were those who thought there had never been anything. Perfect! Done! There was nothing to add. Next were those who thought there were things but never any boundaries. Next were those who thought there were boundaries but never any right or wrong. The Way is lost in the glorification of right and wrong. The Way is lost in the completion of love. But are there such things as loss and completion? Or are there no such things as loss and completion? Loss and completion—that's Master Bright Works playing his lute. No loss and no completion—that's Master Bright Works not playing his lute. Bright Works playing his lute, Shi Kuang holding his baton, Huizi leaning on his desk: the knowledge of these three masters was almost perfect, and they passed their successes on to later years.[29] What they liked they tried to set apart from other things. What they liked they tried to illuminate. But they only succeeded in illuminating the other things and so ended in the gloom of "hard and white."[30] Their followers ended up tangled in the string of works and were incomplete their whole lives. If this counts as completion, then we are all complete, too. If this doesn't count as completion, then none of us have ever been complete. So, the torch of slippery doubt is what the sage steers by. Don't insist, but lodge in the usual: this is what I mean by throwing things open to the light.

Now suppose I say something here. I don't know whether it fits into your category or not. But in terms of the category that includes both things that fit and things that don't, it's no different from anything else. Nonetheless, let me try saying it:

> There is a beginning. There is a not-yet beginning to be a beginning. There is a not-yet beginning to be a not-yet beginning to be a beginning.

> There is something. There is nothing. There is a not-yet beginning to be nothing. There is a not-yet beginning to be a not-yet beginning to be nothing. Suddenly there is nothing. But then I don't know whether nothing is or isn't.

Now I've said something, but I don't know if what I've said meant anything or not.

> Nothing in the world is bigger than the tip of an autumn hair[31] but Mount Tai is small. No one lives longer than a dead child and Pengzu died young. Heaven and earth were born alongside me, and the ten thousand things and I are one.

---

29. On Shi Kuang, see *Important Figures* in the appendices and *Mengzi* 6A7 (in chapter 4 of this volume).

30. "Hard and white" is a stock example from the ancient Chinese philosophy of language. Zhuangzi is using it as synecdoche for all subtle rational arguments. (See also the selections from the "School of Names" in chapter 5 of this volume.)

31. An animal's hair is finest (and hence thinnest) during the autumn.

If we're already one, can I say it? But since I've just said we're one, can I not say it? The unity and my saying it make two. The two and their unity make three. Starting from here, even a clever mathematician couldn't get it, much less an ordinary person! If going from nothing to something you get three, what about going from something to something? Don't do it! Just go along with things.

The Way has never been bounded; words have never been constant. Insist on it and there are boundary-paths. Let me describe these paths. There is left. There is right. There are relations. There is righteousness. There are divisions. There are debates. There is competition. There is contention. These are called the eight Virtues. The sage acknowledges what is beyond the six dimensions but does not discuss it. He discusses what is within the six dimensions but does not deliberate on it. He deliberates on the springs and autumns of successive generations and the records of former kings but does not debate about them. Divisions have something they do not divide. Debates have something they do not debate. "What?" you ask. The sage clasps it to his bosom while ordinary people debate to show it off. Hence it is said, "Debate leaves something undiscriminated."

> The great Way is not announced.
> The great debate is not spoken.
> Great benevolence is not benevolent.
> Great modesty is not reserved.
> Great courage is not aggressive.
> A way that shines does not lead.
> Words in debate do not reach.
> Benevolence that is constant is not complete.
> Modesty that is pure is not trustworthy.
> Courage that is aggressive is not complete.

These five are round but almost square. Therefore, knowledge that stops at what it does not know is perfect. Who knows the unspoken distinction, the unled Way? If you could know it, it would be called the store of Heaven. Pour into it and it does not fill up, draw from it and it does not run dry. Not knowing where it comes from, it is called the shaded glow. Once Yao said to Shun, "I want to attack Zong, Guai, and Xu-ao. I sit on my throne and it bothers me. Why is this?"[32]

---

32. Three backward states that resisted Yao's authority. To see why this bothered him, consider *Analects* 2.1 and 12.19 (in chapter 1 of this volume).

Shun said, "These three small states still dwell among the underbrush. Why are you bothered? Once ten suns came out together and the ten thousand things were all illuminated. Shouldn't Virtue be better than ten suns?"[33]

Gaptooth asked Royal Relativity,[34] "Do you know what all things agree upon as right?"

Royal Relativity said, "How could I know that?"

"Do you know that you don't know it?"

"How could I know that?"

"Doesn't anyone know anything?!"

"How could I know that? But even so, suppose I tried saying something. How could I possibly know that when I say I know something, I don't not know it? How could I possibly know that when I say I don't know something, I don't know it?[35] Let me try asking you something. If people sleep in the damp, their backs hurt and they wake half-paralyzed. But is this true of an eel? If they live in trees they shudder with fear. But is this true of a monkey? Of these three, then, which knows the right place to live? People eat the flesh of cattle, deer eat fodder, maggots like snakes, and hawks enjoy mice. Of these four, which knows the right taste? Monkeys take baboons as partners, deer befriend elk, and eels consort with fish. People say that Maoqiang and Lady Li are beautiful. But if fish saw them, they would dive deep; if birds saw them, they would fly high; if deer saw them, they would cut and run. Of these four, which knows beauty rightly? From where I see it, the sprouts of benevolence and righteousness and the pathways of right and wrong are all snarled and jumbled.[36] How would I know the difference between them?"

Gaptooth said, "If you don't know gain from loss, do perfected people know?"[37]

---

33. The *Huáinánzǐ* 淮南子, a text that was compiled from a set of scholarly debates held at the court of Liú Ān 劉安, Prince of Huainan, sometime before 139 BCE, tells us that the ten suns were too bright, so nine had to be shot down by the archer Yi. Shun's point is that, rather than insist on enlightening these backward states himself, the Virtuous path would be to allow them to find their own way naturally. He is advocating "the shaded glow," "illuminating things with Heaven's light" rather than one's own.

34. The second character in this name, Ni, means end or extreme. Elsewhere, in a portion of the text not translated here, Zhuangzi argues that extremes are extreme only relative to one another: the small is small only in comparison to the large, etc., hence the current translation. Later on, Zhuangzi will speak of "harmonizing things by means of Heaven's relativity," that is, taking advantage of their sameness in difference, like the monkey trainer.

35. Cf. *Analects* 2.17 (in chapter 1 of this volume).

36. The phrase "sprouts of benevolence and righteousness" (rén yì zhī duān 仁義之端) may be a reference to *Mengzi* 2A6 (in chapter 4 of this volume).

37. "Gain" (lì 利) and "loss" (hài 害) are important terms for Mozi—who thinks of them as "benefit" and "harm," respectively—and Mengzi, who contrasts lì, in the sense of "profit," with yì 義, "righteousness."

Royal Relativity said, "Perfected people are spiritual. Though the lowlands burn, they are not hot. Though the He and the Han rivers freeze, they are not cold. When furious lightning splits the mountains and winds thrash the sea, they are not scared. People like this mount the clouds and mists, straddle the sun and moon, and roam beyond the Four Seas. Death and life make no difference to them, how much less the sprouts of benefit and harm!"

Master Nervous Magpie asked Master Long Desk, "I heard from my teacher, Kongzi, that the sage does not make it his business to attend to affairs. He does not seek gain or avoid loss. He does not enjoy being sought out and does not follow any Way. Saying nothing he says something, saying something he says nothing, and he wanders outside the floating dust. My teacher thought this was wild talk, but I thought it captured the mysterious Way. What do you think about it?"

Master Long Desk said, "This would make Huang Di's ears ring. How could Kongzi understand it? But you're getting ahead of yourself. You see an egg and listen for the rooster's crow. You see a crossbow and expect roast owl. I'm going to try saying some crazy things to you, and you listen crazily—how about it? Flank the sun and moon, embrace space and time, and meet like lips, settling in the slippery murk where servants exalt each other. Ordinary people slave away, while the sage is stupid and simple, participating in ten thousand ages and unifying them in complete simplicity. The ten thousand things are as they are, and so are jumbled together.

"How do I know that loving life is not a mistake? How do I know that hating death is not like a lost child forgetting its way home? Lady Li was the daughter of the border guard of Ai. When the duke of Jin got her, her tears fell until they soaked her collar. But once she reached the royal palace, slept in the king's bed, and ate the meats of his table, she regretted her tears. How do I know that the dead don't regret that they ever longed for life?[38]

"One who dreams of drinking wine may weep in the morning. One who dreams of weeping may go for a hunt the next day. In the dream, you don't know it's a dream. In the middle of a dream, you may interpret a dream within it. Only after waking do you know it was a dream. Still, there may be an even greater awakening after which you know that this, too, was just a greater dream. But the stupid ones think they are awake and confidently claim to know it. Are they rulers? Are they herdsmen? Really?! Kongzi and you are both dreaming. And in

---

38. Lady Li, a legendary beauty and villain, was born a member of the non-Chinese Rong people living to the north and west of China. She was given as a hostage to Duke Xian of Jin (r. 676–651 BCE), became his concubine, estranged him from his wife and legitimate heirs, and wreaked havoc in the kingdom. She is an ambiguous figure: a barbarian in China, beautiful yet dangerous. Zhuangzi compounds the ambiguity by retelling the story from her perspective.

saying you are dreaming, I am dreaming, too. These words might be called a puzzle. But if after ten thousand generations we encounter a single sage who knows the solution, it would be no different from what we encounter every morning and evening."

Once you and I have started arguing, if you win and I lose, then are you really right and am I really wrong? If I win and you lose, then am I really right and are you really wrong? Is one of us right and the other one wrong? Or are both of us right and both of us wrong? If you and I can't understand one another, then other people will certainly be even more in the dark. Whom shall we get to set us right? Shall we get someone who agrees with you to set us right? But if they already agree with you, how can they set us right? Shall we get someone who agrees with me to set us right? But if they already agree with me, how can they set us right? Shall we get someone who disagrees with both of us to set us right? But if they already disagree with both of us, how can they set us right? Shall we get someone who agrees with both of us to set us right? But if they already agree with both of us, how can they set us right? If you and I and they all can't understand each other, should we wait for someone else?

Shifting voices waiting on one another may just as well not wait on one another. Harmonize them by means of Heaven's relativity, orient them with the flowing flood, and so live out your years. Forget the years, forget righteousness, but be stirred by the limitless and lodge within it. What do I mean by "harmonize them by means of Heaven's relativity"? I mean right is not right, so is not so. If right were really right, it would be so different from not-right that there would be no room for argument. If so were really so, then it would be so different from not-so that there would be no room for argument.

Penumbra said to Shadow, "First you walk and then you stop. First you sit and then you rise. Why are you so restless?"

Shadow said, "Do I depend on something to be the way I am? Does what I depend on also depend on something to be the way it is? Does a snake depend on its scales to move or a cicada on its wings to fly? How should I know why I am this way? How should I know why I'm not otherwise?"

One night, Zhuangzi dreamed of being a butterfly—a happy butterfly, showing off and doing as he pleased, unaware of being Zhuangzi. Suddenly he awoke, drowsily, Zhuangzi again. And he could not tell whether it was Zhuangzi who had dreamed the butterfly or the butterfly dreaming Zhuangzi. But there must be some difference between them! This is called "the transformation of things."

Chapter Three: The Key to Nourishing Life

Life is bounded. Knowledge is unbounded. Using the bounded to follow the unbounded is dangerous. And if you take that as knowledge, that's really dangerous! If you do good, avoid fame. If you do bad, avoid punishment. Follow the middle line and you can protect yourself, complete your life, raise your family, and finish your years.

A butcher was cutting up an ox for Lord Wenhui.[39] Wherever his hand touched, wherever his shoulder leaned, wherever his foot stepped, wherever his knee pushed—with a zip! with a whoosh!—he handled his chopper with aplomb, and never skipped a beat. He moved in time to the *Dance of the Mulberry Forest*, and harmonized with the *Head of the Line Symphony*.[40] Lord Wenhui said, "Ah, excellent, that technique can reach such heights!"

The butcher sheathed his chopper and responded, "What your servant values is the Way, which goes beyond technique. When I first began cutting up oxen, I did not see anything but oxen. Three years later, I couldn't see the whole ox. And now, I encounter them with spirit and don't look with my eyes. Sensible knowledge stops and spiritual desires proceed. I rely on the Heavenly patterns, strike in the big gaps, am guided by the large fissures, and follow what is inherently so. I never touch a ligament or tendon, much less do any heavy wrenching! A good butcher changes his chopper every year because he chips it. An average butcher changes it every month because he breaks it. There are spaces between those joints, and the edge of the blade has no thickness. If you use what has no thickness to go where there is space—oh! there's plenty of extra room to play about in. That's why after nineteen years[41] the blade of my chopper is still as though fresh from the grindstone.

---

39. This is the same King Hui who gave Huizi the seeds to the giant gourds in *Zhuangzi* chapter 1, above, and who speaks with Mengzi in *Mengzi* 1A1 and 1A3 (in chapter 4 of this volume). This story may be a parody of *Mengzi* 1A7 (also in chapter 4 of this volume), in which Mengzi praises King Xuan of Qi for showing compassion by sparing an ox being led to slaughter, and asserts that "gentlemen keep their distance from the kitchen." In contrast, in Zhuangzi's story, a ruler learns an important lesson precisely by going into the kitchen and watching someone butcher an ox.

40. The *Dance of the Mulberry Forest* celebrates Tang's victory over Jie and the founding of the Shang dynasty. The *Head of the Line Symphony* is part of a larger corpus known as the *Whole Pond Music* commemorating the reign of Yao. The spontaneous harmony of the butcher's movements with traditional music may suggest the inner compatibility of Zhuangzi's Daoism with Confucianism. Cf. *Mengzi* 4A27 (in chapter 4 of this volume).

41. For the significance of this period of time, see note 61 on *Mozi* chapter 31 (in chapter 2 of this volume).

"Still, when I get to a hard place, I see the difficulty and take breathless care. My gaze settles! My movements slow! I move the chopper slightly, and in a twinkling it's come apart, crumbling to the ground like a clod of earth! I stand holding my chopper and glance all around, dwelling on my accomplishment. Then I clean my chopper and put it away."

Lord Wenhui said, "Excellent! I have heard the words of a butcher and learned how to care for life!"

Gongwen Xuan[42] was startled when he saw the Commander of the Right,[43] and he asked, "What kind of man is this? What happened to you? Was it Heaven, or was it human?"

The Commander said, "It was Heaven, not human. Heaven makes each thing unique.[44] People try to look alike. That's how I know it was Heaven, not human. The marsh pheasant has to go ten steps for a peck, a hundred steps for a drink. But it doesn't want to be pampered in a cage. It does the spirit no good even to be king."

When Laozi died, Qin Shi[45] went to mourn him, cried three times, and left. A student asked, "Weren't you our teacher's friend?"

"Yes."

"Then is it okay for you to mourn him this way?"

"Yes. At first, I thought these were his people, but now I see they are not. When I went in earlier, there were old ones crying as though for a child, and young ones as though for their mothers. The one who gathered them here did not want them to talk, but they talk. He did not want them to cry, but they cry. They've run from Heaven, denied their essence, forgotten what they received, and hence suffer what used to be called 'the punishment for running from Heaven.'[46] Our teacher came because it was time and left when the time had passed. If you are content with the time and abide by the passing, there's no room for sorrow or joy. This is what they

---

42. Nothing is known about this person, though the name does not appear to be fictional.

43. The Commander of the Right indicates the supreme military commander.

44. The word for "unique" can also mean "one-footed," so the suggestion is that the Commander is missing a foot. Gongwen's question asks whether he was born that way or lost it later. Amputations, tattoos, and death were common punishments not just for crimes but for bad political advice, and even for good advice that the ruler did not want to hear, and hence were considered indicative of moral as well as physical deformity. Zhuangzi's stories of criminals, the disabled, and outcasts, therefore, address the same theme as the abstract discussions of perfection, completion, and wholeness.

45. Nothing is known about this person, though the name does not appear to be fictional.

46. Cf. *Analects* 3.13 (not in this volume): "When you commit a crime against Heaven, there is nowhere you can turn."

used to call 'the divine release.' You can point to the exhausted fuel. But the flame has passed on, and no one knows where it will end."

Chapter Four: The Human Realm

Yan Hui asked Kongzi for permission to make a trip.[47]

"Where are you going?" he said.

"To Wei."

"What will you do there?"

"I have heard that the lord of Wei is young and willful. He trifles with his state and does not acknowledge his mistakes. He is so careless with people's lives that the dead fill the state like falling leaves in a swamp.[48] The people have nowhere to turn. I have heard my teacher say, 'Leave the well-governed state and go to the chaotic one. There are plenty of sick people at the doctor's door.' I want to use what I have learned to think of a way the state may be saved."

Kongzi said, "Sheesh! You're just going to get yourself hurt. The Way does not like complexity. Complexity quickly becomes too much. Too much leads to agitation, agitation leads to worry, and worry never solved anything. The perfect people of olden times first found it in themselves before looking for it in others. If what you've found in yourself isn't settled yet, what leisure can you spare for this bully's behavior?

"Do you know how Virtue is squandered and where knowledge comes from? Virtue is squandered in fame, and knowledge arises from struggle. People use fame to trample each other and knowledge as a weapon. Both of them are tools of ill-fortune, not the means of finishing your mission.

"Though your Virtue is deep and your faith strong, you have not comprehended the man's *qi*. You've got a reputation for not being contentious, but you have not comprehended the man's heart. If you insist on parading standards of benevolence and righteousness before this bully, you will just make him look bad in comparison to you. That's antagonism, and one who antagonizes others is sure to be antagonized in return. You don't want to antagonize him!

"Or suppose he likes worthy people and dislikes the depraved, then what use is there in changing him? Better not to speak! Kings and dukes love to dominate people and force their submission. He'll want to dazzle you, intimidate you,

---

47. Yan Hui, also known as Yan Yuan, was Kongzi's favorite and most promising student; he died young. See *Analects* 5.9, 6.3, 6.7, 6.11, and 12.1 (in chapter 1 of this volume). However, this dialogue is not supposed to be historically accurate. "Kongzi" is here being used as a spokesperson for anti-Confucian views.

48. This is probably Duke Chu, who first ruled in Wei from 492 to 481 BCE.

tongue-tie you, cue you, and persuade you. Trying to reform this kind of person is like piling fire on fire or water on water. It's called 'adding to the excessive.' Your initial compliance will know no end until he no longer trusts your good word. You will surely die at this bully's hands. . . . Even so, you must have a plan. Come, tell me about it!"

Yan Hui said, "Suppose I am upright but dispassionate, energetic but not divisive. Would that work?"

"No! How could that work?" said Kongzi. "You'd use all your energy to sustain the performance, and your face would be unsettled. Other people can't stand that, so they have to resist what you suggest in order to ease their own hearts. If gradual Virtue wouldn't work, how much less such a great show of force! He'll dig in his heels and resist change. Though he may seem well disposed on the outside, on the inside he'll never consider it. How could that work?"

Yan Hui said, "Then how about being inwardly straight and outwardly bending, having integrity but conforming to my superiors? By being inwardly straight, I could follow Heaven. As a follower of Heaven, I would know that even the Son of Heaven and I are both children of Heaven. If I speak only for myself, why worry about the approval or disapproval of other people? I could be what people call childlike, which is what I mean by being a follower of Heaven.

"By being outwardly bending, I could follow other people. Lifting the ceremonial tablets, kneeling, bending, bowing—this is the etiquette of a minister. Others do it, why shouldn't I? As long as I do what other people do, who can complain? This is what I mean by following people.

"Having integrity and conforming to superiors, one follows olden times. My words, whether they are in fact instructions or even criticisms, belong to antiquity; they are not my own. This way one can be straightforward without causing injury. This is what I mean by following olden times. Would that work?"

Kongzi said, "No! How could that work? You have too many policies. You are planning without reconnaissance. Even if you succeeded in avoiding blame, it would stop there. How could you hope to change him? You're still making the heart your teacher."

Yan Hui said, "I have nothing else to offer. May I ask what to do?"

Kongzi said, "You must fast! Let me explain. Is it easy to do anything with your heart? If you think it is, bright Heaven will not approve."

Yan Hui said, "My family is poor. Indeed, I have not drunk wine or eaten any meat for months. Can this be considered fasting?"

Kongzi said, "That is the fasting one does before a sacrifice, not the fasting of the heart."

"May I ask about fasting of the heart?"

"Unify your attention. Do not listen with your ears but listen with your heart. Do not listen with your heart but listen with your *qi*. Listening stops with the ear. The heart stops with signs. *Qi* is empty and waits on external things. Only the Way gathers in emptiness. Emptiness is the fasting of the heart."[49]

Yan Hui said, "Prior to receiving this instruction, I was full of thoughts of Hui. But having applied it, it's as though Hui never existed. Is this what you mean by emptiness?"

The Master said, "Perfect. Let me tell you. You can go wander in his cage without being moved by his fame. If you're getting through, sing. If not, stop. No schools. No prescriptions. Dwell in unity and lodge in what cannot be helped, and you're almost there.

"To stop leaving tracks is easy. Not to walk upon the ground is hard.[50] It's easy to fake what people do. Faking what Heaven does is hard. You've heard of using wings to fly, but not of using no wings to fly. You've heard of using knowledge to know, but not of using no knowledge to know. Look up at the hole in the wall that fills the empty room with light. The blessed stop stopping. Not stopping means galloping while you sit. If you let the ears and the eyes communicate with the inside and banish knowledge outside the heart, then even ghosts and spirits will come to dwell. Why not men? This is the transformation of ten thousand things, the secret of the ancient sages, not to mention ordinary people!"

Zigao, the Duke of She,[51] was sent to Qi. He said to Kongzi, "The king is putting me on a high-priority mission. Qi treats emissaries very well, but never hurries. You can't budge an ordinary person along, much less a feudal lord! I'm already shaking. You've always told me, 'Few tasks of whatever size are completed happily except by

---

49. In *Mengzi* 2A2 (in chapter 4 of this volume) we learn that the philosopher Gaozi argued that "doctrines" (what you "listen to with your ears") should have priority over both your own heart and *qi,* while Mengzi suggests that the "resolution" or "attention" (zhì 志) of one's cultivated heart has priority over "doctrines" and *qi.* Here Zhuangzi has "Kongzi" disagreeing with both of them by saying that the heart should be made "empty" by "fasting" so that both the heart and doctrines are guided by *qi.* For more on this disagreement, see David S. Nivison, "Philosophical Voluntarism in Fourth Century China," in *The Ways of Confucianism* (Chicago: Open Court Press, 1996), 121–32.

50. Cf. Zhuangzi's criticism of Liezi in *Zhuangzi* chapter 1 (above): "Though he manages to avoid walking, he still relies on something."

51. The Duke of She was an influential politician in the state of Chu in the early fifth century BCE. The *Zuozhuan* describes him as an advocate of the Confucian principle of government by Virtue instead of force who later made good on his word by returning power to the rightful ruler when he was in a position to take over militarily. He and Kongzi spoke about politics and disagreed politely over the priority of obligations to the family and to the state. See *Analects* 7.19, 13.16, and 13.18 (in chapter 1 of this volume).

means of the Way. If you don't complete it, you'll be in trouble with other people. If you do complete it, you'll have trouble with your own *yin* and *yang*.[52] Only someone of Virtue can avoid trouble in success and failure alike.' I'm the kind of person who eats simply and sparingly so my diet doesn't give me indigestion. But I received my orders in the morning and by evening I was gulping ice-water. I'm burning up inside! I haven't even started on the actual job yet and I'm already having trouble with *yin* and *yang*; if the mission doesn't succeed, then I'll also be in trouble with other people. I lose both ways! I can't handle the responsibility of taking on this assignment. Do you have anything you can tell me?"

Kongzi said, "In this world, there are two great concerns. One is destiny. One is righteousness. Children's love for their family is destiny:[53] you can't undo it in your heart. The service of subjects for their rulers is righteousness: there is nowhere you can go and not have rulers, nowhere you can escape between Heaven and earth. These are great concerns. To serve your family, wherever they go, is the perfection of filial piety. To serve your rulers, whatever they ask, is the height of loyalty. To serve your own heart, so that sorrow and joy aren't constantly revolving in front of you, knowing what you can't do anything about and accepting it as though it were destiny, is the perfection of Virtue. As a subject or a child, there will certainly be things you can't avoid. As long as you stick to the actual job and forget about yourself, what leisure do you have to love life or hate death? You'll be able to do it.

"Let me tell you something else I've heard. In relationships, when people are close together, they generate trust through regular contact. When they are far apart, they have to establish loyalty with words, and words require communication. Communicating the words of two happy or two angry people is the hardest thing in the world. Two happy people inevitably exaggerate the good. Two angry people inevitably exaggerate the bad. But any exaggeration is false, and falsehood destroys trust. That's when communication becomes dangerous. So, the *Model Sayings*[54] have it, 'Communicate the real essence; don't communicate exaggerated words.' Then you might come out whole.

"When people pit their strength in games of skill, they start out bright like *yang* but usually end dark as *yin*. They get up to more strange tricks the longer they go. People drinking wine at a ceremony start out orderly enough but usually end in chaos. The party gets stranger the longer it lasts. Everything is like this. What starts

---

52. Success achieved in the wrong way harms a person internally. Good health requires a balanced harmony between the *yin* and *yang*. See *yin* and *yang* under *Important Terms* in the appendices.

53. The word translated here as "destiny" is translated as "orders" in the previous paragraph. In both cases, the character in question is mìng 命 ("fate" or "mandate"). See *ming* under *Important Terms* in the appendices.

54. Another probably fanciful "classical source."

out clean usually ends up dirty. What starts out simple inevitably turns unsupportable.

"Words are like wind and waves. Actions fulfill or disappoint them. Wind and waves are easily moved, and fulfillment and disappointment easily lead to danger. Rage has no other source but clever words and one-sided language.[55] As the hunt draws to a close, the dying animal doesn't choose its sounds but snorts its breath furiously, breeding a similar madness in the hearts of its hunters. Pushing hard toward the conclusion makes people vicious without their knowing it. And if they don't know it, who knows how it will end? So, the *Model Sayings* have it, 'Don't change your orders. Don't strive for completion. Anything over the line is too much.' Changing your orders and striving for completion are dangerous business. A fine completion takes a long time, and a bad one cannot be changed. Can you afford not to be careful?

"Harness things so your heart can wander. Nourish your middle by accepting what cannot be avoided: that's perfection. What is there for you to do in return? Nothing is as good as fulfilling your destiny.[56] That's as hard as it gets." . . .

Splay-limb Shu's chin is sunk in his belly. His shoulders are above his head, pinched together so they point at the sky. His five organs are on top, his thighs tight against his ribs. Plying a needle and taking in laundry he makes enough to fill his mouth. Winnowing leftover grain, he gets enough to feed ten people. When the people in charge are calling out troops, Splay-limb wanders among them waving good-bye. When they are press-ganging workers, he is exempted as a chronic invalid. When they dole out grain to the sick, he gets three measures, and ten bundles of firewood. With splayed limbs, he is still able to keep himself alive and to live out the years Heaven gave him. What if he had splayed Virtue? . . .

Chapter Five: Signs of Abundant Virtue

In Lu there was an amputee named Royal Nag who had as many followers as Kongzi. Chang Ji[57] asked Kongzi, "Royal Nag is an amputee, yet you and he divide Lu for students. He doesn't stand and teach or sit and discuss, yet they go to him

---

55. That is, what matters most is not what people do, but what they say, since it is the words that give the actions meaning.

56. "Fulfilling destiny" could also be translated "following orders."

57. Nothing is known about this person, though the name does not appear to be fictional. He may be connected to the Ji clan, the most powerful of the Three Families that ruled Lu for most of Kongzi's lifetime, reducing the Duke of Lu to little more than a figurehead.

empty and come home full. Can there be teaching without words or a developed heart in a deformed body? What kind of person is he?"

Kongzi said, "He is a sage. I'm just running late and haven't been to see him yet. And if I intend to make him my teacher, is it surprising that others do? Forget about Lu; I'm going to lead the whole world to follow him."

Chang Ji said, "If that amputee can lord it over you, he must be far from ordinary. Someone like that must have a special way of thinking."

Kongzi said, "Death and life are big, but they make no difference to him. Heaven and earth could flip over, and it would not matter to him. He peers into the false-less and does not shift with things. He considers it destiny that they should change and holds on to their ancestor."

Chang Ji said, "What does that mean?"

Kongzi said, "Looked at from their differences, liver and gall are as far apart as the states of Chu and Yue. Looked at from their sameness, the ten thousand things are all one. Someone like him does not know what is appropriate for his ears and eyes but lets his heart wander in the harmony of Virtue. He looks at the way things are one and does not see what they're missing. He looks at losing a foot like shaking off dust."

Chang Ji said, "For his own sake he uses knowledge to gain control of his heart and uses control of his heart to achieve a constant heart. But why should others make so much of him?"

Kongzi said, "People don't mirror themselves in moving water, they mirror themselves in still water.[58] Only the still can still the crowd's stillness. Of those that receive their destiny on earth, only the pine and cypress are green winter and summer. Of those that receive their destiny from Heaven, only the sages Yao and Shun are proper. Those fortunate enough to correct their own lives can correct the lives of the crowd. The proof of guarding the beginning is the fact of not being nervous. A brave soldier will boldly go against the nine armies. If someone can risk his life like this for fame, how much more so one whose palace is Heaven and earth and whose treasure is the ten thousand things, one who only lodges in the form, treats hearing and sight as images, unifies what knowledge knows, and whose heart never tastes death? He will pick his day to transcend the falseness, which is why people follow him. Why would he be willing to make mere things his business?". . .

Mountain-Uncle No-toes, a man from Lu who'd had his foot chopped off, heeled on in to see Kongzi. Kongzi said, "You weren't careful and have already gotten yourself in trouble. Why come to me now?"

---

58. Cf. *Xunzi* chapter 21 (in chapter 9 of this volume).

No-toes said, "I only ignored my responsibilities and took myself lightly, so I'm missing a foot. I come today because there is still something more important than a foot remaining, so I have a responsibility to preserve it. There is nothing that Heaven does not protect, nothing earth does not support. I thought you were like Heaven. How did I know you would be this way?"

Kongzi said, "That was stupid of me. Won't you come in, sir? Let me tell you what I have learned." But No-toes left.

Kongzi said to his students, "You disciples, pay attention! No-toes has had a foot chopped off but still takes responsibility for studying to make up for his former mistake. How much more so should a person whose powers are whole!"[59]

No-toes said to Laozi, "Kongzi is not yet one of the perfect people, is he? What was *he* doing fawning around here to study with you?[60] *He* longs for the sham-glam of reputation; he has no idea that perfect people see this as shackling themselves."

Laozi said, "Why can't you just show him that life and death are two sides of the same strip, that acceptable and unacceptable are strung on a single string? Can't you release his shackles?"

No-toes said, "When Heaven has punished him, how can I release him?"

Duke Ai of Lu[61] asked Kongzi, "There was an ugly man in Wei named Sad Nag. Men hung around with him. They thought about him all the time and couldn't tear themselves away. Women saw him and by the dozen they vowed to their parents that they'd rather be his concubine than another man's wife. No one ever heard him sing the lead, all he ever did was harmonize with others. He had no lordly status to save people from death, no piles of wealth to fill their bellies, and he was ugly enough to shock the world. He harmonized without singing and knew nothing beyond his own borders, but cocks and hens coupled in his presence. There had to be something special about him! So, We summoned him for an audience, and he really was ugly enough to shock the world. He stayed with Us, and before a month was out, We took an interest in his personality. By the time a year passed, We trusted him. Since the state had no minister, We put him in charge. He looked

---

59. Sometimes (as in *Zhuangzi* chapter 4, "The Human Realm," above) Kongzi seems to act as a mouthpiece for Zhuangzi's perspective, but in this passage Kongzi represents dogmatic conventionality. His condescension to No-toes is typical of what disabled people often experience even today. See John Altmann and Bryan W. Van Norden, "Was this Ancient Taoist the First Philosopher of Disability?" *New York Times,* 8 July 2020, online edition, https://www.nytimes.com/2020/07/08/opinion/disability-philosophy-zhuangzi.html.

60. This may be a reference to the legend (found in the *Shiji* 63; see *Sima Qian* under *Important Figures* in the appendices) that Kongzi visited Laozi to learn from him.

61. Duke Ai (r. 494–468 BCE) is depicted asking questions of Kongzi and his disciples in several passages in the *Analects*. For example, see *Analects* 6.3 and 12.9 (in chapter 1 of this volume).

glum and faltered, as though he might even decline. We were embarrassed but eventually got him to take it. Before long, however, he abandoned Us. We were crushed, as though We'd lost a loved one, as though there was no one to enjoy the state with. What kind of man was this?"

Kongzi said, "I was once sent to Chu. On the way I saw piglets feeding at their dead mother. After a while, they all blinked and ran off. They didn't see themselves in her, didn't find their kind. What they loved was their mother—not her form, but what moved her form. When someone dies in battle, his people don't bother with medals at his burial. An amputee's old shoes mean nothing to him. Both have lost the root. Women of the imperial retinue don't pare their nails or pierce their ears. A married man is sent on no more outside missions. When we do this to keep the form whole, how much more should we do to keep Virtue whole! Now this Sad Nag was trusted before he spoke and was loved though he accomplished nothing. He got people to give him their own states and worry he wouldn't take them! He must have completed the potential, though his Virtue took no form."

Duke Ai asked, "What do you mean by completing the potential?"

Kongzi said, "Death, life, survival, loss, failure, success, poverty, wealth, worth, depravity, slander, praise, hunger, thirst, winter, summer—their change is the process of destiny. Day and night they alternate in front of us, but knowledge cannot measure their beginning. Don't let them slip out of harmony or penetrate the spirit store. Indulge them harmoniously. Let them circulate without leaking away. Day and night, without a break, make it springtime with things. As you greet each new circumstance, generate the season in your own heart. This is what I mean by completing the potential."

"What do you mean by Virtue taking no form?"

"Levelness is the height of still water, so it can be used as a standard.[62] Hold it from within and it will not be disturbed from without. Virtue is the cultivation of complete harmony. When Virtue takes no form, things cannot leave it."

Later, Duke Ai told Minzi,[63] "At first when I ruled the empire, I held the reins of the people and worried about their welfare. I thought I had perfected it. Now that I've heard this explanation of the perfect person, I worry that I lacked the real substance and that I damaged the state by neglecting myself. Kongzi and I are not subject and lord, but friends in Virtue." . . .

---

62. Cf. the opening section of *Zhuangzi* chapter 13, below.

63. Min Ziqian is a disciple of Kongzi praised in several passages in the *Analects* that are not included in this volume.

Where sages wander, knowledge is a curse, restrictions are paste, favors are a patch, and effort is for trade. Sages do not plan, so why do they need knowledge? They do not cut, so why do they need paste? They have nothing to lose, so why do they need favors? They're not buying, so why do they need trade? In these four ways they feed at Heaven. Feeding at Heaven, they are nourished by Heaven. Once they are nourished by Heaven, why do they need other people? They have human form but not human essence. Since they have human form, they flock with people. Since they lack human essence, right and wrong do not get to them. Infinitesimally small, they flock with people. Indescribably large, they complete their Heaven alone.

Huizi asked Zhuangzi, "Can people really have no essence?"

Zhuangzi said, "Yes, they can."

Huizi said, "But if they have no essence, how can you call them 'people'?"

Zhuangzi said, "The Way gave them a face. Heaven gave them a form. How can you not call them 'people'?"

Huizi said, "But if you call them 'people,' how can they have no essence?"

Zhuangzi said, "Rights and wrongs (shì/fēi 是非) are what I mean by 'essence.' By 'no essence,' I mean people not letting in good and bad to hurt them. Follow the natural and do not help life along."[64]

Huizi said, "How can people exist without helping life?"

Zhuangzi said, "The Way gave them a face, Heaven gave them a form—by not letting likes and dislikes in to do harm, that's how. But you shut out your spirit, and tire your energies, leaning on a podium ranting, slumping at your desk and napping. Heaven chose a form for you, and you use it to sing of 'hard and white'!"[65]

Chapter Six: The Great Ancestral Teacher

To know what Heaven does and to know what humans do is to have reached perfection. Those who know what Heaven does are born of Heaven.[66] Those who know

---

64. Cf. *Daodejing,* chapter 55 (in chapter 6 of this volume).

65. On "hard and white," see above, note 30. The qíng 情, "essence," is the underlying truth or fact about a thing, as opposed to its reputation or the opinions people have of it. The "human essence" is understood here as the basic emotions or commitments that give rise to judgments of right and wrong. Cf. *Mengzi* 6A6 and 6A8 (in chapter 4 of this volume). Someone without an essence would not necessarily have no emotions but would lack preconceptions about them. Cf. the "perfected people" in chapter 2 above and the "true people" below and elsewhere in the *Zhuangzi.*

66. Translating the word for "Heaven" as "nature," the phrase "born of Heaven" could also be read "live naturally."

what humans do use what they know they know to nurture what they know they don't know, living out their Heavenly years and not dying along the way. This is the flourishing of knowledge.

Even so, there is a problem. Knowledge depends on something before it can be fitting. But what it depends on has not yet been fixed. So how do I know that what I call "Heaven" is not really human and what I call "human" is not really Heaven? Only when there are true people can we have true knowledge. What do I mean by true people? The true people of olden times did not resist poverty. They did not glory in success. They did not plan their affairs. They could miss without regretting it and hit without being pleased. Such people could climb high without shuddering. They could enter water without getting wet and fire without getting burned. Such is the knowledge that is able to climb up to the Way. . . .

The true people of the olden days knew nothing of loving life and nothing of hating death. They emerged without delight and returned without resistance. They came and went briskly, nothing more. They neither forgot their beginning nor sought their end. They enjoyed what they received, forgot it, and handed it back. This is called not using the heart to block the Way, not using the human to help Heaven. These are called true people. . . .

Hence what they liked was one and what they didn't like was one. Their being one was one and their not being one was one. Seeing it as one, they were followers of Heaven. Seeing it as not one, they were followers of humanity. When neither Heaven nor humanity wins out over the other, this is called being a true person. . . .

When the springs dry up, the fish are stuck together on the land. They douse each other with spit and spray each other with drool, but it is not as good as forgetting each other in the rivers and lakes. Praising Yao and condemning Jie is not as good as forgetting them both and transforming with the Way. The Big Lump burdens me with a form, labors me with life, eases me with old age, and rests me with death. So, if I like my life, for the same reason I must also like my death.

You hide your boat in a gully or your net in a swamp and call them secure. But in the middle of the night a strong man could still take them on his back and leave, and you would be asleep and not know. Hiding the small in the large seems fitting, but still you lose. But if you hid the world in the world, you would have nothing to lose. This is the essence of what lasts. You trespass on human form and still delight in it. As a human, you can change ten thousand times without ever reaching the limit. Can you count the different things that have made you happy? So, the sage wanders in what exists everywhere and can't be lost. He likes growing old and he likes dying young. He likes the beginning and he likes the end. People model themselves on the sage. But why not on that to which the ten thousand things are tied and on which every change depends?

The Way has an essence and can be trusted. But it takes no action and has no form. It can be passed on but not received, gotten but not seen. It is its own trunk, its own root. Before Heaven and earth existed, it spiritualized the ghosts and gods, and gave birth to Heaven and earth. It is above the supreme ultimate but not high, below the six limits but not deep. It was born before Heaven and earth but does not age. It is more venerable than high antiquity but is not old.[67] . . .

South Lord Master Flower said to Out-of-step Woman, "You are old in years but have the look of a child. How do you do it?"

She said, "I've heard the Way."

South Lord Master Flower asked, "May I study the Way?"

She said, "How? How could you? You're not the person for it. Huang Di's Dependent had the stuff of a sage but not the way of a sage. I have the way of a sage but not the stuff of a sage. I wanted to teach him, to see if maybe he really could become a sagely person. If not, at least it would be easier to explain the way of a sage to someone with the stuff of a sage. So, I stuck with it, explaining it to him for three days, after which he could put the world outside of himself. Once he'd put the world outside, I kept at it. After seven days he could put things outside. Once he'd put things outside, I kept at it. After nine days he could put life outside himself. Once he'd put life outside himself, the light dawned. After the light had dawned, he could see he was alone. Having seen he was alone, he could have no past or present. With no past or present, he was able to enter no living or dying. What kills life does not die; what lives life is not alive. The kind of thing it is—there is nothing it does not see off, nothing it does not greet, nothing it does not ruin, nothing it does not bring to completion. Its name is Disturbing Peace. The Disturbing Peace completes things only after disturbing them."

South Lord Master Flower asked, "Where did you hear it?"

She said, "I heard it from Ink-Aid's son. Ink-Aid's son heard it from Faltering Recitation's grandson. Faltering Recitation's grandson heard it from Looking-up-at-the-light. Looking-up-at-the-light heard it from Whispered Promise. Whispered Promise heard it from Needs Work. Needs Work heard it from Sing 'Ooh!' Sing 'Ooh!' heard it from Mysterious Darkness. Mysterious Darkness heard it from Present-in-vacancy. Present-in-vacancy heard it from Dubious Beginning."

---

67. Cf. *Daodejing* chapter 25 (in chapter 6 of this volume).

Master Sacrifice, Master Chariot,[68] Master Plow, and Master Arrive all four spoke together, saying, "Who can take nothing as the head, life as the spine, and death as the tail? Who knows death, life, existence, and annihilation as all the same thing? I'll be that person's friend." All four looked at each other and smiled. There was no resistance in their hearts, and so they became friends.

Suddenly, Master Chariot got sick. Master Sacrifice went to ask after him. "How extraordinary of the maker of things to knot me up like this. My back is hunched out. My organs are all out of order. My chin is hidden in my navel. My shoulders are peaked. And my neck bones point to Heaven." But though his *yin* and *yang qi* were fouled, in his heart there was nothing the matter. He hobbled over to look at his reflection in the well. "Sheesh! The maker of things really is knotting me up."

Master Sacrifice said, "Do you dislike it?"

He said, "Not at all. What is there to dislike? If, in time, he turns my left arm into a rooster, I'll use it to crow the day. If he turns my right arm into a bow, I'll shoot down a dove for roasting. If he turns my buttocks into wheels and my spirit into a horse, I'll climb aboard. What better carriage? You get something when it's time. You lose it when it's passed. If you are content with the time and abide by the passing, there's no room for sorrow or joy. This is what the ancients called 'loosing the bonds.' If you don't loose yourself, things will bind you. Nothing has ever beaten Heaven. What is there to dislike?"

Suddenly Master Arrive got sick. Gasping, he was on the point of death. His wife and children circled around him, weeping. Master Plow came to ask after him and said to them, "Stop! Get back! Don't be afraid of the change." Leaning on the doorframe he said, "How extraordinary, the one who makes these changes! What will he do with you next? Where will he send you? Will he make you a rat's liver? Will he make you a bug's arm?"

Master Arrive said, "A child goes wherever its parents say—east, west, north, or south. How much more are *yin* and *yang* to a person than parents! If they bring me to the point of death and I refuse to obey, I would only be being stubborn. What fault is it of theirs? The Big Lump burdens me with a form, labors me with life, eases me with old age, and rests me with death. So, if I like my life, for the same reason I must also like my death. Suppose a great smith were casting metal. If the metal were to rear up and say 'I insist on being a *Moye*!'[69] the great smith would certainly take

---

68. Zi Yu, "Master Chariot," is also the name of Kongzi's disciple Master Zeng. Since none of the other names refer to real people, however, it is probably not significant.

69. Moye was the famous sword of King Helü of Wu (r. 514–496 BCE), the smelting of which was said to have required human sacrifices in order to fuse the alloys. The art of metallurgy was endowed with mystical significance, partly because it was dimly understood, and partly also because of the enormous military advantages it conferred upon its possessors.

it as inauspicious material. If, having once trespassed on the human form, I were to say 'Only a human! Only a human!' then the maker of changes would certainly take me as an inauspicious person. If you take Heaven and earth as a great furnace and the maker of changes as a great smith, then where can you go that will not be all right? I will doze off whole and, drowsily, wake up."

Master Mulberry-door, Anti-Mengzi, and Master Great-Zither were all three friends.[70] They said, "Who can join with others in not joining with them, do for others by not doing for them? Who can climb Heaven, roam the mists, and whirl in the infinite, living forgetful of one another for ever and ever?" The three men looked at each other and smiled. None was reluctant in his heart, so they joined as friends.

Nothing happened for a while and then Master Mulberry-door died. Kongzi heard about it and sent Zigong over to help out. One of them was plaiting frames for silkworms and the other was playing the zither while they harmonized together and sang:

> Oh, Master Mulberry-door,
> Oh, Master Mulberry-door,
> You've returned to your true self,
> While we go on as men-o!

Zigong hurried in and approached them, saying, "Excuse me! But does it accord with the ritual to sing over a corpse?"

The two men looked at each other and smiled, saying, "What does he know about the meaning of ritual?"

Zigong went back and reported this to Kongzi, asking, "What kind of men are those? Correct behavior is nothing to them, as though their physical bodies were something external. They sing overlooking the corpse without even changing expression. I don't know what to say about them. What kind of men are they?"

Kongzi said, "Those are men who wander outside the rules. I am one who wanders within them.[71] Inside and outside don't meet, and it was rude of me to send you to mourn. They are about to join with the generator of things in being human and wander in the single breath of Heaven and earth. They think of life as a hanging tumor and a dangling mole and of death as a wart falling off or a boil bursting.

---

70. These are all allegorical names that bear relation to elements of the following story. For example, "Anti-Mengzi" may reflect his disregard of the funeral rituals held in such high esteem by Confucians (see *Mengzi* 3A5 in chapter 4 of this volume). If this is the correct interpretation, the name of this character is the only direct reference to Mengzi in the *Zhuangzi*. (But see notes 18, 36, 39, and 49 above, regarding possible implicit references to Mengzi.)

71. The word fāng 方 can mean either "rules" or "realm." Both meanings may be implied here. The social realm—that is, the world that people live in and know—comprises, among other things, rules, standards, and definitions. By questioning these things, the friends live simultaneously outside of the rules and outside of the shared social realm.

People such as this, how can they say whether death and life are ground gained or lost? They commit themselves to different things but trust to their all being of one body. They forget liver and gall and abandon the ears and eyes. They exchange the beginning for the end and cannot tell a premonition from an echo. Bemused, they wander about beyond the dirt and dust and play at the business of nonaction.[72] How could they get worked up over conventional politeness just to put on a display for the ears and eyes of the crowd?"

Zigong said, "So why then does my master follow rules himself?"

Kongzi said, "Me, I am one of those who are punished by Heaven. Even so, I share this with you."

Zigong said, "May I ask about these rules?"

Kongzi said, "Fish school together in water. People school together in the Way. For things that school together in the water, dig a pond and they will be provided for. For things that school together in the Way, don't busy yourself with them and their lives will be settled. Hence it is said, 'Fish forget one another in the rivers and lakes; people forget one another in the arts of the Way.'"

Zigong said, "May I ask about deviant people?"

"Deviant people deviate from people but converge with Heaven. Hence it is said, 'Heaven's petty person is a prince among men. The prince among men is Heaven's petty person.'"

Yan Hui questioned Kongzi: "When Mengsun Cai's mother died he cried without tears.[73] In his inner heart he did not mourn; conducting the funeral, he did not grieve. With these three lapses, his reputation as a mourner still covers Lu. Is it really possible to gain the name while lacking the substance? I was shocked."

Kongzi said, "Mengsun is done. He is beyond knowing. He would make it even simpler, but he can't. Still, he did simplify it some. Mengsun does not know why he lives. He does not know why he dies. He's not aware of moving forward. He's not aware of falling back. If he changes into something, he lets the unknown change finish it. When he changes, how does he know he isn't not changing? When he doesn't change, how does he know he hasn't changed already? Take you and me—we're dreaming and haven't woken up! But something can shock his body without

---

72. Wandering beyond the dirt and dust is a potent image that did much later to endear Zhuangzi to the Buddhists. What it probably means in this context is that, trusting to nature, the sages are freed from the anxiety normal people feel in their pursuit of conventional values that are probably wrong anyway. Sages are described as engaging in "nonaction" (wúwéi 無為), because their goals rise spontaneously and not by any act of will on their part. (See *wuwei* in *Important Terms* in the appendices.)

73. The Mengsun clan was one of the Three Families that ruled Lu during Kongzi's lifetime, though nothing specific is known of Mengsun Cai.

harming his heart. He stays here only for a day but feels no death. Mengsun is awake. People cry, so he cries; this is why.

"We say 'I.' But how do I know what I mean by 'I'? You dream you're a bird crossing Heaven or a fish sunk in the depths. There's no telling if the one who speaks now is awake or dreaming. Directing the trip doesn't measure up to smiling, and laughing doesn't measure up to stepping aside. Step aside and leave the changes. Then you will enter the oneness of the vacant sky."

Master Thinker went to see Whence. Whence asked him, "How has Yao rewarded you?"

Master Thinker said, "Yao told me, 'You must submit to benevolence and righteousness to speak clearly about right and wrong.'"

Whence said, "So what did you come here for? Yao's already tattooed your face with benevolence and righteousness and cut off your nose with right and wrong. How can you expect to wander distant, unrestrained, and rolling paths?"

Master Thinker said, "But still, I'd like to wander along the edge."

Whence said, "It's not like that. The blind can't share in the loveliness of faces or the nearsighted in far-off vistas."

Master Thinker said, "But beauties lose their looks and strong men lose their strength. Even Huang Di forgot his knowledge—all in the process of being recast. How do you know the maker of things won't erase my tattoos, replace my nose, and make me whole so I can follow you, sir?"

Whence said, "Ah, you never know! I'll give you the main outlines.

> My teacher! My teacher! He orders ten thousand things but is not righteous. He's kind to ten thousand generations but is not benevolent. He's more venerable than high antiquity but is not old. He roofs Heaven, floors earth, and fashions everything between but is not handy. That's how you wander."

Yan Hui said, "I'm improving."

Kongzi said, "How so?"

"I've forgotten benevolence and righteousness."

"Good, but there's more."

Yan Hui saw him again the next day and said, "I'm improving."

"How so?"

"I've forgotten rites and music."

"Good, but there's more."

Yan Hui saw him again the next day and said, "I'm improving."

"How so?"

"I sit and forget."

Kongzi started and said, "What do you mean by 'sit and forget'?"

Yan Hui said, "I cast off my limbs, dismiss hearing and sight, leave my form, abandon knowledge, and unify them in the great comprehension. That's what I mean by 'sit and forget.'"

Kongzi said, "If you've unified them then you have no preferences. If you've changed then you have no constancy. You really are worthy! I would like to ask to be your follower!"[74] . . .

Chapter Seven: The Proper Way for Emperors and Kings

Gaptooth asked Royal Relativity four times and got four "I-don't-know's" in response.[75] Gaptooth jumped up and down, he was so happy, and went to tell Master Reed Coat.

Master Reed Coat said, "You're just learning that now? Shun didn't measure up to the really ancient sages. Shun still stockpiled benevolence in order to win people. He got people, but he never escaped from not-people. Now the really ancient sages—they slept calmly and woke blankly. Sometimes they took themselves for horses. Sometimes they took themselves for cows. Their knowledge of the essence was trustworthy, and their Virtue was exceptionally true. They never entered into not-people." . . .

Don't make a name for yourself or follow a plan. Don't take responsibility or claim knowledge. Thoroughly embody what can't be exhausted and wander where you can't be seen. Take everything you get from Heaven but don't consider it gain. Just be empty. Perfected people use their hearts like mirrors, not welcoming things as they come or escorting them as they go. They respond without keeping, so they can conquer without harm.

The emperor of the north sea was Whish. The emperor of the south sea was Whoosh. The emperor of the center was All-full. Whish and Whoosh sometimes lodged together at All-full's place and he treated them exceptionally well. Whish and Whoosh decided to return All-full's kindness. "Everyone has seven holes to see, hear, eat, and breathe, but he alone has none. Let's try drilling him some!" Each day they drilled a hole. And in seven days, All-full died.[76]

---

74. Cf. Kongzi's remarks in *Analects* 5.9 and 6.11 (in chapter 1 of this volume).

75. See *Zhuangzi* chapter 2, above.

76. This marks the end of the "Inner Chapters," which many regard as the earliest strata within the *Zhuangzi* and possibly the work of the man Zhuangzi. The "Outer" and "Miscellaneous" chapters often contain profound insights and beautiful writing, but one theory is that they generally express a more simplistic version of Zhuangzi's Way, easier for ordinary humans (like us) to understand and put into practice. See Lee H. Yearley,

Chapter Twelve: Heaven and Earth

. . . Kongzi's student Zigong[77] wandered south to Chu and was returning through Jin. As he passed the south bank of the Han River, he saw an old man gardening a small plot. He'd dug a tunnel for a well and was coming out carrying a jug to water his fields. He was huffing and puffing, working hard for little reward.

Zigong said, "There's a machine now that can water a hundred gardens in one day. You get a big reward for easy work. Wouldn't you like one, sir?"

The gardener raised his head to look at him. "How does it work?"

"You carve the contraption[78] out of a piece of wood. The back is heavy and the front is light. You can lift the water with one hand, until it's practically bubbling over. It's called a well sweep."[79]

The gardener flushed angrily and laughed, "I heard from my teacher that where there are mechanical contraptions there will be mechanical business, and where there is mechanical business there are mechanical hearts. With a mechanical heart, you cannot preserve your simplicity. When you cannot preserve your simplicity, your spiritual life is unsettled, and the Way will not support an unsettled spiritual life. I'm not ignorant of your contraption. I would be embarrassed to use it!" . . .

When the freak gives birth in the middle of the night, she reaches frantically for a torch, gasping, worrying only whether the child looks like her.[80] . . .

Chapter Thirteen: Heaven's Way

. . . The sage is calm, but not because he declares calmness good. None of the ten thousand things are enough to rattle his heart, so he is calm. When water is calm,

---

"The Perfected Person in the Radical Chuang-tzu," in Victor Mair, ed., *Experimental Essays on Chuang-tzu* (Honolulu: University of Hawaii Press, 1983), 125–39.

77. Zigong was arguably Kongzi's most successful student. He was held in high esteem both by the Master and by influential politicians. Kongzi sometimes seemed to worry that things came too easily to him. See, for example, *Analects* 1.15, 5.9, and 5.12 (in chapter 1 of this volume).

78. This word can also mean "shackle."

79. For an image of a well sweep, see the Title Support Page for this volume at www.hackettpublishing.com /rccp-support.

80. This puzzling passage is evocative of several themes in the *Zhuangzi*, including "normality," "abnormality," and "illumination." Is the woman worried that the child looks like her or that it doesn't? On the one hand, one would naturally expect her to hope her child is like others. This would make for a touching but pedestrian passage. On the other hand, perhaps this is meant to be a parody of the Confucian insistence on passing the "normalities" of the past on to future generations.

you can see the wispy hair on your temples in it. Its surface is level and sets the standard for great builders. If water is so clear when calm, how much more so the spirit! The calm heart of the sage is a mirror to Heaven and earth and a looking glass for the ten thousand things. . . .

Duke Huan[81] was reading a book up in his hall. Wheelwright Slab was chiseling a wheel [in the courtyard] below.[82] He put down his hammer and chisel and ascended, asking Duke Huan, "Excuse me. What are you reading?"

The Duke said, "The words of the sages."

"Are the sages still around?"

The Duke said, "They're dead."

"Then what M'Lord is reading is nothing more than the leftovers of the ancients."

Duke Huan said, "How dare a wheelwright criticize what We read? If you have an explanation, okay. If not, you die!"

Wheelwright Slab said, "Your servant looks at it from the point of view of his own business. When I chisel a wheel, if I hit too softly, it slips and won't bite. If I hit too hard, it jams and won't move. Neither too soft nor too hard—I get it in my hand and respond with my heart. But my mouth cannot put it into words. There is an art to it. But your servant can't show it to his own son, and he can't get it from me. I've done it this way seventy years and am growing old chiseling wheels. The ancients died with what they could not pass down. So, what M'Lord is reading can only be their leftovers."

Chapter Fourteen: Heaven's Turning

. . . For traveling on water there's nothing like a boat. For traveling on land, there's nothing like a cart. But though a boat can go on water, if you try pushing it on land, you can push until you die and not go an inch. Aren't past and present like water and land? Aren't the states of Zhou and Lu like boats and carts? Those who insist on using the ways of Zhou in Lu might as well be pushing a boat on land. They exhaust themselves without success and bring certain misfortune on their heads. They do not know the directionless revolution that responds to things without tiring. . . .

---

81. For Duke Huan of Qi, see the entry for Guan Zhong under *Important Figures* in the appendices.

82. The scene in this passage is similar to what we see in *Mengzi* 1A7 (in chapter 4 of this volume; see especially note 3).

The beautiful Xi Shi had a stomach ache and glowered at the villagers. When her ugly neighbor saw how good she looked that way, he went home clasping his stomach and glowering at his neighbors, too, until the wealthy people slammed their windows and doors and the poor grabbed their children and ran. . . .

Chapter Seventeen: Autumn Floods

The monopod envies the millipede; the millipede envies the snake; the snake envies the wind. . . . The monopod[83] said to the millipede, "I just go hippety-flopping on one foot, and am inferior to everyone. How do you manage those ten thousand feet of yours?"

The millipede said, "It's not like that. Haven't you seen a man spit? He just hawks and—drops big as pearls! fine as mist! mixing and falling! You can't count them all! I just put my heavenly mechanism into motion. I don't know how it works!"

The millipede said to the snake, "I use this mob of legs to walk but still don't match up to you with none at all. How do you do it?"

The snake said, "The Heavenly mechanism does it. What could be easier? What use would I have for legs?"

The snake said to the wind, "I move with just my ribs and spine. But I still seem to exist. You bluster up from the north sea and bluster off to the south sea, but you don't seem to be anything at all. How do you do it?"

The wind said, "Yes, I bluster up from the north sea and off to the south sea. But a finger raised against me can stop me. A screen can beat me. Even so, only I can snap huge trees and lift great buildings, because I turn all those little defeats into a great victory. Only the sage is capable of the great victory." . . .

Did you hear about the frog in the collapsed well? He said to the turtle of the eastern sea, "Aren't I happy! I come out and spring on the railing, or I go in and rest in the hollow of a missing brick. When I float in the water, it hugs me under the arms and supports my chin. When I stomp in the mud, my feet sink in until it covers my ankles. Look around at the larvae and shrimp and polliwogs. None of them can match me! To control the water of an entire gully and straddle the happiness of a whole collapsed well—this is really getting somewhere! Why don't you come in some time and see?"

---

83. A monopod (kuí 夔) is a mythical one-legged beast, referred to in both East Asian and European legends.

Before the turtle of the eastern sea could get his left foot in, his right knee was already stuck. He teetered and fell back, and then began to tell of the sea. "A thousand *li* wouldn't measure its breadth. A thousand fathoms wouldn't plumb its depths. In Yu's time there were floods nine years in ten, but its waters never rose. In Tang's time there were droughts seven years in eight, but its shores never receded. Not to change or shift for an instant or ever, not to advance or retreat a little or a lot—that's the happiness of the eastern sea."

When the frog in the caved-in well heard this, he spluttered in surprise and forgot who he was. . . .

Did you hear about the toddler from Shouling who studied walking in Handan? Before he learned the local walk, he'd lost his native gait and had to shuffle home on his hands and knees.[84] . . .

Zhuangzi was angling by the Pu River when the king of Chu sent two officers to him, saying, "We would like to trouble you with administering Our kingdom."

Without looking up from his pole, Zhuangzi said, "I've heard Chu has a sacred turtle. It's been dead three thousand years and the king keeps it wrapped and boxed and stored up in his ancestral hall. Now, would that turtle rather have its bones treasured in death, or be alive dragging its tail in the mud?"

The two officers said, "It would rather be alive dragging its tail in the mud."

Zhuangzi said, "Go! I'll keep my tail in the mud, too." . . .

Zhuangzi and Huizi were wandering on a bridge over the Hao River. Zhuangzi said, "Look at those mottled fish out wandering at ease. That's what fish like!"

Huizi said, "You are not a fish. How do you know what fish like?"

Zhuangzi said, "You are not me. How do you know I don't know what fish like?"

Huizi said, "I'm not you, so I certainly don't know what you know. And since you're not a fish, you don't know what fish like. There, perfect!"

---

84. Shouling was not actually a city but a tomb, construction of which was begun in 335 BCE and probably continued throughout Zhuangzi's lifetime. Handan was the walled capital of Zhao and was also famous for its funerary parks. Assuming that the project at Shouling was to some extent modeled on the one at Handan, Zhuangzi's story may imply a sly criticism of people who follow the past to make sepulchers for themselves in the present.

Zhuangzi said, "Let's go back to the beginning. When you asked how I knew what fish like, you had to know I knew already in order to ask. I know it by the Hao River—that's how."[85]

Chapter Eighteen: Perfect Happiness

. . . When Zhuangzi's wife died, Huizi came to mourn her. At that moment, Zhuangzi was squatting down, beating on a tub, and singing.

Huizi said, "You lived with this person, raised children, and grew old together. Not to cry when she died would be bad enough. But to beat on a tub singing! Isn't that too much?"

Zhuangzi said, "No. When she first died, don't you think I was like everyone else? But then I considered her beginning, before she was alive. Not only before she had life, but before she had form. Not only before she had form, but before she had *qi*.

"In all the mixed-up bustle and confusion, something changed and there was *qi*. The *qi* changed and there was form. The form changed and she had life. Today there was another change and she died. It's just like the round of the four seasons: spring, summer, fall, and winter. She was resting quietly, perfectly at home, and I followed her crying 'Wah-hah!' It seemed like I hadn't comprehended fate. So, I stopped." . . .

Chapter Nineteen: Penetrating Life

On the way to Chu, Kongzi emerged from a forest and saw a hunchback plucking cicadas out of the air on the end of a gummed stick as easily as if he were picking them up off the ground.

Kongzi said, "Are you just getting lucky or is there a Way to do that?"[86]

He said, "I have a Way. For five or six months, I balance balls on the end of a stick. When I can balance two without dropping, the cicadas I miss will be small

---

85. The word translated as "how" can also mean "where." For a discussion of this entertaining but puzzling dialogue, see John R. Williams, "Two Paradigmatic Strategies for Reading Zhuang Zi's 'Happy Fish' Vignette as Philosophy," *Comparative Philosophy* 9, no. 2 (2018): 93–104.

86. This could also be translated, "How clever [qiǎo 巧] you are! Is there a way to do that?" The point, however, seems to be to contrast the Way with mere cleverness or luck. Compare the similar contrast between jì 技, "technique" and the Way in the story of the butcher cutting up the ox in *Zhuangzi* chapter 3, above.

change. When I can balance three without dropping, then I'll only miss one in ten. When I can balance five without dropping, it's like picking them up off the ground.

"I set my body like an old trunk and hold my arm like a dried branch. Despite the size of the world and number of things in it, I know only the cicadas' wings. I don't turn this way or lean that. I would not exchange the myriad things for those cicadas' wings. How could I not catch them?"

Confucius glanced back at his disciples and said, "This old hunchbacked fellow is exactly what I mean by 'undivided attention and concentrated spirit'!"[87]

. . . Yan Hui said to Kongzi, "I once crossed the depths at Goblet Gulf. The ferryman handled the boat like a spiritual being. I asked him, 'Can a person learn to handle a boat like that?' He said, 'A good swimmer can master the ability. And a diver can handle it easily even if he's never seen a boat before.' I asked him for more but he wouldn't tell me. May I ask you what he meant?"

Kongzi said, "A good swimmer can master it because he forgets the water. A diver can handle it easily without ever seeing a boat before because he views the depths like a hillside and a flipped boat like a slipping cart. The ten thousand things could all flip and slip in front of him and they wouldn't get in his front door. Where could he go and not be at ease? Betting for tiles, you're good. Betting for buckles, you worry. Betting for gold, you panic. Your skill is the same, but you care, so you value what is on the outside. Those who value what is on the outside are clumsy on the inside." . . .

Carpenter Qing carved trees into bell stands. When they were done, viewers gasped as though what they saw was the work of ghosts or spirits. The Marquis of Lu saw and asked, "What technique do you use?"

He replied, "I am just a craftsman. How could I have a technique? But there is one thing. When I am going to make a bell stand, I never bother wasting my energies. I always fast to still my mind.[88] After fasting three days, I've stopped bothering about salary or reputation. After five days, I stop bothering with approval or rejection, skill or clumsiness. After seven, I suddenly forget I have four limbs and a body. Once I've gotten to this point, there is no royal court. My abilities focus, and external things fade away. After that I go into the mountain forests to survey

---

87. The closing line sounds like Kongzi might be quoting from a poem. I could find no such poem, but similar phrases are found earlier in the *Zhuangzi*, where the spiritual people of the Maiden Mountain are described as shén níng 神凝 "concentrating their spirit" (in *Zhuangzi* chapter 1, above) and Confucius advises Yan Hui to yí zhì 一志 "unify your attention" (in *Zhuangzi* chapter 4, above).

88. For "fasting," see Yan Hui's conversation with Kongzi (*Zhuangzi* chapter 4, above).

the Heavenly nature of the material. When I arrive at a perfect trunk, I can see a bell stand in it and I lay my hand to it. Otherwise, not. This is just joining Heaven with Heaven. Is not this the reason why people wonder if my bell stands are the work of spirits?"

Chapter Twenty: The Mountain Tree

. . . Zhuangzi was wandering by the edge of the Diaoling preserve when he saw a strange magpie flying up from the south. Her wings were seven feet across and her eyes were an inch around. She bumped into his forehead and then crashed in a chestnut grove. He said, "What kind of bird is this, with such magnificent wings that don't get it anywhere and such big eyes that can't see?"[89] Hitching up his robes and tiptoeing forward, he pursued it, bow in hand. He saw a cicada forgetting itself in a pretty bit of shade. A praying mantis took advantage of the cover to grab for it, forgetting its own body at the sight of gain. The strange magpie was right behind, eyeing the prize and forgetting its truth. Zhuangzi shuddered. "Eeeee! Things certainly entangle one another, each one dragging in the next!" He threw down his bow and ran back the way he came—but then the warden of the grove saw and pursued him, cursing.

Zhuangzi went home and didn't come out for three days. His attendant, Straw, asked, "Sir, why haven't you left the house recently?"

Zhuangzi said, "I was guarding my body but forgot myself. I looked at muddy water and mistook it for clear depths. I've heard my teacher say, 'Out in the world, follow its rules.' Now I was wandering by Diaoling and forgot myself. A strange magpie bumped my forehead, wandered into the chestnut grove, and forgot its truth. And the grove warden took me for a poacher! That's why I haven't been out."[90] . . .

Chapter Twenty-Two: Knowledge Wandered North

. . . Master East Wall asked Zhuangzi, "Where is this so-called Way?"

Zhuangzi said, "There's nowhere it isn't."

Master East Wall said, "You must be more specific."

Zhuangzi said, "It's in an ant."

"How about even lower?"

---

89. The strange magpie could be Breeze on her return journey. See the opening of *Zhuangzi* chapter 1, above.

90. For a discussion of this intriguing story, see Philip J. Ivanhoe, "Zhuangzi's Conversion Experience," *The Journal of Chinese Religions* 19 (Fall, 1991): 13–25.

"It's in the grass."

"How about lower still?"

"In tiles."

"How about even lower than that?"

"It's in dung and urine."

When Master East Wall did not reply, Zhuangzi said, "Your questions don't reach the substance. When the inspector of the hunt asked the superintendent of the market about poking pigs for fatness, he was told the lower the better. But you shouldn't insist on that. There is nowhere it isn't. The perfect Way is like this and so are great words. 'Whole,' 'everywhere,' and 'all' are three different names for the same thing, making a single point." . . .

Chapter Twenty-Three: Mister Gengsang Chu

. . . People who have had their feet cut off forsake jewelry, because they are beyond praise and blame. Chained convicts are not afraid of heights because they have left life and death behind them. They have given up. They do not care. They have forgotten other people, and by forgetting other people they have become people of Heaven. You can honor them and they won't be pleased. You can despise them and they won't be mad. Only those who have identified with Heaven's harmony are like this. . . .

Chapter Twenty-Four: Mister Ghostless Slow

. . . Zhuangzi was accompanying a funeral when he passed by Huizi's grave. Turning to his attendants, he said, "When Plaster Monkey got a speck of mud on his nose as thin as a fly's wing, he would ask Builder Stone to slice it off. Builder Stone would twirl his axe like the wind and chop away obediently, getting all the mud and leaving the nose unharmed, while the plasterer stood there without changing his expression. Years later, when Plaster Monkey had passed away, Lord Yuan of Song[91] heard about the trick and summoned Builder Stone.

"'Do it for Us!' he commanded.

"Builder Stone replied, 'I was able to do it once, but the material I worked with died long ago.'

"Since my own teacher died," Zhuangzi continued, "I have been without material. I have no one to talk to." . . .

---

91. Reigned 531–517 BCE.

Kongzi said, "I have heard the unspoken speech but I've never tried to speak it . . . I wish I had a beak a yard long!"[92] . . .

Chapter Twenty-Six: Outside Things

. . . A trap is for fish: when you've got the fish, you can forget the trap. A snare is for rabbits: when you've got the rabbit, you can forget the snare. Words are for meaning: when you've got the meaning, you can forget the words. Where can I find someone who's forgotten words so I can have a word with him? . . .

Chapter Thirty-Two: Mister Clampdown Lie

. . . When Zhuangzi was about to die, his students wanted to bury him lavishly.[93] He said to them, "I'll have Heaven and earth for a casket, the sun and moon for ornaments, the constellations as pall-bearers, and the ten thousand things as mourners. Isn't everything prepared for the funeral? What could you add?"

"We're afraid the crows and kites will eat you."

"Above ground I'll feed the crows and kites. Below I'll feed the crickets and ants," Zhuangzi said. "Stealing from one to feed the other would be awfully unfair."

---

92. Cf. *Zhuangzi* chapter 2 (above): "We think [human speech] is different from the peeping of fledglings. But is there really any difference or isn't there?"

93. Cf. this passage to *Analects* 9.12 (in chapter 1 of this volume).

SELECTIVE BIBLIOGRAPHY

Translations

Fung, Yu-lan, trans. *A Taoist Classic: Chuang Tzu*. Beijing: Foreign Languages Press, 1989. (An insightful translation, which I have borrowed from at points. The inclusion of Guo Xiang's [265–312 CE] comments gives readers a rare and valuable insight into the commentarial tradition.)

Graham, Angus C., trans. *Chuang-tzu: The Inner Chapters*. London: Unwin Paperbacks, 1986. Reprint, Indianapolis: Hackett Publishing Company, 2001. (A philosophically oriented translation, especially useful when read in conjunction with Graham's other works explaining his reading.)

Lynn, Richard John, trans. *Zhuangzi: A New Translation of the Sayings of Master Zhuang as Interpreted by Guo Xiang*. New York: Columbia University Press, 2022. (This translation includes the insightful and influential commentary of Guo Xiang [265–312 CE].)

Mair, Victor, trans. *Wandering on the Way: Early Taoist Tales and Parables of Chuang Tzu*. Honolulu: University of Hawaii Press, 1998. (A fine recent translation.)

Watson, Burton, trans. *The Complete Works of Chuang Tzu*. New York: Columbia University Press, 1968. (An exquisite translation that I have often made the basis of my own.)

Ziporyn, Brook, trans. *Zhuangzi: The Essential Writings: With Selections from Traditional Commentaries*. Indianapolis: Hackett Publishing, 2009. (This partial translation includes selections from a variety of later commentators.)

Secondary Works

Ames, Roger T., ed. *Wandering at Ease in the Zhuangzi*. Albany, NY: State University of New York Press, 1998. (An anthology of historical and textual as well as philosophical analyses and reflections on Zhuangzi.)

Chinn, Ewing. "Zhuangzi and Relativistic Skepticism." *Asian Philosophy* 7 (1997): 207–20. (A response to the argument that Zhuangzi's skepticism commits him to relativistic skepticism, defending instead a perspectival realist position.)

Cook, Scott, ed. *Hiding the World in the World: Uneven Discourses on the Zhuangzi*. Albany, NY: State University of New York Press, 2003. (An anthology of essays on relativism, skepticism, mysticism, and other issues in the Zhuangzi.)

Fox, Alan. "Reflex and Reflectivity: *Wuwei* in the *Zhuangzi*." *Asian Philosophy* 6 (1996): 59–73. (An interpretation of the idea of *wuwei* based on the image of the hinge of the Way, as productive of a well-adjusted person.)

Graham, A. C. "Chuang-tzu's 'Essay on Seeing Things as Equal.'" *History of Religions* 9, nos. 2–3 (1969–70): 137–59. (A groundbreaking study of technical terms in the second chapter.)

————. *Studies in Chinese Philosophy and Philosophical Literature.* Albany, NY: State University of New York Press, 1990. (The chapter "How Much of Chuang Tzu Did Chuang Tzu Write?" differentiates the text's various contributors and editors.)

Ivanhoe, Philip J. "Zhuangzi's Conversion Experience." *Journal of Chinese Religions* 19 (1991): 13–25. (A useful study of the various interpretations of Zhuangzi's experience at Diaoling. [See *Zhuangzi* chapter 20, above]).

————. "Zhuangzi on Skepticism, Skill, and the Ineffable Dao." *Journal of the American Academy of Religions* 61 (1993): 639–54. (An important analysis of the status of skill.)

Kjellberg, Paul, and Philip J. Ivanhoe, eds. *Essays on Skepticism, Relativism, and Ethics in the Zhuangzi.* Albany, NY: State University of New York Press, 1996. (An anthology of essays on the relation between Zhuangzi's skepticism and his positive philosophical project.)

Liu, Xiaogan, ed. *Dao Companion to Daoist Philosophy.* New York: Springer, 2015. (An anthology of secondary essays with sections on the *Zhuangzi* and other earlier and later "Daoist" texts.)

Mair, Victor, ed. *Experimental Essays on Chuang-tzu.* Honolulu, HI: University of Hawaii Press, 1983. (The earliest of several good anthologies on Zhuangzi. The essays by Graham, Hansen, and Yearley have been especially influential.)

Van Norden, Bryan W. "Competing Interpretations of the Inner Chapters of the 'Zhuangzi.'" *Philosophy East & West* 46 (1996): 247–68. (An analysis of the tensions within the first seven chapters that give rise to conflicting interpretations, along with an interpretation of sagehood that reconciles them.)

CHAPTER NINE

XUNZI

Introduction

Before the unification of China by the Qin state in 221 BCE, which brought to a close the classical period of Chinese philosophy, Confucianism had one last great exponent, Xúnzǐ 荀子, whose work represents the highest development of the school in the Warring States period. (See *Important Periods* in the appendices.) Whereas the views of Kongzi and Mengzi are preserved only in piecemeal sayings, Xunzi's thought has come down to the present in the form of tightly constructed essays that give sustained discussions of various topics and together constitute a remarkably coherent system of arguments. Although his writing is not quite as colorful as that of Zhuangzi, his style is extremely elegant and forceful, occasionally bursting into poetry that movingly conveys his passion for the Confucian way of life.

Much of Xunzi's effort is devoted to ardently defending Confucianism against various challenges. For example, he vehemently condemns Mozi's rejection of ritual and music and argues vigorously that these cultural forms are absolutely necessary. He also attacks Laozi and Zhuangzi for advocating that people adopt the perspective of Heaven and abandon conventional values in favor of yielding to the natural flow of things. Xunzi instead stresses the distinctive importance of the human point of view, and in stark contrast to their emphasis on *wúwéi* 無為, "nonaction" or "non-striving action," he claims that good things are achieved only through *wěi* 偽, "deliberate effort." Yet even as he repudiates rival philosophers, Xunzi also learns from them and incorporates their insights. The influence of Zhuangzi on his thought is particularly evident in his characterization of the heart as mirrorlike and in his description of how it comes to know the Way, though the substance of Xunzi's views differs considerably from that of Zhuangzi.

For Xunzi, the threats to Confucianism come not only from outside the tradition, but also from *within* it, in the form of Mengzi's doctrine that human nature is good. In Xunzi's opinion, such a claim undermines the authority of ritual as a guide to behavior, destroys the necessity of learning, and simply flies in the face of the facts. Xunzi makes the opposite declaration that human nature is bad, but this should not be read as saying that people naturally delight in evil. Rather, his point is that people lack any inborn guide to right conduct, and that without the external restraint of ritual they will fall into wrongdoing and be reduced to a chaotic, impoverished state strongly reminiscent of the "state of nature" depicted by Thomas Hobbes (1588–1679). Nevertheless, Xunzi shares Mengzi's belief that everyone has the potential to achieve moral perfection. However, since we are not inclined to virtue by nature, the process of self-transformation will be slow and difficult, and this idea is reflected in Xunzi's repeated comparison of learning with the harsh processes involved in bending wood.

In his own day, Xunzi was a well-known scholar and was even given high office at one point. Among his students were Han Feizi and Li Si, who was instrumental in bringing about the Qin state's domination of China. Xunzi may even have lived to witness this event. Other students of his were responsible for preserving classic Chinese texts, including the *Odes*. Despite Xunzi's important position in early Chinese intellectual history, when Mengzi's views later came to be favored, Xunzi was rejected for claiming that human nature is bad, and his works were largely neglected for centuries. Recently, however, there has been a renewal of scholarly interest in Xunzi, and he is once again receiving the attention he deserves.

Chapter One: An Exhortation to Learning

The gentleman says: Learning must never stop. Blue dye is gotten from the indigo plant, and yet it is bluer than the plant. Ice comes from water, and yet it is colder than water. Through steaming and bending, you can make wood straight as an ink-line[1] into a wheel. And after its curve conforms to the compass, even when parched under the sun it will not become straight again,

---

1. A carpenter's tool used for marking straight lines.

because the steaming and bending have made it a certain way. Likewise, when wood comes under the ink-line, it becomes straight, and when metal is brought to the whetstone, it becomes sharp.[2] The gentleman learns broadly and examines himself thrice daily,[3] and then his knowledge is clear and his conduct is without fault.

And so, if you never climb a high mountain, you will not know the height of Heaven. If you never approach a deep ravine, you will not know the depth of the earth. If you never hear the words passed down from the former kings, you will not know the magnificence of learning. The children of the Han, Yue, Yi, and Mo[4] peoples all cry with the same sound at birth, but when grown they have different customs, because teaching makes them thus. . . .

I once spent the whole day pondering, but it was not as good as a moment's worth of learning.[5] I once stood on my toes to look far away, but it was not as good as the broad view from a high place. If you climb to a high place and wave, you have not lengthened your arms, but you can be seen from farther away. If you shout from upwind, you have not made your voice stronger, but you can be heard more clearly. One who makes use of a chariot and horses has not thereby improved his feet, but he can now go a thousand *li.* One who makes use of a boat and oars has not thereby become able to swim, but he can now cross rivers and streams. The gentleman is exceptional not by birth, but rather by being good at making use of things. . . .

If you accumulate enough earth to form a mountain, then wind and rain will arise from it. If you accumulate enough water to form a deep pool, then dragons will come to live in it. If you accumulate enough goodness to achieve Virtue, then you will naturally attain to spirit-like powers and enlightenment, and the heart of a sage is complete therein.

And so,

> Without accumulating tiny steps,
> You have no way to go a thousand *li.*
> Without accumulating little streams,
> You have no way to form river or sea.
> Let the horse Qi Ji[6] take a single leap;

---

2. Compare Gaozi's metaphors for self-cultivation in *Mengzi* 6A1–2 (in chapter 4 of this volume) and *Xunzi* chapter 23 (below).

3. Compare *Analects* 1.4 (in chapter 1 of this volume).

4. These are the names of "barbarian" states and tribes.

5. Compare *Analects* 15.31 (in chapter 1 of this volume).

6. The horse Qi Ji was famous for his ability to go a thousand *li* in a single day.

It still would go no farther than ten strides.
Yet old nags ridden ten days equal him;
Not giving up is where success resides.[7]

If you start carving and give up, you will not be able to break even rotten wood, but if you start carving and don't give up, then you can engrave even metal and stone. The earthworm does not have sharp teeth and claws, nor does it have strong bones and muscles. Yet, it eats of the earth above, and it drinks from the Yellow Springs below,[8] because it acts with single-mindedness. In contrast, the crab has six legs and two pincers. Yet were it not for the abandoned holes of water snakes and eels, it would have no place to lodge, because it is frenetic-minded. For this reason,

If you do not first have somber intention,
No brilliant understanding can there be.
If you do not first have determined effort,
No glorious achievements will you see. . . .

Where does learning begin? Where does learning end? I say: Its order begins with reciting the classics, and ends with studying ritual. Its purpose begins with becoming a noble man, and ends with becoming a sage. If you truly accumulate effort for a long time, then you will advance. Learning proceeds until death and only then does it stop. And so, the order of learning has a stopping point, but its purpose cannot be given up for even a moment. To pursue it is to be human, to give it up is to be a beast. Thus:

The *History* is the record of government affairs.
The *Odes* is the repository of balanced sound.
Rituals are the great divisions in the model for things.
Outlines of things' proper classes are in the rituals found.

And so, learning comes to ritual and then stops, for this is called the ultimate point in pursuit of the Way and Virtue. In the reverence and refinement of ritual, the balance and harmony of music, the broad content of the *Odes* and *History,* the subtleties of the *Spring and Autumn Annals,* all things between Heaven and earth are complete.

---

7. In the present translation, passages which rhymed in the original have been translated with rhyming English, mostly using lines with fixed numbers of syllables (but the rhymes do not always follow the Chinese rhyme scheme and the line lengths do not match the length of the original Chinese lines). When a rhyming translation would have significantly obscured an important philosophical point or was otherwise not feasible, such passages in the original are translated as indented prose sections and are pointed out in the footnotes.

8. The Yellow Springs were believed to be deep underground and were thought of as the abode of the spirits of the dead.

The learning of the gentleman enters through his ears, fastens to his heart, spreads through his four limbs, and manifests itself in his actions. His slightest word, his most subtle movement, all can serve as a model for others. The learning of the petty person enters through his ears and passes out his mouth. From mouth to ears is only four inches—how could it be enough to improve a whole body much larger than that? Students in ancient times learned for their own sake, but the students of today learn for the sake of impressing others.[9] Thus the learning of the gentleman is used to improve his own person, while the learning of the petty man is used like gift oxen.[10] To speak without being asked is what people call being presumptuous, and to speak two things when asked only one is what people call being wordy. Being presumptuous is wrong, and being wordy is wrong. The gentleman is simply like an echo.

In learning, nothing is more expedient than to draw near to the right person. Rituals and music provide proper models but give no precepts. The *Odes* and *History* contain ancient stories but no explanation of their present application. The *Spring and Autumn Annals* is terse and cannot be quickly understood. However, if you imitate the right person in his practice of the precepts of the gentleman, then you will come to honor these things for their comprehensiveness, and see them as encompassing the whole world. Thus, in learning there is nothing more expedient than to draw near to the right person.

Of the paths to learning, none is quicker than to like the right person, and exalting ritual comes second. If at best you cannot like the right person, and at worst you cannot exalt ritual, then you will simply be learning haphazard knowledge and focusing your intentions on blindly following the *Odes* and *History*. If so, then to the end of your days you cannot avoid being nothing more than a vulgar scholar.[11] If you are going to take the former kings as your fount and make benevolence and righteousness[12] your root, then rituals are exactly the highways and byways for you.

---

9. Compare *Analects* 14.24 (in chapter 1 of this volume).

10. In ancient China, animals were given as gifts to superiors or honored guests. Xunzi's point is that the petty man likewise shows off his learning to ingratiate himself to others and win official positions.

11. The last word here is *Rú* 儒, which later came to mean simply "Confucian" (see *Important Terms* in the appendices). In Xunzi's time it did not yet have such a specific denotation but instead referred more generally to a "scholar." Compare *Analects* 6.13 (in chapter 1 of this volume).

12. The word here is *yì* 義, an extremely important term for Xunzi. In his writings, it can refer both to a specific set of social standards created by the sages, and to the virtue of abiding by those standards. In the former usage, it is frequently paired with ritual, and the standards to which it refers appear to be higher-order standards for structuring society (e.g., by defining various social roles), from which are derived the more particular directives for behavior contained in ritual. For those contexts, in order to mark that Xunzi is referring to an external set of standards, rather than an internal disposition, it is rendered in this translation as "the standards of righteousness." See *yi* under *Important Terms* in the appendices.

It will be like the action of turning up your fur collar by simply curling your five fingers and pulling on it—it goes smoothly numberless times. If you do not take the regulations of ritual as your way, but instead go at it with just the *Odes* and *History,* then it will be like trying to measure the depth of a river with your finger, or trying to pound millet with a halberd, or trying to eat out of a pot with an awl—you simply will not succeed at it. And so, if you exalt ritual, then even if you are not brilliant, you will still be a man of the proper model. If you do not exalt ritual, then even if you are an acute debater, you will be only a dissolute scholar. . . .

One who misses a single shot out of a hundred does not deserve to be called good at archery. One who falls short of going a thousand *li* by the distance of even a half-step does not deserve to be called good at chariot-driving. One who does not fully comprehend the proper kinds and classes of things, or who is not single-minded in pursuit of benevolence and righteousness, does not deserve to be called good at learning. Learning is precisely learning to pursue them single-mindedly. To depart from it in one affair and adhere to it in another is to be such as common people. To have in oneself little that is good and much that is not good is to be such as Tyrant Jie and Tyrant Zhou and Robber Zhi. Perfect it and complete it, and only then is one truly a learned person.

The gentleman knows that whatever is imperfect and unrefined does not deserve praise. And so, he repeatedly recites his learning in order to master it, ponders it in order to comprehend it, makes his person so as to dwell in it, and eliminates things harmful to it in order to nourish it. He makes his eyes not want to see what is not right, makes his ears not want to hear what is not right, makes his mouth not want to speak what is not right, and makes his heart not want to deliberate over what is not right.[13] He comes to the point where he loves it, and then his eyes love it more than the five colors, his ears love it more than the five tones, his mouth loves it more than the five flavors, and his heart considers it more profitable than possessing the whole world. For this reason, power and profit cannot sway him, the masses cannot shift him, and nothing in the world can shake him.[14] He lives by this, and he dies by this. This is called the state in which Virtue has been grasped.

When Virtue has been grasped, only then can one achieve fixity.[15] When one can achieve fixity, then one can respond to things. To be capable both of fixity and

---

13. Compare *Analects* 12.1 (in chapter 1 of this volume).

14. Compare the last lines of *Mengzi* 3B2 (not in this volume).

15. The Chinese word translated here as "fixity" is *dìng* (定), which is distinct from and etymologically unrelated to the Chinese word *bì* (蔽) that is translated as "fixation" in *Xunzi* chapter 21 (below) and elsewhere. The former word connotes stability and is generally, as seen here, a positive trait for Xunzi, whereas the latter word connotes a failure of understanding (that comes from or leads to an excessive and improper concern for something) and is hence a negative trait.

of responding to things—this is called the perfected person. Heaven shows off its brilliance, earth shows off its breadth, and the gentleman values his perfection.

Chapter Two: Cultivating Oneself

When you observe goodness in others, then inspect yourself, desirous of cultivating it. When you observe badness in others, then examine yourself, fearful of discovering it.[16] If you find goodness in your person, then commend yourself, desirous of holding firm to it. If you find badness in your person, then reproach yourself, regarding it as calamity. And so, he who rightly criticizes me acts as a teacher toward me, and he who rightly supports me acts as a friend toward me, while he who flatters and toadies to me acts as a villain toward me. Accordingly, the gentleman exalts those who act as teachers toward him and loves those who act as friends toward him, so as to utterly hate those who act as villains toward him. He loves goodness tirelessly, and can receive admonitions and take heed. Even if he desired not to improve, how could he avoid it? The petty man is the opposite. He is utterly disorderly, but hates for people to criticize him. He is utterly unworthy, but wishes for people to consider him worthy. His heart is like that of a tiger or wolf, and his conduct like that of beasts, but he hates for people to consider him a villain. To those who flatter and toady to him he shows favor, while those who would admonish him, he keeps at a distance. Those who cultivate correctness he considers laughable, and those truly loyal to him he considers villains. Even though he does not wish to perish, how could he avoid it? The *Odes* says,

> These men conspire and practice slander.
> This is a matter for great sorrow!
> To any plan that's worth adopting,
> Complete resistance is what they show.
> But as for plans not worth adopting,
> These they completely wish to follow![17]

This expresses my meaning.

The measure for goodness in all things is this:

> Use it to control your *qi* and nourish your life,
> Then you will live longer than Peng Zu.
> Use it to cultivate yourself and achieve fame,

---

16. Compare *Analects* 4.17 (in chapter 1 of this volume).

17. *Mao* # 195.

Then you'll be equal to Yao and Yu.
It is fitting in times of prosperity.
It is useful in facing adversity

—truly such is ritual.

If your exertions of blood, *qi*, intention, and thought accord with ritual, they will be ordered and effective.[18] If they do not accord with ritual, they will be disorderly and unproductive. If your meals, clothing, dwelling, and activities accord with ritual, they will be congenial and well regulated. If they do not accord with ritual, then you will encounter dangers and illnesses. If your countenance, bearing, movements, and stride accord with ritual, they will be graceful. If they do not accord with ritual, they will be barbaric, obtuse, perverse, vulgar, and unruly.

Hence,

If their lives are without ritual,
Then people cannot survive.
If affairs are without ritual,
In them success does not thrive.
If state and clan are without ritual,
For them peace does not arrive.

The *Odes* says:

Ritual and ceremony have right measure completely.
Laugh and speak only in complete accord with propriety.[19]

This expresses my meaning.

To lead others along in what is good is called "teaching." To harmonize with others in what is good is called "proper compliance." To lead others along in what is bad is called "flattery." To harmonize with others in what is bad is called "toadying." To endorse what is right and condemn what is wrong is called "wisdom." To endorse what is wrong and condemn what is right is called "stupidity." To attack a good person is called "slander." To injure a good person is called "villainy." To call the right as right and the wrong as wrong is called "uprightness." To steal goods is

---

18. The five sentences after this one are rhymed in the Chinese text, and some scholars suggest that this sentence was originally part of that rhyming group, but became corrupted and so no longer rhymes. Since its grammatical structure is closely parallel to the sentences that follow, I have offset it with the rest of the rhymed lines.

19. *Mao* #209. These lines are also quoted in chapter 19 of the *Xunzi* (see below). In their original context, they describe people ("Their ritual . . . / They laugh . . ."). Without that context, here the lines are ambiguous, and I have rendered them to fit this context best.

called "thievery." To conceal one's actions is called "deceptiveness." To speak too easily of things is called "boastfulness." To be without fixity in one's likes and dislikes is called "lacking constancy." To abandon righteousness in favor of profit is called "utmost villainy." To have heard many things is called "broadness." To have heard few things is called "shallowness." To have seen many things is called "erudition." To have seen few things is called "boorishness."[20] To have difficulty in progressing is called "indolence." To forget things easily is called "leakiness." For one's actions to be few and well-ordered is called "being controlled." For one's actions to be many and disorderly is called "being wasteful."

The methods for controlling the *qi* and nourishing the heart: For unyielding blood and *qi*, soften them with harmoniousness. For overly deep thinking, simplify it with easy goodness. For overly ferocious courage, reform it with proper compliance. For expedience-seeking hastiness, restrain it with regulated movements. For small-minded narrowness, broaden it with expansiveness. For excessive humility, sluggishness, or greed for profit, resist it with lofty intentions. For vulgarity or dissoluteness, expunge it with teachers and friends. For indolence or profligacy, illuminate it with the prospect of disasters. For simpleminded rectitude or scrupulous honesty,[21] make it suitable with ritual and music, and enlighten it with reflection. In each method of controlling the *qi* and nourishing the heart, nothing is more direct than following ritual, nothing is more important than having a good teacher, and nothing works with greater spirit-like efficacy than liking it with single-minded devotion. These are called the methods for controlling the *qi* and nourishing the heart.

If one's intentions and thoughts are cultivated, then one will disregard wealth and nobility. If one's concern is for the Way and righteousness is great, then one will take kings and dukes lightly. It is simply that one examines oneself on the inside, and thus external goods carry little weight. A saying goes, "The gentleman makes things his servants. The petty man is servant to things." This expresses my meaning. If an action tires your body but puts your heart at ease, do it. If it involves little profit but much righteousness, do it. Being successful in the service of a lord who creates chaos is not as good as simply being compliant in the service of an impoverished lord. And so, a good farmer does not fail to plant because of drought, a good

---

20. "Boorishness," *lòu* 陋, is an important term for Xunzi. It is the uncultivated state in which a person has not yet been shown the greatest goods in life (that is, the way of the sages), and so does not properly appreciate them. Compare *Analects* 9.14 (in chapter 1 of this volume, where the same term is translated "uncouthness").

21. In most other places in the text, *duān què* 端愨 ("scrupulous honesty" or "scrupulousness and honesty") is presented as something good, with no sense that there is anything deficient about it. Insofar as it is treated here as being in need of modification through ritual, music, and reflection, perhaps Xunzi has in mind a case where it becomes an excessive moral fastidiousness, something that he warns against in other places.

merchant does not fail to open shop because of losses, and the noble man and the gentleman are not lax in their pursuit of the Way because of poverty.

> If your bearing is reverent and respectful and your heart is loyal and faithful, if your method is ritual and the standards of righteousness and your disposition[22] is concern for others, then you may wander across the whole world, and even if you become trapped among barbarians, no one will fail to value you.[23] If you are eager to take the lead in laborious matters, if you can give way in pleasant matters, and if you show scrupulousness, honesty, integrity, trustworthiness, self-control, and meticulousness, then you may wander across the whole world, and even if you become trapped among barbarians, no one will fail to employ you. If your bearing is arrogant and obtuse and your heart is stubborn and deceitful, if your method is to follow Mozi[24] and your truest essence is polluted and corrupt, then you may wander across the whole world, and even if you reach every corner of it, no one will fail to consider you base. If you try to put off or wriggle out of laborious matters, if you are grasping and will not yield in pleasant matters, if you are perverse and dishonest, if you are not meticulous in work, then you may wander across the whole world, and even if you reach every corner of it, no one will fail to reject you. . . .

He who likes the right model and carries it out is a man of good breeding. He who focuses his intentions upon it and embodies it is a gentleman. He who completely understands it and practices it without tiring is a sage. If a person lacks the proper model, then he will act recklessly. If he has the proper model but does not fix his intentions on its true meaning, then he will act too rigidly. If he relies on the proper model and also deeply understands its categories, only then will he act with comfortable mastery of it.

---

22. The word rendered here as "disposition" is *qíng* 情, an extremely important concept in Xunzi's psychological views. In Xunzi's text, *qing* is most often used as a class term for what in English we call "feelings" (or "emotions") and "desires." Xunzi uses it to refer to specific occasions of feeling and desire but also especially for the general *tendency* to feel and desire in various ways. It is to capture this latter sense that I have rendered *qing* as "disposition," and this translation is used throughout, in order to allow readers to track the term, though this sometimes makes for awkwardness, especially when Xunzi is concentrating on the aspect of it that is closer to "emotion." In those cases, notes have been added to aid the reader. Xunzi believes that a person's *qing* can be changed through habituation. Accordingly, he sometimes uses *qing* to refer to those reformed dispositions, but more often to people's natural dispositions; when he has the second sense in mind, *qing* is sometimes rendered as "inborn dispositions" to make his point clearer.

23. The Chinese text of this and the next three sentences contains rhymed sections.

24. That is, to reject ritual.

Ritual is that by which to correct your person. The teacher is that by which to correct your practice of ritual.[25] If you are without ritual, then how will you correct your person? If you are without a teacher, how will you know that your practice of ritual is right? When ritual is so, and you are also so, then this means your disposition accords with ritual. When the teacher explains thus, and you also explain thus, then this means your understanding is just like your teacher's understanding. If your disposition accords with ritual, and your understanding is just like your teacher's understanding, then this is to be a sage. And so, to contradict ritual is to be without a proper model, and to contradict your teacher is to be without a teacher. If you do not concur with your teacher and the proper model but instead like to use your own judgment, then this is like relying on a blind person to distinguish colors, or like relying on a deaf person to distinguish sounds. You will accomplish nothing but chaos and recklessness. And so, in learning, ritual is your proper model, and the teacher is one whom you take as the correct standard and whom you aspire to accord with. The *Odes* says, "While not knowing, not understanding, he follows the principles of the Lord on High."[26] This expresses my meaning. . . .

In seeking profit, the gentleman acts with restraint. In averting harms, he acts early. In avoiding disgrace, he acts fearfully. In carrying out the Way, he acts courageously. Even if living in poverty, the gentleman's intentions are still grand. Even if wealthy and honored, his demeanor is reverent. Even if he lives at ease, his blood and *qi* are not lazy. Even if weary from toil, his countenance is not disagreeable. When angry he is not excessively harsh, and when happy he is not excessively indulgent. The gentleman retains grand intentions even in poverty, because he exalts benevolence. He maintains a reverent demeanor even when wealthy and honored, because he takes contingent fortune lightly. His blood and *qi* do not become lazy when at ease, because he is heedful of good order. His countenance is not disagreeable even when weary from toil, because he is fond of good relations. He is neither excessively harsh when angry nor excessively indulgent when happy, because his adherence to the proper model overcomes any personal capriciousness. The *History* says:

> Do not create new likes.
> Follow the kings' way.
> Do not create new dislikes.
> On the kings' path stay.[27]

---

25. That is, the teacher shows one both the right rituals to practice and how to practice them rightly.

26. *Mao* # 241.

27. See the chapter of the *History* titled "Hongfan" ("The Great Plan"), translated in Clae Waltham, ed. *Shu Ching: Book of History* (London: George Allen & Unwin, 1971), 128. These same lines are quoted again in *Xunzi* chapter 17, "Discourse on Heaven" (below).

This is saying that through avoidance of prejudice[28] and adherence to righteousness the gentleman overcomes capricious personal desires.

Chapter Five: Against Physiognomy

. . . What is that by which humans are human? I say: It is because they have distinctions. Desiring food when hungry, desiring warmth when cold, desiring rest when tired, liking the beneficial and hating the harmful—these are things people have from birth. These one does not have to await, but are already so. These are what Yu and Jie both share. However, that by which humans are human is not that they are special in having two legs and no feathers, but rather because they have distinctions. Now the ape's form is such that it also has two legs and no feathers. However, the gentleman sips ape soup and eats ape meat. Thus, that by which humans are human is not that they are special in having two legs and no feathers, but rather because they have distinctions. The birds and beasts have fathers and sons but not the intimate relationship of father and son. They have the male sex and the female sex but no differentiation between male and female. And so, for human ways, none is without distinctions. Of distinctions, none are greater than social divisions, and of social divisions, none are greater than rituals, and of rituals, none are greater than those of the sage-kings.[29]

But there are a hundred sage-kings—which of them shall one take as one's model? And so I say: Culture persists for a long time and then expires; regulations persist for a long time and then cease. The authorities in charge of preserving models and arrangements do their utmost in carrying out ritual but lose their grasp. And so, I say: If you wish to observe the tracks of the sage-kings, then look to the most clear among them. Such are the later kings. The later kings were lords of the whole world. To reject the later kings and take one's way from furthest antiquity is like rejecting one's own lord and serving another's lord. And so, I say: If you wish to observe a thousand years' time, then reckon upon today's events. If you wish to understand ten thousand or one hundred thousand, then examine one and two. If

---

28. "Avoidance of prejudice" is my translation for *gōng* 公. It is a virtue opposite both to prejudice in favor of oneself, that is, selfishness, and to prejudice in favor of certain people or certain views, that is, unfair bias. Stated more positively, it combines both public-spiritedness and impartiality. See note 70 in chapter 10 of this volume (re *Han Feizi* chapter 49).

29. Zhuangzi also argues that making normative distinctions sets humans apart from animals, but claims that this tendency is the greatest source of trouble and should be avoided. Here Xunzi turns Zhuangzi's point on its head and glorifies such distinctions as the source of all good. See *Zhuangzi* chapter 2 (in chapter 8 of this volume).

you wish to understand the ancient ages, then examine the way of the Zhou. If you wish to understand the way of the Zhou, then examine the gentlemen whom their people valued. Thus, it is said: Use the near to know the far; use the one to know the ten thousand; use the subtle to know the brilliant. This expresses my meaning. . . .

Chapter Eight: The Achievements of the Ru

The Way of the former kings consists in exalting benevolence. One must cleave to what is central in carrying it out. What do I mean by "what is central"? I say: It is ritual and the standards of righteousness. The Way is not the way of Heaven, nor is it the way of earth.[30] It is that whereby humans make their way, and that which the gentleman takes as his way.

Chapter Nine: The Regulations of a True King

. . . Water and fire have *qi* but are without life. Grasses and trees have life but are without awareness. Birds and beasts have awareness but are without standards of righteousness (*yì* 義). Humans have *qi* and life and awareness, and moreover they have standards of righteousness. And so, they are the most precious things under Heaven. They are not as strong as oxen or as fast as horses, but oxen and horses are used by them. How is this so? I say: It is because humans are able to form communities while the animals cannot. Why are humans able to form communities? I say: It is because of social divisions. How can social divisions be put into practice? I say: It is because of standards of righteousness. And so, if they use standards of righteousness in order to make social divisions, then they will be harmonized. If they are harmonized, then they will be unified. If they are unified, then they will have more force. If they have more force, then they will be strong. If they are strong, then they will be able to overcome the animals. And so, they can get to live in homes and palaces. Thus, the reason why people can order themselves with the four seasons, control the myriad things, and bring benefit to all under Heaven is none other than that they are able to get these social divisions and standards of righteousness. And so, human life cannot be without community. If they form communities but are without social divisions, then they will struggle. If they struggle, then there will be chaos. If there is chaos then they will disband. If they disband then they will be

---

30. This line is probably intended as a polemic against views such as those in *Daodejing* chapter 25 (in chapter 6 of this volume) and *Zhuangzi* chapter 2 (in chapter 8 of this volume), which seem to propose the way of Heaven as the model for human beings. See Xunzi's explicit criticism of this approach in *Xunzi* chapter 21 (below).

weak. If they are weak then they cannot overcome the animals. And so, they will not get to live in homes and palaces. This is the meaning of saying that "one must not let go of ritual and the standards of righteousness for even a moment."

One who can use these to serve his parents is called filial. One who can use these to serve his elder brother is called a proper younger brother. One who can use these to serve his superiors is called properly compliant. One who can use these to employ his subordinates is called a proper lord. The true lord is one who is good at forming community.[31] When the way of forming community is properly practiced, then the myriad things will each obtain what is appropriate for them, the six domestic animals will each obtain their proper growth, and all the various living things will obtain their proper lifespans. And so, when nurturing accords with the proper times, then the six domestic animals will multiply. When reaping accords with the proper times, then the grasses and trees will flourish. If government commands accord with the proper times, then the common people will be united, and good and worthy men will submit and obey.

These are the regulations of a sage-king: When the grasses and trees are flowering and abundant, then axes and hatchets are not to enter the mountains and forests, so as not to cut short their life, and not to break off their growth. When the turtles and crocodiles, fish and eels are pregnant and giving birth, then nets and poisons are not to enter the marshes, so as not to cut short their life, and not to break off their growth. Plow in the spring, weed in the summer, harvest in the fall, and store in the winter. These four activities are not to miss their proper times, and then the five grains will not be depleted, and the common people will have a surplus to eat. Be vigilant in the seasonal prohibitions concerning ponds, rivers, and marshes, and then turtles and fish will be fine and plentiful, and the common people will have a surplus to use. Cutting and nurturing are not to miss their proper times, and then the mountains and forests will not be barren, and the common people will have surplus materials.

This is the way a sage-king operates: He observes Heaven above, and applies this knowledge on earth below. He arranges completely everything between Heaven and earth and spreads beneficence over the ten thousand things.

> His actions are subtle, yet they are shining.
> Though they are brief, their results are long-lasting.
> Their scope is narrow; their impact, wide-ranging.

---

31. Here Xunzi is playing upon that fact that the words "lord" (*jūn* 君) and "community" (*qún* 群) were very similar in both pronunciation and written form during ancient times (a similarity that one can still perceive in their present pronunciations and written forms).

He has spirit-like powers of intelligence that are broad and vast, yet work by the utmost restraint. Thus, it is said: The person who by even the slightest movements always does what is right is called a sage.[32] . . .

Chapter Twelve: The Way to Be a Lord

There are chaotic lords; there are no states chaotic of themselves. There are men who create order; there are no rules[33] creating order of themselves. The rules of Archer Yi have not perished, but not every age has an Archer Yi who hits the target precisely. The rules of Yu still survive, but not every age has a Xia dynasty to reign as true kings. Thus, rules cannot stand alone, and categories cannot implement themselves. If one has the right person, then they will be preserved. If one loses the right person, then they will be lost. The rules are the beginning of order, and the gentleman is the origin of the rules. And so, with the gentleman present, even if the rules are sketchy, they are enough to be comprehensive. Without the gentleman, even if the rules are complete, one will fail to apply them in the right order and will be unable to respond to changes in affairs, and thus they can serve to create chaos. One who tries to correct the arrangements of the rules without understanding their meaning, even if he is broadly learned, is sure to create chaos when engaged in affairs. And so, the enlightened ruler hastens to obtain the right person.

Chapter Seventeen: Discourse on Heaven

The activities of Heaven are constant.[34] They do not persist because of Yao. They do not perish because of Jie. If you respond to them with order, then you will have good fortune. If you respond to them with chaos, then you will have misfortune.

If you strengthen the fundamental works[35] and moderate expenditures, then Heaven cannot make you poor. If your means of nurture are prepared and your actions are timely, then Heaven cannot make you ill. If you cultivate the Way and do not deviate from it, then Heaven cannot ruin you. Thus, floods and drought

---

32. The text of this paragraph is very difficult, and the translation is tentative.

33. "Rules" here is *fa* 法, which generally connotes a rule-like standard for doing things. As such, it can also mean a "method" or "model" or "law." Here it is translated as "rules" to try to cover all these senses, but it is usually rendered elsewhere as "model." Xunzi often describes ritual as a kind of *fa* (see *Xunzi* chapter 2, above).

34. This and the next few sentences are rhymed in the original.

35. The "fundamental works" are agriculture and textile production.

cannot make you go hungry or thirsty, cold and heat cannot make you sick, and aberrations and anomalies cannot make you misfortunate.

If the fundamental works are neglected and expenditures are extravagant, then Heaven cannot make you wealthy. If your means of nurture are sparse and your actions are infrequent, then Heaven cannot make you sound in body. If you turn your back on the Way and act recklessly, then Heaven cannot make you fortunate. And so, although floods and drought have not yet come, you still will go hungry. Although heat and cold are not yet pressing, you still will become sick. Although aberrations and anomalies have not yet come, you still will be misfortunate. To receive the benefit of the seasons is the same as having an ordered age, but calamities and disasters are incompatible with there being an ordered age. You must not complain against Heaven; its way is simply thus. And so, one who understands clearly the respective allotments of Heaven and humankind can be called a person of utmost achievement.

That which is accomplished without anyone's doing it and which is obtained without anyone's seeking it is called the work of Heaven. With respect to what is like this, even though he thinks deeply, a proper person does not try to ponder it. Even though he is mighty, he does not try to augment it by his own abilities. Even though he is expertly refined, he does not try to make it more keenly honed. This is called not competing with Heaven's work. When

> Heaven has its proper seasons,[36]
> Earth has its proper resources,
> And humankind has its proper order,

—this is called being able to form a triad. To neglect that whereby we form a triad and wish instead for those things to which we stand as the third is a state of confusion. The arrayed stars follow each other in their revolutions, the sun and the moon take turns shining, the four seasons proceed in succession, *yin* and *yang* undergo their great transformations, and winds and rain are broadly bestowed.

> Their harmony[37] keeps the myriad things alive.
> Their nurturing helps the myriad things to thrive.

What is such that one does not see its workings but sees only its accomplishments—this is called spirit-like power. What is such that everyone knows how it comes about but no one understands it in its formless state—this is called the accomplishment of Heaven. Only the sage does not seek to understand Heaven.

---

36. This and the following two lines are rhymed in the original.

37. I.e., the harmonious operations of the various natural elements that are mentioned in the sentence immediately prior to this remark.

When the work of Heaven has been established and the accomplishments of Heaven have been completed, then the body is set and spirit arises. Liking, dislike, happiness, anger, sorrow, and joy are contained therein—these are called one's "Heavenly dispositions." The abilities of eyes, ears, nose, mouth, and body each have their respective objects and are not able to assume each other's abilities—these are called one's "Heavenly faculties." The heart dwells in the central cavity so as to control the five faculties—this is called one's "Heavenly lord."[38] Using what is not of one's kind as a resource for nourishing what is of one's kind—this is called one's "Heavenly nourishment." To be in accordance with what is proper for one's kind is called "happiness," and to go against what is proper for one's kind is called "disaster"—this is called one's "Heavenly government." To becloud your Heavenly lord, disorder your Heavenly faculties, abandon your Heavenly nourishment, go against your Heavenly government, and turn your back on your Heavenly dispositions, so that you lose the accomplishments of Heaven—this is called the "greatest misfortune." The sage keeps clear his Heavenly lord, sets straight his Heavenly faculties, makes complete his Heavenly nourishment, accords with his Heavenly government, and nurtures his Heavenly dispositions, so as to keep whole the accomplishment of Heaven. A person who is thus is someone who knows what he is to do and what he is not to do. Then Heaven and earth will have their proper positions and the myriad things will all be servants to him. His conduct will be completely ordered, his nourishment will be completely appropriate, and his life will suffer no harm—*this* is called "knowing Heaven."

Thus, the greatest cleverness lies in not doing certain things, and the greatest wisdom lies in not pondering certain things.

> With respect to Heaven, focus only on those manifest phenomena to which you can align yourself. With respect to earth, focus only on those manifest places which are suitable for growing. With respect to the four seasons, focus only on that manifest order by which work is to be arranged. With respect to *yin* and *yang*, focus only on those manifest harmonies that can be used to order things.[39]

Let the officials keep watch over Heaven and yourself keep watch over the Way. . . .

If stars fall or trees groan, the people of the state are filled with fear and say, "What is this?" I say: It is nothing. These are simply rarely occurring things among the changes in Heaven and earth and the transformations of *yin* and *yang*. To marvel at them is permissible, but to fear them is wrong. Eclipses of the sun and moon, unseasonable winds and rain, unexpected appearances of strange stars—there is

---

38. Xunzi is playing on the fact that the character *guān* 官 (here translated as "faculty") means both "organ" and "official." Compare *Mengzi* 6A15 (in chapter 4 of this volume), where the same term is translated "office."

39. These lines are rhymed in the original.

no age in which such things do not occur. If the superiors are enlightened and the government is stable, then even if all these things come about in the same age, there is no harm done. If the superiors are benighted and the government is unstable, then even if none of these things come to pass, it is of no benefit. The falling of stars and the groaning of trees are simply rarely occurring things among the changes in Heaven and earth and the transformations of *yin* and *yang*. To marvel at them is permissible, but to fear them is wrong.

Of things that come to pass, it is human ill omens that are to be feared. When poor plowing harms the planting, when the cutting loses control over the weeds, when the government is unstable and loses control over the people, such that the fields are overgrown with weeds and the planting is bad, buying grain is expensive and the people face famine, and there are corpses lying in the roads—these are called "human ill omens." When efforts are not exerted in a timely fashion, such that cows and horses will give birth to each other and the six domestic animals produce monstrous offspring, when government orders are not clear, when policies are not timely, when the fundamental tasks are not well-ordered—these are called "human ill omens." When ritual and the standards of righteousness are not cultivated, when insiders and outsiders are not properly differentiated, when men and women engage in perverse, disorderly conduct, then fathers and sons are suspicious of one another, superiors and inferiors desert one another, and bandits and other difficulties arrive together—these are called "human ill omens." Ill omens thus arise from disorder. . . .

One performs the rain sacrifice and it rains. Why? I say: There is no special reason why. It is the same as when one does not perform the rain sacrifice and it rains anyway. When the sun and moon suffer eclipse, one tries to save them. When Heaven sends drought, one performs the rain sacrifice. One performs divination and only then decides on important affairs. But this is not to be regarded as bringing one what one seeks, but rather is done to give things proper form. Thus, the gentleman regards this as proper form, but the common people regard it as connecting with spirits. If one regards it as proper form, then one will have good fortune. If one regards it as connecting with spirits, then one will have misfortune. . . .

> To exalt Heaven and long for it—[40]
>
> How can this compare to nourishing things and overseeing them?
> To obey Heaven and praise it—
>
> How can this compare to overseeing what Heaven has mandated and using it?
> To observe the seasons and wait upon them—
>
> How can this compare to responding to the seasons and employing them?

---

40. From here down to the word "confusion" in the next paragraph, the original text is rhymed.

To follow along with things and increase them—

    How can this compare to developing their powers and transforming them?

To long for things and appraise them—

    How can this compare to ordering things and never losing them?

To desire that from which things arise—

    How can this compare to taking hold of that by which things are completed?

Thus, if one rejects what lies with humankind and instead longs for what lies with Heaven, then one will have lost grasp of the disposition of the myriad things.[41]

The unchanging element among the reigns of the hundred kings can serve as the binding thread of the Way. As one thing passes by and another arises, respond to them with this thread. If one has mastered the thread, there will be no chaos. If one does not know the thread, one will not know how to respond to changes. The major substance of the thread has never perished, but chaos arises from falling short of it, whereas order arises from adhering to it meticulously. And so as for what is counted good in light of the Way, courses of action conforming to it may be followed, but those veering from it may not be followed. Those that obscure it will create great confusion.

Those who cross waters mark out the deep places, but if the markers are not clear, then people will fall in. Those who order the people mark out the Way, but if the markers are not clear, then there will be chaos. The rituals are those markers. To reject ritual is to muddle the world, and to muddle the world is to create great chaos. And so, when the Way is in no part unclear, and that which is within the bounds and that which is outside the bounds have different markers, and that which is inglorious and that which is illustrious have constant measures, then the pitfalls of the people will be eliminated.

The myriad things are but one facet of the Way. A single thing is but one facet of the myriad things. Foolish people take a single facet of a single thing and think themselves to know the Way—this is to lack knowledge.

Shenzi saw the value of hanging back, but did not see the value of being in the lead.[42] Laozi saw the value of yielding, but did not see the value of exerting oneself.

---

41. The Chinese text of the last part of the sentence is ambiguous between two possible meanings: (1) failing to understand how the myriad things actually operate (because one mistakenly thinks Heaven exercises greater influence over them than it really does), and (2) missing the opportunity to control the condition of the myriad things (because one mistakenly focuses on Heaven's influence over them). Both senses are probably intended, and the translation here is worded to allow both construals.

42. From here down to the quote from the *History*, the original text is rhymed. Shenzi is Shen Dao (see chapter 7 of this volume). For more on Songzi, see *Important Figures* in the appendices.

Mozi saw the value of making things uniform, but did not see the value of establishing differences. Songzi saw the value of having few desires, but did not see the value of having many desires. If there is only hanging back and no being in the lead, the masses will have no gateway to advancing. If there is only yielding and no exerting oneself, the noble and the lowly will not be distinguished. If there is only uniformity and no difference, governmental orders cannot be promulgated. If there are only few desires and not many desires, the masses cannot be transformed.

The *History* says:

> Do not create new likes.
> Follow the kings' way.
> Do not create new dislikes.
> On the kings' path stay.[43]

This expresses my meaning. . . .

Chapter Nineteen: Discourse on Ritual

From what did ritual arise? I say: Humans are born having desires. When they have desires but do not get the objects of their desires, then they cannot but seek some means of satisfaction. If there is no measure or limit to their seeking, then they cannot help but struggle with each other. If they struggle with each other then there will be chaos, and if there is chaos then they will be impoverished. The former kings hated such chaos, and so they established rituals and the standards of righteousness in order to divide things among people, to nurture their desires, and to satisfy their seeking. They caused desires never to exhaust material goods, and material goods never to be depleted by desires, so that the two support each other and prosper. This is how ritual arose.[44]

Thus, ritual is a means of nurture. Meats and grains, the five flavors and the various spices are means to nurture the mouth. Fragrances and perfumes are means to nurture the nose. Carving and inlay, insignias and patterns are means to nurture the eyes. Bells and drums, pipes and chimes, lutes and zithers are means to nurture the ears. Homes and palaces, cushions and beds, tables and mats are means to nurture the body. Thus, ritual is a means of nurture. The gentleman not only obtains its nurturing, but also loves its differentiations. What is meant by "differentiations"? I say: It is for noble and lowly to have their proper ranking, for elder and youth to have their proper distance, and for poor and rich, humble and eminent each to have

---

43. Quoted earlier: see *Xunzi* chapter 2, "Cultivating Oneself" (above).

44. Cf. *Mozi* chapter 11 (in chapter 2 of this volume).

their proper weights. And so, in the Grand Chariot of the Son of Heaven there are cushions, as a means to nurture his body. On the sides are carried sweet-smelling angelica, as a means to nurture his nose. In front there is a patterned crossbar, as a means to nurture his eyes. The sounds of the attached bells match the tunes *Wu* and *Xiang*[45] when proceeding slowly, and they match the tunes *Shao* and *Hu*[46] when proceeding quickly, as a means to nurture his ears. There is a dragon pennant with nine tassels, as a means to nurture his ability to inspire trust. There are insignias of a crouching rhinoceros and kneeling tiger, serpent-decorated coverings for the horses, silk curtains, and dragon patterns on the chariot hooks, as a means to nurture his awe-inspiring authority. And so, the horses of the Grand Chariot are repeatedly given training to be obedient, and only then will they be harnessed, as a means to nurture his safety.

Know well that in going out, to abide by the proper measure even at risk of death is the means to nurture one's life. Know well that to make expenditures is the way to nurture wealth. Know well that reverence, respect, and deference are the way to nurture safety. Know well that ritual, the standards of righteousness, good form, and proper order are the way to nurture one's dispositions. And so, if a person has his eyes only on living, such a one is sure to die. If a person has his eyes only on benefiting himself, such a one is sure to be harmed. If a person seeks safety only in laziness and sluggishness, such a one is sure to be endangered. If a person takes pleasure only in delighting his inborn dispositions, such a one is sure to be destroyed. And so, if a person puts even one amount of effort into following ritual and the standards of righteousness, he will get back twice as much. If he puts even one amount of effort into following his inborn dispositions and nature, he will lose twice as much. And so, the Confucians are those who will cause people to gain twice as much, and the Mohists are those who will cause people to lose twice as much. This is the difference between the Confucians and the Mohists.

Ritual has three roots. Heaven and earth are the root of life. Forefathers and ancestors are the root of one's kind. Lords and teachers are the root of order. Without Heaven and earth, how would one live? Without forefathers and ancestors, how would one have come forth? Without lords and teachers, how would there be order? If even one of these three roots is neglected, no one will be safe. And so, ritual serves Heaven above and earth below, it honors forefathers and ancestors, and it exalts lords and teachers. These are the three roots of ritual. . . .

In every case, ritual begins in that which must be released, reaches full development in giving it proper form, and finishes in providing it satisfaction. And so,

---

45. The *Wu* and the *Xiang* were pieces of music associated with King Wu.

46. The *Shao* and *Hu* were pieces of music associated with Shun and Tang, respectively.

when ritual is at its most perfect, the requirements of inner dispositions and proper form are both completely fulfilled.[47] At its next best, the dispositions and outer form overcome one another in succession. Its lowest manner is to revert to the dispositions alone so as to subsume everything in this grand unity.

> By ritual, Heaven and earth harmoniously combine;
> By ritual, the sun and the moon radiantly shine;
> By ritual, the four seasons in progression arise;
> By ritual, the stars move orderly across the skies;
> By ritual, the great rivers through their courses flow;
> By ritual, the ten thousand things all thrive and grow;
> By ritual, for love and hate proper measure is made;
> By ritual, on joy and anger fit limits are laid.
> By ritual, compliant subordinates are created,
> By ritual, enlightened leaders are generated;
> With ritual, all things can change yet not bring chaos,
> But deviate from ritual and you face only loss.

Is not ritual perfect indeed! It establishes a lofty standard that is the ultimate of its kind, and none under Heaven can add to or subtract from it. In it, the fundamental and the secondary accord with each other, and beginning and end match each other. In its differentiations of things, it is the utmost in patterning. In its explanations, it is the utmost in keen discernment. Those under Heaven who follow it will have good order. Those who do not follow it will have chaos. Those who follow it will have safety. Those who do not follow it will be endangered. Those who follow it will be preserved. Those who do not follow it will perish. The petty man cannot fathom it. Deep indeed is the pattern of ritual! Investigations into the hard and the white, the same and the different drown when they try to enter into it.[48] Vast indeed is the pattern of ritual! Those expert in creating institutions and the purveyors of perverse, vulgar doctrines are lost when they try to enter it. High indeed is the pattern of ritual! Those who take violent arrogance, haughty indulgence, and contempt of custom for loftiness fall when they try to enter it.

And so, when the ink-line is reliably laid out, then one cannot be deceived by the curved and the straight. When the scale is reliably hung, then one cannot be deceived by the light and the heavy. When the compass and carpenter's square

---

47. Here and in many other places in "Discourse on Ritual," Xunzi is relying on the sense of *qing,* "dispositions," that is closer to our notion of "emotions." (For more on *qing,* see note 22, above.) In this case, his point seems to be that the perfect form of ritual is one in which inner feeling and outer expression are perfectly balanced and matched. Cf. *Analects* 6.18 (in chapter 1 of this volume).

48. This refers to debates among members of the so-called School of Names (see chapter 5 of this volume).

are reliably deployed, then one cannot be deceived by the circular and the rectangular. The gentleman examines ritual carefully, and then he cannot be deceived by trickery and artifice. Thus, the ink-line is the ultimate in straightness, the scale is the ultimate in balance, the compass and carpenter's square are the ultimate in circular and rectangular, and ritual is the ultimate in the human way. Those who nevertheless do not take ritual as their model nor find sufficiency in it are called "standardless commoners." Those who take ritual as their model and find sufficiency in it are called "men of standards." To be able to reflect and ponder what is central to ritual is called "being able to deliberate." To be able to be undeviating in what is central to ritual is called "being able to be firm." When one can deliberate and be firm, and adds to this fondness for it, then this is to be a sage. Thus, Heaven is the ultimate in height, earth is the ultimate in depth, the boundless is the ultimate in breadth, and the sage is the ultimate in the Way. And so, learning is precisely learning to be a sage—one does not learn solely so as to become a standardless commoner.

Ritual takes resources and goods as its implements. It takes noble and lowly as its patterns. It takes abundance and scarcity as its differentiations. It takes elevating some and lowering others as its essentials. When patterning and order are made bountiful, and the dispositions and implements are limited, this is the most elevated state of ritual. When the dispositions and implements are made bountiful, but the patterning and order are limited, this is the lowest state of ritual. When patterning and order, dispositions and implements are in turn central and peripheral, so that they proceed together and are mixed evenly, this is the intermediate course of ritual. And so, at his greatest, the gentleman achieves the most elevated state of ritual, and at the least he fulfills completely its lowest form, and when in intermediate circumstances, he dwells in its intermediate form. Whether going slowly, quickly, or at full gallop, he never departs from this, for this is the gentleman's home and palace. If a person grasps this, he is a man of good breeding or a gentleman. If he departs from this, he is but a commoner. Thus, to be able to travel everywhere in its midst and in every case obtain its proper arrangement is to be a sage. And so, being generous is due to the accumulated richness of ritual. Being great is due to the vastness of ritual. Being lofty is due to the elevated nature of ritual. Being enlightened is due to the exhaustive nature of ritual. The *Odes* says:

> Ritual and ceremony have right measure completely.
> Laugh and speak only in complete accord with propriety.[49]

---

49. *Mao* # 209. These same lines are quoted earlier: see *Xunzi* chapter 2, "Cultivating Oneself," (above).

This expresses my meaning.

Ritual is that which takes care to order living and dying. Birth is the beginning of people, and death is the end of people. When beginning and end are both good, then the human way is complete. Thus, the gentleman is respectful of the beginning and careful about the end. When end and beginning are treated alike,[50] this is the way of the gentleman, and the proper form contained in ritual and the standards of righteousness. To treat people generously while alive but stingily when dead is to show respect to those with awareness and show arrogance to those without awareness. This is the way of a vile person and is an attitude of betrayal. The gentleman considers it shameful to use such a betraying attitude in dealing with servants and children—how much more so in the case of those he exalts and those he loves! . . .

For the funeral of the Son of Heaven, one notifies all within the Four Seas and summons the feudal lords. For the funeral of a feudal lord, one notifies all allied states and summons the grand ministers. For the funeral of a grand minister, one notifies all within his state and summons those distinguished among the well-bred. For the funeral of a distinguished, well-bred man, one notifies all in his county and summons his associates. For the funeral of a common person, one gathers together his family and friends and notifies all within the neighborhood and district. For the funeral of an executed convict, one is not allowed to assemble his family and friends but rather summons only his wife and children. The coffin's thickness may be only three inches. There may be only three layers of burial clothing and coverings. One is not allowed to decorate the coffin. One is not allowed to have the funeral procession during the day but must rather perform the interment at night. One goes out to bury him wearing ordinary clothing, and upon returning, there are to be no periods of crying, no wearing of mourning garb, and no differentiation of mourning periods for closer and more distant relatives. Everyone is to return to their normal ways and revert to their original state. When a person has just been buried, but it is as though there had never been a funeral and the matter has simply come to an end, this is called the greatest disgrace.[51]

Ritual takes care that fortunate and unfortunate events do not intrude upon each other. When it comes to the point where one has to place gauze on the person's face[52] and listen for breathing, then the loyal minister and filial son know that the

---

50. I.e., with one and the same care.

51. Commentators note that Xunzi's description of this last kind of funeral largely resembles the kind of mourning regulations prescribed by Mozi for everyone (see *Mozi* chapter 25, in chapter 2 of this volume), and thus this passage serves as a criticism of Mozi by implying that Mozi would have us treat even our dearest loved ones as no better than executed criminals.

52. I.e., as a means of detecting breath visually.

person's illness is serious indeed. Even so, they do not yet seek the items for dressing the corpse and the lying-in-state. They weep and are filled with fear. Even so, they do not stop in their feelings of hoping that miraculously the person will live, and they do not cease their attempts to maintain the person's life. Only when the person has truly died do they then make and prepare the necessary items.

Thus, even the best-equipped households are sure to pass a day before the lying in state, and three days before the mourning garments are complete. Only then do those sent to notify people far away set out, and only then do those responsible for preparing things get to work.

And so, at its longest, the lying in state is not to last for more than seventy days, and at its quickest, it is not to last less than fifty days. Why is this? I say: It is so that those far away can come, so that many needs can be fulfilled, and so that many matters can be accomplished. The loyalty expressed in this is of the highest sort. The proper regulation involved in this is of the greatest type. The good form displayed in this is of the greatest kind. . . .

The standard practice of funeral rites is that one changes the appearance of the corpse by gradually adding more ornamentation, one moves the corpse gradually further away, and over a long time one gradually returns to one's regular routine. Thus, the way that death works is that if one does not ornament the dead, then one will come to feel disgust at them, and if one feels disgust, then one will not feel sad. If one keeps them close, then one will become casual with them, and if one becomes casual with them, then one will grow tired of them. If one grows tired of them, then one will forget one's place, and if one forgets one's place, then one will not be respectful. If one day a person loses his lord or father, but his manner in sending them off to be buried is neither sad nor respectful, then he is close to being a beast. The gentleman is ashamed of this, and so the reason that he changes the appearance of the corpse by gradually adding more ornamentation is to eliminate any disgust. The reason that he moves the corpse gradually further away is to pursue respectfulness. The reason that only over a long time does he gradually return to his regular routine is to properly adjust his life.

Ritual cuts off what is too long and extends what is too short. It subtracts from what is excessive and adds to what is insufficient. It achieves proper form for love and respect, and it brings to perfection the beauty of carrying out the standards of righteousness. Thus, fine ornaments and coarse materials, music and weeping, happiness and sorrow—these things are opposites, but ritual makes use of them all, employing them and alternating them at the appropriate times. And so, fine ornaments, music, and happiness are that by which one responds to peaceful events and by which one pays homage to good fortune. Coarse mourning garments, weeping, and sorrow are that by which one responds to threatening events and by which one pays homage to ill fortune. Thus, the way ritual makes use of fine ornaments is such as not to lead to exorbitance and indulgence. The way it makes use of coarse mourning garments is such as not to lead to infirmity or despondency. The way it makes use of music and happiness is such as not to lead to perversity or laziness. The way it makes use of weeping and sorrow is such as not to lead to dejection or self-harm. This is the midway course of ritual.

Thus, when the changes in disposition and appearance are sufficient to differentiate good fortune and ill fortune and to make clear the proper measures for noble and lowly, close relations and distant relations, then ritual stops. To go beyond this is vile, and even should it be a feat of amazing difficulty, the gentleman will still consider it base. And so, to measure one's food and then eat it, to measure one's waist and then tie the mourning sash, to show off to those in high positions one's emaciation and infirmity—this is the way of a vile person. It is not the proper patterning of ritual and the standards of righteousness; it is not the true disposition of a filial son. It is rather the behavior of one acting for ulterior purposes.

And so, a joyful glow and a shining face, a sorrowful look and a haggard appearance—these are the ways in which the dispositions in good fortune and ill fortune,[53] happiness and sorrow are expressed in one's countenance. Singing and laughing, weeping and sobbing—these are the ways in which the dispositions in good fortune and ill fortune, happiness and sorrow are expressed in one's voice. Fine meats and grains and wine and fish, gruel and roughage and plain water—these are the ways in which the dispositions in good fortune and ill fortune, happiness and sorrow are expressed in one's food and drink. Ceremonial caps and embroidered insignias and woven patterns, coarse cloth and a mourning headband and thin garments and hempen sandals—these are the ways in which the dispositions in good fortune and ill fortune, happiness and sorrow are expressed in one's dress. Homes and palaces and cushions and beds and tables and mats, a thatched roof and mourning lean-to and rough mat and earthen pillow—these are the ways in which the dispositions in good fortune and ill fortune, happiness and sorrow are expressed in one's dwelling.

When people are born, the beginnings of these two dispositions are originally present in them. If you cut these dispositions short and extend them, broaden them and narrow them, add to them and subtract from them, make them conform to their proper classes and fully express them, make them abundant and beautify them, cause root and branch, beginning and end all to go smoothly and fit together, then they can serve as the model for ten thousand ages—and just such is what ritual does! None but a devotedly and thoroughly cultivated gentleman can understand it.

---

53. Here *qing*, "dispositions," seems to refer specifically to people's feeling positive or negative emotions in response to good or bad events. See note 47, above.

Thus, I say that human nature is the original beginning and the raw material, and deliberate effort (*wěi* 偽) is what makes it patterned, ordered, and exalted. If there were no human nature, then there would be nothing for deliberate effort to be applied to. If there were no deliberate effort, then human nature would not be able to beautify itself. Human nature and deliberate effort must unite, and then the reputation of the sage and the work of unifying all under Heaven are thereupon brought to completion. And so, I say, when Heaven and earth unite, then the myriad creatures are born. When *yin* and *yang* interact, then changes and transformations arise. When human nature and deliberate effort unite, then all under Heaven becomes ordered. For Heaven can give birth to creatures, but it cannot enforce distinctions among creatures. Earth can support people, but it cannot order people. In the world, all members of the myriad things and the human race must await the sage, and only then will they be appropriately divided up. The *Odes* says, "He mollifies the hundred spirits, and extends this to the rivers and towering peaks."[54] This expresses my meaning.[55] . . .

For the burial offerings,[56] among the hats there is to be a helmet but no straps for binding the hair. There are to be various vessels and containers, but they are to be empty and unfilled. There are to be mats but no bedding materials. The wooden utensils are not to be completely carved, the pottery utensils are not to be finished products, and the utensils woven from reeds are not to be capable of holding things. A set of music pipes is to be prepared, but they are not to be harmonized. A lute and zither are to be laid out, but they are not to be tuned. A chariot is to be included in the burial, but the horse returns home. This is to indicate that these things will not be used.

One prepares the utensils used by the person in life and takes them to the tomb, and this resembles the way one acts when moving house. The burial goods are to be simple and not perfect. They are to have the appearance of the regular items but are not to be functional. One drives a chariot out to the tomb and buries it, but the bit ornaments, bridle, and harness are not to be included. This makes clear that these things will not be used. One uses the semblance of moving house but also makes clear that the things will not be used, and these are all means by which to heighten sorrow. . . .

---

54. *Mao # 273*.

55. This paragraph does not fit well with the context. Burton Watson (*Hsün Tzu: Basic Writings* [New York: Columbia University Press, 1963]) suggests that it may have fallen out of place from chapter 23. Nonetheless, it expresses very important ideas relating to Xunzi's view of human nature.

56. In this paragraph, Xunzi speaks mainly of the *míng qì* 明器, or so-called "spirit goods," items made specifically to be buried along with the deceased.

Depriving the dead to give to the living is called Mohism.[57]
Depriving the living to give to the dead is called confusion.
Killing the living to send off the dead is called villainy.[58] . . .

Among all the living things between Heaven and earth, those that have blood and *qi* are sure to have awareness, and of those that have awareness, none fails to love its own kind. Now if one of the great birds or beasts loses its group of companions, then after a month or a season has passed, it is sure to retrace its former path and go by its old home. When it does, it is sure to pace back and forth, cry out, stomp the ground, pause hesitatingly, and only then is it able to leave the place. Even among smaller creatures such as swallows and sparrows, they will still screech for a moment before being able to leave. Thus, among the creatures that have blood and *qi*, none has greater awareness than man, and so man's feeling for his parents knows no limit until the day they die. Will we follow foolish, ignorant, perverse men? Those who have died that morning they forget by that evening. If one gives way to this, then one will not even be as good as the birds and beasts. How could such people come together and live in groups without there being chaos? Will we follow cultivated gentlemen? For them the twenty-five months of the three-year mourning period pass by as quickly as a galloping horse glimpsed through a crack. If one acquiesces in this, then mourning will continue without end. Therefore, the former kings and sages accordingly established a middle way and fixed a proper measure for it, such that once mourning is made sufficient to achieve good form and proper order, then one stops it.

That being the case, then how is it divided up? I say: The mourning for those most close is broken off at one year. Why is that? I say: By then, Heaven and earth have already gone through their alterations, the four seasons have already completed their course, and everything in the world changes and begins again. Thus, the sage-kings accordingly took this and made it their image. That being the case, then why the three-year mourning period? I say: To add loftiness to it, they accordingly made the period double, and thus it continues for another year. What about the mourning of nine months and below? I say: They accordingly made it not reach as long. Thus, the three-year mourning period is the most lofty, the *sima* and *xiaogong* mourning periods are the most slight,[59] and the year-long and nine-month mourning periods are in between. The sage-kings took an image from

---

57. This sentence and the two that follow it are rhymed in the original.

58. The term *zéi* 賊, here translated as "villainy," often had the connotation of murder in particular. Xunzi here is criticizing the practice of "accompanying burials," in which people were sacrificed to serve the deceased in death.

59. The *sima* lasted for three months, and the *xiaogong* lasted for five months.

Heaven above, they took an image from earth below, they took a standard from humans in the middle, and then the order by which people are to live together in harmony and unity was complete. . . .

The sacrificial rites are the refined expression of remembrance and longing. To be moved and feel upset are things that cannot but come upon one at times. And so, on occasions when people are happy and join together harmoniously, then a loyal minister or filial son will also be moved and such feelings will come to him. When the feelings that come to him stir him greatly but simply play themselves out and stop, then with regard to the refined expression of remembrance he will feel anguished and unsatisfied, and his practice of ritual and proper regulation would be lacking and incomplete. And so, the former kings accordingly established a proper form for it, and thereby was set what is righteous in venerating those esteemed and loving those intimate. Thus, I say: The sacrificial rites are the refined expression of remembrance and longing. They are the utmost in loyalty, trustworthiness, love, and respect. They are the fullest manifestation of ritual, proper regulation, good form, and proper appearance. If one is not a sage, then one will not be able to understand them. The sage clearly understands them. The well-bred man and the gentleman are at ease in carrying them out. The officials take them as things to be preserved. The common people take them as their set customs. The gentleman regards them as the way to be a proper human being. The common people regard them as serving the ghosts. . . .

For the ritual sacrifices, one engages in divination and determines the appropriate day.

> One fasts and sweeps out the site, sets out tables and food offerings, and has the "announcement to the assistant," as if the deceased were attending a banquet.[60] The impersonator of the dead takes the goods and from each of them makes a sacrifice, as if the deceased were tasting them. One does not use a helper to raise a toast, but rather the host himself takes hold of the cup, as if the deceased were engaging in the toast. When the guests leave, the host sends them off and bows to them as they go, then returns and changes his clothing.[61] He goes back to this position and cries, as if the deceased had left. How full of sorrow! How full of respect! One serves the dead as if one were serving the living, and one serves the departed as if one were serving a surviving person. One gives a shape to that which is without physical substance and magnificently accomplishes proper form.

---

60. The "announcement to the assistant" is a part of the ceremony in which the impersonator of the dead gives blessings to the host of the ceremony. The idea seems to be that just as guests come with expressions of thankfulness for the host of a feast, so the spirit of the dead expresses thanks for the sacrifice. Also, from here to the end of the chapter, the text is rhymed in the original.

61. According to commentators, the host changes from the sacrificial robes back into the robes of mourning.

Chapter Twenty: Discourse on Music

Music is joy, an unavoidable human disposition.[62] So, people cannot be without music; if they feel joy, they must express it in sound and give it shape in movement. The way of human beings is that changes in the motions of their nature are completely contained in these sounds and movements. So, people cannot be without joy, and their joy cannot be without shape, but if it takes shape and does not accord with the Way, then there will inevitably be chaos. The former kings hated such chaos, and therefore they established the sounds of the *Ya* and the *Song*[63] in order to guide them. They caused the sounds to be enjoyable without becoming dissolute.[64] They caused the patterns to be recognizable without becoming degenerate. They caused the progression, complexity, intensity, and rhythm of the music to be sufficient to move the goodness in people's hearts. They caused perverse and corrupt *qi* to have no place to attach itself to them. This is the manner in which the former kings created music, and so why is Mozi denouncing it?[65]

And so, when music is performed in the ancestral temple and the ruler and ministers, superiors and inferiors listen to it together, none fail to become harmoniously respectful. When it is performed within the home and father and sons, elder and younger brothers listen to it together, none fail to become harmoniously affectionate. And when it is performed in the village, and old and young people listen to it together, none fail to become harmoniously cooperative. Thus, music observes a single standard in order to fix its harmony, it brings together different instruments in order to ornament its rhythm, and it combines their playing in order to achieve a beautiful pattern. It is sufficient to lead people in a single, unified way, and is sufficient to bring order to the myriad changes within them. This is the method by which the former kings created music, and so why is Mozi denouncing it?[66] . . .

Chapter Twenty-One: Undoing Fixation

In most cases, the problem with people is that they become fixated on one twist and are deluded about the greater order of things. If they are brought under control,

---

62. That is, people have a natural tendency to feel joy in response to certain things, and this tendency is sure to manifest itself in such feelings sooner or later. For more on *qing*, "dispositions," see note 22, above.

63. The names of parts of the *Odes*. See the entry for the *Odes* in *Important Texts* in the appendices.

64. Compare *Analects* 3.20 (in chapter 1 of this volume).

65. See *Mozi* chapter 32 (in chapter 2 of this volume).

66. The repetition of this sentence may be meant to mock Mozi's own repetitive style.

then they will return to the right standards. If they are of two minds, then they will be hesitant and confused. There are not two Ways for the world, and the sage is not of two minds. Nowadays, the feudal lords have different governments, and the hundred schools have different teachings, so that necessarily some are right and some are wrong, and some lead to order and some lead to chaos. The lords of chaotic states and the followers of pernicious schools all sincerely seek what they consider correct and put themselves into achieving it. They hate what they consider erroneous views of the Way, and others are seduced into following their same path. They selfishly favor the approach in which they have accumulated effort and only fear to hear it disparaged. They rely on it when regarding other approaches and only fear to hear those others praised. Therefore, they depart further and further from getting under control and think they are right not to stop. Is this not because they have become fixated on one twist and missed the true object of their search? If the heart does not apply itself to the eyes, then black and white can be right in front of you and the eyes will not see them. If the heart does not apply itself to the ears, then drums and thunder can be right at your side and the ears will not hear them. How much more so in the case of that which is applying itself in the first place![67] The person of true Virtue and the true Way is denounced from above by the lords of chaotic states, and denounced from below by the followers of pernicious schools. Is this not lamentable?

Thus, among the cases of fixation, one can be fixated on desires, or one can be fixated on dislikes. One can be fixated on origins, or one can be fixated on ends. One can be fixated on what is far away, or one can be fixated on what is nearby. One can be fixated by broad learning, or one can be fixated by narrowness. One can be fixated on the ancient past, or one can be fixated on the present. In whatever respect the myriad things are different, they can become objects of fixation to the exclusion of each other. This is the common problem in the ways of the heart. . . .

Mozi was fixated on the useful and did not understand the value of good form. Songzi was fixated on having few desires and did not understand the value of achieving their objects. Shenzi was fixated on laws and did not understand the value of having worthy people. Shen Buhai was fixated on power and did not understand the value of having wise people. Huizi was fixated on wording and did not understand the value of what is substantial. Zhuangzi was fixated on the Heavenly and did not understand the value of the human.

Thus, if one speaks of it in terms of usefulness, then the Way will consist completely in seeking what is profitable. If one speaks of it in terms of desires, then

---

67. That is, just as the heart must apply itself to the sense organs in order for them to perceive correctly, so it must watch over itself in order to avoid obsession and apprehend the truth.

the Way will consist completely in learning to be satisfied. If one speaks of it in terms of laws, then the Way will consist completely in making arrangements. If one speaks of it in terms of power, then the Way will consist completely in finding what is expedient. If one speaks of it in terms of wording, then the Way will consist completely in discoursing on matters. If one speaks of it in terms of the Heavenly, then the Way will consist completely in following along with things. These various approaches are all merely one corner of the Way. As for the Way itself, its substance is constant, yet it covers all changes. No one corner is sufficient to exhibit it fully.

People of twisted understanding observe one corner of the Way and are unable to recognize it as such. So, they think it sufficient and proceed to embellish it. On the inside, they use it to disorder their own lives. On the outside, they use it to confuse other people. As superiors, they use it to transfix their subordinates. As subordinates, they use it to transfix their superiors. This is the disaster of being fixated and blocked up in one's thinking. Kongzi was benevolent, wise, and was not fixated, and so through his study of various methods, he was worthy of being one of the former kings. His one line alone grasped the way of the Zhou and upheld and used it, because he was not fixated by accumulated deeds. Thus, his Virtue equals that of the Duke of Zhou, and his name ranks with those of the three kings. This is the good fortune that comes from not being fixated.

The sage knows the problems in the ways of the heart, and sees the disaster of being fixated and blocked up in one's thinking. So, he is neither for desires, nor for dislikes, is neither for the origins, nor for the end results, is neither for what is near, nor for what is far away, is neither for what is broad, nor for what is shallow, is neither for the ancient past, nor is for the present. He lays out all the myriad things, and in their midst suspends his scales. For this reason, the various different things are unable to become fixating and so disorder his categories of judgment.

What am I calling his "scales"? I say: It is the Way. Thus, one's heart must not be ignorant of the Way. If the heart does not know the Way, then it will not approve of the Way, but will rather approve what is not the Way. For what person would wish to be so dissolute as to keep to what they disapprove and reject what they approve? If one chooses people using a heart that does not approve of the Way, then one is sure to accord with people who do not follow the Way, and one will not know to accord with people who *do* follow the Way. To use a heart that does not approve of the Way and to join together with people who do not follow the Way when judging people who do follow the Way—this is the root of chaos.

How will one know [which are the people who follow the Way]? I say: The heart must know the Way, and only then will it approve of the Way. Only after it approves of the Way will it be able to keep to the Way and reject what is not the Way. If one chooses people using a heart that approves of the Way, then one will accord with people who follow the Way, and one will not accord with people who do not follow the Way. To use a heart that approves of the Way and to join together with people who follow the Way when judging what is not the Way—this is the essential thing for good order. What problem of not knowing [those who follow the Way] could there be? Thus, the essential thing for good order rests in knowing the Way.

How do people know the Way? I say: With the heart. How does the heart know the Way? I say: It is through emptiness, single-mindedness, and stillness. The heart is always holding something. Yet, there is what is called being "empty." The heart is always twofold. Yet, there is what is called being "single-minded." The heart is always moving. Yet, there is what is called being "still." Humans are born and have awareness. With awareness, they have focus.[68] To focus is to be holding something. Yet, there is something called being "empty." Not to let what one is already holding harm what one is about to receive is called being "empty."[69] The heart is born and has awareness. With awareness, there comes awareness of differences. These differences are known at the same time, and when they are known at the same time, this is to be twofold. Yet, there is what is called being "single-minded." Not to let one idea harm another idea is called being "single-minded." When the heart sleeps, then it dreams. When it relaxes, then it goes about on its own. When one puts it to use, then it forms plans. Thus, the heart is always moving. Yet, there is what is called being "still." Not to let dreams and worries disorder one's understanding is called being "still."

For those who have not yet grasped the Way but are seeking the Way, I say: Emptiness, single-mindedness, and stillness—make these your principles. If one who would search for the Way achieves emptiness, then he may enter upon it. If one who would work at the Way achieves single-mindedness, then he will exhaustively obtain it. If one who would ponder the Way achieves stillness, then he will discern it keenly. One who knows the Way and observes things by it, who knows the Way and puts it into practice, is one who embodies the Way. To be empty, single-minded, and still—this is called great clarity and brilliance. For such a one, none of the myriad things takes form and is not seen. None is seen and not judged. None is judged and loses its proper position. He sits in his chamber yet sees all

---

68. "Focus" is *zhi* 志. This is the character that appears in the text, but most other commentators and translators read it as *zhi* 誌, "memory." Cf. *Mengzi* 2A2 (in chapter 4 of this volume, where *zhi* is translated "resolution"; see also the accompanying note 19) and *Zhuangzi* chapter 4 (in chapter 8 of this volume, where *zhi* is translated "attention"; see also the accompanying note 49).

69. From this explanation, it is clear that what Xunzi means by "emptiness" is *not* having no thoughts or clearing out one's mind, but rather the ability to take up new ideas and objects of attention. Thus, his "emptiness" is more akin to what nowadays would be called "receptiveness."

within the Four Seas.[70] He dwells in today yet judges what is long ago and far away in time. He comprehensively observes the myriad things and knows their true dispositions. He inspects and examines order and disorder and discerns their measures. He sets straight Heaven and earth, and arranges and makes useful the myriad things. He institutes great order, and the whole world is encompassed therein.

> So vast and broad is he! Who grasps his true limits?
> So lofty and broad is he! Who grasps his true Virtue?
> So active and varied is he! Who grasps his true form?[71]

His brilliance matches the sun and moon. His greatness fills all the directions. Such a one is called the "Great Man." What fixation could there be in him?

The heart is the lord of the body and the master of one's spirit and intelligence. It issues orders, but it takes orders from nothing: *it* restrains itself, *it* employs itself; *it* lets itself go, *it* takes itself in hand; *it* makes itself proceed, *it* makes itself stop. Thus, the mouth can be compelled either to be silent or to speak, and the body can be compelled either to contract or to extend itself, but the heart cannot be compelled to change its thoughts. What it considers right, one accepts. What it considers wrong, one rejects. And so, I say: If the heart allows its choices to be without restraint, then when it reveals its objects[72] they will surely be broadly varying. Its perfected disposition is to be undivided. The *Odes* says,

> I pick and pick the *juan-er* leaves,
> but cannot fill my sloping basket.
> Oh, for my cherished one!
> He is stationed on the Zhou campaign.[73]

A sloping basket is easy to fill, and the *juan-er* leaves are easy to get, but one must not be divided with thoughts of the Zhou campaign. And so, I say: If the heart is split, it will be without understanding. If it deviates, it will not be expertly refined. If it is divided, then it will be confused. If one guides its examinations, then the myriad things can all be known together, and if the person thoroughly develops his original substance, then he will be truly beautiful.

---

70. Compare *Daodejing* chapter 47 (in chapter 6 of this volume).

71. The first two of these lines are rhymed in the original. The third does not rhyme in its current form, and Gu Qianli suggests emending the word "form" to make it rhyme. I have not adopted his emendation, but given the parallel structure here, it is likely that the third line was supposed to be part of the rhymed set, so I have grouped it with the others.

72. The word here is *wù* 物 (lit. "things"), which in this context could refer to one's thoughts and/or to one's purposes; rendering it as "objects" is intended to cover both possibilities.

73. *Mao # 3*. These lines are rhymed in the original.

The proper classes of things are not of two kinds. Hence, the person with understanding picks the one right object and pursues it single-mindedly. The farmer is expert in regard to the fields, but cannot be made Overseer of Fields. The merchant is expert in regard to the markets, but cannot be made Overseer of Merchants. The craftsman is expert in regard to vessels, but cannot be made Overseer of Vessels. There is a person who is incapable of any of their three skills, but who can be put in charge of any of these offices, namely the one who is expert in regard to the Way, not the one who is expert in regard to things. One who is expert in regard to things merely measures one thing against another. One who is expert in regard to the Way measures all things together.[74] Thus, the gentleman pursues the Way single-mindedly and uses it to guide and oversee things. If one pursues the Way single-mindedly, then one will be correct. If one uses it to guide one in examining things, then one will have keen discernment. If one uses correct intentions to carry out discerning judgments, then the ten thousand things will all obtain their proper station. . . .

The human heart can be compared to a pan of water. If you set it straight and do not move it, the muddy and turbid parts will settle to the bottom, and the clear and bright parts will be on the top, and then one can see one's whiskers and inspect the lines on one's face. But if a slight breeze passes over it, the muddy and turbid parts will be stirred up from the bottom, and the clear and bright parts will be disturbed on top, and then one cannot get a correct view of even large contours. The heart is just like this.[75] Thus, if one guides it with good order, nourishes it with clarity and nothing can make it deviate, then it will be capable of determining right and wrong and deciding what is doubtful. If it is drawn aside by even a little thing, then on the outside one's correctness will be altered, and on the inside one's heart will deviate, and one will be incapable of discerning the multifarious patterns of things. . . .

In the caves there lived a man named Ji.[76] He was good at guessing riddles because he was fond of pondering things. However, if the desires of his eyes and ears were aroused, it would ruin his thinking, and if he heard the sounds of mosquitoes or gnats, it would frustrate his concentration. So, he shut out the desires of his eyes and ears and put himself far away from the sounds of mosquitoes and gnats, and by dwelling in seclusion and stilling his thoughts, he achieved comprehension. But can pondering benevolence in such a manner be called "true sublimeness"? Mengzi hated depravity and so expelled his wife—this can be called "being able to force

---

74. Compare *Analects* 2.12 (in chapter 1 of this volume; see also the accompanying note 23).

75. Compare *Zhuangzi* chapter 5 (in chapter 8 of this volume).

76. This person is unattested elsewhere, and the pronunciation of the name is uncertain.

oneself."[77] Youzi[78] hated dozing off and so burned his palm to keep awake—this can be called "being able to steel oneself." These are not yet true fondness. To shut out the desires of one's eyes and ears can be called "forcing oneself." It is not yet truly pondering. To be such that hearing the sounds of mosquitoes or gnats frustrates one's concentration is called "being precarious." It cannot yet be called "true sublimeness." One who is truly sublime is a perfected person. For the perfected person, what forcing oneself, what steeling oneself, what precariousness is there? Thus, those who are murky understand only external manifestations, but those who are clear understand internal manifestations. The sage follows his desires and embraces all his dispositions, and the things dependent on these simply turn out well-ordered. What forcing oneself, what steeling oneself, what precariousness is there? Thus, the person of benevolence carries out the Way without striving, and the sage carries out the Way without forcing himself. The benevolent person ponders it with reverence, and the sage ponders it with joy. This is the proper way to order one's heart.

Chapter Twenty-Two: On Correct Naming[79]

In setting names for things, the later kings followed the Shang in names for punishments, followed the Zhou in names for official titles, and also followed their rituals in names for cultural forms. In applying various names to the myriad things, they followed the set customs and generally agreed usage of the various Xia states. Villages in distant places with different customs followed along with these names and so were able to communicate.

As for the ways the various names apply to people, that by which they are as they are at birth is called "human nature." The close connection of response to stimulus, which requires no effort but is so of itself, and which is produced by the harmonious operation of the nature, is also called "human nature." The feelings of liking and disliking, happiness and anger, and sadness and joy in one's nature are called the "dispositions" (*qíng* 情).[80] When there is a certain disposition and the

---

77. For an account of this incident, see D. C. Lau, trans., *Mencius* (New York: Penguin Books, 1970), 217.

78. Youzi, also known as You Ruo, was a disciple of Kongzi.

79. "On Correct Naming" deals, among other things, with issues raised by the School of Names (see chapter 5 of this volume). For the phrase "Correct Naming," see *Analects* 13.3 (in chapter 1 of this volume; see also the accompanying note 118). "Name" in both passages is *míng* 名, which can refer not only to proper names, but to words in general.

80. For more on *qing,* "dispositions," see note 22 above. Here Xunzi most clearly has in mind the aspect of *qing* we call "emotions."

heart makes a choice on its behalf, this is called "deliberation."[81] When the heart deliberates and one's abilities act on it, this is called "deliberate effort." That which comes into being through accumulated deliberations and training of one's abilities is also called "deliberate effort." Actions performed for the sake of profit are called "work." Actions performed for what is required by the standards of righteousness are called "personal conduct." That by which people understand things is called the "understanding." When the understanding connects to things, this is called "knowledge." That by which people are able to do things is called "ability." When ability connects to things, these are also called "abilities."[82] When the nature is injured, this is called "illness." When one encounters unexpected circumstances, this is called "fate" (*ming* 命). These are the ways the various names apply to people. These are the ways the later kings set names for things.

So, when the kings established names, the names were fixed, and the corresponding objects were thus distinguished. This way was followed, and the kings' intentions were thus made understood. They then carefully led the people to adhere to these things single-mindedly. Thus, they called it great vileness to mince words and recklessly create names so as to disorder the correct names and thereby confuse the people and cause them to engage in much disputation and litigation. This wrongdoing was considered to be just like the crime of forging tallies and measures. Hence, none of their people dared rely on making up strange names so as to disorder the correct names, and so the people were honest. Since they were honest, they were easy to employ, and since they were easy to employ, tasks were accomplished. Because none of the people dared rely on making up strange names so as to disorder the correct names, they were unified in following the proper model of the Way and were conscientious in following commands. Because they were like this, the legacy of the kings was long-lasting. To have such a long-lasting legacy and to achieve such accomplishments is the height of good order. Such is what can be accomplished by diligently preserving the agreed names.

Nowadays, the sage-kings have passed away, and the preservation of these names has become lax. Strange words have arisen, the names and their corresponding objects are disordered, and the forms of right and wrong are unclear. As a result, even officers who diligently preserve the proper models and scholars who diligently recite the proper order for things are also all thrown into chaos. If there arose a true king, he would surely follow the old names in some cases and create new names

---

81. That is, when one is disposed a certain way, such as feeling anger, and the heart reflects and chooses whether and how one will act on that feeling, this is to engage in deliberation.

82. That is, when the potential to do something is manifested in a certain activity, it is called a particular ability (e.g., one is said to have the *ability* to drive when one performs the activities specific to that skill).

in other cases.[83] Thus, one must examine the reason for having names, the proper means for distinguishing like and unlike, and the essential points in establishing names.

When different forms make contact with the heart, they make each other understood as different things. If the names and their corresponding objects[84] are tied together in a confused fashion, then the distinction between noble and base will not be clear, and the like and the unlike will not be differentiated. If this is so, then the problem of intentions not being understood will surely happen, and the disaster of affairs being thereby impeded and abandoned will surely occur. Thus, the wise person draws differences and establishes names in order to point out their corresponding objects. Most importantly, he makes clear the distinction between noble and base, and, at the least, he distinguishes the like and the unlike. When noble and base are clearly distinguished, and like and unlike are differentiated, then the problem of intentions not being understood will not happen, and the disaster of affairs being thereby impeded and abandoned will not occur. This is the reason for having names. . . .

Names have no predetermined appropriateness. One forms agreement in order to name things. Once the agreement is set and has become custom, then they are called "appropriate," and what differs from the agreed usage is called "inappropriate." Names have no predetermined objects. One forms agreement in order to name objects. Once the agreement is set and has become custom, then they are called "names of objects."[85] Names do have a predetermined goodness. If they are straightforward, simple, and do not conflict, then they are called "good names." Some things have a like appearance but reside in unlike classes, and others have unlike appearances but reside in the like class, and these two can be differentiated. For those which have a like appearance but reside in unlike classes, even though they could be combined into one class, they are called two separate objects. If the appearance changes but the object does not become different so as to belong to an unlike class, this is called a transformation. When there is transformation without such difference, it is still called one and the same object. These are what to rely

---

83. A noteworthy alternative way of reading this line is proposed by the commentator Wang Xianqian, who interprets it as saying, "If a true king were to arise, he would surely follow along with the old names [that are still in use] and change back the new [i.e., bad] names."

84. Xunzi's word "object" (shí 實) appears to include both the meaning and referent of a term, as distinguished by modern philosophers.

85. Xunzi's point seems to be that only after usage is set do the names have any meaning, rather than being mere sound.

upon in observing the objects and determining their numbers.[86] This is the essential point in establishing names, and the names established by the later kings must not go unexamined.

Claims such as "To be insulted is not disgraceful,"[87] "The sage does not love himself,"[88] and "To kill a robber is not to kill a man"[89] are cases of confusion about the use of names leading to disordering names. If one tests them against the reason why there are names, and observes what happens when they are carried out thoroughly, then one will be able to reject them. Claims such as "Mountains and gorges are level,"[90] "The desires of one's natural dispositions are few,"[91] "Fine meats are not any more flavorful," and "Great bells are not any more entertaining"[92] are cases of confusion about the use of objects leading to disordering names. If one tests them against the proper means for distinguishing like and unlike, and observes what happens when they are thoroughly practiced, then one will be able to reject them. Claims such as [. . .][93] "Oxen and horses are not horses"[94] are cases of confusion about the use of names leading to disordering the objects. If one tests them against the agreement on names, using the fact that what such people accept goes against what they reject, then one will be able to reject them. In every case of deviant sayings and perverse teachings that depart from the correct Way and recklessly innovate, they will belong to one of these three classes of confusion. Thus, the enlightened lord understands their kind and does not dispute with such people.

The people can easily be unified by means of the Way, but one should not try to share one's reasons with them. Hence, the enlightened lord controls them with his power, guides them with the Way, moves them with his orders, arrays them with his judgments, and restrains them with his punishments. Thus, his people's

---

86. Xunzi here seems to be talking about identifying and individuating classes, rather than identifying and individuating particular entities.

87. This claim was put forth by Songzi.

88. It is unknown who put forth this claim.

89. This is a famous Mohist argument.

90. This claim was put forth and defended by Huizi (see chapter 5 in this volume).

91. This is another of Songzi's famous claims.

92. The origin of these last two statements is uncertain.

93. Here the text seems very corrupt. I have translated the clearest part of the sentence, and omitted the rest.

94. It is uncertain who maintained this thesis, but its similarity to the famous claim that "a white horse is not a horse" made by Gongsun Longzi suggests that it might also be his (see "On the White Horse," in chapter 5 in this volume). We also find the similar phrase "Oxen and horses are not [only] oxen and they are not [only] horses" in a passage that is apparently part of a rebuttal to Gongsun Longzi in *Mohist Canon* B (not in this volume).

transformation by the Way is spirit-like. What need has he for demonstrations[95] and persuasions? Nowadays the sage-kings have all passed away, the whole world is in chaos, and depraved teachings are arising. The gentleman has no power to control people, no punishments to restrain them, and so he engages in demonstrations and persuasions.

When objects are not understood, then one engages in naming. When the naming is not understood, then one tries to procure agreement. When the agreement is not understood, then one engages in persuasion. When the persuasion is not understood, then one engages in demonstration. Thus, procuring agreement, naming, discrimination, and persuasion are some of the greatest forms of useful activity, and are the beginning of kingly works. When a name is heard and the corresponding object is understood, this is usefulness in names. When they are accumulated and form a pattern, this is beauty in names. When one obtains both their usefulness and beauty, this is called understanding names. Names are the means by which one arranges and accumulates objects. Sentences combine the names of different objects in order to discuss a single idea. Persuasion and demonstration use fixed names of objects in order to make clear the proper ways for acting and remaining still. Procuring agreement and naming are the functions of demonstration and persuasion. Demonstration and persuasion are the heart's way of representing the Way. The heart is the craftsman and overseer of the Way. The Way is the warp and pattern of good order. When the heart fits with the Way, when one's persuasions fit with one's heart, when one's words fit one's persuasions, then one will name things correctly and procure agreement, will base oneself on the true disposition of things and make them understood, will discriminate among things without going to excess, and will extend by analogy the categories of things without violating them. When listening to cases, one will accord with good form. When engaging in demonstration, one will cover thoroughly all the reasons. One will use the true Way to discriminate what is vile, just like drawing out the carpenter's line in order to grasp what is curved and what is straight. Thus, deviant sayings will not be able to cause disorder, and the hundred schools will have nowhere to hide. . . .

All those who say that good order must await the elimination of desires are people who lack the means to guide desire and cannot handle the mere having of desires. All those who say good order must await the lessening of desires are people who lack the means to restrain desire and cannot handle abundance of desires.

---

95. The word here is *biàn* 辨, which literally means "to discriminate among things." This character was interchangeable with another, also read *biàn* 辩, which means "to argue, dispute." The text seems to play on a fusion of these senses in the idea that true differences between things will be presented and defended through argument. Therefore, I have rendered it "demonstration" to convey the sense both of pointing out differences and arguing for a position.

Having desires and lacking desires fall under two different kinds, namely being alive and being dead, not order and disorder. Having many desires and having few desires also fall under different kinds, namely the numbers of people's dispositions, not order and disorder.

The occurrence of desires does not wait upon the permissibility of fulfilling them, but those who seek to fulfill them follow what they approve of.[96] That the occurrence of desires does not wait upon the permissibility of fulfilling them is something which is received from Heaven. That those who seek to fulfill them follow what they approve is something which is received from the heart. When a single desire received from Heaven is controlled by many things received from the heart, then it will be difficult to classify it as something received from Heaven.

Life is what people most desire, and death is what people most despise. However, when people let go of life and accomplish their own death, this is not because they do not desire life and instead desire death. Rather, it is because they do not approve of living in these circumstances, but do approve of dying in these circumstances.[97] Thus, when the desire is excessive but the action does not match it, this is because the heart prevents it. If what the heart approves conforms to the proper patterns, then even if one's desires are many, what harm would they be to good order? When the desire is lacking but one's action surpasses it, this is because the heart compels it. If what the heart approves misses the proper patterns, then even if the desires are few, how would it stop short of chaos? Thus, order and disorder reside in what the heart approves, they are not present in the desires from one's dispositions. If you do not seek for them where they reside, and instead seek for them where they are not present, then even though you say, "I have grasped them," you have simply missed them.

Human nature is the accomplishment of Heaven. The dispositions are the substance of the nature. The desires are the responses of the dispositions to things. Viewing the objects of desire as permissible to obtain and seeking them are what the dispositions cannot avoid. Deeming something permissible and guiding one are

---

96. This section is difficult to translate, because the word *kě* 可 is used multiple times in senses that cannot always be easily rendered consistently into English, and it is not clear that Xunzi is using it consistently in the first place. When used as a verb, I have rendered it as "approve." When used adjectivally or adverbially in this section, I have usually rendered it as "permissible" (where I take it that Xunzi really intends something like "should be approved"). *Ke* also has the sense of "possible [to do]," and in certain places, it seems necessary to take it this way (which I have rendered as "can" or "cannot"). One could try to use this latter sense throughout, substituting "possible" for "permissible" and "think possible" for "approve," which would give the argument a very different sense, but it seems to me that such a reading is less preferable given the overall context.

97. This might be a denial of the claim about the role of desire in moral motivation made in *Mengzi* 6A10 (in chapter 4 of this volume).

what the understanding must provide. Thus, even were one a gatekeeper, the desires cannot be eliminated, because they are the necessary equipment of the nature. Even if one were the Son of Heaven, one's desires cannot be completely satisfied. Even though the desires cannot be completely satisfied, one can get close to complete satisfaction. Even though desires cannot be eliminated, one's seeking can be regulated. (Even though what is desired cannot be completely obtained, the seeker can approach complete satisfaction. Even though desires cannot be eliminated, when what is sought is not obtained, one who deliberates about matters desires to regulate his seeking.[98]) When the Way advances, then one approaches complete satisfaction. When it retreats, then one regulates one's seeking. In all under Heaven there is nothing as great as it. Among all people, no one fails to follow that which they approve and to abandon that which they do not approve. For a person to know that there is nothing as great as the Way and yet not follow the Way—there are no such cases. Suppose there were a person who did not have much desire for heading south, but did have no little dislike for heading north. How would it be that, because of the impossibility of going all the way south, he would depart from the south and instead go north? Now in the case of people who have not much desire for something, but do have no little dislike for something else, how would they, because of the impossibility of completely fulfilling their desires, depart from the way of obtaining their desires and instead take what they dislike? Thus, if one approves of the Way and follows it, how would lessening things lead to disorder? If one does not approve of the Way and departs from it, then how would increasing things lead to order? Thus, those who are wise judge the Way and that is all, and the things the lesser schools wish for in their prized doctrines will all decline.

Chapter Twenty-Three: Human Nature Is Bad

People's nature is bad. Their goodness is a matter of deliberate effort. Now people's nature is such that they are born with a fondness for profit. If they follow along with this, then struggle and contention will arise, and yielding and deference will perish therein. They are born with feelings of hate and dislike. If they follow along with these, then cruelty and villainy will arise, and loyalty and trustworthiness will perish therein. They are born with desires of the eyes and ears, a fondness for beautiful sights and sounds. If they follow along with these, then lasciviousness and chaos will arise, and ritual and the standards of righteousness, proper form and

---

98. The repetitive character of these sentences makes them seem very much like glosses that were miscopied into the main text.

good order, will perish therein. Thus, if people follow along with their inborn dispositions and obey their nature, they are sure to come to struggle and contention, turn to disrupting social divisions and disorder, and end up becoming violent. So, it is necessary to await the transforming influence of teachers and models and the guidance of ritual and the standards of righteousness, and only then will they come to yielding and deference, turn to proper form and order, and end up becoming controlled.[99] Looking at it in this way, it is clear that people's nature is bad, and their goodness is a matter of deliberate effort.

Thus, crooked wood must await steaming and straightening on the shaping frame, and only then does it become straight. Blunt metal must await honing and grinding, and only then does it become sharp.[100] Now since people's nature is bad, they must await teachers and proper models, and only then do they become correct. They must obtain ritual and the standards of righteousness, and only then do they become well-ordered. Now without teachers or proper models for people, they will be deviant, dangerous, and not correct. Without ritual and the standards of righteousness, they will be unruly, chaotic, and not well-ordered. In ancient times, the sage-kings saw that because people's nature is bad, they were deviant, dangerous, and not correct, unruly, chaotic, and not well-ordered. Therefore, for their sake they set up ritual and standards of righteousness, and established proper models and measures. They did this in order to straighten out and beautify people's nature and inborn dispositions and thereby correct them, and in order to train and transform people's nature and inborn dispositions and thereby guide them, so that for the first time they all came to order and conformed to the Way. Among people of today, those who are transformed by teachers and proper models, who accumulate culture and learning, and who make ritual and the standards of righteousness their path, become gentlemen. Those who give rein to their nature and inborn dispositions, who take comfort in being utterly unrestrained, and who violate ritual and the standards of righteousness, become petty men. Looking at it in this way, it is clear that people's nature is bad, and their goodness is a matter of deliberate effort.

---

99. Here and elsewhere, this chapter deploys two terms in rapid succession, *li* 理 and *zhi* 治, which both mean "order" or "well-ordered," and their close proximity makes it difficult to translate the text without making it sound as if Xunzi is simply repeating himself. In such cases, I have kept *li* as "order," while rendering *zhi* as "controlled," in the sense of disciplined restraint. *Zhi* can also carry the connotation of good government in particular, though that sense seems less relevant in the instances where *li* and *zhi* are closely juxtaposed. When not so juxtaposed, both *li* and *zhi* have been rendered here as "order" or "well-ordered," depending on context.

100. Compare Gaozi's metaphor in *Mengzi* 6A1 (in chapter 4 of this volume), and the opening paragraph of *Xunzi* chapter 1 (above).

Mengzi says: When people engage in learning, this manifests the goodness of their nature. I say: This is not so. This is a case of not attaining knowledge of people's nature and of not inspecting clearly the division between people's nature and their deliberate efforts. In every case, the nature of a thing is the accomplishment of Heaven. It cannot be learned. It cannot be worked at. Ritual and the standards of righteousness are what the sage produces. They are things that people become capable of through learning, things that are achieved through working at them. Those things in people that cannot be learned and cannot be worked at are called their "nature." Those things in people that they become capable of through learning and that they achieve through working at them are called their "deliberate efforts." This is the division between nature and deliberate effort.[101]

Now people's nature is such that their eyes can see, and their ears can hear. The brightness by which they see does not depart from their eyes, and the acuity by which they hear does not depart from their ears. Their eyes are simply bright, and their ears are simply acute. One does not learn this brightness. Mengzi says: People's nature is good, but they all wind up losing their nature and original state.[102] I say: If it is like this, then he is simply mistaken. People's nature is such that they are born and then depart from their original simplicity, depart from their original material; they are sure to lose them. Looking at it in this way, it is clear that people's nature is bad. The so-called goodness of people's nature would mean for one not to depart from one's original simplicity and instead beautify it, not to depart from one's original material and instead make use of it. It would be to cause the relation of one's original simplicity and original material to beauty, and the relation of the heart's thoughts to goodness, to be like the way the brightness by which one sees does not depart from one's eyes, and the acuity by which one hears does not depart from one's ears. Thus, I have said: "The eyes are simply bright and the ears are simply acute." . . .

Someone asks: If people's nature is bad, then from what are ritual and the standards of righteousness produced? I answer: In every case, ritual and the standards of righteousness are produced from the deliberate effort of the sage; they are not produced from people's nature. Thus, when the potter mixes clay and makes vessels, the vessels are produced from the deliberate efforts of the craftsman; they are not produced from people's nature. Thus, when the craftsman carves wood and makes utensils, the utensils are produced from the deliberate efforts of the craftsman; they are not produced from people's nature. The sage accumulates reflections and deliberations and practices deliberate efforts and reasoned activities in order to produce

---

101. Compare Xunzi's definitions in *Xunzi* chapter 22, "On Correct Naming" (above).

102. Cf. *Mengzi* 6A6, 6A8, 7A15, and 7B31 (in chapter 4 of this volume).

ritual and standards of righteousness and in order to establish proper models and measures.[103] So, ritual and the standards of righteousness and proper models and measures are produced from the deliberate efforts of the sage; they are not produced from people's nature.

As for the way that the eyes like pretty colors, the ears like beautiful sounds, the mouth likes good flavors, the heart likes what is beneficial, and the bones and flesh like what is comfortable—these are produced from people's inborn dispositions and nature. These are things that come about of themselves in response to stimulation, things that do not need to await being worked at before being produced. Those things that are not immediate responses to stimulation, that must await being worked at before they are so, are said to be produced from deliberate effort. These are the things that nature and deliberate effort produce, and their different signs.

So, the sage transforms his nature and establishes deliberate effort. In establishing deliberate effort, he produces ritual and the standards of righteousness. In producing ritual and the standards of righteousness, he institutes proper models and measures. Thus, ritual and the standards of righteousness and proper models and measures are produced by the sage. Thus, that in which the sage is like the masses, that in which he is no different than the masses, is his nature. That in which he differs from and surpasses the masses is his deliberate efforts.

Liking what is beneficial and desiring gain are people's inborn dispositions and nature. Suppose there were brothers who had some property to divide, and that they followed the fondness for benefit and desire for gain in their inborn dispositions and nature. If they were to do so, then the brothers would conflict and contend with each other for it. However, let them be transformed by the proper form and good order of ritual and the standards of righteousness. If so, then they would even give it over to their countrymen. Thus, following along with inborn dispositions and nature, even brothers will struggle with each other. If transformed by ritual and the standards of righteousness, then they will even give it over to their countrymen.[104]

In every case where people desire to become good, it is because their nature is bad. The person who has little longs to have much. The person of narrow experience

---

103. There is a noteworthy alternative way of reading this line, which construes it as being in the past tense, and with a plural subject: "Sages accumulated reflections and thoughts and practiced deliberate efforts and reasoned activities. . . ." This reading would fit well with the suggestion by David S. Nivison ("Critique of David B. Wong, 'Xunzi on Moral Motivation,'" in *Chinese Language, Thought, and Culture: Nivison and His Critics*, ed. Philip J. Ivanhoe [Chicago: Open Court, 1996], 323–31) that Xunzi's view can allow for a series of sages to produce ritual and the standards of righteousness by working in a piecemeal fashion over time, perhaps without even being fully aware of what they were doing.

104. This seems to be a reference to the story of Bo Yi and Shu Qi. See *Important Figures* in the appendices.

longs to be broadened. The ugly person longs to be beautiful. The poor person longs to be rich. The lowly person longs to be noble. That which one does not have within oneself, one is sure to seek for outside. Thus, when one is rich, one does not long for wealth. When one is noble, one does not long for power. That which one has within oneself, one is sure not to go outside oneself for it. Looking at it in this way, people desire to become good because their nature is bad.

Now, people's nature is originally without ritual and without the standards of righteousness. Thus, they must force themselves to engage in learning and seek to possess them. Their nature does not know of ritual and the standards of righteousness, and so they must reflect and deliberate and seek to know them. So, going only by what they have from birth, people lack ritual and the standards of righteousness and do not know of ritual and the standards of righteousness. If people lack ritual and the standards of righteousness, then they will be chaotic. If they do not know of ritual and the standards of righteousness, then they will be unruly. So, going only by what they have from birth, unruliness and disorder are within them. Looking at it in this way, it is clear that people's nature is bad, and their goodness is a matter of deliberate effort.

Mengzi says: People's nature is good. I say: This is not so. In every case, both in ancient times and in the present, what everyone under Heaven calls good is being correct, ordered, peaceful, and controlled. What they call bad is being deviant, dangerous, unruly, and chaotic. This is the division between good and bad. Now does he really think that people's nature is originally correct, ordered, peaceful, and controlled? Then what use would there be for sage-kings? What use for ritual and the standards of righteousness? Even though there might exist sage-kings and ritual and the standards of righteousness, whatever could these add to its correctness, order, peaceful, and controlled state? Now, that is not the case, because people's nature is bad. Thus, in ancient times the sage-kings saw that because their nature is bad, people were deviant, dangerous, and not correct; unruly, chaotic, and not well-ordered. Therefore, for the people's sake they set up the power of lords and superiors in order to oversee them. They made ritual and the standards of righteousness clear in order to transform them. They set up laws and standards in order to make them well-ordered. They multiplied punishments and fines in order to restrain them. As a result, they caused all under Heaven to come to order and conform to goodness. Such are the ordering influence of the sage-kings and the transformative effects of ritual and the standards of righteousness.

Now suppose one were to try doing away with the power of lords and superiors, try doing without the transformation from ritual and the standards of righteousness, try doing away with the order of laws and standards, try doing without the restraint of punishments and fines, then relying on these things and observing how all the people of the world treat each other. If it were like this, then the strong would harm the weak and take from them. The many would tyrannize the few and shout them down. One would not have to wait even a moment for all under Heaven to arrive at unruliness and chaos and perish. Looking at it in this way, it is clear that people's nature is bad, and that their goodness is a matter of deliberate effort.

So, those who are good at speaking of ancient times are sure to have some measure from the present. Those who are good at speaking of Heaven are sure to have some evidence from among mankind. For any discourse, one values it if things conform to its distinctions, and if it matches the test of experience. Thus, one sits and propounds it, but when one stands up then one can implement it, and when one unfolds it then one can put it into practice. Now Mengzi says: People's nature is good. Nothing conforms to his distinctions, and this does not match the test of experience. He sits and propounds it, but when he stands up then he cannot implement it, and when he unfolds it then he cannot put it into practice. Is his error not great indeed! Thus, if human nature is good then one may do away with the sage-kings and put ritual and the standards of righteousness to rest. If human nature is bad, then one simply must side with the sage-kings and honor ritual and the standards of righteousness. . . .

Someone suggests: Ritual and the standards of righteousness and the accumulation of deliberate effort are people's nature, and that is why the sage is able to produce them. I answer: This is not so. The potter mixes clay and produces tiles. Yet, how could the clay of the tiles be the potter's nature? The craftsman carves wood and makes utensils. Yet, how could the wood of the utensils be the craftsman's nature? The relationship of the sage to ritual and the standards of righteousness can be compared to mixing up clay and producing things. So, how could ritual and the standards of righteousness and the accumulation of deliberate effort be people's original nature? In every aspect of human nature, the nature of Yao and Shun was one and the same as that of Tyrant Jie and Robber Zhi. The nature of the gentleman is one and the same as that of the petty man. Now will you take ritual and the standards of righteousness and the accumulation of deliberate effort to be a matter of human nature? Then for what do you value Yao and Shun? For what do you value the gentleman? Everything that one values in Yao and Shun and the gentleman is due to the fact that they were able to transform their nature and to establish deliberate effort. In establishing deliberate effort, they produced ritual and the standards of righteousness. Thus, the relationship of the sage to ritual and the standards of righteousness and the accumulation of deliberate effort is like mixing up clay and producing things. Looking at it in this way, then how could ritual and the standards of righteousness and the accumulation of deliberate effort be people's nature? What one finds base in Jie and Robber Zhi and the petty man is due to the fact that they follow along with their inborn dispositions and obey their nature and take comfort in utter lack of restraint, so that they come to greed for profit and to struggle and contention. Thus, it is clear that people's nature is bad, and that their goodness is a matter of deliberate effort. Heaven did not favor Zengzi, Minzi Qian, and Xiao Yi[105] and exclude the masses. Then why is it that only Zengzi, Minzi Qian, and Xiao Yi were rich in the true substance of filial piety and were perfect in their reputation for filial piety? It is because they exerted themselves to the utmost in ritual and the standards of righteousness. Heaven does not favor the people of Qi and Lu and exclude the people of Qin. Then why is it that with regard to the standards of righteousness for father and son, and the distinction between husband and wife, the people of Qin are not as good at filial reverence and respectful good form as those of Qi and Lu? It is because the people of Qin obey their inborn dispositions and nature, take comfort in utter lack of restraint, and are lax in regard to ritual and the standards of righteousness. How could it be because their nature is different?

Anyone on the streets could become a Yu. How do I mean this? I say: That by which Yu was Yu was that he was benevolent, righteous, lawful, and correct. Thus, benevolence, righteousness, lawfulness, and correctness have patterns that can be known and can be practiced. However, people on the streets all have the material for knowing benevolence, righteousness, lawfulness, and correctness, and they all have the equipment for practicing benevolence, righteousness, lawfulness, and correctness. Thus, it is clear that they can become a Yu. Now if benevolence, righteousness, lawfulness, and correctness originally had no patterns that could be known or practiced, then even Yu would not know benevolence, righteousness, lawfulness, and correctness and could not practice benevolence, righteousness, lawfulness, and correctness. Shall we suppose that people on the streets originally do not have the material to know benevolence, righteousness, lawfulness, and correctness, and that they originally do not have the equipment for practicing benevolence, righteousness, lawfulness, and correctness? If so, then within the family, people on the streets could not know the standards of righteousness for father and son, and outside the family, they could not know the proper relations of lord and minister. This is not so. Now it is the case that anyone on the streets can know the standards of righteousness for father and son within the family, and can know the proper relations of lord and minister outside the family. Thus, it is clear that the material for understanding these things and the equipment for practicing them is present in people on the

---

105. Zengzi (Master Zeng) and Minzi Qian were both disciples of Kongzi. Xiao Yi (or "Filial Yi") was heir to the throne of Gaozong, ruler of the Shang dynasty. All three were famous for their displays of filial piety.

streets. Now, if people on the streets were to use their material for understanding these things and the equipment for practicing them to base themselves upon the knowable patterns and practicable aspects of benevolence and righteousness, then it is clear that anyone on the streets could become a Yu. Now, if people on the streets were to submit themselves to study and practice learning, if they were to concentrate their hearts and make single-minded their intentions, if they were to ponder, query, and thoroughly investigate—then if they add to this days upon days and connect to this long period of time, if they accumulate goodness without stopping, then they will break through to spirit-like powers and understanding, and will form a triad with Heaven and earth.

Thus, becoming a sage is something that people achieve through accumulation. Someone says: Sageliness is achieved through accumulation, but why is it that not all can accumulate thus? I say: They can do it, but they cannot be made to do it. Thus, the petty man can become a gentleman, but is not willing to become a gentleman. The gentleman can become a petty man, but is not willing to become a petty man.[106] It has never been that the petty man and gentleman are incapable of becoming each other. However, the reason they do not become each other is that they can do so but cannot be made to do so. Thus, it is the case that anyone on the streets can become a Yu, but it is not necessarily the case that anyone on the streets will be able to become a Yu. Even if one is not able to become a Yu, this does not harm the fact that one could become a Yu. One's feet can walk everywhere under Heaven. Even so, there has not yet been anyone who has been able to walk everywhere under Heaven. It has never been that craftsmen, carpenters, farmers, and merchants cannot do each other's business. However, none have ever been able to do each other's business. Looking at it in this way, one is not always able to do what one can do. Even if one is not able to do it, this is no harm to the fact that one could do it. Thus, the difference between being able and unable, and can and cannot, is far indeed. It is clear, then, that [the gentleman and the petty man] can become one another.

Yao asked Shun, "What are people's inborn dispositions like?" Shun answered, "People's inborn dispositions are most unlovely! Why ask about them? When one has a wife and son, then one's filial piety to one's parents declines. When one's appetites and desires are fulfilled, then one's faithfulness to friends declines. When one's rank and salary are full, then one's loyalty to one's lord declines. People's inborn dispositions? People's inborn dispositions? They are most unlovely. Why ask about them? Only the worthy man is not like that." . . .

---

106. Cf. *Mengzi* 6A15 (in chapter 4 of this volume).

Chapter Twenty-Five: Working Songs

There are warp threads for weaving good order:
Rites and punishments are exactly these.
The gentleman takes and cultivates them.
The common folk are thereby put at ease.
Make virtue bright. Treat penalties with care.
This orders the state and its families,
And peace comes to all within the Four Seas.

Chapter Twenty-Seven: The Grand Digest

The gentleman dwells in benevolence by means of righteousness,[107] and only then is it benevolence. He carries out righteousness by means of ritual, and only then is it righteousness. In conducting ritual, he returns to the roots of things and completes the branches of things, and only then is it ritual.[108] When all three are thoroughly mastered, only then is it the Way. . . .

Chapter Twenty-Nine: The Way to Be a Son

To be filial upon entering and to be a good younger brother upon going out is lesser conduct. To be compliant to one's superiors and devoted to one's subordinates is middle conduct. To follow the Way and not one's lord, to follow righteousness and not one's father, is the greatest conduct. If one's intentions are at ease in ritual, and one's words are put forth in accordance with the proper classes of things, then the Confucian way is complete. Even Shun could not improve on this by so much as a hair's breadth.

There are three cases in which the filial son does not follow orders. When following orders will endanger one's parents, but not following orders will make them safe, then the filial son will not follow orders, and this is having scruples. When following orders will disgrace one's parents, but not following orders will bring them honor, then the filial son will not follow orders, and this is being righteous. When following orders requires a beastly act, but not following orders requires cultivation

---

107. The wording here recalls *Analects* 4.1 (in chapter 1 of this volume).

108. Commentators offer different suggestions about how to construe the "roots" and "branches." Perhaps the most plausible is the Tang commentator Yang Liang's view that "roots" refers to benevolence and righteousness, and "branches" refers to particular regulations of ritual.

and decorum, then the filial son will not follow orders, and this is being respectful. And so, not following orders when it is permissible to do so is to behave as though one is not a son. Following orders when it is not permissible to do so is to lack any scruples. If one understands the proper purposes of following and not following orders, and if one can be reverent, respectful, loyal, trustworthy, scrupulous, and honest so as to carry these out vigilantly, then this can be called the greatest filial piety. A proverb states, "Follow the Way, not your lord. Follow righteousness, not your father." This expresses my meaning.

SELECTIVE BIBLIOGRAPHY

Translations

Hutton, Eric L., trans. *Xunzi: The Complete Text*. Princeton, NJ: Princeton University Press, 2014. (A handy, one-volume English rendering of the entire text of the *Xunzi* by the translator of this chapter. There are some minor differences between the present selections and the full-length translation, due mostly to different conventions adopted for this volume.)

Knoblock, John, trans. *Xunzi: A Translation and Study of the Complete Works*, vols. 1–3. Stanford, CA: Stanford University Press (vol. 1, 1988; vol. 2, 1990; vol. 3, 1994). (The first full translation of Xunzi's works in English. Includes detailed information on historical and philosophical background, as well as an extensive bibliography of works pertaining to Xunzi.)

Watson, Burton, trans. *Xunzi: Basic Writings*. New York: Columbia University Press, 2003. (A slightly updated version of Watson's highly readable selective translation of the *Xunzi*, first published as *Hsün Tzu: Basic Writings* in 1963.)

Secondary Works

Goldin, Paul R. *Rituals of the Way: The Philosophy of Xunzi*. La Salle, IL: Open Court Press, 1999. (A wide-ranging study of Xunzi's thought. Examines in detail his views on human nature, Heaven, ritual, and language.)

Hutton, Eric L., ed. *Dao Companion to the Philosophy of Xunzi*. Dordrecht: Springer, 2016. (Provides thorough and in-depth discussion of many different aspects of Xunzi's thought. Also contains lengthy discussions of Xunzi's influence in the later history of China, Japan, and Korea.)

Kim, Sungmoon. *Theorizing Confucian Virtue Politics: The Political Philosophy of Mencius and Xunzi*. New York: Cambridge University Press, 2020. (Provides a detailed account of the similarities and differences between the political theories of Xunzi and Mengzi, with special attention to how they responded to the challenges of their times.)

Kline, T. C., III, and Philip J. Ivanhoe, eds. *Virtue, Nature, and Moral Agency in the "Xunzi."* Indianapolis, IN: Hackett Publishing Company, 2000. (An anthology containing many of the most influential modern essays on Xunzi's thought in English.)

Kline, T. C., III, and Justin Tiwald, eds. *Ritual and Religion in the "Xunzi."* Albany, NY: State University of New York Press, 2014. (An anthology focusing on the religious dimensions of Xunzi's thought. Includes discussion of ecological concerns in Xunzi's views, as well as comparisons between Xunzi and Sigmund Freud, Peter Berger, and other thinkers concerned with religious themes.)

Lewis, Colin J. "Ritual Education and Moral Development: A Comparison of Xunzi and Vygotsky." *Dao* 17, no. 1 (2018): 81–98. (Argues that Xunzi's model of moral education fits well with and complements a highly influential modern theory of learning that is also supported by empirical studies.)

Machle, Edward J. *Nature and Heaven in the Xunzi: A Study of the "Tian Lun."* Albany, NY: State University of New York Press, 1993. (Considers Xunzi as a religious thinker through his views on *tian* ["Heaven"]. Argues against reading *tian* as amoral, scientific "Nature.")

Nivison, David S. "Critique of David B. Wong, 'Xunzi on Moral Motivation.'" In *Chinese Language, Thought, and Culture: Nivison and His Critics*, edited by Philip J. Ivanhoe, 323–31. Chicago: Open Court, 1996. (Offers an innovative account of how Xunzi can explain the development of human morality in history, despite believing that human nature is bad.)

Stalnaker, Aaron. *Overcoming Our Evil: Human Nature and Spiritual Exercises in Xunzi and Augustine*. Washington, DC: Georgetown University Press, 2006. (Develops a methodology for cross-cultural studies and provides a detailed Confucian-Christian comparison, focused on the topic of self-cultivation.)

Sung, Winnie. "Xunzi" in *Oxford Bibliographies Online: Chinese Studies*. Oxford University Press, 2018. DOI: 10.1093/obo/9780199920082-0124. (A substantial annotated bibliography covering many significant publications on the *Xunzi* in English and other languages, updated periodically.)

Tang, Siufu. *Self-Realization through Confucian Learning: A Contemporary Reconstruction of Xunzi's Ethics*. Albany, NY: State University of New York Press, 2016. (An in-depth study arguing that Xunzi's view can meet the modern demand that ethical theories answer people's need for self-realization.)

Van Norden, Bryan W. "Hansen on Hsün Tzu." *Journal of Chinese Philosophy* 20 (1993): 365–82. (Investigates the extent to which Xunzi may be considered a "conventionalist" in language and in ethics.)

Wang, Ellie Hua. "Moral Reasoning: The Female Way and the Xunzian Way." In *The Bloomsbury Research Handbook of Chinese Philosophy and Gender*, edited by Ann A. Pang-White, 141–56. New York: Bloomsbury Academic, 2016. (Argues that Xunzi's view of moral judgment is not as incompatible with certain feminist views as it might first appear, and that Xunzi's ethics—and Confucian ethics more broadly—overlaps with but also constitutes a noteworthy rival to feminist care ethics.)

CHAPTER TEN

HAN FEIZI

Introduction

Hán Fēizǐ 韓非子 (ca. 280–233 BCE) was the last great philosopher active before the unification of China by the ruler of the state of Qin in 221 BCE. Like the Confucians and Mohists, he was interested in how to ensure a strong, stable, and flourishing state. Unlike the Confucians, however, Han Feizi did not think that moral cultivation was the answer. Unlike the Mohists, he did not think that it was possible to unify the people's sense of right and wrong. And unlike Laozi, he did not think that order could naturally be achieved simply by reducing desires and according with the Way.

Agreeing with Shen Dao, and in opposition to the Confucians, Mohists, and Daoists, Han Feizi did not believe that any substantive change in an individual's fundamental desires, dispositions, and interests was possible. Therefore, any attempt to create social harmony or political stability that relied on substantive changes in people's desires, interests, and values was doomed to failure. However, this did not mean that there was only a tenuous possibility of social and political order. Rather, since most people's dispositions include a healthy dose of self-interest, they could be guided into actions that they would not otherwise engage in by means of the two handles of reward and punishment. These rewards and punishments did nothing to change people's actual desires and interests; rather, they worked by changing which activities would allow individuals to obtain the things that they desired.

Thus, in Han Feizi's account, it was laws, rather than moral cultivation, that were fundamental to guiding and shaping human behavior. This had a range of implications: in order for laws to be effective, they (and the rewards and punishments attached to them) had to be clearly promulgated throughout the state in a fashion that was easy for everyone to understand, and their enforcement had to be viewed by the people as guaranteed. This required the establishment of a thoroughgoing bureaucratic apparatus

323

pervading all levels of society. Furthermore, since those who staffed the bureaucratic offices were no different from the average person, they could not be expected to serve the state out of loyalty—any time they saw it as being in their self-interest to take advantage of their position to serve their own private ends, they would do so. This then required the establishment of a set of bureaucratic techniques that the ruler could utilize to reign in and control his ministers in much the same way that the laws reigned in and controlled the masses. However, in order to effectively implement these techniques and ensure that the laws were reliably being followed, it was necessary for the ruler to avail himself of the power inherent in the position of ruler, rather than in any particular contingent qualities that the ruler himself happened to possess. This positional power (shì 勢), the power of the ruler *qua* ruler, must be carefully guarded from those who wished to appropriate it, else the entire edifice of state power, order, and control would come crumbling down.

Han Feizi himself was a member of the ruling house of the state of Hán (韓); according to his biography found in the *Shiji* (*Records of the Historian*), written more than a century after his death, he was a stutterer who found it difficult to speak in court and thus turned to writing to express his ideas. He is also purported to have been a student of Xunzi at one point early in his life, and, while he never mentions Xunzi in his writings, it is clear throughout the *Han Feizi* that he is familiar with Xunzi's ideas. Although he vociferously attacks Xunzi's virtue-based political philosophy, he draws substantially on other aspects of Xunzi's views. At some point around 234 BCE, Han Feizi was dispatched as an envoy to the Qin court, where he attempted to gain the attention of the king of Qin (who would later become the first emperor of a united China). Afraid of what this might mean to his own position, the prime minister of Qin, Li Si, had him imprisoned. While he was in prison, Li Si offered him poison, which he took as a less painful alternative to execution.

Chapter Five: The Way of the Ruler

The Way is the beginning of the myriad things, the guideline of right and wrong. Because of this, the clear-sighted ruler abides by the beginning so as to understand the source of the myriad things, and puts into order the guidelines so as to understand the beginnings of success and failure. Therefore, empty and still he waits, causing names to name themselves and affairs to settle themselves. Empty, he understands the essence of things; still, he understands the proper ordering of activities.

Those who have proposals will provide their own names for them; those who engage in tasks will provide their own form for them.[1] When form and name are inspected and found to correspond to one another, the ruler has nothing else to do, and things return to their essence. Thus, it is said: "A ruler must not reveal his desires, for if he does so, his ministers will carve and polish themselves accordingly. A ruler must not reveal his intentions, for if he does so, his ministers will display themselves differently." So, it is said: "Discard likes, discard dislikes, and ministers will thereupon reveal their true colors. Discard the old, discard knowledge, and the ministers will thereupon take precautions."[2]

Therefore, while [a clear-sighted ruler] has knowledge, he does not employ it to make plans, thus causing the myriad things to know their places. While he possesses worthiness,[3] he does not act from it, but observes the reasons behind his ministers' actions. While he has courage, he does not exhibit it through bouts of anger, but rather causes his assembled ministers to exhaust their own martial courage. Hence, discarding knowledge leads to clarity; discarding worthiness leads to achievements; discarding courage leads to strength. When the assembled ministers keep watch over their respective duties, when the hundred offices keep to their regular routines, when rulers employ them on the basis of their abilities, this is called practicing constancy.[4] Thus it is said: "Silent, he dwells without actively governing; empty, no one can ascertain his whereabouts." When a clear-sighted ruler practices nonaction from above, his assembled ministers will be apprehensive and frightened below.

The Way of a clear-sighted ruler is such that it causes those who are intelligent to exhaust themselves in making plans, while the ruler is able to decide affairs on this basis without exhausting his own intelligence. The worthy organize their

---

1. This refers to the ministers. The division between míng 名 "name" and xíng 形 "form" is the division between what one says and what one actually does. These terms are also often translated as "achievements" and "claims." For more discussion of this, see later in this chapter as well as *Han Feizi* chapter 7 (below).

2. By saying that the old should be discarded, Han Fei likely is referring to traditional patterns of governing, in which the ruler makes clear his desires, preferences, etc.

3. "Worthy" and "worthiness" here and below are xián 賢 (see *Important Terms* in the appendices), but in Han Feizi this term refers not to any moral qualities but rather to politically or bureaucratically relevant talents.

4. This same line occurs at the end of *Daodejing* chapter 52 (in chapter 6 of this volume), though translated differently.

talents, and the ruler assigns them posts on this basis without exhausting his own ability.[5] When there are achievements, the ruler takes the credit for their worthiness; when there are errors, ministers shoulder the blame for their faults. As such, the ruler does not exhaust himself in the pursuit of fame.[6] Consequently, though not a worthy himself, such a ruler becomes the masters of the worthies; though not intelligent himself, he sets straight the intelligent. The ministers do the work, while the ruler achieves success. This describes the guiding principles of the worthy ruler.

The Way [of the ruler] lies in what cannot be seen; its use lies in what cannot be understood. Be empty and tranquil without engaging in affairs, and from the darkness observe others' faults. Observe but do not be observed; listen but do not be heard; understand but do not be understood.[7] Upon understanding others' words, do not change, do not transform, but rather inspect and compare [name and form] in order to assess [their correspondence]. Ensure that each position has only a single occupant and do not permit them to communicate among themselves, and then the myriad things will all reach fruition. Cover your tracks and hide your motivations, and those below will be unable to trace back to your source. Discard your knowledge, leave behind your ability, and those below will be unable to understand your intentions. Hold on to what has been previously said and examine whether actions accord with this. Carefully grasp the handles [of governance] and hold them tightly.[8] Cut off others' hope of using them, destroy others' intentions to employ them, and let not others desire them.

If you are not careful in barring your door and do not strengthen your gate, then tigers will continue to arise. If you are not cautious in your affairs, and do not hide your dispositions, then thieves will continue to be born. Some assassinate their rulers and take their place, with none not supporting them. Thus, they are called tigers. Some dwell by the side of their rulers, in service of villainous ministers, listening for their rulers' mistakes. Thus, they are called thieves. Disperse their henchmen, gather up their remains, bolt their doors, and seize their supporters, and no tigers will be left in the state. Be so great that you cannot be measured, so deep that you cannot be fathomed. Ensure the correspondence between achievements and claims, examine laws and rules, execute those who act without authorization. If you do these things, then your state will have no thieves.

---

5. While I translate chì 敕 as "to organize," it could also be taken to mean "to be careful." This would give the idea that in these conditions the ministers are careful about the uses to which they put their talent.

6. This can also be read as saying that the ruler never impoverishes his own reputation.

7. This line might also be read as "Observe while appearing not to observe; listen while appearing not to listen; understand while appearing not to understand."

8. For a fuller discussion of the handles of governance, see *Han Feizi* chapter 7, below.

And so, the ruler faces five obstructions: the obstruction of ministers blocking their ruler, the obstruction of ministers controlling wealth and profits, the obstruction of ministers exceeding their authority in their actions and orders, the obstruction of ministers who do what they think is right, and the obstruction of ministers who cultivate their own disciples. If ministers block their rulers, then their ruler will lose his status. If ministers control wealth and profits, then their ruler will lose his potency.[9] If ministers exceed their authority in their actions and orders, then their ruler will lose control. If ministers do what they think is right, then their ruler will lose his people. If the ministers can cultivate their own disciples, then their ruler will lose his supporters. These are the means by which the ruler monopolizes power and ministers must not be allowed to grasp hold of them.

As for the Way of the ruler, it takes tranquility and withdrawal as its treasures. [One who follows this Way] does not personally handle affairs, but understands the difference between clumsiness and skill in others. He does not personally calculate and plan, but understands the difference between good and bad fortune. Therefore, while he does not personally make proposals, he is nonetheless good at responding to the proposals of his ministers; while he does not personally restrain his ministers, the good results of these ministers' actions intensify. When such a ruler responds to a minister's proposal by giving him a task, he holds on to his portion of the contractual tally. And when the affair is finished, this ruler holds up the actual result and compares it with the initial tally. By examining the correspondence between actions and words, such a ruler is able to produce rewards and punishments. Therefore, when ministers lay out their proposals, such a ruler uses these proposals to assign them tasks, and on the basis of the success of their tasks calls them to account. If their results correspond to their assigned tasks, and their tasks correspond to their proposals, they are rewarded. If their results do not correspond to their assigned tasks or their tasks do not correspond to their proposals, they are punished.

As for the Way of the clear-sighted ruler, it ensures that ministers cannot make proposals that do not correspond to subsequent achievements. Therefore, in giving rewards, the clear-sighted ruler is timely like the seasonal rain, and the people benefit from his favor. In inflicting punishments, he is dreadful like roaring thunder, so that even spirits and sages cannot escape. Therefore, the clear-sighted ruler does not give secret rewards nor does he pardon crimes. If he gives secret rewards, successful ministers' work will degenerate, while if he pardons crimes, unscrupulous ministers will easily err. Because of this, those who provide genuine accomplishments, even

---

9. "Potency" here is Dé 德, which is translated elsewhere in this volume as "Virtue." However, in the *Han Feizi*, as in the *Shenzi Fragments* (in chapter 7 of this volume), it does not connote a moral power. Rather, it refers to a "potency" that need not have moral characteristics.

if distant and lightly regarded, must be rewarded, while those who commit errors, even if near and dear, must be punished. When even those distant and lightly regarded are rewarded and even those near and dear are punished, then those distant and lightly regarded will not become negligent and those near and dear will not become arrogant.

Chapter Six: Having Standards

No state is eternally strong; no state is eternally weak. When whose who uphold the law are strong, the state is strong. When those who uphold the law are weak, the state is weak. King Zhuang of Chu[10] annexed 26 states and opened up 3,000 square *li* of land. But with the sweeping away of his ancestral shrine, the state of Chu fell to ruin. Duke Huan of Qi[11] annexed 30 states and developed 3,000 square *li* of land. But with the sweeping away of his ancestral shrine, the state of Qi fell to ruin. King Zhao of Yan[12] extended his borders to the Yellow River, established his capital at Ji, made surprise attacks on Zhuo and Fangcheng, wiped out Qi, and flattened Zhongshan. Those who had Yan as an ally were strong, while those who did not were weak. But with the sweeping away of his ancestral shrine, the state of Yan fell to ruin. King Anxi of Wei[13] attacked Yan and saved Zhao. He captured lands east of the Yellow River and completely overran the lands of Tao and Wei. He sent his troops into Qi and made the city of Pinglu his own. He attacked Han, captured Guan, and was victorious at the Qi River. In the battle at Suiyang, the Chu army fled in exhaustion, while in the battle at Cai and Zhaoling, the Chu army was defeated. His army spread to the four corners of the world, and his awe-inspiring might was accepted in all states where caps and belts were worn.[14] And yet, when King Anxi died, the state of Wei fell to ruin.

And so, while King Zhuang of Chu and Duke Huan of Qi were alive, the states of Chu and Qi were hegemonic.[15] While King Xiang of Yan and King Anxi of Wei were alive, the states of Yan and Wei were strong. Now, as for why these states have

---

10. King Zhuang of Chu (r. 613–591 BCE) was the fourth of the Five Lord Protectors. See bà 霸, lord protector, under *Important Terms* in the appendices.

11. Duke Huan of Qi (r. 685–643 BCE) was the first of the Five Lord Protectors.

12. King Zhao of Yan (r. 311–279 BCE) substantially increased the strength of the state of Yan.

13. King Anxi of Wei (r. 276–243 BCE) increased the military might of his state.

14. This is a reference to places where Chinese attire was worn, with the implication that these were the "civilized" rather than "barbarian" states.

15. "Hegemonic" is the adjectival form of bà 霸 "lord protector" (see *Important Terms* in the appendices).

all fallen to ruin, their assembled ministers and officials were all focused on actions bringing about disorder, and none of them were focused on actions bringing about good order. When a state is already disordered and weak, and moreover everyone casts aside the laws of the state and pursues private interests beyond their purview, this is like trying to put out a fire while carrying kindling on one's back—disordered and weak to the extreme.

And so, in the present time, if one can eliminate private crookedness and attend to public laws, one's people will be secure and one's state well-ordered. If one can eliminate private actions and implement public law, one's army will be strong and one's enemies weak. Thus, if in examining gains and losses, one employs a system of laws and standards and applies these to the assembled ministers from above, such a ruler cannot be cheated by duplicity or deception. If in examining gains and losses, one employs an objective scale for weighing them, in attending to distant affairs, such a ruler cannot be cheated with respect to the relative importance of world affairs.

Now, if promotion of the capable is based upon their public acclaim, ministers will stray away from those above, colluding with and assisting those below.[16] If promotion in office is based upon one's political faction, the people will devote themselves to making connections and will not strive to apply themselves in accordance with the law. And so, offices will lack those who are truly capable, and such states will fall into disorder. If rewards are based on public acclaim and punishments are based on defamation, the people, who like rewards and dislike punishments, will cast aside public-spirited actions, engage in private schemes, and collude with and assist one another so as to advance each other's interests. If they forget their ruler, and make external connections in order to promote their associates, those below will be of scant assistance to their superiors. If their external connections are numerous and their associates many, if both externally and internally they have associates and factions, even if their transgressions are grave, their means of hiding them will be plentiful. In such situations, loyal ministers will be in danger of death through no crime of their own, while unscrupulous and wicked ministers will attain security and profits through no achievements of their own. If loyal ministers are in danger of death but not because of any crimes of their own, good ministers will conceal themselves away. If unscrupulous and wicked ministers attain security and profits but not because of their achievements, unscrupulous ministers will advance. This is the root of ruin.

In such situations, the assembled ministers will discard the law; in their actions they will treat their private interests as important while treating public laws as

---

16. Since reputation depends on how one is viewed by the masses, one's focus will be on them, rather than on the ruler.

unimportant. They will repeatedly attend the gates of "the capable" while not once attending their ruler's court. They will consider their own private families' benefit a hundred times while not once making plans for their ruler's state. Even though the numbers of those in the ruler's employ are numerous, they will not be the sort to exalt their ruler. Even though the hundred offices are filled, these officeholders will not be the sort who can be entrusted with the state. That being so, while such rulers will have the title of ruler, in reality they have arrogated authority to the clans of the assembled ministers. As such, it is said: "There are no people in the court of a moribund state." The saying "there are no people in the court" does not mean that there is a decline in the actual number of people in court. Rather it is that clans work toward their mutual benefits, rather than working for the state's enrichment. Great ministers work to exalt one another rather than working to exalt their ruler. Minor ministers accept their salaries while nourishing their connections rather than attending to the tasks of their office. This situation arises from the fact that such rulers do not decide things on the basis of the law from above, but rather entrust those below to engage in the appropriate actions. Thus, a clear-sighted ruler ensures that people are chosen in accordance with the law rather than raising them up based on his own feelings. He utilizes the law to measure achievement rather than measuring it himself. When ability cannot be hidden, when blunders cannot be dressed up, when reputation alone is insufficient for advancement, when gainsayers cannot cause the capable to withdraw, there is a clear differentiation between ruler and minister and it is easy to govern. And so, if the ruler employs the law, all this will be accomplished.

When the worthy enter service, they face north[17] to present their tokens of allegiance, showing that their loyalties are not divided. At court, they do not presume to decline lowly tasks; in the military, they do not presume to decline difficult tasks. They follow their superior's actions and accord with their ruler's laws. With empty minds they await orders and make no determinations of right and wrong. Thus, while they have mouths, they do not use them to speak for their private interests. While they have eyes, they do not use them to look for private gain. And so, those above completely control them. One who serves as a minister can be compared to a hand. Reaching up, it tends to the head, reaching down, it tends to the feet. When cool or warm, cold or hot, the hand cannot help but save the body. When the *Moye* sword threatens the body, the hand does not dare not to strike it away.[18] One should

---

17. As rulers traditionally sat facing south in the court, those addressing them faced north. Cf. *Analects* 2.1 and 15.5 (in chapter 1 of this volume).

18. For more on the *Moye* sword, see *Zhuangzi* chapter 6 and the accompanying note 69 (in chapter 8 of this volume).

not make private use of worthy and wise ministers; one should not make private use of officials who are useful and capable. And so, the people will not go beyond their villages to establish relationships or be concerned about happenings a hundred *li* away. The noble and the base will not transgress one another's bounds, the foolish and the wise will both hold up the objective standard (of the law) to find their position. This is the pinnacle of good order.

Now, as for those who treat rank and emoluments lightly, who readily abscond in search of another ruler, these I do not describe as having integrity. As for those who engage in duplicitous persuasions and go against the law, who defy their ruler with forceful admonishments, these I do not describe as loyal. As for those who act compassionately and distribute benefits so as to gain the support of those below and make a name for themselves, these I do not describe as benevolent. As for those who withdraw from the world and live in seclusion, employing these actions to attack their superiors, these I do not describe as righteous. As for those who serve feudal lords abroad while squandering resources at home; who keep an eye out for dangerous situations that they can use to scare their ruler, saying "Without me, your relations with others will not be close, without me, grudges cannot be resolved," so that their ruler will trust them and the state listen to them; who debase their ruler's reputation in order to celebrate themselves; who destroy the prosperity of the state in order to profit their clans: these I do not describe as wise.

These various things [integrity, loyalty, benevolence, righteousness, and wisdom] are the doctrines of a dangerous age and were precluded by the laws of the former kings. The laws of the former kings said: "Ministers should not work to create their own awe-inspiring might or to create their own benefit, but should follow the guidance of their king. They should not engage in vice but should follow their king's path." In the past, the people of well-ordered ages upheld public laws, discarded private schemes, focused their attention, and unified their actions, making preparations to deal with their assigned tasks.

Now, if a ruler personally examines each of the hundred governmental offices, the days will be insufficient and his strength will not allow it. Furthermore, if those above use their eyes, those below will dress up what those above see. If those above use their ears, those below will dress up what those above hear. If those above use their intellectual faculties, those below will make their explanations more complicated. The former kings took these three things (eyes, ears, and intellect) to be insufficient for governing and so set aside their own personal abilities, relying on laws and techniques and carefully examining rewards and punishments. The former kings kept to the essentials, and so their laws were simple but not infringed upon. Alone, they controlled all within the Four Seas: the clever and wise were unable to employ their duplicity, the sharp-tongued talkers were unable to find an opening for their flattery, and the unscrupulous and wicked had nothing they could rely upon. Even those as far as a thousand *li* away did not dare to change their words, while those in positions of power (shì 勢) in the court did not dare to cover up goodness or dress up wrongdoing. The ministers of the court simply brought together their individually weak abilities, never daring to transgress or infringe upon one another's duties. As such, the task of ordering the state was insufficient (to exhaust the ruler) and they had a surplus of time in their days. It was the way that these superiors relied upon the power of their position (*shi*) that made it so.[19]

Now, as for how ministers infringe upon their rulers, it is like the contours of terrain, gradually shifting as one continues on, causing rulers to lose their starting point, turning from east to west and not realizing it. Thus, the former kings established markers pointing south in order to establish the directions of sunrise and sunset.[20] Therefore, a clear-sighted ruler ensures that his assembled ministers do not allow their thoughts to roam beyond the scope of the law, and does not grant favors even within the scope of the law, so that none of their actions fail to conform to the law. Laws are the means by which to put a stop to excesses and eliminate selfishness. Strict punishments are the means by which to ensure that orders are fulfilled and those below are constrained. Awe-inspiring might must not arise from two sources; control must not have a shared gate. If awe-inspiring might and control are held in common, a multitude of vices will be on display. If the law is not trusted, the ruler's actions will be endangered. If punishments are not cut short, wickedness will not flourish.

Therefore, it is said: "Skillful carpenters' visual estimations will hit the ink line, and yet they are certain to begin by taking the compass and square as their standard. The snap judgments of the supremely wise will hit the heart of affairs, and yet they are certain to take the laws of the former kings as their standard for comparison." Thus, so long as the ink line is straight, warped wood can be cut straight; so long as the level is even, high spots can be planed down; so long as the steelyard is properly hung, what is heavy will be seen to be greater than what is light; so long as the peck and bushel measures[21] are appropriately calibrated, larger volumes will be seen to be greater than smaller ones.

Thus, employing the law to order the state is merely a matter of promoting what accords with the law and putting a stop to what does not. The law does not incline toward the noble, just as the ink line does not bend around what is crooked.

---

19. For more on the concept of "positional power" (shì 勢), see *Han Feizi* chapter 40 (below).

20. Cf. *Mozi* chapter 35 and the accompanying notes 88 and 89 (in chapter 2 of this volume).

21. I translate dòu 斗 as "peck" and hú 斛 as "bushel," following Endymion Wilkinson (*Chinese History: A New Manual*, 6th ed. [Cambridge, MA: Harvard University Asia Center, 2022]).

As for what the law confers, even the wise cannot shirk from it and even the brave do not dare to dispute it. Punishments for transgressions do not bypass great ministers, while rewards for goodness do not leave the common people behind. Thus, in straightening out the mistakes of those above, in bringing charges against the wickedness of those below, in bringing order to disorder and unraveling what is tangled up, in reducing envy and bringing into line the disobedient, in unifying the paths of the people, nothing compares to the law. In motivating those in office and demonstrating awe-inspiring might over the people, in eliminating licentiousness and dangerous behavior, in putting a stop to duplicity and deception, nothing compares to punishment. When punishments are weighty, the noble will not dare to treat the base lightly. When laws are meticulously followed, those above will be exalted and their authority not infringed upon. When those above are exalted and their authority not infringed upon, the ruler will be strong and keep to the essentials. This is why the former kings valued these things and transmitted them. If rulers cast aside the law and follow their own private interests, it will be impossible to distinguish superior and subordinate.

Chapter Seven: The Two Handles

The means by which the clear-sighted ruler guides and controls his minister are the two handles and that is all. The two handles are punishment and favor. What is meant by "punishment" and "favor"? Killing and executing are cases of "punishment." Venerating and rewarding are cases of "favor." Those who serve as ministers dread execution and punishments, but see veneration and rewards as beneficial. Therefore, if the ruler personally employs his powers of punishment and favor, the assembled ministers will dread his awe-inspiring might and turn toward the benefits he offers. However, the unscrupulous ministers of this age are not like this. When there are those whom they hate, they can utilize their ruler's awe-inspiring might to punish them. When there are those whom they care about, they can utilize their ruler's awe-inspiring might to reward them. Now, if the ruler does not ensure that the awe-inspiring might and benefits of rewards and punishments emanate from him alone, but rather listens to the advice of his ministers in implementing rewards and punishments, his state's people will all respect the ministers and slight their ruler, turn toward the ministers and dismiss their ruler. This is the calamity of the ruler losing the handles of punishment and favor.

The reason the tiger can subdue the dog is because of its claws and fangs. If the tiger were to cast aside its claws and fangs and allow the dog to use them, then the tiger would instead be subdued by the dog. The ruler controls ministers by means of punishment and favor. Now, if he were to cast aside his control over punishments and favor and allow his ministers to use them, then the ruler would instead by controlled by his ministers. Thus, Tian Chang requested control over ranks and emoluments from his superior and distributed them among the assembled ministers, while toward those below, he increased the size of the peck and bushel measures when distributing (grain) to the people. Because of this, Duke Jian lost his power over favor while Tian Chang employed it, and as a result, Duke Jian was assassinated (by Tian Chang).[22] Zi Han said to the ruler of Song: "The granting and issuing of venerations and rewards are things that the people like, so you should implement them yourself. Killing, executing, punishing, and penalizing are things that the people hate, so allow me to manage these." At this point, the ruler of Song lost his power over punishments and Zi Han used it, and so the ruler of Song was robbed (of his authority).[23] When Tian Chang alone had power over favors, Duke Jian was killed. When Zi Han alone had power over punishments, the ruler of Song was robbed of his authority.[24] Therefore, if, in the present age, ministers have the combined power to employ both punishment and favor, then the rulers of the present age are in more extreme danger than even Duke Jian and the ruler of Song. Thus, when rulers end up being robbed of their authority, assassinated, blocked, or kept in the dark, inevitably it is because they have endangered and ruined themselves by losing control over punishment and favor, allowing their ministers to use them.

If the ruler desires to eliminate unscrupulousness, he will examine the correspondence between form and name and whether proposals made differ from subsequent tasks.[25] Those who serve as ministers lay out proposals and rulers use these proposals to assign them tasks. And it is exclusively by means of the achievement of these tasks that they are to be held accountable. If their results correspond to their assigned tasks and their tasks correspond to their proposals, they are to be rewarded. If their results do not correspond to their assigned tasks or their tasks do not correspond to proposals, they are to be punished. Therefore, if among the assembled ministers there are those whose proposals are grand while their results are small,

---

22. Tian Chang was a senior minister in the state of Qi. According to records, he utilized larger peck and bushel measurements when making loans to the people, while calculating the grain due in taxes by means of smaller peck and bushel measurements, thus gaining the favor of the people. He subsequently murdered his ruler, Duke Jian of Qi, in 481 BCE, and took control of the state.

23. Zi Han tricked his ruler, Marquis Huan of Song, into allowing him to administer rewards and punishments. This allowed him to gain the favor of the people and depose Marquis Huan in 370 BCE.

24. For further discussion of Tian Chang and Zi Han, see *Han Feizi* chapter 49 (below).

25. See also *Han Feizi* chapter 5 (above) for a discussion of form and name.

they are to be punished. It is not because their achievements are small that they are punished; rather they are punished because their results did not match their proposals. If among the assembled ministers there are those whose proposals are small while their results are grand, they are also to be punished. It is not that the ruler is not pleased by these grand achievements, but rather because he takes the harm of results not matching proposals to outweigh the good of great achievements, and thus punishment is meted out.

In the past, Marquis Zhao of Han became drunk and fell asleep. The Keeper of Caps saw that his ruler was cold and thereupon placed some clothing over him. When the Marquis woke up, he was pleased and asked his attendants, "Who placed clothing over me?"

The attendants replied, "The Keeper of Caps." The ruler therefore punished both the Keeper of Caps and the Keeper of Clothing. He punished the Keeper of Clothing because he took him to have failed his task, and he punished the Keeper of Caps because he had gone beyond his duty. It was not that he did not fear the cold; it was that he considered the harm of intruding upon [other ministers'] offices to be greater than the harm of the cold. Thus, a clear-sighted ruler, in training his ministers, ensures that they cannot achieve results by transgressing beyond the bounds of their office and that they cannot lay out proposals and fail to match them [with subsequent results]. If they transgress beyond the bounds of their office, they must die. If their achievements do not match their proposals, they must be punished. If they keep to the tasks of their office and their proposals are pure, the assembled ministers will not be able to gain associates and factions in order to help one another.

The ruler faces two potential calamities: if he employs the worthy, then ministers will avail themselves of [the appearance of] worthiness in order to coerce their ruler; if he haphazardly promotes people, then his affairs will be obstructed and not succeed. Thus, if the ruler is fond of worthiness, the assembled ministers will dress up their actions in order to accord with their ruler's desires, and thus the true dispositions of the assembled ministers will not be evident. If the true dispositions of the assembled ministers are not evident, the ruler will have no way of differentiating among his ministers. Thus, since the King of Yue was fond of bravery, many of his people treated death lightly. Since King Ling of Chu was fond of slender waists, there were many starving people in his state.[26] Since King Huan of Qi was jealous and fond of his harem, Shu Diao castrated himself in order to take control of the harem. Since Duke Huan was fond of exotic flavors, Yi Ya steamed his son's head

---

26. For additional discussion of these two stories, see *Mozi* chapter 16 (in chapter 2 of this volume).

and offered it to the Duke.[27] Since Zikuai of Yan was fond of worthiness, Zi Zhi made a great show of not accepting the state.

Therefore, if the ruler displays what he hates, the assembled ministers will hide their motivations. If the ruler displays what he is fond of, the assembled ministers will misrepresent their abilities. If the ruler's desires are displayed, the true dispositions and attitudes of the assembled ministers are given the resources they need to succeed. Therefore, Zi Zhi relied upon worthiness in order to wrest away his ruler's power. Shu Diao and Yi Ya followed their ruler's desires in order to appropriate his power. In the end, Zikuai died in the chaos (following his abdication) and Duke Huan remained unburied as the worms devouring his corpse came out from under his door. What is the reason for all this? These calamities arose because rulers allowed their ministers to use their rulers' true dispositions as a pretext for action. The true dispositions of ministers are not necessarily such that they can care for their rulers, and some act in ways most profitable to themselves. Now, if rulers do not conceal their true dispositions, if they do not hide their motivations, but rather provide their ministers with opportunities to appropriate their power, then the assembled ministers will find that becoming a Zi Zhi or a Tian Chang is not difficult. So, it is said: "Discard likes, discard dislikes, and the assembled ministers will reveal their true colors. When the assembled ministers reveal their true colors, the great ruler will not be kept in the dark."

Chapter Twelve: The Difficulty of Persuasion

In general, the difficulty of persuasion is not the difficulty of gaining knowledge and using this knowledge to persuade others. Nor does it lie in the difficulty of expressing yourself in such a way as to clarify your meaning. Nor does it lie in the difficulty of daring to speak out all that you know without impediment. The difficulty of persuasion lies in understanding the heart of the person being persuaded such that you can ensure that your persuasion matches it.

If the person to be persuaded is someone who wishes to elevate their reputation, and you utilize the promise of substantial profits to persuade them, you will be seen as possessing an inferior character, be treated as vulgar and base, and your ideas are certain to be discarded and you will be kept at a distance. If the person to be persuaded is someone who wishes for substantial profits, and you utilize the promise

---

27. Shu Diao and Yi Ya were, respectively, the harem master and the cook of Duke Huan of Qi. While Duke Huan had an able prime minister in Guan Zhong, upon Guan's death, Shu Diao and Yi Ya gained influence by catering to Duke Huan's desires. They subsequently conspired against him and, according to some records, locked him in his room until he starved to death.

of an elevated reputation to persuade them, you will be seen as witless, kept at a distance from the essence of affairs, and your ideas are certain not to be accepted. If the person to be persuaded is someone who inwardly wishes for substantial profits but makes an appearance of being concerned with elevating their reputation, and you utilize the promise of an elevated reputation to persuade them, they will openly admit you to their vicinity while in reality paying no heed to you. If, on the other hand, you utilize the promise of substantial profits to persuade them, they will secretly employ your words while making an appearance of discarding you. These are things that you must not fail to examine.

Moreover, affairs that are kept secret will succeed, while discussions that are divulged will fail. Even if you do not divulge a secret, if your discussions happen to touch upon affairs that the ruler wishes to keep hidden, you are endangered. If the ruler makes an appearance of carrying out some set of affairs, but is doing so for ulterior reasons, and you know not only how the ruler wishes to appear but also what is behind his actions, you are endangered. If you give advice about an exceptional undertaking and the ruler accepts it, but a clever person from outside the undertaking figures it out for themself and divulges it to the world, the ruler will assume that you divulged it, and you are endangered. If your connection with the ruler is not yet intimate, but your discussions demonstrate the acme of intelligence, if your persuasions are implemented and the ruler is successful, your rewards will be forgotten. If, on the other hand, your persuasions are not implemented, and the ruler meets failure, you will be viewed with suspicion, and you are endangered. If someone esteemed by the ruler makes a slight mistake and you speak openly of ritual propriety and righteousness in order to poke at their vice, you are endangered. If someone esteemed by the ruler obtains a plan from someone else and wishes to count it as their own success, but you know where it came from, you are endangered. If you try to force the ruler to do what they are incapable of doing and try to stop them from doing what they cannot stop doing, you are endangered.

So, if you discuss great people with the ruler, the ruler will assume you are drawing a distinction between the great people and him. If you discuss inconsequential people with the ruler, he will assume you are selling your own importance. If you discuss someone whom the ruler is fond of, he will assume you are trying to make use of that person's abilities. If you discuss someone whom the ruler dislikes, he will assume you are trying to test them. If you are direct and economical with your persuasions, he will assume that you lack intelligence and treat you unfairly. If you discuss extensively and in great detail, he will assume that you are excessive and discard you. If you are too brief in sketching out your ideas, he will say that you are too timid and weak to try your best. If you consider affairs broadly and extensively, he will say that you are unpolished and arrogant. These are the difficulties of persuasion that you must not fail to understand.

The gist of the task of persuasion lies in understanding how to dress up that which the person to be persuaded is proud of and to minimize that which they are ashamed of. If this person has pressing private concerns, you must display and strengthen them by showing them to be a matter of public righteousness. If their intentions are base and yet they cannot stop themselves, you must accordingly dress up those aspects of their intentions that can be beautified and minimize those that cannot. If they have lofty ambitions but, in reality, cannot achieve them, you must bring up the excessiveness and display the errors of these ambitions, praising the person for not implementing them. If they wish to brag about their wisdom and ability, you must bring up different examples in the same category, providing them with more material, allowing them to avail themselves of your persuasions while pretending not to understand, so as to bolster their [belief in their own] wisdom.

If you wish to put forward a proposal for peaceful coexistence within the state, be certain to employ beautiful words to clarify your proposal while subtlety allowing them to see how it fits in with their personal interests. If you wish to explain how some situation is dangerous and harmful, you must make clear to them the sort of destruction and criticism that could arise as a result, while subtly allowing them to see how it leads to personal misfortune. You should praise other people who have acted in the same way as those whom you are persuading and hold up other policies that employ the same strategies as those employed by them as a model. If there are those who share similar blemishes as those whom you are persuading, you must gloss them as harmless. If there are those who have shared similar defeats, you must gloss them as not truly being defeats. If there are those who overestimate their own strength, you must not point out their past difficulties to cut them back down. If they regard their resolve as courageous, you must not anger them by pointing out their past errors. If they regard their own plans as clever, do not embarrass them by referencing their past failures. Ensure there is nothing in your overall ideas that opposes or contradicts those whom you are persuading, that in your phrasing and language there is nothing to bind things up—only then can you give full rein to your wisdom and eloquence. Once this way of acting has been achieved, then you will become intimate and close with those whom you wish to persuade and be able to fully express yourself without arousing suspicion.

Yi Yin took a position as a cook and Boli Xi allowed himself to be enslaved, each doing so as a means of bringing about their own advancement.[28] These two

---

28. Yi Yin and Boli Xi were both traditionally viewed as paragons of virtue. For Yi Yin, see *Analects* 12.22 (in chapter 1 of this volume), *Mozi* 8 (in chapter 2 of this volume), and *Mengzi* 2A2 (in chapter 4 of this volume). For Boli Xi, see *Mengzi* 5A9 (in chapter 4 of this volume).

people were both sages, and yet they were still unable to advance without subjecting themselves to servitude and defiling themselves in these ways. If, for the sake of promoting one's own proposals, one becomes a cook or allows oneself to be enslaved, and thus is listened to and employed, enabling one to save the world, this is not something that an official would regard as shameful.

In the past, Duke Wu of Zheng desired to attack the state of Hu. He thus first married his daughter to the ruler of Hu so as to divert his attention. Following this, he queried his assembled ministers, "I wish to direct a military operation—whom should I attack?" His minister Guan Qisi responded, "You could attack the state of Hu." Duke Wu became enraged and executed him, saying, "The state of Hu is our brother, how can you speak of attacking it?!" Upon hearing of this, the ruler of Hu regarded the state of Zheng as being a close ally and thereupon made no preparations against Zheng. When the people of Zheng engaged in a surprise attack on Hu, it was taken.

In the state of Song there lived a rich man. It rained and a wall [around his compound] collapsed. His son said, "If we do not rebuild, thieves will certainly come." The father of one of his neighbors also said the same thing. Evening came and resulted in great losses of his property. The rich man's family took his son to be extremely wise but were suspicious of their neighbor's father. What these two people [Guan Qisi and the neighbor's father] said was both appropriate. If in the more serious case, it resulted in execution, while in the slighter case it resulted in being viewed with suspicion, then the problem is not a difficulty of knowledge but rather a difficulty in managing this knowledge. Thus, while Rao Zhao's words were appropriate and he was considered a sage by the state of Jin, he was still executed by the state of Qin.[29] One cannot fail to examine this.

In the past, Mi Zixia was favored by the ruler of the state of Wey.[30] According to the laws of the state of Wey, secretly riding in the carriage of the ruler carried the punishment of having one's feet amputated. When Mi Zixia's mother fell ill, someone came to the palace at night in secret to tell Mi Zixia. Mi Zixia faked an order from the ruler so as to use the ruler's carriage to go out and see his mother. When the ruler heard of this, he considered it to be worthy behavior, saying, "How filial! For the sake of his mother, he disregarded the punishment

---

29. Rao Zhao was a minister in the state of Qin who advised his duke to be wary of an envoy from the state of Jin. Though his advice was correct, he fell subject to slander initiated by the Jin envoy and was executed by the duke.

30. The names of two different states are romanized as Wéi, 衛 and 魏. In this chapter, I have transliterated 魏 as Wei and 衛 as Wey, following Burton Watson.

of amputation." On a different day, Mi Zixia was walking through the orchard with the ruler. He was eating a peach that was particularly sweet and rather than finishing it, gave half of it to the ruler to eat. The ruler said, "You love me so much that you disregard the taste of the peach and offer it to me to eat!" But when Mi Zixia's beauty had declined and the ruler's love for him had slackened, he committed an offense against the ruler, and the ruler said, "After all, he once faked an order so as to use my carriage and once gave me a half-eaten peach." Therefore, while Mi Zixia's actions had not changed, those that in the past led to him being viewed as worthy were the same as those that later led to him being seen as a criminal. This is because love had turned to hate. Therefore, if one is loved by their ruler, one's wisdom will be deemed appropriate and the two will become increasingly close. If one is hated by one's ruler, one's knowledge will be deemed inappropriate and one will be accused of crimes and kept at a distance. Therefore, persuaders and orators cannot fail to examine whether the ruler feels love or hatred and only then speak.

The dragon as a creature is such that it is pliant and can become accustomed to being ridden. However, on the underside of its throat is a square foot of inverted scales. If someone brushes against them, the dragon will certainly kill them. The ruler of men also has his "inverted scales," and if, in speaking, you are able to avoid brushing against the ruler's "inverted scales," that is a success.

Chapter Twenty-Seven: Employing the People

I have heard that those in the past who were good at employing people certainly followed Heaven, accorded with people's [dispositions], and clarified rewards and punishments. If one follows Heaven, one will need to employ little effort in order to achieve great results. If one accords with people's [dispositions], punishments will be rare while one's orders will be implemented. If one clarifies rewards and punishments, neither [the paragon] Bo Yi nor Robber Zhi[31] can create chaos. In this way, black and white will be clearly separated.

The ministers of a well-ordered state obtain administrative status on the basis of their accomplishments in service to the state, receive appointments on the basis of demonstrations of ability in their posts, and are appointed to important positions on the basis of having exhausted their strength in upholding objective standards. Ministers all have positions that suit their abilities and so succeed in their offices while finding their responsibilities light. None holds back excess

---

31. For more on Bo Yi and Robber Zhi, see *Important Figures* in the appendices.

energy in his heart, and none shoulders the burden of serving in more than one post for his ruler. Therefore, within the state there is no chaos arising from hidden resentments while abroad there are no calamities of the sort experienced in Ma Fu.[32]

A clear-sighted ruler ensures that different positions do not interfere with one another, and thus there is nothing to dispute. He ensures that officials do not hold more than one post, and thus their abilities develop. He ensures that multiple people do not have responsibility for the same achievements, and thus there is no conflict. When conflicts and disputes have ceased and circumstances allowing the development of abilities have been established, the strong and the weak will not contend with one another, and ice and hot coals will not be mistaken for one another. When no one in the world harms one another, this is the pinnacle of good order.

If one cast aside laws and techniques and attempted to bring the state to order based on one's own ideas, in this way even the sage-king Yao could not set straight a single state. If one discarded the compass and carpenter's square and measured based on one's own rash ideas, even the lauded wheelwright Xi Zhong could not complete a single wheel.[33] If one got rid of the foot and inch measurements and tried to determine different lengths, even the famous carpenter Wang Er could not find the middle. If a mediocre ruler abides by laws and techniques, or if a clumsy carpenter abides by the compass and square and the foot and inch measurements, in ten thousand attempts, he will not go wrong. If the lord can discard that which the talented and clever are incapable of and abides by what the mediocre and clumsy cannot get wrong in ten thousand attempts, then the people's power will be used to the utmost, and the ruler's achievements and fame will be established.

A clear-sighted ruler establishes rewards that can be obtained and sets up punishments that can be avoided. Therefore, those of ability will be motivated by rewards and avoid the calamity of Zixu.[34] The unworthy will rarely commit crimes

---

32. Ma Fu was a fiefdom in the state of Zhao ruled by Zhao Gua (d. 260 BCE). Zhao Gua was extremely fond of military texts, and had a great deal of theoretical knowledge but no practical military experience. Soon after being appointed General by King Xiaocheng of Zhao, he died in a battle at Changping where the Zhao forces were defeated by the Qin army, leading to the loss of more than 400,000 men, according to records. He is referred to as the "Lord of Ma Fu" in *Han Feizi* chapter 50 (below), where this story is also referenced.

33. Xi Zhong is credited with inventing the horse-drawn cart. Cf. *Xunzi* chapter 21 (not in this volume).

34. Zixu was a famous general from the state of Wu who was forced to commit suicide for issuing a warning about the dangers of the neighboring state of Yue that his ruler, King Fucha, did not wish to heed. Subsequent to his death, Yue attacked, Wu was destroyed, and Fucha was killed.

and hunchbacks will avoid being dissected.[35] The blind will live on level ground and avoid [falling into] steep ravines. The ignorant will remain quiet and not fall into danger and peril. When circumstances are like this, then the affection between those above and those below will be tightly intertwined.

The ancients said: "Their minds are difficult to understand, what delights and angers them is difficult to ascertain." Therefore, [the ruler should] use visible signs to show things to the people's eyes, drums to speak to their ears, and laws to instruct their minds. If the ruler casts aside these three simple methods and tries to accord with those whose minds are difficult to understand, then anger will accumulate in those above and resentment will accumulate in those below. If one tries to control accumulated resentment with accumulated anger, this brings danger to both sides.

A clear-sighted ruler's signs are easy to see, and so his covenants are solidly established. His teachings are easy to understand, and so what he says is implemented. His laws are easy to carry out, and so his orders are followed. When these three are solidly established and those above do not pursue their private wishes, those below will follow the law and be well-ordered. Observing the signs, they will move; following the ink line, they will cut; and according with the needle pattern, they will sew. When circumstances are like this, those above will not be poisoned by the pursuit of awe-inspiring might for their private interests and those below will not be punished for ignorant and stupid actions. Thus, the ruler above will be clear-sighted and rarely angry, while those below will exhaust themselves in their loyalty and rarely commit crimes.

I have heard it said that "As for engaging in affairs without fear, even the sage-king Yao could not achieve this." Yet the world is never such that there are no affairs to deal with. A ruler who does not readily proffer rank and emoluments or freely extend wealth and noble rank is not one with whom one can save an endangered state.[36] Therefore, a clear-sighted ruler will raise up those with integrity and a sense of shame and attract the benevolent and righteous. In the past, Jie Zitui had no rank or emolument but followed Duke Wen out of a sense of righteousness.[37] He could not bear the Duke being hungry and so cut off his own flesh [to feed him]

---

35. This is a reference to the time of the Tyrant Jie, who followed no set standards, punishing those who were not guilty, rewarding those without achievements, and dissecting hunchbacks simply because they were different.

36. The claim here is not that the ruler should hand out benefits willy-nilly to all who ask. Rather, it is that all those who meet the requisite standards will, as a matter of course, receive their rewards.

37. Jie Zitui was loyal to the Jin prince Chong'er (697–628 BCE) during his time of exile, but retreated to live as a hermit in the mountains once Chong'er returned to take the throne and become Duke Wen of Jin.

out of a sense of benevolence. Therefore, the Duke recorded his potency and both books and pictures inscribed his reputation.

A ruler finds happiness in making others exhaust their strength for the public good and finds bitterness in seizing awe-inspiring might for his private interests. Ministers find peacefulness in accepting their duties and bitterness in shouldering two separate responsibilities at the same time. Therefore, the clear-sighted ruler gets rid of that which causes bitterness in his ministers and implements that in which the ruler finds happiness. As for what is mutually advantageous for superior and subordinate, nothing is greater than this.

If one does not investigate what happens behind closed doors; if one contemplates serious affairs lightly; if one implements substantive punishments for minor crimes; if one long harbors resentment for slight transgressions; if one continually humiliates those who have secret pleasures; if one time and again courts disaster for the sake of potency; this is to cut off one's arm and replace it with jade, and thus the world will see this calamity of a ruler being replaced.

If the ruler establishes requirements that are difficult to achieve and punishes those who do not attain them, personal resentments are born. If ministers lose what they are good at and have to offer up what is difficult for them to provide, hidden resentments will develop.[38] Those who toil and suffer hardship will not be comforted and accommodated, while those with worries and sorrows will not be treated with compassion and pity. When delighted, the ruler will honor those who are inferior, and the worthy and unworthy will be rewarded alike. When angry, he will defame even the gentleman, humiliating Bo Yi and Robber Zhi alike. As such, ministers will have a rebellious ruler.

Suppose the king of Yan loathed the people of his own state and loved those from the state of Lu. He would be unable to employ the people of Yan and those of Lu would not be attached to him. If his own people see that they are loathed, they will not exhaust their strength in working to succeed. And even if the people of Lu see that he is pleased with them, they will not risk their lives in order to draw near another ruler. When circumstances are like this, ministers will hide in crevices and holes and the ruler will be left standing alone. If a ruler standing alone is served only by ministers hidden in crevices and holes, this is called danger and peril.

If you cast aside your target and shoot rashly, then even if you hit something small, this is not skill. If you cast aside laws and regulations and express your anger rashly, then even if you kill and execute, those who are unscrupulous will

---

38. Cf. *Shenzi Fragments* sections 1 and 6 (in chapter 7 of this volume) for a discussion of the source of resentment.

feel no dread. If the crime arises from "Person A" while the ruin falls on "Person B," then hidden resentments will thereupon develop. Thus, in the most well-ordered of states, there are rewards and punishments but no feelings of delight or anger.

Therefore, when a sage carries out executions, death is in accordance with the penal codes and without any poisonous anger, and thus the unscrupulous will submit. When the arrows shot hit their mark, rewards and punishments are suitable and appropriate. Thus, the sage-king Yao is reborn, and the great Archer Yi rises again. If circumstances are like this, those above will not suffer the disasters that befell the Shang and Xia dynasties while those below will not suffer the calamity of Bi Gan.[39] The ruler can rest high above while his ministers delight in their work. His Way will cover all of Heaven and earth while his potency will extend for myriad generations.

If the ruler does not block up the crevices and holes, but expends his strength in adorning things with ocher and chalk powder, then violent rains and strong winds are certain to destroy his work. If he does not eliminate those disasters that are right in front of him, but admires how the legendary strongmen Ben and Yu died; if he is not concerned with dangers to the walls surrounding his inner quarters, but strengthens the solid walls of his distant borders; if he does not employ the ideas of the worthies near at hand, but entangles himself in associations with large states over a thousand *li* away; then, when a whirlwind suddenly arises, Ben and Yu will not be able to save him, and his associates will not arrive in time. No calamity is greater than this.

In the present time, one who loyally makes plans for his ruler must not allow the king of Yan to love those from the state of Lu; he must not allow the present generation's admiration of the sages of antiquity; he must not yearn for the people of [the coastal state of] Yue to save someone from an interior state from drowning.[40] In this way, then, those above and those below will be close to one another, one's achievements will be established within one's state, and one's reputation will be achieved beyond one's borders.

Chapter Twenty-Nine: The Great Whole

Those in ancient times who perfected the great whole gazed out at Heaven and earth, observed the rivers and seas, and followed the mountains and valleys. They

---

39. On Bi Gan, see note 13 on "Robber Zhi" (in chapter 3 of this volume).

40. For a further discussion of this point, see *Han Feizi* chapter 40 (below).

were like the sun and the moon in their illumination and like the four seasons in their actions. Like the clouds they spread out and like the wind they moved. They did not clutter their minds with cleverness nor clutter their selves with private interests. They entrusted questions about order and chaos in governing to laws and techniques, entrusted questions about right and wrong to rewards and punishments, and subordinated questions about weight to steelyards. They did not oppose the patterns of Heaven, nor did they harm their own dispositions or natures.[41] They did not blow on hairs to seek out trifling flaws, nor did they wash away filth in order to scrutinize those things that are difficult to understand. They did not draw things in from beyond the ink line, nor did they push things out from within the ink line. They were not anxious about what was outside the purview of the law, nor were they hesitant about what was within the purview of the law. They abided by the established pattern and accorded with what was naturally so.[42]

Misfortune and fortune arose from the Way and the law, and not from the ruler's likes and dislikes. The responsibility for honor and shame lay with the people themselves, and not with others. Therefore, the generation was completely peaceful, and the law was like the morning dew: pure, simple, and undiluted. Within the hearts of men there were no knotted-up resentments, and from their mouths came no vexing words. Thus, chariot-drawing horses were not exhausted by distant journeys into battle, and battle flags and banners did not become disordered in the great marshes. The myriad people did not lose their lives at the weapons of invaders, and the powerful and talented did not cut short their life spans among the banners and pennants of battle. Those of extraordinary talent and ability did not have their names inscribed in tableaux or books, nor did they have their achievements recorded on bronze plates and basins, and the wooden tablets for the chronicles remained uninscribed. Thus, it is said, "There is no advantage that lasts longer than simplicity, and there is no fortune more long-lasting than peace."

If one ordered the skilled Mason Stone[43] to spend a thousand years of his life grasping his hook, observing his compass and square, and holding up his ink line in order to set straight Mount Tai, or if one ordered the legendary strongmen Meng Ben and Xia Yu to use the *Ganjiang* sword to bring into line the myriad people, then, even if they exhausted the power of their skills and even if their lives were extremely long, neither would Mount Tai be set straight, nor would the people be brought into line. Thus, it is said, those in ancient times who shepherded the world

---

41. "Dispositions" and "natures" here are qíng 情 and xìng 性. For more, see *Important Terms* in the appendices.

42. "Naturally" here is zìrán 自然. For more, see *Important Terms* in the appendices.

43. "Mason Stone" is the name of a stonemason legendary for his great skill.

did not order Mason Stone to use all of his skill in order to destroy the fundamental shape of Mount Tai, nor did they order Meng Ben and Xia Yu to exhaust their awe-inspiring might to damage the basic nature of the myriad people.

If one accords with the Way to perfect the law, those of noble rank will be delighted, and great villainies will cease. One will be tranquil, idle, and still, according with the mandate of Heaven, and holding on to the great whole. Thus, one will ensure that people do not commit crimes by departing from the law, and that fish do not suffer the calamity of being out of water. When it is like this, there is little in the world that cannot be achieved.

If those above are not [broad like] Heaven, those below will not be universally protected. If one's mind is not [vast like] the earth, it cannot contain all things. Mount Tai has no established preferences [with regard to the material composing it], and so it achieves its great height. Rivers and oceans are not picky with regard to their tributaries, and so they achieve abundance. Therefore, the great man entrusts his form to Heaven and earth and the myriad things are all provided for. He places his mind in the mountains and seas, and his state has abundance. Those above will not be poisoned by anger or rage and those below will not suffer the calamities of hidden resentments. Those above and those below will interact naturally and dwell within the Way. Therefore, lasting achievements can be accumulated, great accomplishments can be established, one's fame will be established in the present, and one's potency will be transmitted to future generations. This is the pinnacle of good order.

Chapter Thirty-Two: Collected Illustrations
• Outer Part • Upper Left Section

. . . Duke Xiang of Song[44] was fighting the people of Chu on the Zhuogu River. The people of Song had already formed their battle ranks while the people of Chu had not yet forded the river. The Commander of the Right, Gou Qiang, hastened forward and remonstrated: "The people of Chu are numerous while the people of Song are few. Please order the attack while the people of Chu are only halfway across the river and have not yet formed ranks, and they are certain to be defeated."

Duke Xiang replied, "I have heard a gentleman say, 'Do not wound someone more than once, do not capture those whose hair is turning gray, do not push people into danger, do not compel people into impossible situations, do not sound

---

44. Duke Xiang of Song ruled from 650 to 637 BCE.

the attack drums when the enemy has not yet formed ranks.' Now, attacking Chu when they have not yet forded the river is a harm to righteousness. I request that you wait until the people of Chu have finished fording the river and formed their battle array and only after that sound the attack drums to send the officers forward."

The Commander of the Right said, "My lord does not care about the people of Song or whether their stomachs are cut open and their hearts scooped out. You are only concerned with righteousness and that is all."

The Duke responded, "If you do not return to your ranks, I shall enforce the law [i.e., punish you]."

The Commander of the Right returned to the ranks. Only after the people of Chu had formed their ranks and composed their battle array did the duke thereupon drum his troops forward. The people of Song suffered a great defeat and the duke was wounded in the thigh, dying three days later. This is the disaster arising from a personal admiration for benevolence and righteousness. . . .

Chapter Thirty-Five: Collected Illustrations
• Outer Part • Lower Right Section

. . . Order and strength arise from law while weakness and disorder arise from leniency. If the ruler is clear-sighted with respect to this, he will set straight rewards and punishments and will not treat those below with benevolence. Rank and emoluments will arise from achievement, while punishments and penalties will arise from crimes. If his ministers are clear-sighted with respect to this, they will exert their strength to the point of death, but not because of loyalty to the ruler. If the ruler thoroughly understands not to be kind, and his ministers thoroughly understand not to be loyal, he can become a true king. King Zhaoxiang[45] understood the proper disposition of the ruler and did not release supplies from the Five Gardens. . . .

There was a great famine in the state of Qin. The Marquis of Ying[46] said: "As for the plants and roots of the Five Gardens, these vegetables, acorns, jujubes, and chestnuts would be sufficient to allow the people to survive. I ask that we distribute them."

---

45. King Zhaoxiang (325–251 BCE) set the state of Qin on the road to dominance in the Warring States Period, (see *Important Periods* in the appendices), with the result that his grandson gained unified control over all the states, becoming the first emperor in 221 BCE.

46. The Marquis of Ying, Fan Ju, was originally from the state of Wei, but served as prime minister of Qin from 266 to 256 BCE.

King Zhaoxiang said: "Our laws of the state of Qin ensure that people have achievements and only then receive rewards, that they commit crimes and only then are punished. Now, if we distribute the plants from the Five Gardens, this will enable those who have achievements along with those who lack achievements all to be rewarded. Now, if we enable those who have achievements along with those who lack achievements all to be rewarded, this is the way of disorder. Distributing food from the Five Gardens and having disorder is not as good as throwing away these jujubes and vegetables and having order."

Another source says: King Zhaoxiang replied, "Ordering the distribution of melons, vegetables, jujubes, and chestnuts would be sufficient to allow the people to survive, but this would cause those who have achievements and those without achievements to struggle over getting these things. Now, keeping them alive but having disorder is not as good as letting them die but having order. May you, Grand Minister, cast aside this thought!" . . .

Chapter Forty: A Critique of the Doctrine of Positional Power

Shenzi[47] said: "The flying dragon rides the clouds, and the winged snake travels on the mists. But when the clouds are gone and the mists dissipate, the dragon and snake become the same as worms and ants, because they have lost that upon which they were riding. If worthies yield to an unworthy, it is because their authority is slight and their status low. If unworthies put up with submitting to a worthy, it is because his authority is strong and his status exalted. When Yao was a commoner, he could not order [even] three people, but when Jie was the Son of Heaven, he could bring chaos to the world. From this I know that positional power (shì 勢) and status are sufficient to rely upon, while worthiness and wisdom are not sufficient to be esteemed. If a crossbow is weak but its arrow flies high, it is because it is pushed forward by the wind. If one is unworthy and yet one's orders are carried out, it is because one has attained the assistance of the masses. When Yao tried to teach the lower classes, the people would not listen to him. [However,] when he came to face south and rule over the world, his orders were carried out, and what he prohibited ceased. From this, we can see that worthiness and knowledge are insufficient to control the masses while positional power and status are sufficient to cause worthies to submit."

In response to Shenzi, a critic says, "As for the flying dragon riding the clouds, and the winged snake traveling on the mists, I am not claiming that

---

47. Shenzi refers to Shen Dao. Cf. *Shenzi Fragments* (chapter 7 in this volume).

the dragon and the snake are not indebted to the clouds and the mists for their positional power. Nonetheless, if one casts aside worthiness and relies exclusively upon positional power, is this sufficient to create order? This I have never seen. When positional power arising from clouds and mists is available, dragons and snakes can ride and travel on them, but this is because their abilities are excellent. Now, even if clouds are abundant, still the worm cannot ride upon them; even if the mists are thick, the ant cannot travel upon them. When positional power arising from an abundance of clouds and thick mists is available, they are still unable to ride and travel upon them; this is because the abilities of worms and ants are meager. Now, when the tyrants Jie and Zhou faced south and ruled over all the world, employing the awe-inspiring might of the Son of Heaven as their clouds and mists, all the world could not avoid chaos; this was because the abilities of Jie and Zhou were meager."

[The critic continues,] "Furthermore, Shenzi takes Yao's positional power as being what allowed him to bring order to the world, but in what way is Yao's positional power different from Jie's positional power, which brought chaos to the world? Positional power is not something that can be restricted such that [only] the worthy will employ it and the unworthy will not. If the worthy employ it, then the world will be well-ordered, while if the unworthy employ it, then the world will be brought to chaos. The inborn dispositions and natures of people are such that the worthy are few while the unworthy are numerous. Thus, if one employs the efficaciousness of awe-inspiring might and positional power to rescue the unworthy who would bring chaos to the age, then those who bring chaos to the world by means of positional power will be many, while those who bring order to the world by means of positional power will be few."

[The critic continues,] "Positional power is such that it is both advantageous for creating order and beneficial for creating chaos. Therefore, the *Documents of Zhou*[48] says, "Do not apply wings to a tiger or it will fly into the city, snatching people up and eating them." Giving positional power to the unworthy to ride upon is the same as applying wings to a tiger. The tyrants Jie and Zhou built high pavilions and deep pools, and by doing so exhausted the strength of the people. They employed roasting pillars and by doing so harmed people's lives.[49] The reason that Jie and Zhou were able to succeed in this wanton behavior is because the awe-inspiring

---

48. This quotation is found in the "Wu jing" chapter of the *Yi Zhou shu* (*Lost Documents of the Zhou*). While this book dates to the Western Han, the *Documents of Zhou* likely refers to the core of this text, which dates to an earlier time.

49. These "roasting pillars" were metal pillars heated over pits of fire. Tyrant Zhou was infamous for forcing people to walk across these pillars barefooted as a punishment. As the soles of their feet burned, they would lose their balance, falling into the fire below and being roasted alive.

might of their south-facing [position] served as their wings. If Jie and Zhou had been commoners, they would have suffered the punishment of execution before they had begun to carry out even one [of these actions]. If positional power nourishes the hearts of tigers and wolves, and gives rise to violent and chaotic affairs, this is the greatest disaster in the world. Positional power fundamentally has no fixed status in relation to order or chaos, and when [Shenzi's] words say that positional power is sufficient to bring order to the world, then the place where his wisdom has reached is shallow indeed!"

[The critic continues,] "As for fine horses and a sturdy chariot, if one allows a common slave to drive them, then he will be laughed at by the people. But if Wang Liang drives them, then they will manage a thousand *li* in a single day.[50] If it is not that the chariot or the horses are different, but one manages a thousand *li* while the other is laughed at, this is because the difference between skillfulness and clumsiness is vast indeed. Now, if we take the chariot to represent one's status in the state, the horses to represent one's positional power, the bridle to represent one's commands and orders, and the whip to represent one's punishments, then when the sage-kings Yao and Shun drove them, then the world was well-ordered, while when the tyrants Jie and Zhou were driving, then the world was in chaos, because the difference between worthiness and unworthiness is vast indeed. If one wishes to go fast and far, but does not know to rely upon a Wang Liang, or if one wishes to accrue benefits and eliminate harms, but does not know to rely upon worthiness and ability, this will be a disaster of failing to understand how to properly categorize things. Yao and Shun were the Wang Liangs of bringing people to order."

In response, I[51] say: Shenzi takes positional power to be sufficient to rely upon in bringing order to the offices of the state, while the previous critic says that it is necessary to await the worthy and only then will there be order. This is not so! As for "positional power," it is a single term, but its variations in meaning are innumerable. If this term necessarily refers to the way that things are of themselves, then there is no reason to speak of this term. When I speak of this term, I speak of that which people set up.[52]

---

50. Wang Liang was a famous charioteer, mentioned throughout ancient literature as the epitome of excellence.

51. The "I" here indicates that it is Han Fei himself speaking in response to the criticism that he has just laid out.

52. This paragraph and the following one are particularly tricky to translate, in part because the term shì 勢 is being used in two senses: that which people set up and which is thus under human control, and that which is not. In English, the former can be translated as "positional power," as I have done. However, the latter is closer to what we would render in English as "circumstances beyond human control." Since the

Now, it is said that in the past when Yao and Shun gained the upper hand due to circumstances (shì 勢), they brought about good order, while when Jie and Zhou gained the upper hand due to circumstances, they brought about chaos— and I do not claim that this was not the case with Yao and Jie. Nonetheless, this is not something that a person can set up. If a Yao or a Shun was born with a high status, then even if there were ten Jies or Zhous, they would not be able to create chaos, because the circumstances would favor good order. But if a Jie or a Zhou was born with a high status, then even if there were ten Yaos or Shuns, they would not be able to create order, because the circumstances would favor chaos. Thus, it is said, "When the circumstances favor good order, then chaos cannot arise. When the circumstances favor chaos, then good order cannot arise." This refers to circumstances arising from the way that things are of themselves, not what is set up by people. As for what I am talking about, it is the positional power set up by people, and that is all. How could worthiness have anything to do with this?

How can I make clear that this is the case? A visitor once told me the following story: There was a man who sold spears and shields. He praised the strength of his shields, claiming that nothing could pierce them. After a while, he praised his spears, saying, "My spears are so sharp that there is nothing that they cannot pierce." Someone responded to him, saying, "What about if I try to pierce one of your shields with one of your spears?" The salesman could not respond.

"Unpierceable shields" and "all-piercing spears" are two claims that cannot coexist. Now, [if one claims that] the Way of the worthy is such that he cannot be stopped and [simultaneously claims that] the Way of positional power (shì 勢) is such that there is nothing that it cannot stop, or tries to use unstoppable worthiness to overtake an all-stopping positional power, this is like

---

following paragraph deals with the latter, I have opted to translate *shi* as "circumstances" to clarify this meaning.

While reading, please keep in mind that, according to Han Feizi, whether one succeeds or fails depends both upon the *shi* that is within one's control and the *shi* that is beyond one's control. Throughout the text, Han Feizi argues that there is a range of things the ruler can control due to the power inherent in his position, including administering the two handles of reward and punishment and ensuring that achievements match prior proposals. Properly employing these tools results in the positional power set up by individuals. However, there is also a range of *shi* outside of human control that nevertheless plays a significant role in success and failure. This includes factors involving the natural world. However, more importantly for present purposes, it includes the natural dispositions and natures of individual rulers, those unique qualities specific to particular rulers. Thus, the tyrants Jie and Zhou were only able to bring about chaos because of a variety of things that Han Feizi takes to be outside of human control—being born as the heir to the throne as well as being born with deviant, perverted, and chaotic dispositions, natures, and desires.

[what the salesman] said about shields and spears. That [unstoppable] worthiness and positional power [that can stop anything] do not accommodate one another is also clear.

Moreover, if a Yao, Shun, Jie, or Zhou emerged once per thousand generations, this would be for them to be born shoulder to shoulder, heel to heel. Those who govern each generation are typically mediocre. Those for whom I speak of positional power are the mediocre. The mediocre, at their highest, do not reach up to the heights of a Yao or a Shun, while at their lowest, they also do not sink to the depths of a Jie or a Zhou. If they embrace the law and dwell in positional power, then there will be order. If they turn their back on the law and abandon positional power, then there will be chaos. Now, abandoning positional power and turning away from the law while awaiting a Yao or a Shun, on the assumption that when a Yao or a Shun arrives, there will thereupon be order—this is to have a thousand generations of chaos for every generation of order. Embracing the law and dwelling in positional power while awaiting a Jie or a Zhou, on the assumption that when a Jie or a Zhou arrives, there will thereupon be chaos—this is to have a thousand generations of order for every generation of chaos. Moreover, the difference between the case of having a thousand generations of order for every one of chaos and that of having one generation of order for every thousand generations of chaos is as vast as the result of riding two fast horses galloping in opposite directions.

If one abandons the models for shaping wood and gets rid of the technique for measuring length and then asks the excellent wheelwright Xi Zhong to construct a chariot, he could not make even a single wheel. Without the encouragement of veneration and rewards or the awe-inspiring might of punishments and fines, having cast aside positional power and tossed away the law, if Yao or Shun were to go door to door, speaking to people and debating them, they would not be able to bring order to even three families. That positional power is sufficient to be employed is certainly clear, and to say that it is necessary to await the worthy is certainly not so.

Moreover, if one goes a hundred days without eating while awaiting the finest of millet and meat, such a starving person will not survive. Now, awaiting a worthy such as Yao or Shun and only then bringing to order the people of the present age, doing so would be like saying that one should await the finest of millet and meat to save one from starvation. As for saying that if one allows a common slave to drive fine horses and a sturdy chariot, the people will laugh, while only if Wang Liang drives them will they manage a thousand *li*, I do not take it to be so. If one awaits an excellent sea swimmer from the [coastal] state of Yue in order to save someone drowning in an interior state, the person from Yue will be excellent at swimming, and yet the drowning person will not be rescued.[53] If one awaits antiquity's Wang Liang in order to guide the reins of today's horses, this also is like saying that we should use the swimmer from Yue to save the drowning person. That this is inappropriate is also certainly clear. If one has fine horses and a sturdy chariot and places [replacement horses] at intervals of fifty *li*, and has a mediocre charioteer drive them, then one can go fast and far, and it is possible to manage a thousand *li* in a single day. How could it be necessary to await antiquity's Wang Liang?! Moreover, [saying that] if in driving a chariot, one does not have a Wang Liang, then one will certainly have failure resulting from the use of a common slave, or [saying that] if in ordering the state, one does not have a Yao or a Shun, then one will certainly have the chaos of a Jie or a Zhou, this is like [saying that] if flavors are not sweet like honey, then they are certainly bitter like herbs and mustard greens. This, then, is simply piling up meaningless rhetoric and accumulating empty phrases, straying from the principles and neglecting the techniques [of effective methods], by discussing the two extremes. How could this criticize the words [of Shenzi], based on the principles of the Way? The discussions of the critic do not approach the level of [Shenzi's] theory.

Chapter Forty-Three: Establishing Methods of Government

Someone asked, "As for the words of Shen Buhai and Gongsun Yang,[54] between the two, which is more critical for the state?"

In response, I say, "They cannot be measured [against one another]. If someone does not eat, they will die within ten days. But, in the depths of winter, without clothing, one will also die. If one asks whether clothing or food is more critical for people, isn't it that one cannot lack either? They are both tools for nourishing life. Now, Shen Buhai discussed administrative techniques while Gongsun Yang implemented laws. Administrative techniques dictate awarding offices on the basis of qualifications, following proposals in evaluating results, grasping the handles of life and death, and examining the abilities of the assembled ministers. This is what the ruler controls. [Employing] laws means that statutes and decrees are promulgated through the governmental offices and bureaus, punishments and fines are felt as inevitable in the hearts of the people, rewards accrue to those who are scrupulous with respect to the laws, and punishments are conferred upon those who violate

---

53. See also *Han Feizi* chapter 27 (above).

54. While Han Fei drew many ideas from these two figures, he also attacked them vociferously at times. For more, see *Important Figures* in the appendices.

decrees. These are what provide models for the ministers. If rulers lack administrative techniques, they will be blinded from above, while if the ministers lack the laws, they will be chaotic below. There cannot be a lack of either one—they are the tools of emperors and kings."

Someone asked, "What would be wrong with merely employing administrative techniques but not the law or merely employing the law but not administrative techniques?"

In response I say, "Shen Buhai was an aide to Marquis Zhao of Han, and the state of Han was created from the division of the state of Jin. Even before the old laws of Jin had been suspended, the new laws of Han had already arisen. Even before the decrees of the former ruler had been put aside, the decrees of the new ruler had already been handed down. Since Shen Buhai did not take sole control over the laws, nor did he unify statutes and decrees, there were many instances of unscrupulousness. If there was benefit to be had by following the old laws and the former decrees, then they were followed, while if there was benefit to be had by following the new laws and the later decrees, then they were followed. The benefits arising from the new and the old laws were mutually contradictory while those arising from the former and the later decrees were contrary to one another. And so, even though Shen Buhai ten times instructed Marquis Zhao of Han on the use of administrative techniques, unscrupulous ministers could still deceive him with their words. Thus, while the Marquis of Han had control over the strength of ten thousand war chariots for seventeen years, he was unable to achieve the status of lord protector or king. This disaster arose since, even though he employed administrative techniques from above, laws were not diligently arranged within government offices.

When Gongsun Yang governed the state of Qin, he established a system by which people had to report one another and were responsible for the truth of their claims. He linked people together in groups of five and ten households and held them all equally responsible for the crimes of any one member. His rewards were magnanimous and trusted while his punishments were severe and certain. Because of this, his people exhausted their strength in laboring without rest and pursued their enemies into danger without retreating. Thus, his state was rich and its army strong. Even so, due to a lack of administrative techniques for identifying the unscrupulous, the state's riches and strength simply supported its ministers, and that was all. Upon the deaths of Duke Xiao and Gongsun Yang, King Hui ascended the throne.[55] While the laws of Qin had not yet been defeated, Zhang

---

55. Duke Xiao of Qin (r. 361–338 BCE) employed Gongsun Yang as his prime minister. Upon his death, his son, King Hui of Qin (r. 337–211 BCE) ascended the throne and had Gongsun Yang executed for an earlier punishment against the king's tutor.

Yi sacrificed [the interests of] Qin to the states of Han and Wei.[56] Upon the death of King Hui, King Wu ascended the throne and Gan Mao sacrificed [the interests of] Qin to the House of Zhou.[57] When King Wu died, King Zhaoxiang ascended the throne and Marquis Rang passed over the states of Han and Wei to attack the state of Qi in the east. Over a period of five years, Qin did not gain a single foot of land, but the Marquis of Rang enlarged his fiefdom around Tao Yi.[58] The Marquis of Ying attacked the state of Han for eight years, enlarging his fiefdom south of the Ru River.[59]

Ever since, all of those who made use of Qin have been in the same category as Ying and Rang. And so, when battles were won, the great ministers were exalted; when territories were increased, private fiefdoms were established. Rulers lacked the administrative techniques allowing them to understand who was unscrupulous. Even though Gongsun Yang refined his laws ten times, it was the ministers who were able to make use of the state's resources. Thus, if one has availed oneself of the resources of the strong state of Qin and yet after several decades has not become an emperor or king, this is a disaster arising because even though laws were diligently arranged within government offices, rulers lacked administrative techniques above.

Someone asked, "If a ruler employs the techniques of Shen Buhai and implements the laws of Gongsun Yang in governmental offices, would that do?"

I respond, "Shen Buhai did not completely understand administrative techniques and Gongsun Yang did not completely understand laws. Shen Buhai said, 'Do not transgress the bounds of your office; even if you know, do not speak.' As for 'not transgressing the bounds of your office,' this describes keeping to one's own duties, and is appropriate. However, 'knowing but not speaking,' this is to not call out [others'] faults. The ruler sees with the eyes of all within the state, and thus in terms of seeing, none is more clear-sighted than him. He listens with the ears of all within the state, and thus in terms of hearing, none is more keen-eared than him.

---

56. Zhang Yi was a wandering statesman originally from the state of Wei, but who served in a variety of ministerial positions in Qin and Wei. On Han Fei's interpretation, Zhang Yi played the rulers of these states off of one another so as to gain his own private fortune.

57. Gan Mao was another wandering statesman who served King Wu of Qin (r. 310–307 BCE) and who was instrumental in King Wu's plans to destroy the remnants of the House of Zhou. Again, Han Fei seems to understand Gan Mao as having pursued his own private interests to the detriment of those of the state of Qin.

58. King Zhaoxiang of Qin (r. 306–251 BCE) was the son of King Hui. The Marquis of Rang, Wei Ran, served as his prime minister from 300 to 266 BCE and utilized Qin forces to expand his own private holdings.

59. The Marquis of Ying, Fan Sui, served as prime minister to King Zhaoxiang of Qin from 266 to 256 BCE, using this position to enrich himself.

Now, if his people know things but do not speak up, how can the ruler above avail himself of their eyes and ears?"

The laws of Gongsun Yang said, "Someone who chops off one head in battle shall be raised one level in rank, and if this person desires to take office, it will be to a position with a salary of 50 bushels of grain. One who chops off two heads in battle shall be raised two levels in rank, and if this person desires to take office, it will be to a position with a salary of 100 bushels of grain." Position and rank [in this system] corresponded to achievements in beheading. Now, if there were a law that said: "Those who chop off heads are ordered to become doctors and carpenters," houses would not be constructed and illnesses would not be cured. A carpenter requires skilled hands while a doctor requires a comprehensive understanding of medicine, and if one takes success at beheading as the standard for handing out these positions, positions will not correspond with abilities. Now, managing governmental offices depends upon knowledge and ability. Beheading people depends upon bravery and strength. Employing the brave and the strong to manage governmental offices that require knowledge and ability is the same as making success at beheading the criterion for becoming doctors or carpenters.

Therefore, I say, "With regard to laws and administrative techniques, neither of these two were fully competent."

Chapter Forty-Seven: Eight Explanations

. . . As for a caring mother's relation to her infant son, her love is such that nothing comes before him. Even so, if her infant son engages in perverse actions, she makes him submit to a teacher. If he has a serious sickness, she makes him submit to a doctor. If he does not submit to a teacher, he will fall victim to punishment, while if he does not submit to a doctor, he will draw near to death. If even a caring mother's love is of no help in avoiding punishment or saving one who is dying, that which preserves the child is not love.

The nature of the relationship between a son and a mother is one of love. The relationship between a minister and a ruler is one of power and strategy. If a mother cannot use love to preserve her family, how can a ruler use love to uphold the state? The clear-sighted ruler understands how to achieve wealth and power, and thus he can attain his desires. So, he is careful in governing, for it is the method for achieving wealth and power. He makes laws and prohibitions clear and examines his schemes and plans. If laws are clear, then within the state there will not be the calamity of disorder. If his plans are attained, then outside the state, he will not suffer the disaster of death or capture on the battlefield.

Therefore, what preserves the state is neither benevolence nor righteousness Those who are benevolent are caring and compassionate and take wealth lightly. Those who are cruel have hearts that are harsh and easily punish. If one is caring and compassionate, one cannot bear to do certain things. If one takes wealth lightly, one is fond of giving to others. If one is harsh, a hate-filled heart will manifest itself toward subordinates. If one easily punishes, rash executions will be applied to the people. If there are things that one cannot bear to do, punishments will often be forgiven and waived. If one is fond of giving to others, rewards in many cases will lack corresponding achievements. If a hate-filled heart manifests itself, those below will resent their superiors. If rash executions are instituted, the people will rebel.

So, when a benevolent individual is in power, those below will be unrestrained and think little of violating prohibitions and laws. They will look to luck and be lazy, and will hope for good things from their superior. When a cruel individual is in power, laws and orders will be rashly applied, and the relationship between ministers and their ruler will be one of opposition. The people will be resentful and hearts bent on disorder will arise. Therefore, it is said: "Both those who are benevolent and those who are cruel will ruin the state." . . .

Chapter Forty-Nine: The Five Vermin

In the age of upper antiquity, human beings were few while the birds and beasts were numerous, so the people could not prevail against the birds, beasts, insects, and serpents. Then there arose a sage who taught the people how to interlace branches to form nests so they could escape all harm. The people were pleased by this and made him king of the world, giving him the name "The Nester." The people ate fruits, berries, mussels, and clams, but they were rancid, repulsive, and fetid and hurt the people's stomachs so that they often became sick and ill. Then there arose a sage who taught the people how to use a fire drill and flint to obtain fire, so they could cook their rancid, repulsive foods. The people were pleased by this and made him king of the world, giving him the name "The Kindler." In the age of middle antiquity, the world was submerged by great floods, but [the great kings] Gun and Yu of the Xia dynasty dug drainage ditches. In the age of lower antiquity, the [tyrants] Jie and Zhou were violent and caused chaos, but [the sage-kings] Tang and Wu led campaigns to overthrow them.

Now, were someone to have interlaced branches or used a fire drill and flint during the age of the rulers of the Xia dynasty, they would certainly have been laughed at by Gun and Yu. If someone were to have dug drainage ditches during the age of the Yin or Zhou dynasties, they would certainly have been laughed at by Tang and Wu. This being so, if one were to praise the Ways of Yao, Shun, Yu, Tang, and Wu in the present age, they would certainly be laughed at by the new sages. Hence, [true] sages do not expect to cultivate antiquity or take as their model an unchanging standard for what is appropriate. They evaluate the affairs of their age and make preparations on this basis.

A man in the state of Song was plowing his field, which had within it a tree stump.[60] A rabbit ran through his field, collided with the stump, broke its neck, and died. At this point, the man from Song laid down his plow and kept watch over the tree stump, hoping that he would get another rabbit. However, getting another rabbit in this manner was impossible, and so this man was laughed at by all within the state of Song. Now, if one desires to bring order to the people of the present age by means of the ordering methods of the former kings, this is in the same category as keeping watch over the tree stump.

In antiquity, adult men did not engage in agriculture, for the fruits of bushes and trees provided sufficient nourishment. Adult women did not weave, for the hides of wild animals provided sufficient clothing. They did not exert their strength and yet there was enough to nourish them. The people were few while material resources were abundant, and so the people did not fight [among themselves]. Therefore, magnanimous rewards were not handed out, and strict punishments were not employed, and yet the people were well-ordered of themselves. In the present, having five sons is not considered many, and these sons in turn each have five sons of their own, so that before they pass away, grandfathers already have twenty-five grandsons. Thus, the number of people increases while goods and material resources grow scarce. The people exhaust their strength for meager supplies of nourishment. Thus, the people fight among themselves, and even if rewards are doubled and punishments are piled on, chaos cannot be avoided.

When Yao was king of the world, the thatching on his roof was not trimmed, and his painted rafters were left uncarved. He ate cakes of coarsely ground rice and drank thick soup made of the leaves of lamb's quarters and pulses. In the winter he wore the hide of fawns, while in the summer he wore clothing woven from vines. Even the clothing and food of a gatekeeper was of no less a quality than this. When Yu was king of the world, he personally took hold of plow and spade so as to lead his people, [working until] there was no hair on his thighs and his shins no longer grew hair. Even the labor of captured slaves was no more bitter than this.

---

60. People from the state of Song were often the butt of jokes about their stupidity in the literature of the time. Compare *Mengzi* 2A2 (in chapter 4 of this volume).

Speaking from this perspective, those in antiquity who abdicated the throne over the world were discarding the life of a gatekeeper and abandoning the labor of a captured slave. Thus, their handing over the world is not worth making much of. As for the district magistrates of the present, once they die, their sons and grandsons for generations ride around in carriages. Therefore, the people take these positions to be important. As for people's attitude toward yielding, they would have found it easy to take their leave from the position of Son of Heaven in antiquity, but find it difficult to leave the position of today's district magistrates. This is because of the differences in the available benefits.

Those who live in the mountains who must descend into the valleys to gather water give one another gifts of water during the festivals of the second and twelfth months, while those who live in swamplands and suffer from flooding hire laborers to dig ditches to drain away the water. In the spring after a crop failure, even young children are not given food, while in the autumn after an abundant harvest, even passing strangers are certain to be fed. It is not that they neglect their own flesh and blood while caring for passing strangers; it is that there are differences in available resources.

Thus, when those of antiquity treated resources lightly, it was not because they were benevolent, but because material resources were plentiful. When those of today fight and contend with one another, it is not because they are vulgar, but because material resources are scarce. If one easily takes his leave from the position of Son of Heaven, it is not because he is high-minded, but because the benefits of the position are slight. When people fight over gaining official positions and connections to the powerful, it is not because they are base, but because the benefits to be gained are substantial. Thus, sages deliberate about the quantity [of material resources] and discuss the benefits [of governmental positions] and on these bases implement their government. Thus, when penalties are slight, it is not because of compassion. When punishments are severe, it is not because of cruelty. [Sages] simply accord with local circumstances in their actions. Thus, circumstances depend upon the particular age and methods of preparing must be focused on these circumstances.

Antiquity's [sage] King Wen lived in between Feng and Hao, on land of 100 square *li*. He implemented benevolence and righteousness, embraced the Western barbarians, and subsequently became king of the world. King Yan of Xu lived east of the Han River, on land of 500 square *li*.[61] He implemented benevolence and righteousness, and 36 states paid him allegiance by giving him pieces of their

---

61. King Yan of Xu was a semi-legendary ruler who is described in the *Huainanzi* as having lost his state due to his adherence to righteousness and benevolence.

territory. King Wen of Jing [Chu], fearful that he himself would be harmed, raised an army to attack the state of Xu and subsequently exterminated Xu.[62] Thus, King Wen implemented benevolence and righteousness and became king of the world, while King Yan implemented benevolence and righteousness and lost his state. This is because benevolence and righteousness were useful in antiquity, but not useful in the present. Thus, I say, "When the age differs, circumstances differ."

During the time of the sage-king Shun, the Youmiao tribe[63] would not submit, and Yu [wished to send] an expedition against them. Shun said, "That would not be acceptable. For a ruler to engage in warfare before his potency is filled out, this is not in accordance with the Way." Thereupon, Yu devoted himself to his education for three years before taking up his shield and battle-ax and performing a war dance, and the Youmiao thereupon submitted. But in the war with Gong Gong, long, sharp iron weapons were used to reach the enemy, and those whose armor and helmet were not strong were injured.[64] Thus, shields and battle-axes were useful in antiquity but are not useful in the present. Thus, I say, "When circumstances differ, methods of preparation must change."

In upper antiquity, people competed by means of the potency of the Way. In middle antiquity, people expelled one another by means of clever stratagems. In the present, people fight by means of vital energy and power. When the state of Qi was about to attack the state of Lu, Lu dispatched Zigong to speak for them. The people of Qi said, "As for your words, it is not that they lack eloquence. But what we desire is land, and this is something that your words have not discussed." Thereupon they raised their army and attacked Lu, establishing a border ten *li* from the gates of Lu's capital. Thus, King Yan was benevolent and righteous but his state of Xu was lost. Zigong was eloquent and wise, but the state of Lu was carved up. On the basis of these examples, we can say this: benevolence, righteousness, eloquence, and wisdom are not the means by which a state can be maintained. Discard the benevolence of King Yan, cease with the wisdom of Zigong, develop the power of Xu and Lu to the point where they can oppose enemies fielding ten thousand war chariots, and the states of Qi and Chu will no longer be able to do what they want with these two states.

Antiquity and the present are faced with different circumstances. The new and the old require different methods of preparation. If one desires to use a lenient and

---

62. King Wen of Chu, a contemporary of King Yan of Xu, was fearful of the power that King Yan was gaining due to his benevolence and righteousness.

63. The Youmiao, also known as the Sanmiao, were an ancient southern tribe.

64. According to *Mengzi* 5A3 (not in this volume), Gong Gong was a rebellious minister of works exiled by the sage-king Shun.

relaxed government to bring to order the people of an anxious age, this would be like trying to drive untamed horses without reigns or whip. This is the disaster of ignorance.

Now, the Confucians and the Mohists all praise the former kings for loving everyone in the world and viewing the people as parents do their children. How do we know it is so? They say, "When the minister of justice carries out punishments, the ruler does not hold musical performances. When he hears a report of the death penalty being carried out, the ruler sheds tears." They praise the former kings for this. Now, if it were the case that when the relationship between ruler and minister is like that between father and son, there is necessarily good order, then, if we extrapolate from this saying, it would mean that there is no disorder in the relationships between fathers and sons. The dispositions and natures of people are such that no one comes before one's parents. They all express their love, but this does not necessarily lead to good order. Even if love is substantial, why would there not be disorder? Now, the love that the former kings had for their people could not exceed the love that parents have for their children. If [this love] cannot prevent children from being chaotic, how can it ensure that the people are orderly?!

Moreover, if, when one carries out punishments in accordance with the law, the ruler sheds tears, this is for the sake of conforming to benevolence, not for the sake of creating order. To shed tears and not desire to punish is benevolence, while ensuring the inevitability of punishment is the law. Since the former kings ensured that the laws were triumphant and did not listen to their tears, the fact that benevolence cannot create order is certainly clear. Furthermore, the people can assuredly be made to submit by means of positional power, but few embrace righteousness.[65]

Kongzi was the greatest sage in the world. He traveled throughout the land within the Four Seas, cultivating his actions and clarifying the Way. Throughout the land within the Four Seas, people were pleased by his benevolence and praised his righteousness, and yet his disciples numbered only seventy. It seems that those who value benevolence are few and being righteous is difficult. Therefore, in the vastness of the world, [Kongzi only] had seventy disciples, and among them, only one was fully benevolent and righteous.[66]

Duke Ai of Lu was an inferior ruler, and yet when he faced south and governed the state, among the people within his borders, none dared not to serve him. The

---

65. For an extended discussion of positional power, see *Han Feizi* chapter 40 (above).

66. There is some ambiguity in this passage. Han Fei is saying either that among Kongzi's disciples, only one (Yan Hui) was fully benevolent and righteous, or that only Kongzi himself was truly benevolent and righteous.

people can assuredly be made to submit by means of positional power, and it is genuinely easy to make them so submit. Therefore, Kongzi, despite [his benevolence and rightness] was a subject, while Duke Ai, on the other hand, was a ruler. It was not that Kongzi embraced righteousness, it was that he submitted to positional power. Thus, if he had relied upon righteousness, Kongzi would not have submitted to Duke Ai, but since he relied upon positional power, Duke Ai was able to make Kongzi his subject. Now, when scholars provide counsel to rulers, they do not advise them to rely upon the invincibility of positional power but tell them instead to strive to carry out benevolence and righteousness, so as to become kings. This is to demand that the ruler rise to the level of Kongzi and that all the people of the age be like his disciples. Such a technique is certain not to succeed.

Take the case of a no-account child. His parents getting angry at him will not cause him to reform. His neighbors reprimanding him will not lead him to budge. His teachers and elders instructing him does not lead him to change. So, even when the love of his parents, the actions of his neighbors, and the wisdom of his teachers and elders—these three excellent influences—are brought to bear upon him, in the end he will not change even a hair on his shin and will not reform. But when the officials of the local magistrate take up the weapons of their office so as to enforce public laws and search out the unscrupulous, he will thereupon become terrified and filled with dread, transforming his character and changing his actions. Therefore, the love of parents is insufficient to reform their children's behavior, and it is necessary to await the strict punishments of the local magistrate, since people naturally become arrogant from love but listen to awe-inspiring might.

Thus, even Louji[67] could not climb over an 80-foot-high wall, because its face is too steep, but even a lame sheep can easily graze on the side of an 8,000-foot-high mountain when the slope is gradual. So a clear-sighted king ensures that his laws are steep and his punishments are severe. Ordinary people are unwilling to discard even a yard of cloth or silk, but even Robber Zhi would not pick up 2,000 taels of molten gold. Without certainty of harm, even a yard of silk will not be discarded, while with certainty of harm to one's hands, even 2,000 taels of gold will not be picked up. Therefore, a clear-sighted ruler ensures that his punishments are certain. Because of this, in handing out rewards, nothing is better than ensuring that they are magnanimous and reliable, so as to cause the people to benefit from them. In handing out punishments, nothing is better than ensuring that they are weighty and certain, so as to cause the people to dread them. Of laws, none are better than those that are uniform and fixed, so as to cause the people to understand

---

67. Louji was particularly famous for his ability to climb, as well as for his overall agility, strength, and courage.

them. Therefore, the ruler must not make changes in the dispensation of rewards or issue exemptions to the implementation of punishments. If praise accompanies his rewards and condemnation follows along with his punishments, both the worthy and the unworthy will exhaust their strength [in service to the state].

Now, though, this is not the case. Titles are given to those who have meritorious achievements, and yet their assigned offices are disdained. Rewards are given to those who engage in agricultural activities, and yet their profession is belittled. Those who refuse to accept official positions are banished, and yet they are esteemed for treating the world lightly. Those who violate prohibitions are blamed, and yet their bravery is praised. That which is praised and blamed and that which is rewarded and punished are completely at odds with one another. Thus, laws and prohibitions are ruined, and the people become increasingly disordered.

Nowadays, if someone attacks anyone who assaults his brothers, he is treated as having integrity, and if someone gets revenge on anyone who insults his friends, he is treated as pure. In perfecting such actions of integrity and purity, the laws of the ruler above are violated. Rulers exalt such actions of integrity and purity and forget to punish violations of their prohibitions, and so the people manifest bravery such that magistrates cannot restrain them. If those who obtain clothing and food without engaging in agriculture are described as capable, and those who are exalted without serving meritoriously in battle are described as worthy, then in perfecting such capable and worthy actions, the army is weakened and fields lie fallow. If rulers praise such capable and worthy actions and forget the calamity of a weakened army and fallow fields, then actions promoting private interests will be established, and those promoting public benefit will be extinguished.

Confucians bring disorder to the law with their culture (wén 文), while knights-errant violate the laws with their weapons, and yet rulers treat them both with ritual courtesy. This is the cause of disorder. Those who deviate from the law should be charged, and yet scholars are chosen on the basis of their cultural arts (wén xué 文學). Those who violate prohibitions should be punished, and yet groups of knights-errant support themselves by means of their privately employed swords. Thus, those whom the law forbids are those whom rulers seek; those whom magistrates seek to punish are those whom their superiors nourish. What the laws require, what rulers base their choices upon, what high officials want, and what lower officials implement—when these four things are all at odds with one another and there is no means by which to establish a fixed standard, even ten Yellow Emperors would be unable to bring about good order. Therefore, those who carry out benevolence and righteousness must not be praised, for to praise them is to harm genuine achievements. Scholars must not be employed, for to employ them is to bring chaos to the law.

In the state of Chu there was one called "Upright Gong." When his father stole a sheep, he reported this to the authorities. The magistrate said, "Execute him!" because, while he considered Gong to be upright with respect to his lord, he considered him crooked with respect to his father. Thus [Upright Gong] was reported to authorities and charged.[68] From this case it can be seen that one who is an upright subject to his ruler can at the same time be a cruel son to his father. A man from the state of Lu followed his ruler into battle. In three battles, he turned tail and ran three times. Kongzi asked the reason for this, and the man replied, "I have an elderly father; if I die there would be no one to care for him." Kongzi considered him to be filial and so raised him up and had him promoted. Looking at it from this perspective, someone who is a filial son to his father can be a disloyal subject to his ruler. Therefore, the magistrate [in Chu] executed a man, subsequently preventing superiors from hearing about unscrupulous activities within the state. Kongzi rewarded a man, leading to the people of Lu easily surrendering and running away. Since what benefits superiors and subordinates are different in this way, if a ruler raises up the actions of the common people while at the same time seeking blessings for his altars of soil and grain, he certainly will not succeed.

In antiquity, when Cang Jie[69] invented writing, he used the character "private" (sī 私) to refer to that which revolved around the self. That which was opposed to "private" he referred to as "public" (gōng 公).[70] The mutual opposition between public and private [benefit] is thus something that Cang Jie certainly already understood. Now, to take these two types of benefit to be identical, this disaster arises from a lack of scrutiny.

And so, in making plans from the perspective of an individual, nothing is as good as cultivating righteous actions and practicing cultural arts. If someone cultivates righteous actions, he will be viewed as trustworthy. If he is viewed as trustworthy, he will be entrusted with governmental tasks. If someone practices the cultural arts, he will become an illuminating teacher. If he becomes an illuminating teacher, he will become illustrious and honored. This is what is attractive for an individual. However, [this results in] those without accomplishments being entrusted with governmental tasks and those without rank becoming illustrious and honored. When government is conducted in this fashion, the state is certain to

---

68. See *Analects* 13.18 (in chapter 1 of this volume) for another take on this story.

69. Cang Jie was the legendary creator of the Chinese writing system.

70. Han Fei's argument here is based on the appearance of the Chinese graphs for "private" and "public." The graph for "public" (gōng 公) is composed of two parts: 八 and 厶. The graph 八 can mean "opposed to," while the graph for "private" (sī 私) was originally written using the simpler graph 厶. Therefore, the graph for "public" (公) is written by combining a graph meaning "opposed to" (八) and one meaning "private" (厶).

be chaotic and the ruler is certain to be endangered. Therefore, private and public interests are incompatible and the two cannot be simultaneously established.

Bestowing rewards upon those who decapitate the enemy while at the same time esteeming acts of care and compassion; bestowing rank and emoluments upon those who capture the cities of one's enemies while at the same time trusting speeches about integrity and love; strengthening one's armor and honing one's weapons in preparation for difficulties while at the same time praising the elaborate ornamentation on the clothing of the gentry; enriching the state by means of agriculture and relying on soldiers to ward off the enemy while at the same time valuing scholars of the cultural arts; dismissing those who respect their superiors and dread the law while at the same time supporting wandering knights-errant and private swordsmen—if one acts in this way, a strong government cannot be attained. If, when the state is at peace, Confucian scholars and knights-errant are supported, but when difficulties arise, armored soldiers are employed, those who truly benefit the state will not be those who are employed, and those who are employed will not be those who truly benefit the state. Therefore, those in charge of affairs are negligent in their duties and traveling scholars increase daily. Such is the reason for the chaos of our age.

Moreover, those whom this age describes as worthy are those whose actions are pure and trustworthy. Those whom this age describes as wise are those whose words are abstruse and mysterious. Abstruse and mysterious words are difficult for even the wisest to understand. Now, if one makes laws for the sake of the masses by using words that even the wisest find difficult to understand, the people will have no way to understand and follow them. So, someone who cannot even get enough dregs and husks to fill their stomach should not pursue the finest of millet and meat. Someone who has only a threadbare short coat of rough cloth should not wait for fine embroidered silk. The work of governing this age is the same: if you cannot deal with what is urgent, do not focus on what is unimportant. The task of government is to put the affairs of the people in order. If you do not employ methods that any man or woman can clearly understand, but rather admire the discussions of the wisest of people, this is at odds with good order. Thus, abstruse and mysterious words are not the business of the people.

People who consider those whose actions are excellent, pure, and trustworthy to be worthy certainly do so because they value officers who will not deceive them. But people who value officers who will not deceive them also lack techniques to deal with those who do deceive them. When the common people engage with one another, they lack the wealth and resources by which to benefit one another, and they lack the awe-inspiring might and positional power by which to intimidate one another. Thus, they seek out those who will not deceive them.

Now, the ruler dwells in a position of power whereby he has control over others, along with the resources of the entire state, and so he can employ substantial rewards and strict punishments. If he grasps these handles so as to cultivate what his clear-sighted techniques illuminate, even if he had ministers such as Tian Chang or Zi Han, they would not dare to deceive him.[71] Why is it necessary to await virtuous officers who would not deceive him? Nowadays, there are no more than ten officers who are excellent, pure, and trustworthy, and yet within the state's borders are hundreds of governmental offices. If it is necessary to rely upon excellent, pure, and trustworthy officers, then they will be insufficient to fill up the governmental offices. If they are insufficient to fill up the governmental offices, then those promoting good order will be rare while those promoting chaos will be numerous. Therefore, the Way of the clear-sighted ruler is to unify the law and not to seek out the wise, to solidify administrative techniques and not to admire trustworthiness. Thus, the law will not fail and among the assembled ministers there will be none who are unscrupulous or duplicitous.

Nowadays, when the ruler listens to speeches, he is pleased by their eloquence and does not demand that they be appropriate. When he employs people for some task, he is attracted to their claims [about what they will accomplish] but does not demand that actual achievements [live up to the promises].[72] Therefore, when the people in the world talk or give speeches, they work on their eloquence and are not attentive to the applicability of their words. Thus, those who hold up the former kings and speak of benevolence and righteousness fill the courts, and in governing it is impossible to avoid disorder. In their personal conduct, people compete for lofty reputations but lack corresponding achievements. Thus, wise officers withdraw from service to live in cliffside caves, returning their official salaries and refusing to serve. When the army cannot avoid being weakened and the government cannot avoid disorder, what is the reason for this? It is because what the people praise and what superiors treat with ritual courtesy are those techniques that bring disorder to the state.

Now, the people within the state's borders all speak about good order, everyone has the books of Gongsun Yang and Guan Zhong in their homes, and yet the state gets progressively poorer. Those who talk about agricultural work are numerous, while those who actually pick up a plow are few. Those within the state's borders all talk about the military, and everyone has the books of Sun Wu and Wu Qi in their

---

71. For more on these duplicitous ministers, as well as the "two handles," see *Han Feizi* chapter 7 (above).

72. For a fuller discussion of the correspondence between achievements and claims, couched in terms of "name" and "form," see *Han Feizi* chapter 7 (above).

homes,[73] and yet the army gets progressively weaker, because those who talk about war are numerous, while those who put on armor are few.

Therefore, the clear-sighted ruler employs people's strength but does not listen to their words. He rewards achievements and completely prohibits useless activities. Thus, the people will exhaust their strength to the point of death in following their superiors. Employing one's strength in farming is laborious, and yet the people will do it, saying, "In this way I can become rich." The undertaking of war is dangerous, and yet the people will do it, saying, "In this way I can become ennobled."

Now, if people can, by cultivating the cultural arts and practicing eloquent speeches, obtain the fruits of wealth without the labor of farming, or obtain the respect of nobility without the dangers of war, who would not do so? Thus, for every hundred who pursue wisdom, there will be only one who employs his physical strength to farm or fight. If those who pursue wisdom are numerous, the law will be defeated. If those who employ their physical strength are few, the state will become poor. This is why the age is in disorder.

Thus, in the state of a clear-sighted ruler, there is no literature inscribed on bamboo strips; only the law is used for education. There are no words of the former kings; only magistrates serve as teachers. There are no valiant private swordsmen; only cutting off heads in battle [in the service of the state] counts as bravery. In this way, the people within the state's borders will ensure that their orations follow the tracks of the law, that their actions return to actual achievements, that their displays of bravery are exhausted within the ranks of the military. Because of this, in times of peace, the state will be rich, while in times of war, its army will be strong. These are called the resources of a king. Once one has accumulated the resources of a king, one can avail oneself of weaknesses in enemy states. One who wishes to surpass the Five Emperors and be equal to the Three Kings must employ such a method.[74]

Nowadays, though, things are not like this. Officers and the people indulge themselves at home while orators work at their positional power abroad. Making preparations for a strong enemy when those at home and abroad are both up to no good, is this not dangerous?! So, when the assembled ministers discuss foreign affairs, if they are not divided between the Vertical Alliance and the Horizonal Alliance, they are devoted to appropriating the strength of the state

---

73. Sun Wu (ca. 544–496 BCE) was the purported author of the *Sunzi bingfa* (*Master Sun's Art of War*), while Wu Qi (440–381 BCE) was the purported author of the *Wuzi bingfa* (*Master Wu's Art of War*).

74. The Five Emperors refer to the mythical Tai Hao, Yan Di, Huang Di, Shao Hao, and Zhuan Xu. The Three Kings refer to the sage-kings Tang, Wen, and Wu. On Huang Di (the Yellow Emperor), Tang, Wen, and Wu, see *Important Figures* in the appendices.

for vengeance against personal enemies.[75] The Vertical Alliance is focused on bringing together numerous weaker states in order to fight a single strong one, while the Horizontal Alliance is focused on employing a strong state in order to fight numerous weaker ones; neither is the means by which to preserve one's own state.

Now, those who speak in favor of the Horizontal Alliance all say, "If we do not serve a powerful state, then when we are attacked by enemies, we will suffer disaster." When one serves a powerful state, one cannot be certain of positive results, but one must offer up one's maps, entrusting them to the powerful state, and hand over one's official seals when requesting assistance. But if one hands over one's maps, one's lands will be cut away, and if one offers up one's official seals, one's reputation will be diminished. If one's lands are cut away and one's reputation is diminished, one's government will be chaotic. If one serves a powerful state and joins the Horizontal Alliance, one will never see benefit, but will, rather, lose one's land and bring disorder to one's government.

Those who speak in favor of the Vertical Alliance all say, "If we do not save the small states and attack the powerful one, we will lose the rest of the world. If we lose the rest of the world, our state will be endangered. If our state is endangered, our ruler will be diminished." When one works to save small states, one cannot be certain of positive results but must still raise an army and make an enemy of a powerful state. It is not certain whether one can save the smaller states, and one cannot ensure that there will be no divisions in one's own alliance against the powerful state. If there are divisions, one will be at the mercy of the powerful state. If one sends out one's army, one's troops will be defeated. If one retreats to protect one's territory, one's cities will be captured. If one attempts to rescue smaller states and joins the Vertical Alliance, one will never see benefit, but will, rather, lose one's land and leave one's army defeated.

Thus, if one serves a strong state, then powerful foreigners will serve in the offices of one's state; if one seeks to save small states, then the powerful men from within one's own state will seek profits abroad. Before any benefits to one's own state have been achieved, [these men] will have achieved fiefdoms and abundant

---

75. The Vertical Alliance and Horizontal Alliance referred to ever-changing alliances among the states of the Warring States Period. (See *Important Periods* in the appendices.) The Vertical Alliance, so called because its members were on a roughly north-south axis, was an alliance of smaller states who wished to prevent the state of Qin from gaining too much power and influence. The Horizontal Alliance, so called because its members were on a roughly east-west axis, was a group of states that allied with the more powerful state of Qin, either to avoid being invaded by Qin or simply to increase their own strength and power. These ever-shifting alliances were often the result of rulers listening to wandering persuaders who held no particular allegiance, such as Zhang Yi and Gan Mao, discussed in *Han Feizi* chapter 43 (above).

emoluments. Even if their ruler above is diminished, these ministers will be exalted. Even if the state's land is cut away, private families will be rich. If their plans succeed, their resultant authority will extend their importance, while if their plans fail, they will retreat with their wealth. If the ruler listens to what his ministers have to say, honoring them with rank and emoluments before their plans have succeeded, and failing to punish them when their plans fail, among wandering persuaders, who would not employ words like stringed arrows in hopes of a subsequent benefit?[76] Why listen to the superficial words of such orators that destroy states and ruin rulers? This is the result of the ruler not being clear about the difference between public benefit and private benefit, not being able to distinguish between words that are appropriate and those that are not, and not ensuring that punishments follow failure.

Rulers all say, "If I focus on international affairs, then, at best, I can become a king, while at worst I can ensure my security." A king is one who can attack others, while security lies in being invulnerable to attack. If one is strong, one can attack others. If one's state is well-ordered, one is invulnerable to attack. But order and strength cannot be appropriated from abroad; they arise from the way one governs one's state internally. Now, if one does not employ the law and administrative techniques internally but relies on wisdom in foreign affairs, order and strength cannot be achieved.

A proverb says, "If you have long sleeves, you will be a good dancer. If you have a lot of money, you will be a good merchant." This means that if you have abundant resources, it is easy to work. Therefore, good order and strength make it easy to enact schemes, while weakness and disorder make it difficult to enact plans. Thus, those employed by the [strong] state of Qin can change their schemes ten times and rarely fail, while those employed by the [weak] state of Yan may change their plans only once and yet rarely succeed. This is not because those employed by Qin are necessarily wise while those employed by Yan are necessarily foolish. Undoubtedly, it is because their resources—good order [in the case of Qin] and chaos [in the case of Yan]—are different.

Therefore, the state of Zhou abandoned Qin to join the Vertical Alliance, and within a year they were conquered. The state of Wey abandoned the state of Wei to join the Horizontal Alliance, and within half a year they were extinguished. Thus, Zhou was annihilated by the Vertical Alliance and Wey was extinguished by the Horizontal Alliance. If Zhou and Wey had slowed down their plans to join the Horizontal and Vertical Alliances respectively, and had instead been strict about

---

76. If one has an arrow tied to a string, one need not worry about whether the arrow hits its mark or not, for it can always be retrieved.

imposing good order within their own borders, clarifying their laws and prohibitions, making their rewards and punishments certain, exhausting the resources of their land so as to stockpile material, ensuring that their people were willing to die in defense of their walls and that if anyone tried to take their land their benefit would be slight while if anyone tried to attack their states their harm would be great, then, even among states with ten thousand war chariots, none would dare to exhaust their strength against the solid walls of such states, allowing their strong enemies to cut them down in their weakened condition. Such a technique guarantees that one will not be extinguished. To abandon a technique that guarantees that one will not be extinguished and follow a path of guaranteed annihilation is an error in governance. If the wise find themselves in difficulties abroad and governance is chaotic at home, one's state cannot be saved from extinction.

When the people make plans, they all move toward security and benefit just as they avoid danger and poverty. Now, if, when one is engaged in warfare, advancing would result in death by the enemy while retreating would result in death by punishment, one is endangered. If one must abandon the affairs of one's own family and work like a sweating horse, and when one's family encounters difficulties, one's superior does not address this, one is impoverished. Under conditions of danger or poverty, who among the people would not flee? Thus, they serve at the private gates of influential officials to guarantee exemption from military service. Since they are guaranteed exemptions from military service, they remain far from the battlefield, and since they remain far from the battlefield, they are secure. They offer gifts and bribes and follow along behind influential officials, obtaining appointments, for when they obtain appointments, they will be secure. Under conditions where they can obtain the benefits of security, who would not move toward this? Because of this, people who are public-spirited are few, while those who are private-minded are many.

Thus, the governing method employed by a clear-sighted ruler to bring order to the state is to reduce the numbers of merchants and artisans who make their living by traveling around and to ensure that their reputation is low, because [otherwise] few will pursue the primary occupations [agriculture and warfare], desiring, rather, to go after the auxiliary ones. In the present age, the requests of those close to the ruler are granted and so office and rank can be purchased. When office and rank can be purchased, the reputations of merchants and artisans will not be low. When ill-gotten gains and money can be used in the marketplaces, the number of merchants will not be low. When those who gain wealth by taxation make twice as much as farmers and gain more respect than those who engage in agriculture and warfare, dedicated and upright officers will be few, while merchants will be numerous.

These, then, are the customs of a disordered state: its scholars praise the Way of the former kings as a pretext for implementing benevolence and righteousness; they pay careful attention to their appearance and clothing and dress up and embellish their speech so as to cast suspicion on the laws of the present age and create divisions in their ruler's mind. Its orators fabricate and implement duplicitous claims, borrowing the strength of foreign powers so as to accomplish their private goals while neglecting that which would benefit the state's altars of soil and grain. Its swordsmen gather up bands of followers, establishing their own [codes of] character so as to display their reputation and violate the prohibitions of the five offices.[77] Those who are anxious about being driven into battle gather at the private gates of influential officials, exhausting their wealth in bribes and using the recommendations of important people so as to avoid having to work like sweating horses. The merchants and artisans among its people make cheap and shoddy goods and hoard up extravagant wealth, accumulating these things and waiting for the best time to sell so as to take advantage of farmers. These five are the vermin of the state. If the ruler does not eliminate these five vermin, if he does not nourish dedicated and upright officials, then even if the states within the Four Seas are broken and extinguished, their ruling houses cut away and destroyed, this certainly should not be seen as strange!

Chapter Fifty: On the Illustrious Schools of Thought

The illustrious schools of thought of this age are Confucianism and Mohism. The greatest Confucian was Kongzi, and the greatest Mohist was Mozi. After the death of Kongzi, there arose Confucians following Zizhang, Confucians following Zisi, Confucians following the Yan Clan, Confucians following the Meng Clan, Confucians following the Qidiao Clan, Confucians following the Zhongliang Clan, Confucians following the Sun Clan, and Confucians following the Yuezheng Clan. After the death of Mozi, there arose Mohists following the Xiangli Clan, Mohists following the Xiang Fu Clan, and Mohists following the Dengling Clan.

Thus, after the deaths of Kongzi and Mozi, the Confucians divided into eight groups while the Mohists separated into three. The doctrines that each accepts and rejects are mutually contradictory and not the same, and yet each group claims that they are the true representatives of Kongzi or Mozi. Kongzi and Mozi cannot be

---

77. This likely refers to the Ministry of Education, the Ministry of War, the Ministry of Works, the Ministry of Taxation, and the Ministry of Criminal Justice.

brought back from the dead, so who should decide which of the schools of our age is correct?

Kongzi and Mozi both followed the Way of Yao and Shun, but the doctrines that each accepted and rejected were not the same. They each said that they were the true representatives of Yao and Shun. Yao and Shun cannot be brought back from the dead, so who should decide whether the Confucians or the Mohists are correct?

The Yin and the Zhou dynasties go back more than 700 years, while the Yu[78] and Xia dynasties go back more than 2,000 years before that. We cannot even establish whether the Confucians or the Mohists are correct, and yet we still desire to examine the Ways of Yao and Shun from 3,000 years ago! How could we possibly be certain of their ideas?! Those who claim to be certain without examining the evidence are fools. Those who base their ideas on what they cannot be certain of are frauds. Thus, it is clear that those who base their views on the former kings or who are certain about [the Way of] Yao and Shun, if they are not fools, they are frauds. The teachings of fools or frauds and confused and contradictory [guides to] action, a clear-sighted ruler will never accept these.

As for Mohist funeral rituals, if in winter, mourners wear winter clothing; if in summer, they wear summer clothing. The coffin is made of Paulownia wood, three inches thick, and mourners wear mourning garments for three months. Rulers of the present age view this as frugal and honor them. Confucians impoverish their households for the sake of funeral rituals. They wear mourning garments for three years. They so greatly damage their health that they must walk with the support of a cane. Rulers of the present age view this as filial and honor them. But to approve of Mozi's frugality is to condemn Kongzi's extravagance, while to approve of Kongzi's filial piety is to condemn Mozi's filial impiety. Now within Confucianism and Mohism, there are both filial piety and impiety, both frugality and extravagance, yet those above simultaneously honor them both.

According to the views of Qidiao,[79] one should never flinch or look away from the gaze of another. If one's actions are crooked, one should avoid even the lowliest of servants, while if one's actions are upright, one should call to account even feudal lords. Rulers of the present age regard his conduct as displaying integrity and honor him. According to the views of Song Rongzi,[80] one should set oneself up

---

78. Yu refers to the dynasty of the sage-king Shun.

79. This unknown individual does not seem to have been a member of the Qidiao Clan referred to at the beginning of this chapter.

80. Song Rongzi appears, named "Songzi," in *Zhuangzi* chapter 1(in chapter 8 of this volume), and is likely the same Songzi that appears in *Xunzi* chapters 17 and 21 (in chapter 9 of this volume).

in opposition to fighting and contending and refuse to repay insults. One should not consider it shameful to be imprisoned or view being humiliated as disgraceful. Rulers of the present age regard his conduct as broad-minded and honor him. Now, to approve of Qidiao's integrity is to condemn Song Rongzi for being so forgiving. To approve of Song Rongzi's broad-mindedness is to condemn Qidiao for being too violent. Now, within the views of these two, there are both broad-mindedness and integrity, both forgiveness and violence, yet rulers simultaneously honor them both.

This derives from the teachings of fools or frauds and debates among confused and contradictory views, and yet rulers listen to them all. Therefore, the officers within the Four Seas have no fixed technique with regard to speaking and no fixed views with regard to acting. Ice and hot coals cannot remain long in the same container; winter and summer cannot arrive at the same time. Confused and contradictory teachings cannot be established at the same time and lead to order. Now, if one at the same time listens to confused teaching and tangled views of proper behavior, and to mutually contradictory words, how can chaos be avoided? If one listens and acts in this fashion, the way that one governs the people will also necessarily be like this.

When the educated officers of the present age speak about governing, they all say, "Give land to the poor and impoverished so as to provide for those without resources." Now, if people have the same opportunities but even without the benefit of a bumper crop or side income someone is able to ensure that they are fully supplied, if it is not because of their hard work, it is because of their frugality. Now, if people have the same opportunities, but even without the calamity of famine, sickness, or other misfortune someone is poor and impoverished, if this is not because of their wastefulness, it is because of their indolence. Those who are wasteful and indolent become poor, while those who are hardworking and frugal become rich. Now, if superiors collect taxes from the rich in order to distribute it to poor households, this is to expropriate from those who are hardworking and frugal so as to give to those who are wasteful and indolent. And if one desires by such a means to exhort the people to work hard while reducing their expenditures, this cannot be accomplished.

Suppose there is someone like this: he regards it as righteous to avoid entering cities that are endangered and to avoid dwelling in an army camp and would not change even a hair on his chin in order to greatly benefit the world. Rulers of the present age are certain to thereby honor him. They will value his wisdom and hold up his actions, taking him to be an officer who looks lightly upon material things while valuing his life. So, the reason why superiors hand out good farmland and large houses and establish ranks and emoluments is in order to make it easy for the people to risk their lives for them. Now, if superiors exalt officers who look lightly upon material things while valuing their lives, and yet hope to exhort the people to go forth with a willingness to die, considering sacrificing themselves in the service of their superior as important, this cannot be accomplished.

As for those who collect books written on bamboo strips, study rhetoric, gather together disciples, and devote themselves to the cultural arts, speaking and discussing them, rulers of the present age are certain to thereby honor them, saying, "Respecting worthy officers, this is the Way of the former kings." So, those from whom the magistrates collect taxes are the farmers, but those whom their superiors nourish are the scholars. Heavily taxing farmers while substantially rewarding scholars and yet hoping to exhort the people to work hard while spending little time in discourse, this cannot be accomplished.

As for those who establish [codes of] character and gather together bands of followers, who hold on to their standards of character, allowing no encroachment, who are sure to respond with swords when spiteful words reach their ears, rulers of the present age are certain to thereby honor them, considering them to be officers who care about their reputation. If the ruler does not reward those who labor to take heads in battle but displays respect for those who show bravery in squabbles among households and yet hopes to exhort people to fight vigorously in opposing the enemy while not engaging in private squabbles, this cannot be accomplished.

When the state is at peace, it nourishes Confucians and knights-errant, but when difficulties arrive, it needs to employ armored officers. Those whom it nourishes are not those whom it employs, while those whom it employs are not those whom it nourishes. This is the reason for chaos. Furthermore, when the ruler listens to scholars, if he approves of their views, he should promulgate this throughout his government offices and employ these people. If he condemns their views, he should dismiss these scholars and eliminate the sources of their views. But nowadays, even when the ruler approves of something, he does not promulgate this throughout his governmental offices, and even when he condemns something, he does not extinguish its source. To approve of something without using it or to condemn something without extinguishing it, this is the Way of chaos and ruin.

Tantai Ziyu had the appearance of a gentleman, and after examining his appearance, Kongzi took him as a disciple. However, after spending a long time with him, Kongzi recognized that his actions did not match his appearance. Zai Yu's speech was elegant and refined, and so after examining his speech, Kongzi took him as a disciple. However, after spending a long time with him, Kongzi recognized that his wisdom did not accord with his eloquence.[81] Thereupon, Kongzi said, "By choosing someone on the basis of their appearance, I made a mistake with Ziyu; by choosing someone on the basis of their words, I made a mistake with Zai Yu." Thus, even one of Kongzi's wisdom can make inaccurate pronouncements. Now, the eloquence of the new orators of today is even more overflowing than that of Zai Yu, while the understanding of the rulers of this age is far more muddled than that of Kongzi. If, being pleased with someone's words, they appoint them for that reason, how could they possibly not make mistakes?! Thus, the state of Wei appointed Meng Mao because of his eloquence and suffered disaster beneath Mount Hua.[82] The state of Zhao appointed the Lord of Ma Fu because of his eloquence and suffered calamity at Changping.[83] These two cases demonstrate the mistake of appointing people based on their eloquence.

Simply by examining the amount of tin used in an alloy and the color of fire in the forge, even the great swordsmith Ou Ye could not discern the quality of a sword. But if the sword is used to strike swans and geese in the water or to decapitate colts and horses on land, even a common slave would have no doubt about whether it was dull or sharp. Simply by examining its teeth and shape, even the great horse trainer Bo Le could not discern the quality of a horse. But if one harnesses the horse to a chariot and drives it forward so as to observe how fast it reaches the end of the road, even a common slave would have no doubts about whether it was a nag or a fine horse. Simply by observing someone's appearance or clothing or listening to their speech, even Kongzi could not be certain about an officer. But if he is tested by placing him in an official capacity and examining his achievements, even a mediocre person would not be in doubt about whether he is foolish or wise. Therefore, in the administrative ranks of a clear-sighted ruler, the prime minister necessarily rises from the ranks of the district magistrates, while fierce generals rise up through the ranks. Since those with achievements are certain to be rewarded, rank and emoluments become increasingly generous, and they are motivated to work ever harder. If they are promoted up through the ranks of governments offices, their official responsibilities will become increasingly greater, and the state will become increasingly well-ordered. Thus, to ensure that rank and

81. Zai Yu, also known as Zai Wo, is praised for his elegant speech in *Analects* 11.3 (not in this volume), but chastised for his lack of Goodness (*Analects* 17.21) and his laziness (*Analects* 5.10; both in chapter 1 of this volume).

82. Meng Mao was a general for the state of Wei in a disastrous battle against the state of Qin at the foot of Mount Hua. Records indicate the loss of some 130,000 men.

83. The Lord of Ma Fu, Zhao Gua, was killed in a battle with the state of Qin at Changping, losing some 400,000 troops. See *Han Feizi* chapter 27 and the accompanying note 32 (above).

emoluments are vast and that governmental offices and duties are well-ordered, this is the Way of the king.

One who has a thousand square *li* of rocky land cannot be called rich. One who has a million funerary statues cannot be called strong. It is not that the rocks are not large or that [the statues] are not numerous and so one cannot be called rich and strong. Rather, rocky land cannot grow grain, and funerary statues cannot be sent to fight the enemy. Now, merchants who buy their offices and expert artists do not cultivate land, and yet sustain themselves. But uncultivated land is no different than rocky land. If Confucians and knights-errant do not serve in the military and yet gain illustriousness and honor, then the people cannot be used any more than funerary statues. Now, to understand the disaster of having only rocky land and funerary statues, but not to understand the disaster of having merchants who buy their offices, Confucians, and knights-errant who ensure that land is not cultivated and that the people cannot be used, this is to not understand things of the same category.

Thus, even if the ruler of a hostile state is pleased by your righteousness, you cannot make him come to offer tribute and become your subject. Even if the lords within your borders disapprove of your actions, you can make them present the ceremonial tribute of birds in your court. Therefore, if your strength is great, people will attend your court, while if your strength is slight, you must attend the court of others. Therefore, the clear-sighted ruler works to build up strength. Now, in a strict household, there are no headstrong slaves, though caring mothers often have wastrel sons. Because of this, I know that awe-inspiring might and positional power are sufficient to put a stop to violence, while even the deepest of kindness is insufficient to put a stop to chaos.

When a sage governs a state, he does not wait for people to do good for his sake; he ensures that they can do no wrong. If he waits for people to do good for his sake, within his borders there will be fewer than ten who do so; if he ensures that people can do no wrong, the entire state can be brought into line. Those who govern employ what works for the many and abandon what works for the few. Therefore, they do not work on their kindness, they work on their laws.

If one waits for arrow shafts that are naturally straight, in a hundred generations there will not be a single arrow. If one waits for a piece of wood that is naturally round, then in a thousand generations there will not be a single wheel. Naturally straight arrow shafts and naturally round pieces of wood cannot be found in a hundred generations, and yet every generation rides in carriages and shoots birds. Why is this? It is because they employ the techniques of bending and straightening. And even if, without awaiting the use of these techniques, there was a naturally straight arrow or a naturally round piece of wood, excellent artisans would not value them.

Why is this? Because more than one single person wants to ride in carriages, and archers need more than a single shot. Even if, without awaiting the imposition of rewards and punishments, there was someone who was good of himself, the clear-sighted ruler would not value him. Why is this? The laws of the state cannot be abandoned, since it is necessary to govern more than one person. Therefore, the ruler who understands techniques does not pursue accidental goodness but rather employs the Way of certain success.

Now, if someone says to others, "I can make you wise and long-lived [if you do what I say]," then the world would certainly take him to be deceitful. Wisdom is a matter of one's nature, while long life is a matter of fate. One's nature and fate are not things that can be learned from others; Telling others that one can do something that is not within the realm of human ability, this is the reason the world takes such a person as deceitful. . . .[84] Persuading someone [to act in a certain way] on the basis of [its providing] benevolence and righteousness, this is tantamount to persuading someone that one can provide wisdom and long life, and rulers who have a system will not accept this.

Thus, praising the beauty of Mao Qiang and Xi Shi[85] will do nothing to improve your own looks, while if you use makeup, polish, powder, and eyeliner, you can double your attractiveness. Talking about the benevolence and righteousness of the former kings will do nothing to improve your governance, while making clear your system of laws and making certain your rewards and punishments, this is the makeup, polish, powder, and eyeliner of the state. Therefore, a clear-sighted ruler is urgently focused on what helps and slow to extol [the former kings]. Therefore, he does not take benevolence and righteousness as his Way.

Now, when shamans pray for the people, they say, "May you live a thousand autumns and ten thousand years!" But the sound of "a thousand autumns and ten thousand years" is just so much noise, and there is no proof that it increases one's life by even a single day. This is why people ignore shamans. Now, Confucians of the present age, when they speak to their ruler, do not praise the things that bring good order in the present but rather talk about things that brought about good order in the past. They do not investigate the workings of governmental offices and laws; they do not scrutinize the conditions leading to villainy and wickedness. Rather, they all follow the path transmitted down from high antiquity and praise the accomplishments of the former kings. Confucians embellish their words,

---

84. The dozen or so characters in this lacuna are indecipherable as they stand. Some commentators argue that they constitute an early commentary accidentally written into the original text. In any case, no proposed reconstruction makes full sense of these characters or adds to our understanding of the broader passage.

85. Mao Qiang and Xi Shi were women renowned for their beauty.

saying, "If you listen to our words, you can become a lord protector or king." These are the shamans among advisers, and a ruler who has a system will not accept them. Therefore, the clear-sighted ruler acts on practical affairs and gets rid of what is useless. He does not take stories of benevolence and righteousness as his path and does not listen to the words of scholars.

Now, those who do not understand how to order the state are certain to say, "It is necessary to attain the hearts of the people." If it were possible to order the state by attaining the hearts of the people, there would be no need for the likes of Yi Yin and Guan Zhong; one would need only to listen to the people and that would be all.[86] The wisdom of the people cannot be employed because their minds are like those of babes in arms.[87] If a baby's head is not shaved, it will be in greater pain, while if a boil is not lanced, the infection will gradually spread. When shaving a baby's head or lancing its boil, it is necessary for someone to hold the baby while its caring mother deals with it, and still the baby will weep and cry without end. The baby does not understand that enduring this small pain will result in a great benefit.

Now, when superiors are urgently focused on plowing the land and opening up wastelands, this is in order to enrich the people's means of livelihood, and yet the people view their superiors as cruel. They compile legal codes and heavy punishments so as to put a stop to wickedness, and yet the people view them as harsh. They levy taxes in money and grain in order to fill the government storehouses, and moreover, they do this so they can provide food for the starving and pay for military expeditions, and yet the people view their superiors as greedy. They ensure that everyone within their borders knows how to put on armor and that there are no private exemptions from military service. They ensure that the strength of the state is unified and that it fights fiercely so as to take captives, and yet the people view their superiors as violent. These four are the means by which to obtain good order and peace, and yet the people do not understand enough to be pleased by this. Why do rulers seek out officers with sagely understanding? It is because the understanding of the people is insufficient to learn from and use.

In the past, [the great king] Yu opened channels for the Yangzi River and dredged the Yellow River, and yet the people gathered up tiles and stones [to throw at him]. Zichan opened up lands for cultivation and planted mulberry trees [for

---

86. Yi Yin was minister to the sage-king Tang, while Guan Zhong was minister to Duke Huan of Qi. See *Important Figures* in the appendices.

87. Cf. *Mengzi* 4B12 (in chapter 4 of this volume).

raising silkworms], and yet the people of Zheng defamed and slandered him.[88] Yu benefited the world and Zichan saved the state of Zheng, but they were both defamed. That the understanding of the people is insufficient to be used is certainly clear. Therefore, searching for those with sagely knowledge when promoting officers or seeking to satisfy the people in governing, these are both sprouts of disorder. They can never be joined with good order.

---

88. Zichan was minister under Duke Mu of Zheng (r. 627–606) and was responsible for numerous political, agricultural, and economic reforms that strengthened the state, but which were not initially well-received by the people.

SELECTIVE BIBLIOGRAPHY

Translations

Liao, Wên-kuei, trans. *The Complete Works of Han Fei tzu: A Classic of Chinese Legalism*. 2 vols. London: A. Probsthain, 1939/1959. (The only complete English-language translation of the *Han Feizi*. However, inaccuracies abound, and care should be exercised when using it.)

Watson, Burton, trans. *Han Feizi: Basic Writings*. New York: Columbia University Press, 2003. (Generally accurate and readable partial translations of twelve core chapters of the *Han Feizi*. First published in 1964 under the name *Han Fei Tzu: Basic Writings*.)

Secondary Works

Bárcenas, Alejandro. "Xunzi and Han Fei on Human Nature." *International Philosophical Quarterly* 52, no. 2 (2012): 135–48. (Examines the relationship between Xunzi's and Han Feizi's conceptions of human nature.)

Flanagan, Owen, and Jing Hu. "Han Fei Zi's Philosophical Psychology: Human Nature, Scarcity, and the Neo-Darwinian Consensus." *Journal of Chinese Philosophy* 38, no. 2 (2011): 293–316. (Examines Han Fei's conception of human nature and works to explain why his negative conception has received less attention than Mengzi's more positive one.)

Goldin, Paul R., ed. *Dao Companion to the Philosophy of Han Fei*. New York: Springer, 2013. (This anthology includes a range of essays on various aspects of Han Feizi's philosophy, as well as those from whom he drew ideas.)

Harris, Eirik Lang. "Is the Law in the Way? On the Source of Han Fei's Laws." *Journal of Chinese Philosophy* 38, no. 1 (2011): 73–87. (Argues that Han Feizi develops a nonmoral political theory that takes as its core an understanding of human dispositions as well as the natural world.)

Harris, Eirik Lang, and Henrique Schneider, eds. *Adventures in Chinese Realism: Classic Philosophy Applied to Contemporary Issues*. Albany, NY: State University of New York Press, 2022. (A collection of essays that draw on Han Feizi's political realism and examine how it may be applicable in the contemporary world.)

Hutton, Eric L. "Han Feizi's Criticism of Confucianism and Its Implications for Virtue Ethics." *Journal of Moral Philosophy* 5 (2008): 423–53. (Analyzes Han Feizi's criticism of Confucian virtue politics and its relevance to debates in contemporary virtue ethics.)

Ivanhoe, Philip J. "Hanfeizi and Moral Self-Cultivation." *Journal of Chinese Philosophy* 38, no. 1 (2011): 31–45. (Examines the influence of Laozi and Mozi on Han Feizi's political philosophy, highlighting fundamental differences between Laozi's conception of self-cultivation and Han Fei's borrowing of Laozian vocabulary in his advice to the ruler.)

Lundahl, Bertil. *Han Fei Zi: The Man and the Work.* Stockholm: Institute of Oriental Languages Stockholm University, 1992. (A study of the authenticity of the various chapters composing the *Han Feizi.* Includes a translation of Han Fei's biography in the *Shiji* as well as brief overviews of other thinkers that have fallen under the label of "Legalist.")

Makeham, John. "The Legalist Concept of *Hsing-ming*: An Example of the Contribution of Archaeological Evidence to the Re-interpretation of Transmitted Texts." *Monumenta Serica, Journal of Oriental Studies* 39 (1990): 87–114. (An excellent analysis of Han Feizi's discussion of *xing ming*, form and name, and its role in his political philosophy.)

Martinich, A. P. "The Sovereign in the Political Thought of Hanfeizi and Thomas Hobbes." *Journal of Chinese Philosophy* 38, no. 1 (2011): 64–72. (Examines similarities between Han Feizi's vision of the sovereign and that found in Thomas Hobbes's *Leviathan*.)

Schneider, Henrique. *An Introduction to Hanfei's Political Philosophy.* Newcastle upon Tyne: Cambridge Scholars Publishing, 2018. (Interesting introduction that examines Han Fei's thought and draws from it ideas on welfare, justice, truth, and constitutionalism.)

Winston, Kenneth. "The Internal Morality of Chinese Legalism." *Singapore Journal of Legal Studies* (December 2005): 313–47. (Draws on the work of the legal sociologist Lon Fuller to argue that Han Fei's conception of law includes an articulation of morality.)

明倫堂

乾隆庚午四月穀旦

大學之道在明明德在新民在
止於至善知止而后有定定而
后能靜靜而后能安安而后能
慮慮而后能得物有本末事有
終始知所先後則近道矣古之
欲明明德於天下者先治其國
欲治其國者先齊其家欲齊其
家者先脩其身欲脩其身者先
正其心欲正其心者先誠其
意欲誠其意者先致其知致
知在格物物格而后知至知至
而后意誠意誠而后心正心正
而后身脩身脩而后家齊家齊
而后國治國治而后天下平自
天子以至於庶人壹是皆以
脩身為本其本亂而末治者否矣
其所厚者薄而其所薄者厚未之有
也

後學趙孟頫書

CHAPTER ELEVEN

GREAT LEARNING AND *MEAN*

Introduction

The *Great Learning* (*Dàxué* 大學) and the *Mean* (*Zhōngyōng* 中庸) were originally chapters from the *Record of Rites* (*Lǐjì* 禮記), and were probably composed either late in the Warring States Period (403–221 BCE) or early in the Han dynasty (202 BCE to 220 CE). However, due to the influence of the Song dynasty philosopher Zhū Xī 朱熹 (1130–1200), they were singled out to be part of the Four Books (*Sìshū* 四書) (along with the *Analects* and *Mengzi*) that became the basis of the Chinese civil service examinations. Zhu Xi claimed that the *Great Learning* consists of a Classic section, composed by Kongzi, and a Commentary section, composed by his disciple Master Zeng, while the *Mean* was composed by Kongzi's grandson Zisi.

Whatever the facts of their composition, the *Great Learning* and the *Mean* are philosophically intriguing works. For example, the Classic section of the *Great Learning* eloquently expresses the Confucian belief that the well-being of the community is dependent upon the Virtue of individuals. In addition, chapter 6 of the Commentary section offers a famous metaphor that one should love the good "like loving a lovely sight" and hate evil "like hating a hateful smell." Wáng Yángmíng 王陽明 (1472–1529 CE), a Ming dynasty critic of Zhu Xi, argued that this metaphor means that moral knowledge and motivation are intrinsically combined, so that it is impossible to know what is good without doing what is good.

The *Mean* opens with definitions that explain that the right "Way" to live is to follow one's "nature," which has been dictated by a higher power ("Heaven"). "Education" thus has a distinctively moral purpose: helping students to understand and follow their Heaven-given nature.[1] The *Mean* goes on to defend the view (also found in Aristotle) that Virtue is a mean

---

1. Similar teleological foundations for ethics are found in many premodern civilizations, although the detailed understanding of the higher power, human nature, and educational process differ substantially. For more on the concept of human "nature," see the "Yangist Writings" (in chapter 3 of this volume) and *Nature Comes from the Mandate* (in chapter 12 of this volume).

between extreme states, and suggests that "sympathetic understanding" (shù 恕; see *Analects* 4.15 and 15.24 in chapter 1 of this volume) must be grounded in the obligations that go with our specific social roles.

One of the key terms in both works is "Sincerity" (chéng 誠). Although it was not a significant concept in the thought of Kongzi, Mengzi, or Xunzi, Sincerity became a key term in later Confucianism, where it referred to ethical and metaphysical integrity or wholeness. Intuitively, we might say that to be Sincere is to be true to one's genuine self, whereas to lack Sincerity is to be alienated from one's most fundamental self, and thus to have warring motivations.

Great Learning (selections)

"CLASSIC SECTION"

1. The Way of Great Learning lies in enlightening one's enlightened Virtue.[2] It lies in renewing the people.[3] It lies in resting in the ultimate good.

2. When one knows the place to rest, only then is one settled. When one is settled, only then is one able to be tranquil. When one is tranquil, only then is one able to be at peace. When one is at peace, only then is one able to ponder. When one ponders, only then is one able to understand it.

3. Things have their roots and their branches. Situations have their endings and their beginnings. To know what to put first and last is to come close to the Way.

4. The ancients who desired (i) to enlighten the enlightened Virtue of the world would first (ii) put their states in order. Those who desired to put their states

---

2. "Great Learning" has been variously interpreted as learning appropriate to "a government official," "higher education," or "a morally advanced individual." Zhu Xi argued that "enlightened Virtue" refers to the moral knowledge one has innately, which has to be "enlightened" again because it has been obscured by selfish physical desires. On this and other aspects of Zhu Xi's interpretation, see Zhu Xi, *Collected Commentaries on the "Great Learning,"* in Justin Tiwald and Bryan W. Van Norden, eds., *Readings in Later Chinese Philosophy: Han Dynasty to the Twentieth Century* (Indianapolis: Hackett Publishing Company, 2014), 184–94.

3. The original text of this line says: "It lies in loving the people." Zhu Xi argued that "loving" (qīn 親) was a scribal error for "renewing" (xīn 新). Wang Yangming defended the original version. On this and other aspects of Wang's interpretation, see his, "Questions on the *Great Learning*," in Tiwald and Van Norden, *Readings in Later Chinese Philosophy*, 238–50.

in order would first (iii) regulate their families. Those who desired to regulate their families would first (iv) cultivate their selves. Those who desired to cultivate their selves would first (v) correct their hearts. Those who desired to correct their hearts would first (vi) make their thoughts have Sincerity. Those who desired to make their thoughts have Sincerity would first (vii) extend their knowledge. Extending knowledge lies in (viii) getting a handle on things.[4]

5. Only after one (viii) gets a handle on things does (vii) knowledge reach the ultimate. Only after knowledge has reached the ultimate do (vi) thoughts have Sincerity. Only after thoughts have Sincerity is (v) the heart correct. Only after the heart is correct is (iv) the self cultivated. Only after the self is cultivated is (iii) the family regulated. Only after the family is regulated is (ii) the state ordered. Only after the state is ordered is (i) the world at peace.

6. From the Son of Heaven on down to the common people, all regarded cultivating one's self as the root.

7. A tree with gnarled roots never has straight branches. What you treat as significant will never become insignificant, and what you treat as insignificant will never become significant.

"COMMENTARY SECTION"

Chapter 6

What is meant by "making thoughts have Sincerity" is to let there be no self-deception. It is like hating a hateful odor, or loving a lovely sight. This is called not being conflicted. Hence the gentleman must be careful even when alone.

Mean (selections)

Chapter 1

(1) "Nature" means what is mandated by Heaven. The "Way" means following one's nature. "Education" means cultivating the Way. (2) The Way is something

---

4. "Getting a handle on things" is gé wù 格物. It is often translated "investigating things," following the interpretation of Zhu Xi, who thought it meant achieving intellectual understanding by "reaching [the Pattern in] things," but many other interpretations are defensible. Wang Yangming argued that it meant "correcting things."

that one cannot depart from for even a moment. If one could depart from it, it would not be the Way. For this reason, the gentleman is careful even before he sees anything; he is concerned even before he hears anything. (3) Nothing is more evident than what is hidden; nothing is more manifest than what is subtle. Hence, the gentleman is careful even when alone. (4) When happiness, anger, sadness, and joy have not yet been expressed, it is called the "mean." When they are expressed but all hit the right points, it is called "harmony." The mean is the great foundation of the world. Harmony is the universal Way of the world. (5) If one achieves the mean and harmony, Heaven and Earth will find their places, and the myriad things will be nurtured.

Chapter 4

The Master[5] said, "I realize that the Way is not put into practice: the clever overshoot it; the foolish do not come up to it. I realize that the Way is not understood: the worthy overshoot it; the unworthy do not come up to it. There are no people who do not eat and drink, but few are those who are able to appreciate the flavors!"

Chapter 13

The Master said, "Dutifulness and sympathetic understanding are not far from the Way.[6] Do not inflict upon others what you would be unwilling to accept if it were inflicted upon yourself. There are four aspects to the Way of a gentleman, and I, Kongzi, have been unable to attain even one. 'Serve one's father with what one seeks from his own son'—I have been unable to do this. 'Serve one's ruler with what one seeks from one's own ministers'—I have been unable to do this. 'Serve one's elder brother with what one seeks from one's younger brother'—I have been unable to do this. 'First do for one's friends what one seeks from them'—I have been unable to do this."

Chapter 20

The Master said, "The universal Way of the world has five aspects, and there are three things by means of which one puts it into action. The five aspects are the

---

5. As in the *Analects*, the "Master" refers to Kongzi.

6. Compare this passage to *Analects* 4.15 (in chapter 1 of this volume).

relationships between ruler and minister, father and son, husband and wife, elder and younger brothers, and friends. These five make up the universal Way of the world. Wisdom, benevolence, and courage—these three things—are the universal Virtues of the world. But that by means of which one puts them into action is one."[7]

---

7. Zhu Xi claims that the "one" is Sincerity. On the five relationships, compare *Mengzi* 3A4 (in chapter 4 of this volume). This is perhaps the earliest passage in which the term "Virtue" (dé 德) is used as a countable noun to refer to good character traits, as opposed to its earlier use to refer to the "moral charisma" that results from the possession of such traits. Cf. *Analects* 2.1 (in chapter 1 of this volume), and see David S. Nivison, "The Paradox of 'Virtue,'" in *The Ways of Confucianism: Investigations in Chinese Philosophy* (Chicago: Open Court Press, 1996), 31–43.

SELECTIVE BIBLIOGRAPHY

Translations

Gardner, Daniel K., trans. *The Four Books: The Basic Teachings of the Later Confucian Tradition*. Indianapolis: Hackett Publishing, 2007. (Selections from the Four Books with helpful supporting materials.)

Johnston, Ian, and Wang Ping, trans. *Daxue and Zhongyong: Bilingual Edition*. Hong Kong: Chinese University Press, 2012. (In addition to providing the Chinese texts, this edition provides two translations, one according to the Han dynasty understanding of the texts, and one according to Zhu Xi's interpretation.)

Legge, James, trans. *Confucian Analects, the Great Learning, and the Doctrine of the Mean*. Reprint, New York: Dover Books, 1971. (This reprint of James Legge's 1893 translation incudes the Chinese text and extensive explanatory notes.)

Plaks, Andrew, trans. *Ta Hsüeh and Chung Yung (The Highest Order of Cultivation and On the Practice of the Mean)*. New York: Penguin Books, 2003. (A valuable literary interpretation.)

Van Norden, Bryan W., trans. "Collected Commentaries on the *Great Learning*" and "Collected Commentaries on the *Mean*." Sections 33 and 36 in *Readings in Later Chinese Philosophy: Han Dynasty to the 20th Century*, edited by Justin Tiwald and Bryan W. Van Norden. Indianapolis: Hackett Publishing, 2014. (Includes partial translations of both works and selections from Zhu Xi's commentaries on them.)

Secondary Works

Gardner, Daniel K. *Chu Hsi and the Ta-hsueh: Neo-Confucian Reflections on the Confucian Canon*. Cambridge, MA: Harvard University Asia Center, 1986. (Scholarly study of the role of the *Great Learning* in the later Confucian tradition.)

Tu, Wei-ming. *Centrality and Commonality: An Essay on Confucian Religiousness*, rev. ed. New York: State University of New York Press, 1989. (Speculations inspired by the *Mean*.)

Van Norden, Bryan W. "'Few Are Able to Appreciate the Flavours': Translating the *Daxue* and the *Zhongyong*." *Journal of Chinese Studies* 56 (January 2013): 295–314. (Overview of the major translations and some of the issues raised by the texts.)

———. "Moral Failure, Ethical Roles, and Metaphysics in the *Great Learning* and the *Mean*." In the *Oxford Handbook of Chinese Philosophy*, edited by Justin Tiwald. New York: Oxford University Press, forthcoming. (Discussion of some of the philosophical issues raised by these texts.)

性自命出

CHAPTER TWELVE

NATURE COMES FROM THE MANDATE[1]

Introduction

Nature Comes from the Mandate (*Xìng zì Mìng Chū* 性自命出) is a work from a cache of manuscripts written on bamboo slips found, in 1993, in a tomb located near the town of Guōdiàn 郭店, in Jīngmén 荊門, Húběi Province 湖北省. The text can be dated with confidence to around 300 BCE, as that is when the tomb was sealed. Its authorship is contested, as is its affiliation, but it concerns a number of concepts such as human nature (xìng 性), dispositions (qíng 情), the heart (xīn 心), the mandate (mìng 命), ritual (lǐ 禮), right (yì 義), music (yuè 樂), Heaven (Tiān 天), sages (shèng 聖), etc. that are characteristic of Confucianism. Moreover, it discusses the central importance of the *Odes* (Shī 詩), *History* (Shū 書), *Rites* (Lǐ 禮), and *Music* (Yuè 樂) in education and moral self-cultivation, though it is not certain to what texts these names refer. Like several of the other works in the Guodian corpus, *Nature Comes from the Mandate* was lost some time between the late Warring States (403–221 BCE) and the Western Han (206 BCE–9 CE) periods and was not transmitted to future generations. While echoes of its influence can be heard throughout a wide range of later texts, the exact relationship between it and later philosophers and traditions remains highly speculative.

1. Though all human beings have a nature, their hearts lack a fixed intention. The heart waits until it encounters things and only then becomes aroused; it waits until it encounters what is pleasing and only then becomes active; it waits until it

---

1. Thanks to Eirik L. Harris and Justin Tiwald for helpful comments and suggestions on earlier drafts of this translation.

practices repeatedly and only then becomes fixed. The *qi* of joy, anger, grief, and sorrow are the nature. When they are manifested on the outside, things have taken hold of them. The nature comes from the mandate; the mandate descends from Heaven. The Way begins in dispositions and dispositions arise from the nature.[2] In the beginning, one is close to one's dispositions;[3] in the end, one is close to the right. Those who understand the dispositions are able to draw them out; those who understand the right are able to draw it in. Likes and dislikes are the nature. What one likes and dislikes are things. Approval and disapproval are the nature. What one approves and disapproves of are circumstances.[4]

2. The nature is most basic and important; things take hold of it. The sounds of metal [bells] and stone [chimes] do not come forth unless they are struck. Though human beings possess the nature, if things do not take hold of their hearts it is not brought forth. Whenever the heart has an intention, it must be engaged with something. The heart cannot implement itself on its own, just as the mouth cannot converse on its own [i.e. without having something to talk about]. Oxen are born and grow large; geese are born and spread their wings; their natures cause this to be so. Human beings are born and learn; something causes this to be so.

3. All things display differences. Strong things are used as pillars; they are chosen for this purpose because they are strong. Pliable things are used as bindings; they are chosen for this purpose because they are pliable. All [people] within the Four Seas have the same nature, but each uses their heart differently; instruction causes this to be so.

4. As for the nature, some things move it, some things attract it, some things regulate it, some things hone it, some things draw it out, some things nurture it, some things grow it.

5. What moves the nature are things. What attracts the nature are pleasures. What regulates the nature are [proper] influences.[5] What hones the nature is the

---

2. Cf. the opening lines of the *Mean* (in chapter 11 of this volume).

3. "Dispositions" (qíng 情) refers to our innate repertoire of emotional responses or reactive attitudes, the characteristic ways in which people tend to respond to certain things, events, or circumstance. See also *Xunzi* chapter 2, note 22, in chapter 9 of this volume.

4. Literally, "Good and not good [shàn bú shàn 善不善] are the nature. What one regards as good and regards as not good are circumstances." Cf. the notion of "the heart of approval and disapproval" (shì fēi zhī xīn 是非之心) in *Mengzi* 2A6 (in chapter 4 of this volume).

5. The sense is obscure but this probably means the norms, classical texts, and institutions that influence proper behavior and development that were intentionally designed "to bring about some specific effect." For the latter idea, see the following two sections.

right.[6] What draws out the nature are circumstances. What nurtures the nature is practice. What grows the nature is the Way.

6. Whatever can be seen is called a thing. Whatever gratifies the self is called a pleasure. The circumstance [brought about by] a thing is called its circumstance.[7] What is done to bring about some specific effect is called an influence. The right is the sum of the various things that are approved. Practice is what one uses to train the nature. The Way is the Way of the various things.

7. The working of the heart is the most basic and important of Ways. Of the four workings of the Way,[8] only the human Way can be taken as the Way [i.e. only it can be chosen as a method for guiding the heart]. The other three workings [of the Way] are simply followed [as parts of the natural course of things].

8. When the *Odes*, *History*, *Rites*, and *Music* first came forth, they arose from human beings. The *Odes* was composed to bring about some specific effect; the *History* was enunciated to bring about some specific effect; the *Rites* and *Music* were held up to bring about specific effects.

9. The sages compared the different types [of classical texts] and sorted and collected them; they surveyed what came earlier and later and arranged them properly; they embodied the right and regulated and embellished it; they gave good order to the dispositions and brought forth [what should be manifested] and took in [what should be internalized]. Only then did they apply them to instruction. Instruction is how one gives rise to Virtue within.

10. The rites are created from the dispositions but elevate them. The rites regulate the dispositions by fitting them to what is proper for each affair; the order of what

---

6. The word "right" is a translation of the character yì 義, which is often translated as "righteousness." For a discussion of its diverse meanings, see *Xunzi* chapter 1, note 12, in chapter 9 of this volume. See also *yi* under *Important Terms* in the appendices.

7. The point being that the nature's circumstances are *set by* and depend upon external things and not the nature itself. Thanks to Justin Tiwald for insights on this issue.

8. What the four workings of the Way are is a matter of controversy and speculation. Perhaps this refers to the workings of Heaven, earth, ghosts and spirits, and humanity. Only the last concerns forming a fixed intention for one's heart and following it *as the Way*. The others are all things that are simply so of themselves (zìrán 自 然). Compare the second sentence of this section with the opening line of *Daodejing* chapter 1 (in chapter 6 of this volume).

comes earlier and what comes later results in the moral Way.[9] The moderation of this order results in a refined pattern. Assuming an appropriate demeanor and expression is how one achieves a refined pattern and moderation. Noble people refine their dispositions, ennoble what is right, enhance their moderation, perfect their demeanor, find happiness in the Way, and take pleasure in instruction; this is how they become reverent. Doing obeisance is how they manifest their reverence. The praises they offer accord with a refined pattern. By presenting bolts of silk they attest to their trustworthiness.[10] Their words are in accord with the moral Way.

11. Laughter is the shallow release of joy; happiness is the profound release of joy.

12. When sounds that come forth from dispositions are trustworthy, only then do they enter deeply into and profoundly stir the hearts of people. When one hears the sound of laughter, one is refreshed and feels delight. When one hears songs and ballads, one is pleased and feels elation. When one hears the sounds of zithers, one is anxious and sighs. When one observes the Lai or Wu [dances], one is angered and roused to take action. When one observes the Shao or Xia [dances], one makes effort and feels restraint. When singing out thoughts of longing, one's heart is moved as if letting out a sigh. When one resides in moderation for a long time, one takes care to return to what is fine and reverts to the beginning; one follows along in bringing forth and taking in [what is proper]—this is the beginning of Virtue. The music of Zheng and Wei is not the music one should listen to or follow.[11]

13. All ancient music moves the heart; licentious music moves the lustful [inclinations]. Both types instruct those [who listen to them]. The Lai and Wu [dances] express happiness about the conquest [of the Shang];[12] the Shao and Xia [dances] express happiness in [proper] dispositions.[13]

14. Whenever one feels utmost happiness, one will come to feel sorrow; weeping in grief too, of course, is an expression of sorrow. These are all expressions of

---

9. "Moral Way" here and below is literally yì dào 義道, "Way of right" or "Way of righteousness."

10. Cf. "Twelfth Year of Duke Ai" in the *Zuozhuan*, which describes how one offers "jade and silk" to attest to the covenants one signs.

11. Cf. *Analects* 15.11 (in chapter 1 of this volume).

12. These dances celebrate the Zhou king Wu's conquest of the Shang dynasty, which had come to oppress and harry its people.

13. Cf. *Analects* 7.14 and 15.11 (in chapter 1 of this volume).

dispositions. Grief and happiness are close to one another as natural dispositions. For this reason, as states of the heart, they are not far removed from one another. When weeping moves the heart, one is mired in depression; when such intense feelings linger on, one remains grief-stricken until the end. When happiness moves the heart, one is profoundly elated; when such intense feelings begin to slip away, one feels sorrow and becomes lost in distant longing.

15. Whenever one feels anxious and thinks longingly about it, one will feel sorrow. Whenever one feels happiness and thinks longingly about it, one will feel delight.

16. In longing [for something], one uses one's heart to the extreme. Sighing is the art or working[14] of longing. When the sound [one makes] changes, the heart changes [with it]. When the heart changes, the sound [one makes] will change accordingly. A groan is the playing out of grief. An exclamation [of delight] is the playing out of happiness. Babbling is the playing out of [a child's] voice; chattering is the playing out of the heart.

17. Joy leads to being pleased. Being pleased leads to elation. Elation leads to singing. Singing leads to swaying. Swaying leads to dancing. Dancing is the culmination of joy. Anger leads to anxiousness. Anxiousness leads to indignation. Indignation leads to sighing. Sighing leads to beating one's breast. Beating one's breast leads to stomping one's feet. Stomping one's feet is the culmination of anger.

18. In learning, the most difficult thing is to seek for one's heart.[15] By keeping track of what someone does, one can get close [to finding it], but this is not as fast a route as [seeking it] through music. Those who are capable of handling affairs but incapable of handling their hearts are not esteemed. Those who seek for their hearts through artifice will fail to obtain it. It is easy to understand why one cannot obtain the heart through artifice. Those who commit no error in carrying out ten consecutive undertakings must have their hearts in it.[16] If one examines what is clearly manifest [about a person], how can one fail to grasp their dispositions?

---

14. Here and below, "art" means the method or workings of some state of the mind or character.

15. Cf. *Mencius* 6A11 (not in this volume).

16. Similar thoughts are expressed in *Xunzi* chapter 9 (in chapter 9 of this volume) and chapter 13 (not in this volume).

19. Conferring benefits is the art or working of the right.[17] The right is the art or working of reverence. Reverence is moderation in regard to things. Sincerity is the art or working of benevolence.[18] Benevolence is the art or working of the nature; the nature, in some respects, gives rise to it. Dutifulness is the art or working of trustworthiness. Trustworthiness is the art or working of the dispositions. The dispositions come forth from the nature.

20. There are seven types[19] of care, but only care [that arises from] the nature is close to benevolence. There are five types of wisdom, but only that pertaining to the right is close to dutifulness. There are three types of loathing, but only the loathing of what is not benevolent[20] is close to the right. There are four Ways that are regarded as the Way, but only the human Way can be taken as the Way.[21]

21. Among the agitations that can arise from the exercise of the heart, the greatest involve longings. Among the anxieties that can arise from the exercise of the intelligence, the greatest involve worries. Among the states that can arise from the exercise of the dispositions, the greatest involve grief and joy. Among the comforts that can arise from the exercise of the body, the greatest involve pleasure. Among the ways exhaustion can arise from the exercise of one's strength, the greatest involve [the pursuit of] profit. The eyes' fondness for beauty, the ears' delight in sounds [arouse] profoundly pleasing forms of *qi*. People do not find it difficult to die in pursuit of these.[22]

22. Those who are moderate but lack a forthright heart will become pretentious.[23] Those who are forthright but lack a happy personality will become unrestrained.

---

17. For this line and the line below about the "art or working of benevolence," see *Analects* 6.30 (in chapter 1 of this volume), which begins with a disciple asking Kongzi whether someone who extensively confers benefits to the people is Rén 仁 ("Good" or "benevolent") and ends by saying that relying on the Confucian version of the Golden Rule to "draw the inference [about how to treat others] from what is near at hand [i.e. oneself] is the art or working of benevolence."

18. Here, "sincerity" is dǔ 篤, not chéng 誠 ("Sincerity"), as in chapter 11. The same is true with "sincerely" below.

19. There is no other reference in this or collateral texts to the seven types of care mentioned here or the five types of wisdom mentioned in the following line.

20. Cf. *Analects* 4.6 (in chapter 1 of this volume) for the idea of loathing what is not benevolent.

21. Cf. note 8 (on paragraph 7), above.

22. Compare *Daodejing* chapter 12 (in chapter 6 of this volume).

23. The structure of the argument in much of this passage is reminiscent of *Analects* 8.2 (in chapter 1 of this volume).

Those who have clever words and crafty speech but lack a compliant heart will become degenerate.[24] Those who can pleasantly harmonize and be at home with others but lack an ardent and enterprising disposition will be disgraced. Those who are quick-witted must be guided. Those who are honest must be assisted.

23. Everyone loathes those who employ artifice. Artifice leads to secrecy. Secrecy leads to deception. Deception leads to none wanting to associate with you. Carefulness is the art or working of benevolence;[25] even its excesses[26] do not elicit blame.

Haste is the art or working of scheming, and its excesses elicit blame. For people not to be careful is itself a mistake; of this, one can be sure.

24. Everyone delights in those who possess [genuine] human dispositions. As long as one acts in accord with one's [genuine] dispositions, even one's excesses will not elicit loathing. If one does not act in accord with one's [genuine] dispositions, even though one [conquers] difficulties one will not win esteem. People trust those who act in accord with their [genuine] dispositions, even before they act.

25. Those who are trusted without having spoken[27] are those with refined dispositions. Those who cause the people to show constancy without having taught them are those whose nature is good. Those who inspire the people to follow without having rewarded them harbor wealth within. Those who cause the people to stand in awe without having punished them are those with majestic hearts.

26. Those who, though lowly, are esteemed by the people are those with Virtue. Those who, though poor, draw the people to them are those who have the Way. Those who dwell alone but are full of joy[28] are those who have inner discrimination. Those who, though loathed, cannot be shown to be wrong are those who comprehend the right. Those who, though wrong, cannot be loathed are those who

---

24. Compare *Analects* 1.3 (in chapter 1 of this volume) and 5.25, 15.27, and 17.17 (not in this volume).

25. See note 17 (on paragraph 19) above.

26. The word translated here and in the following section as "excesses" (guò 過) refers to a transgression or simply a mistake. Here, though, I think the author is playing on the idea that an excess of carefulness (like kindness) is not regarded as a mistake.

27. A number of other early texts contain the same line, for example, *Xunzi* chapter 8, "The Achievements of the Ru" (in a section of that chapter not in this volume), and the "Record of Music" (Yuèjì 樂記) and "Record of Examples" (Biǎojì 表記) chapters of the *Book of Rites*.

28. The same line appears in a section of *Xunzi* chapter 8, "The Achievements of the Ru," not included in this volume.

are sincerely benevolent. Those whose actions are free of excesses are those who understand the Way.

27. Those who hear the Way and bring it back to those above have dealings with those above.[29] Those who hear the Way and bring it back to those below have dealings with those below. Those who hear the Way and bring it back to themselves cultivate themselves. Having dealings with those above is close to serving a lord; having dealings with those below and winning over the masses is close to administering the government. Cultivating the self is close to attaining benevolence.

28. One uses the Way when dealing with those who share the same orientation. One uses the right when dealing with those who do not share the same orientation. One uses Virtue when dealing with those who delight in the same things. One uses planning when dealing with those who do not delight in the same things. For bringing good order within the home, one seeks leniency. For bringing good order outside the home, one seeks regulation.

29. Whenever setting out to persuade others, do not hold back; one must personally follow through with whatever one advocates and in speech clearly own up to it without any artifice. Whenever dealing with others, do not be overly intense, and always ensure your affairs reach a conclusion. Whenever summoned [to court], do not be afraid and do not offer monologues. Whenever living at home, practice [what you have learned]. If there are minor faults in what brings joy to your father and elder brothers, accept them, as long as they do no great harm. Once such things have passed, do not mention them again.

30. Whenever there are distressing or worrisome affairs, what is needed is to take responsibility. Whenever there are happy affairs, what is needed is to put oneself last. When it comes to one's self, what is needed is to be calm and free from envy. When it comes to contemplation, what is needed is to be profound and without artifice. When it comes to action, what is needed is to be courageous and persevere to the end. When it comes to appearance, what is needed is to be serious and unpretentious. When it comes to the heart, what is needed is to be pure and peaceful. When it comes to joy, what is needed is wisdom and disregarding what is not

---

29. The terms "have dealings with those above" (shàng jiāo 上交) and "have dealings with those below" (xià jiāo 下交) are found in the Great Appendix to the *Changes* (Part II), where Kongzi is quoted as saying, "The superior man, in his dealings with those above, does not flatter; in his dealings with those below, he shows no disrespect."

essential. When it comes to happiness, what is needed is good measure and a place to stop. When it comes to anxiety, what is needed is restraint without discouragement. When it comes to anger, what is needed is to wax full but not explode. When it comes to taking office, what is needed is to be modest and not deceitful. When it comes to retiring from office, what is needed is to be solemn and not insouciant. In regard to all of these, one must be finely patterned and without artifice.

31. When noble people maintain a firm commitment, they must have a broad and accommodating heart. When they speak, they must have resolute and straightforward trustworthiness. When they entertain guests, they must have a humble and reverent countenance. When they carry out sacrificial rituals, they must have chaste and perfect reverence. When they conduct mourning, they must have cherishing and longing feelings of grief. Noble people take their character as most basic and important.

SELECTIVE BIBLIOGRAPHY

Translations

Cook, Scott. *The Bamboo Texts of Guodian: A Study and Complete Translation. Volumes I & II.* Ithaca, NY: Cornell University East Asia Program, 2013. (A magisterial study of the text, both its history and philosophy, along with a very good translation.)

Middendorf, Ulrike. "Again on *Qing*: With a Translation of the Guodian *Xing zi ming chu*." *Oriens Extremus* 47 (2008): 97–159. (A thorough analysis of the notion of *qing*, widely informed by contemporary psychological accounts of the emotions, along with a translation that reflects the analysis.)

Secondary Works

Brindley, Erica Fox. "Music and 'Seeking One's Heart' in the 'Xing Zi Ming Chu.'" *Dao: A Journal of Comparative Philosophy* 5, no. 2 (2006): 247–55. (A revealing study focusing on issues relating to the role of music in ethical cultivation as described in the text.)

Chan, Shirley. "Human Nature and Moral Cultivation in the Guodian 郭店 Text of the *Xing Zi Ming Chu* 性自命出 (Nature Derives from Mandate)." *Dao: A Journal of Comparative Philosophy* 8, no. 4 (2009): 361–82. (An insightful account of the process of self-cultivation in the text and how it is designed to shape our first-nature.)

Goldin, Paul Rakita. "Xunzi in the Light of the Guodian Manuscripts." *Early China* 25 (2000): 113–46. (A stimulating exploration of ways in which the philosophy of the *Xunzi* may well be related to ideas found in the text.)

Meyer, Dirk. *Philosophy on Bamboo: Text and Production of Meaning in Early China.* Leiden: Brill, 2012. (A general study of textual composition and its effects on the development of thought in early China.)

Perkins, Franklin. "Human Motivation and the Heart (*xin*) in the *Xing Zi Ming Chu*." *Dao: A Journal of Comparative Philosophy* 8, no. 2 (2009): 117–31. (A work focused on views about the human heart and motivation as described in the text.)

Puett, Michael. "The Ethics of Responding Properly: The Notion of *Qing* 情 in Early Chinese Thought." In *Love and Emotions in Traditional Chinese Literature*, edited by Halvor Eifring. Leiden: Brill, 2004. (A splendid and inspiring study of the notion of *qing*, an idea that plays a central role in the text.)

APPENDICES

IMPORTANT FIGURES[1]

Bó Yí 伯夷. Elder brother of Shu Qi (see below). The brothers were royal princes in a small state loyal to the Shang dynasty (see *Important Periods*). The younger brother was designated as heir by his father but, upon the latter's death, he deferred to his elder brother. However, Bo Yi refused to contravene his father's wishes, and with both brothers mutually deferring to one another, they decided to withdraw from the state and live in isolation at the foot of Mount Shou Yang. When King Wu (see below) subsequently defeated the Shang and established the Zhou dynasty (see *Important Periods*), the brothers refused to serve the Zhou, regarding it as an illegitimate regime established by brute force. As a consequence, they starved to death. They are regarded as paragons of propriety and rightness.

Fú Xī 伏羲 ("Tamer of Oxen"). The first of three mythical cultural heroes known as the "Three Sovereigns" (see Huang Di and Shen Nong below) who were credited with discovering or implementing the inventions and institutions that made Chinese civilization possible. Fu Xi is credited with the domestication of animals, inventing methods for fishing and trapping, and establishing the basic structure of the family.

Gōngmíng Yí 公明儀. A disciple of Kongzi's disciple Master Zeng, who is quoted favorably by Mengzi in several passages. The Chinese expression "playing the zither to cows" (duì niú tán qín 對牛彈琴, roughly equivalent to the English "casting pearls before swine") is also attributed to him.

Gōngshūzǐ 公輸子. Famed craftsman and contemporary of Kongzi whose skill was so great that he was said to have made mechanical birds of bamboo that could continue flying for three days and wooden horses propelled by springs that could draw carriages. He became the patron deity of carpenters.

Gōngsūn Lóng 公孫龍 (b. 380 BCE?). Along with Huizi (see below), an important figure within the *Mingjia*, "School of Names" (see *Important Terms*). Gongsun

---

1. Owing to the uncertainty of historical dates in China prior to the Eastern Zhou dynasty, we only provide the most commonly accepted traditional dates for historical figures and periods earlier than 771 BCE, with the caveat that these dates are unlikely to be accurate. (See also note 6 in the Introduction to this volume, and note 2 in chapter 1 of this volume.)

Long was renowned for his paradoxes; the most famous is in his dialogue "On the White Horse" (in chapter 5 of this volume), which claims that "A white horse is not a horse."

Gōngsūn Yāng 公孫鞅 (d. 338 BCE). Also known as Shāng Yāng 商鞅 or "Lord Shang." He was chief minister for Duke Xiào of Qín 秦孝公 (r. 361–338 BCE) and the purported author of the *Book of Lord of Shang* (Shāngjūnshū 商君書), an important work of the *Fajia*, "Legalist School" (see *Important Terms*). Gongsun Yang is credited with developing the notion of government through "laws" or "legal standards" (fǎ 法), in which a ruler establishes clearly defined and easily understood standards of duty and behavior for his subjects and then motivates his people to accord with them through the use of rewards and punishments. This idea directly influenced the thought of Han Feizi.

Guǎn Zhòng 管仲 (d. 645 BCE). Guan Zhong was the chief minister for Duke Huán of Qí 齊桓公 (r. 685–643 BCE) and the purported author of the Legalist work (see *Fajia* under *Important Terms*) the *Guǎnzǐ* 管子. Under his guidance, Duke Huan became first of the *ba*, "lord protectors" (see *Important Terms*). Primarily as a consequence of this event, Guan Zhong was either praised or criticized by later thinkers.

Hòujì 后稷 ("Duke of Millet"). Originally an official title but now regarded as a proper name for Qì 棄, who served as the minister of agriculture under Emperor Shun (see below).

Huáng Dì 黃帝 ("Yellow Emperor"). Third of the "Three Sovereigns" (see Fu Xi above and Shen Nong below). He is credited with the invention of wooden houses, boats, and carts, as well as the military and police forces. One of his ministers supposedly invented Chinese characters, inspired by the tracks left by birds, and his wife is credited with inventing the methods of sericulture (raising silkworms to produce silk).

Huìzǐ 惠子 (ca. 380–305 BCE). Also known as Huì Shī 惠施, and along with Gongsun Long (see above) a prominent figure within the *Mingjia*, "School of Names" (see *Important Terms*). Though he was a prodigious author, few of Huizi's works are extant today. He is best-known for his ten paradoxes (in chapter 5 of this volume), which purportedly show that distinctions are arbitrary, so there is an underlying unity to the universe. He concludes from this that we should show compassion to all things. Huizi was a friend of and philosophical influence on Zhuangzi.

Jié 桀 ("Tyrant Jie"). Purportedly, the evil last ruler of the Xia dynasty (see *Important Periods*). His traditional reign dates are 1818–1766 BCE.

Lì 厲 ("King Li"). An incompetent, cruel Western Zhou dynasty ruler. Traditionally, he is said to have ascended to the throne in 878 BCE, and the year he was forced into exile (842 BCE) is generally considered the first reliably known date in Chinese history.

Lí Lóu 離婁. Also known as Lí Zhū 離朱. A contemporary of Huang Di (see above), Li Lou was renowned for his acute vision. It was said that at a hundred paces he could see the tip of an autumn hair. (In autumn an animal's hair is finest and thinnest.)

Lóngzǐ 龍子. According to the commentaries, he is an "ancient worthy" who is cited by Mengzi but otherwise unknown to us.

Péngzǔ 彭祖 ("Ancestor Peng," or "Old Peng"). The Chinese Methuselah, purported to have lived seven hundred years. He is referred to in both *Analects* 7.1 (in chapter 1 of this volume) and *Zhuangzi* chapter 1 (in chapter 8 of this volume).

Robber Zhi (Dào Zhí 盜跖). On some accounts, a contemporary of Huang Di, but more commonly regarded as an infamous and shameless brigand of the Spring and Autumn Period (see *Important Periods*). Some sources say that he came from Lu, Kongzi's home state. He is used as a mouthpiece for the philosophical ideas of Yang Zhu in the "Robber Zhi" dialogue (in chapter 3 of this volume).

Shēn Búhài 申不害 (d. 377 BCE). Prime minister of the state of Han under Marquis Zhāo of Hán 韓昭候 (r. 358–333 BCE) and an important figure within the *Fajia*, "Legalist School" (see *Important Terms*). Shen Buhai is credited with developing the idea of "administrative methods" (shù 術), an elegant, though somewhat inflexible, system for evaluating the performance of government officials by comparing the objectives or duties that ministers "name" (míng 名) for themselves, when they propose an action or accept a government position, with the actual "form" or "situation" (xíng 刑 or 形) that results when they carry out said duties. If "form" and "name" match, the minister has properly performed his duties and should be rewarded; if they do not match, the minister has failed in his duties and should be punished. This idea directly influenced the thought of Han Feizi.

Shén Nóng 神農 ("Divine Farmer"). Second of the "Three Sovereigns" (see Fu Xi and Huang Di above), he is credited with the discovery of the hoe and the plow, the invention of agriculture, and establishing the basic institutions of trade and commerce.

Shènzǐ 慎子 (ca. 350–275 BCE). Also known as Shèn Dào 慎到, an important figure within the *Fajia*, "Legalist School" (see *Important Terms*). Shenzi developed the doctrine of "the power of position" (shì 勢), an idea that directly influenced Han Feizi's thought. According to the doctrine of *shi*, the key to a ruler's success lies in his ability to maintain his sociopolitical superiority over his subjects so that he can use the power and prestige of his position to intimidate people into obeying his commands. This idea can be understood as an amoralized, institutional version of the earlier notion of government through "moral charisma" (Dé 德) advocated by the Confucians. But whereas the Confucians maintained that the power of moral charisma is generated through the cultivation of the ruler's character, Shen Dao and Han Fei believed that the power of status is simply a concomitant feature of the ruler's sociopolitical position. See chapter 7 in this volume for selections from the *Shenzi Fragments*.

Shī Kuāng 師曠 ("Music Master Kuang"). A blind musician of the sixth century BCE who could reportedly foretell the outcome of a battle by listening to the hoofbeats of the enemy cavalry or the fortunes of a king by listening to the grumblings of his people. He is often cited as the standard for musical taste and a paradigm for connoisseurs in general.

Shùn 舜 ("Emperor Shun"). Second of the mythical "Three Sage-Kings" (see Yao and Yu below). His traditional reign dates are 2255–2205 BCE. Shun was renowned for his filial piety: his father—known as the "Blind Man"—and stepmother treated him remarkably badly and even attempted to kill him on several occasions in order to benefit his spoiled and generally worthless half-brother. Shun's continued love and respectfulness in the face of this abuse eventually won over his parents and brother, moving them to reform.

Shū Qí 叔齊. Younger brother of Bo Yi (see above).

Sīmǎ Qiān 司馬遷 (ca. 145–90 BCE). A Han dynasty (see *Important Periods*) figure who completed the *Shǐjì* 史記 (*Records of the Historian*), a work begun by his father, Sima Tan. The *Shiji* is the first comprehensive account of Chinese history from its beginnings to the time of composition. It had a tremendous influence on later Chinese views of history and historiography and was treasured as a fount of moral and political exemplars and insights.

Sòngzǐ 宋子 (ca. 360–290 BCE). Also known as Sòng Róngzǐ 宋榮子, Sòng Jiān 宋鈃, or Sòng Kēng 宋牼, a pacifist who encouraged people to simplify their lives and avoid conflict by minimizing their desires, particularly what he considered to be artificial desires for things such as prestige, wealth, and power.

Tāng 湯 ("King Tang," also known as Chéng Tāng 成湯, "Tang the Successful"). Tang's traditional reign dates are 1766–1753 BCE. He defeated the tyrant Jie (see above) and founded the Shang dynasty (see *Important Periods*).

Wén 文 ("King Wen"). A virtuous vassal of the Tyrant Zhou (see below), his name means "cultured." King Wen ruled over a state called Zhōu 周. (Note that the name of this state, though romanized the same way as the name of Tyrant Zhòu—see below—is written with a different graph and pronounced with a different tone.) While having good warrant for rebellion, King Wen remained loyal to his ruler, sustained by the hope of reforming him. Although he did not reign as king during his lifetime, he is traditionally referred to as "King Wen" in honor of his great Virtue.

Wǔ 武 ("King Wu"). Wu's traditional reign dates are 1122–1115 BCE. He was the son of King Wen (see above), and his name means "martial." After succeeding his father, he overthrew Tyrant Zhou (see below) and founded the Zhou dynasty (see *Important Periods*), which was named after the state over which he ruled.

Yáo 堯 ("Emperor Yao"). First of the mythical "Three Sage-Kings" (see Shun above and Yu below). His traditional reign dates are 2356–2255 BCE. He is credited with the invention of the calendar, developing rituals and music, and establishing the basic structure of government. Yao skipped over his own unworthy son and designated a peasant named Shun as his successor, based upon the latter's remarkable filial piety. Yao is said to have trained Shun to rule and shared power with him during the last twenty-eight years of his reign.

Yì Yá 易牙. Famed as a remarkably talented chef who worked in the kitchen of Duke Huan of Qi (see Guan Zhong above), Yi Ya's ability to harmonize various flavors in ways that people in general found delicious and appealing was seen as emblematic of the way sages are able to hit upon those ethical principles and practices that all people approve of and take delight in.

Yī Yǐn 伊尹. An able minister of King Tang's (see above). According to some accounts, Yi Yin was working as a farmer when his talents were recognized and he was promoted by the king. Others say that he attracted the king's attention through his cooking.

Yōu 幽 ("King You"). An incompetent, cruel Zhou dynasty ruler. He ascended to the throne in 781 BCE. His incompetence and cruelty as a ruler led to his murder, and the end of the Western Zhou dynasty, in 771 BCE. (See the Introduction to this volume for more on King You.)

Yǔ 禹 ("Emperor Yu"). Third of the mythical "Three Sage-Kings" (see Yao and Shun above) and founder of the Xia dynasty. His traditional reign dates are 2205–2197 BCE. Yu is credited with overseeing the first successful state efforts at flood control, a remarkably important project given the topography of central China. Yu is said to have so selflessly dedicated himself to this work that he wore off all the hair of his thighs and shins, and passed by his own house three times without pausing, even though he could hear his wife and children weeping over his absence. While cited by many early thinkers, Yu was a particular favorite of Mozi, perhaps because his dedication to public duty seemed to trump his devotion to his own family.

Zhòu 紂 ("Tyrant Zhou"). The evil last ruler of the Shang dynasty (see *Important Periods*). His traditional reign dates are 1154–1122 BCE, though many modern scholars think the end of his reign must be closer to 1045 BCE. See also the entry for Wen, above.

Zhōu Gōng 周公 ("The Duke of Zhou"). Brother of King Wu (see above). According to traditional accounts, when King Wu died, his infant son became ruler of the newly founded Zhou dynasty (see *Important Periods*). The Duke purportedly served the young king as a wise and virtuous regent and did not attempt to wrest power from him for his own gain. The Duke of Zhou thus served as a paragon for selfless devotion to the greater good.

IMPORTANT PERIODS

Xià 夏 dynasty. Traditional dates: 2205–1766 BCE. See Yu and Jie under *Important Figures*.

Shāng 商 dynasty, also known as the Yīn 殷 dynasty. Traditional dates: 1765–1123 BCE. See Tang and Tyrant Zhou under *Important Figures*.

Zhōu 周 dynasty. Traditional dates: 1122–221 BCE. Often divided into "Eastern" and "Western" Zhou (see below). See Wén, Wǔ, and Zhōu Gōng 周公 ("The Duke of Zhou") under *Important Figures*.

> Western Zhou (Xīzhōu 西周). The earlier part (1122–771 BCE) of the Zhou dynasty. Widely regarded as a golden age of peace, stability, and prosperity.

> Eastern Zhou (Dōngzhōu 東周). The latter part (770–221 BCE) of the Zhou dynasty. It began when disgruntled vassals, together with "barbarian" (i.e., non-Chinese) forces, sacked the Zhou capital and killed the ruling monarch (King You, see *Important Figures*). Remnants of the Zhou royal family escaped and founded a new capital far to the east at Loyang, installing the king's son as ruler. However, the dynasty never again had real control of China. (The last Zhou ruler was deposed in 256 BCE, but traditionally the dynasty is said to have lasted until the start of the next dynasty, the Qin, in 221 BCE.)

>> Spring and Autumn Period (Chūnqiū shídài 春秋時代). The period 722–481 BCE, covered by the court chronicle of Lu, Kongzi's native state (see the *Spring and Autumn Annals* in *Important Texts*). This period saw the rise of the institution of bà 霸 ("lord protector," see *Important Terms*). The philosophers Kongzi and Mozi lived during this period.

>> Warring States Period (Zhànguó shídài 戰國時代). The period 403–221 BCE. It began when the Zhou king officially recognized the partitioning of the state of Jìn 晉, which had been carved up by and divided among the members of an alliance of other states, into the states of Han, Zhao, and Wei. Soon after, in 335, the rulers of these and other allegedly "vassal" states began to usurp the title wáng 王, "king" (see *Important Terms*), which rightfully only the

Zhou king could claim. Most of the philosophers in this volume lived during this period.

Qín dynasty 秦. A short-lived dynasty (221–207 BCE) that marked the end of the "Warring States Period" by unifying the various states into a single empire. It is from the name "Qin" that we get our word "China."

Hàn dynasty 漢. 206 BCE–220 CE. A long-lasting and largely stable dynasty consisting of an "Earlier" or "Western" and a "Later" or "Eastern" period, on either side of a brief interregnum. See Sima Qian under *Important Figures*.

"Earlier" or "Western Han" (206 BCE–9 CE).

"Later" or "Eastern Han" (25–220 CE).

IMPORTANT TEXTS

The *Changes* (Yì 易), sometimes called the "I Ching." A multilayered composition whose earliest strata originate in divinatory texts of extremely old provenance, perhaps as early as the beginning of the first millennium BCE. There is little evidence of it playing a major role in the thought of any of the philosophers covered in this volume, though it was known to them in some form. It becomes profoundly important to the history of Chinese thought beginning in the Han dynasty, after the addition of various *Appendices* (which probably occurred in the third to second century BCE).

The *History* (Shū 書 or Shàngshū 尚書), also called the *Documents*. The original text purportedly contained the pronouncements and judgments of important figures at critical junctures in history. Along with the *Odes* (see below), the *History* was regarded as a classic from the very earliest period. Both were seen as repositories of traditional wisdom and cited as support by a wide range of Chinese thinkers. The present version of the text contains some genuine Zhou dynasty-era (see *Important Periods*) writings, though its purportedly pre-Zhou material remains suspect.

The *Music* (Yuè 樂). A no longer extant text that was probably more concerned with the proper effects and meaning of music and its contribution to social and ethical well-being than with any analysis of the nature of music itself. The *Liji* (see the *Rites* below) contains a chapter called the "Record of Music" (Yuèjì 樂記), but the relationship between this text and the ancient classic is uncertain at best.

The *Odes* (Shī 詩), also called the "Songs" or "Book of Poetry." A collection of rhymed poems derived from early folk songs and ceremonial incantations. Tradition claims that Kongzi edited an earlier group of three thousand poems down to three hundred, but modern scholars regard this as myth. The text existed in a number of versions during the early period and, like the *History*, was regarded as a classic. The message of the *Odes* was thought to be more allusive and allegorical in nature, and interpreting the poems has been a preoccupation of thinkers from Kongzi on down to contemporary times. The text we have today, called the Mao version, is named after and can be directly traced to a student of Xunzi's. It contains three hundred and five poems divided into three types: Fēng 風 ("The Airs"), Yǎ 雅 ("The Elegies"), and Sòng 頌 ("The Hymns").

The *Rites* (Lǐ 禮). By the end of the Han dynasty (see *Important Periods*) there were several texts that purported to describe the proper form of ancient ceremonies and their significance. Among the most important of these are the *Rites of the Zhou Dynasty* (Zhōulǐ 周禮), *On Etiquette and Rites* (Yílǐ 儀禮), the *Record of Rites* (Lǐjì 禮記), and the *Rites of the Elder Dai* (Dà Dài Lǐjì 大戴禮記). While none of these descend from any known pre-Han text, it is clear that at least large sections of the first two texts existed and were known as early as the fourth century BCE.

The *Spring and Autumn Annals* (Chūnqiū 春秋). The court chronicle of Lu, Kongzi's native state. It takes its name from the generic name for such chronicles, which literally meant "Springs and Autumns" (i.e., the regular passage of time). Tradition says that Kongzi edited this remarkably terse work. Two influential commentaries on it, the *Gongyang zhuan* and *Guliang zhuan*, present interpretations of the text that see it as offering "praise and blame" judgments of various historical individuals and events. A third text, the *Zuozhuan* (*Zuo's Commentary*, see below) is not so much an interpretation as a complement to the text. It fills in historical details of the events recorded in the *Spring and Autumn Annals* rather than offering interpretations of its cryptic pronouncements.

Zuo's Commentary (Zuǒzhuàn 左傳). A substantial historical text that augments the *Spring and Autumn Annals* by providing a wealth of detail concerning the events recorded in the original court chronicle.

IMPORTANT TERMS

bà 霸 ("lord protector" or "hegemon"). Lord protectors were rulers of states who, although nominally vassals to the Zhou king, actually ruled in the king's place, with the mutual political and military support of their fellow "vassals." See Spring and Autumn Period under *Important Periods*.

bǎijia 百家 ("Hundred Schools"). A collective name for the various schools of thought that proliferated during the late Spring and Autumn and Warring States Periods (see *Important Periods*). The notion of a "school" of thought in early Chinese philosophy is quite loose. Usually, it is a concept applied retrospectively (often by Sima Qian, see under *Important Figures*) to identify groups of thinkers who shared common themes or approaches or who studied with or were inspired by a common thinker.

Dào 道 ("Way"). One of the basic meanings of early forms of this character was a physical "path," but it came to refer more generally to a way of doing something—either *one* way of doing something, or *the* right Way of doing it. For illustrations of these senses, see *Analects* 8.7, 4.20, and 12.19 (in chapter 1 of this volume). *Dao* could also refer to an oral or written account of such a way, and, when used as a verb, the giving of such an account. For this sense, see *Daodejing* chapter 1 (in chapter 6 of this volume, especially note 1). Daoists later appropriated the term to refer to a transcendent entity that is responsible for the underlying pattern of the universe (on this last sense, see *Daodejing* chapter 25, in chapter 6 of this volume).

Dàojiā 道家 ("Daoist School" or "Daoism"). A term applied retrospectively, by Sima Qian in the Han dynasty (see *Important Figures* and *Important Periods*), to a varied collection of thinkers, especially Laozi and Zhuangzi, who rejected both the Confucians' particular conceptions of ethical cultivation and the Mohists' rationalistic consequentialism. See chapters 6 and 8 of this volume for selections from Daoist writings.

Dé 德 ("Virtue"). One of the most important senses of early forms of this character was "Royal Virtue"—the spiritual force a king cultivates through proper sacrifice and deportment that allows him to gain and maintain his rule. This sense of *De* being a kind of power remained central to many of its later meanings. Most generally, it could designate the natural effect or power—good, bad, or indifferent—that a person or thing had upon those nearby. For Kongzi, *De* came to mean something like "moral charisma"—a property that any person could cultivate through developing character traits like "Goodness" and "wisdom" (see Rén 仁 and zhì 智, below). It retained the connotation of having a "magnetic" capacity to draw, influence, and inspire others that was part of the earlier notion of "Royal Virtue." Daoists embraced a related but distinctive sense of *De*, describing it in terms of the natural therapeutic effect Daoist sages had upon the people, creatures, and things within their presence. For illustrations of these uses, see *Analects* 2.1, 2.3, 4.25, 7.23, 9.18, 12.19 (in chapter 1 of this volume) and *Daodejing* chapters 10, 38, and 55 (in chapter 6 of this volume). By the end of the Warring States Period, the term *De* was used as a countable noun to refer to what we call "virtues"—positive character traits such as benevolence, wisdom, and courage (see *Mean* chapter 20, in chapter 11 of this volume). For more on this concept, see David S. Nivison, "The Paradox of 'Virtue,'" in *The Ways of Confucianism: Investigations in Chinese Philosophy*, ed. Bryan W. Van Norden (Chicago, IL: Open Court Press, 1996), 31–43, and Philip J. Ivanhoe, "The Concept of *de* ('Virtue') in the *Laozi*," in Mark Csikszentmihalyi and Philip J. Ivanhoe, eds., *Essays on Religious and Philosophical Aspects of the "Laozi"* (Albany, NY: State University of New York Press, 1999), 239–57.

Fǎjiā 法家 ("Legalist School" or "Legalism"). A term applied retrospectively by Sima Qian in the Han dynasty (see *Important Figures* and *Important Periods*) to an intellectual movement, centered on the writings of Gongsun Yang (Lord Shang), Shen Dao, Shen Buhai, and Han Feizi (see *Important Figures*), that took an amoral approach to the problems of social and political organization and management. For selections from Shen Dao, see chapter 7 of this volume; for selections from Han Feizi, see chapter 10 of this volume.

Four Seas. See Sìhǎi 四海, below.

jūnzǐ 君子 ("gentleman"). Literally, this term means "son of a lord," and hence originally referred to someone possessing a particular social status. However, Kongzi emphasized living up to the ethical implications of this social role, so that being a genuine gentleman is a goal to strive for, rather than something simply bestowed by noble birth. The opposite of a "gentleman" is a "petty person" (literally, "small person," xiǎo rén 小人). For illustrations of these senses, see, for example, *Analects* 4.5, 4.16, 6.13, 6.18, 9.6, 9.14, 12.5, 12.8, 12.19, 15.2, 15.21, 16.8, and 17.23 (in chapter 1 of this volume).

lǐ 禮 ("rites," "rituals," or "propriety"). This term originally referred to religious rituals, such as sacrifices of food and wine to the spirits of one's ancestors, but it came to have a much broader application, including matters of etiquette and aspects of one's entire way of life, including dress, behavior, and demeanor. For examples, see *Analects* 1.12, 4.13, 9.3, 12.1, 17.11, 17.21 (in chapter 1 of this volume) and *Mengzi* 4A17 and 4A27 (in chapter 4 of this volume). *Li* sometimes seems coextensive with all of ethics and can even extend to what seems like the patterns of nature. See, for example, *Xunzi* chapter 19, "Discourse on Ritual" (in chapter 9 of this volume). Mengzi also uses the term to refer to a virtue associated with following the rites. See *Mengzi* 2A6 and 6A6 (in chapter 4 of this volume).

lǐ 里. A unit of length equal to about one-third of a mile.

mìng 命 ("fate" or "mandate"). Most broadly, *ming* refers to what is determined independently of human agency or choice. It is a concept closely related to Tiān 天 ("Heaven," see below), and like *Tian* has both descriptive and normative senses. Thus, unavoidable future events (such as one's death) and inescapable natural facts (such as the need to eat) are said to be *ming*. However, *ming* can also refer to what is normatively mandated, such as the right to rule of a sage-king (which is referred to as Tiān Mìng 天命, the "Mandate of Heaven"). See, for example, *Analects* 2.4, 6.10, 12.5, 14.36, 16.8, 20.3 (in chapter 1 of this volume); *Mozi* chapters 35 and 39 (in chapter 2 of this volume); *Mengzi* 7A1–3 and 7B24 (in chapter 4 of this volume); and the "Announcement to the Prince of Kang" and "Announcement of the Duke of Shao" (both on the Title Support Page for this volume at www.hackettpublishing.com/rccp -support). See also Edward Slingerland, "The Conception of *Ming* in Early Chinese Thought," *Philosophy East & West* 46, no. 4 (1996): 567–81.

Míngjiā 名家 ("School of Names" or "Sophists"). A term applied retrospectively by Sima Qian in the Han dynasty (see *Important Figures* and *Important Periods*) to a varied collection of thinkers who shared a common interest in the nature of language, debate, and paradox, including Gongsun Longzi and Huizi. See chapter 5 of this volume for selections from these thinkers.

Mòjiā 墨家 ("Mohist School" or "Mohism"). The school of thought that grew around and out of the teachings of Mozi. See chapter 2 for a selection of Mohist writings.

mǔ 畝. A unit of area equal to about 733 square yards, a little less than one-seventh the area of a football field.

qì 氣. Perhaps originally referring to the mist that arose from heated sacrificial offerings, this term later came to refer to vapor in general and human breath in particular. In a more technical sense, *qi* was thought of as a kind of vital energy found in both the atmosphere (hence the expression "clouds and *qi*") and the human body (hence the expression "blood and *qi*"), and existing in various densities and levels of clarity or turbidity, that is responsible, among other things, for the intensity of one's emotions. For illustrations of its uses, see *Analects* 16.7 (in chapter 1 of this volume), *Mengzi* 6A8 (in chapter 4 of this volume), *Xunzi* chapters 2 and 9 (in chapter 9 of this volume), and *Nature Comes from the Mandate* 1 (in chapter 12 of this volume). There were different theories about how *qi* should be related to the heart. Mengzi argues that the *qi* should be guided by one's cultivated heart (see *Mengzi* 2A2, in chapter 4 of this volume), while Zhuangzi recommends emptying the heart so that one can be guided by the *qi* (see *Zhuangzi* chapter 4, in chapter 8 of this volume), presumably because he regarded it as more objective and impersonal than the promptings of one's own heart. In later Chinese philosophy, *qi* was thought of as the fundamental "stuff" out of which everything in the universe condenses and into which it eventually dissipates.

qíng 情 ("the genuine," "essence," or "disposition"). The *qing* of something is what it genuinely is, as opposed to what it might appear to be (see *Mengzi* 6A6, in chapter 4 of this volume). This is often conceived of in terms of how it would spontaneously behave and develop if given a proper environment and support. More specifically, some interpreters have argued that the *qing* of a thing can be the essential characteristics of that thing. Toward the end of the Warring States Period, *qing* came to refer to human emotions or dispositions (perhaps because some thinkers regarded these as essential to human beings). On this later use, see, for example, *Xunzi* chapter 2 (in chapter 9 of this volume, and especially note 22). For more on this term, see Angus C. Graham, "The Background of the Mencian Theory of Human Nature," in his *Studies in Chinese Philosophy and Philosophical Literature* (Albany, NY: State University of New York Press, 1990), 7-66.

Rén 仁 ("Goodness" or "benevolence"). For Kongzi, this term refers to the sum total of virtuous qualities, or the perfection of human character. It is etymologically related to the character for "human" (rén 人) and thus has previously been rendered as "humaneness" or "manhood-at-its-best," but in our *Analects* translation it is "Goodness." For Mohists it is the universal and impartial concern one should manifest toward all people, so beginning with the Mozi we translate the term as "benevolence." Later thinkers are influenced by this Mohist use; for Confucians like Mengzi, however, benevolence is "graded," stronger for family members than for strangers. See, for example, *Mengzi* 7A45 (in chapter 4 of this volume). For more on this concept, see Lin Yu-sheng, "The Evolution of the Pre-Confucian Meaning of *Jen* 仁 and the Confucian Concept of Moral Autonomy," *Monumenta Serica* 31 (1924): 172–204.

Rú 儒 or Rújiā 儒家 ("Confucians" or "Erudites"). Although traditionally translated as "Confucian," the Chinese term has no etymological relationship with the name Kǒngzǐ 孔子 (Confucius). The term appears to have already been in use by the time of Kongzi (see *Analects* 6.13 in chapter 1 of this volume), but there is considerable scholarly debate over exactly what its original meaning was. After Kongzi, however, it is clearly used to refer to those who think of themselves as carrying on the tradition of culture and learning that Kongzi defended and came to represent, so we normally translate it as "Confucian." (See, for example, *Mozi* chapter 39, in chapter 2 of this volume.) However, the Confucians often disagreed vehemently among themselves about how to interpret this tradition.

shén 神 ("spirit," "spiritual," or "spirit-like"). *Shen*, like guǐ 鬼 ("ghost"), can refer to a spiritual being, such as the spirit of a dead ancestor. However, some philosophers speak of living people as *shen*, "spiritual" or "spirit-like," when they accomplish things beyond the range of normal human capacities, such as morally transforming people through the power of Virtue.

shèng 聖 ("sage"). A *sheng* is a person who has achieved the greatest possible human excellence. Sages may possess special abilities (see *De*, "Virtue," above), but they are still human beings. For illustrative uses, see *Analects* 6.30, 7.34, 9.6, 16.8 (in chapter 1 of this volume) and *Mengzi* 2A2 (in chapter 4 of this volume). Famous sages include the kings Yao, Shun, Yu, Tang, Wen, Wu, Zhou Gong aka the Duke of Zhou (see *Important Figures*), and Kongzi himself. Lower classes of human excellence include *shi*, "scholar," and *xian*, "worthy"; see below.

shì 士 ("scholar," "scholar-official," "knight," or "literatus"). Speaking most generally, a *shi* is a member of the social elite. However, the precise nature of that elite varies with historical period and society. Early on, the *shi* were members of the warrior nobility (hence "knight"), but already by the time of Kongzi "shi" often referred to someone who was literate, hence it is sometimes translated "literatus." (Much later, in Japan, *shi* was one of the characters for *samurai*, who were often both warriors and scholars.) As with *junzi*, "gentleman" (see above), later philosophers emphasize living up to the duties implied by the social role rather than simply enjoying the prerogatives of one's often hereditary position. See also *sheng*, "sage" (above) and *xian*, "worthy" (below).

Sìhǎi 四海 (Four Seas). It was a common belief in ancient China that the earth is square and Heaven is round (or spherical). Along with this typically went a belief that there are "Four Seas," one on each side of the square earth. Consequently, the expression "within the Four Seas" became a common way to refer to the inhabited world.

sī 思 ("to concentrate," "think," or "reflect"). *Si* refers to a directing of the attention to something either external or mental. Although the term is often translated as "thinking," it does not generally refer to ratiocination or theoretical reasoning. However, *si* does not exclude what we would commonly call "reflection." For illustrative uses, see *Analects* 2.15, 4.17, 15.31 (in chapter 1 of this volume) and *Mengzi* 6A6, 6A15 (in chapter 4 of this volume). See also Arthur Waley, trans., *The Analects of Confucius* (New York: Vintage Books, 1989), 44–46.

Son of Heaven. See Tiānzǐ 天子, below.

Tiān 天 ("Heaven"). This term can refer to the sky, hence the standard translation "Heaven." However, Heaven can also be a sort of higher power. Various thinkers conceive of this higher power in different ways, though. Thus, Heaven seems to be very much like a personal god in the Mohist writings, more like the impersonal processes of nature in the writings of Zhuangzi and Xunzi, and somewhere in the middle in the sayings of Kongzi and Mengzi. In the period covered in this anthology, Heaven is *not* primarily thought of as a place, and is not connected with any explicit views about an afterlife. For illustrative uses, see *Analects* 2.4, 3.24, 5.13, 6.28, 7.23, 8.19, 9.5, 9.6, 11.9, 12.5, 14.35, 16.8, 17.19 (in chapter 1 of this volume); *Mozi* chapters 26 and 31 (in chapter 2 of this volume); *Mengzi* 2B13, 3A5, 7A1 (in chapter 4 of this volume); *Xunzi* chapter 17 (in chapter 9 of this volume); *Mean* chapter 1 (in chapter 11 of this volume); and *Nature Comes from the Mandate* chapter 1 (in chapter 12 of this volume).

Tiānxià 天下 ("all under Heaven," or "the world"). An expression referring to the entire world.

Tiānzǐ 天子 ("Son of Heaven"). A title for the legitimate ruler of the world (i.e., a true king; see *wang*, "king," below).

wáng 王 ("king"). A genuine king should rule by Virtue (see *De*, above), not by brute force. In addition, there should be only one genuine king at a time. As in the case of *junzi* and *shi* (see above), there is a distinction between the de facto social and political role and its idealized, normative conception. See also the entry on *ba* ("lord protector") above, and the entries for Spring and Autumn Period and Warring States Period in the list of *Important Periods*.

wúwéi 無為 ("nonaction" or "effortless action"). Although it literally means "the absence of doing," *wuwei* does not refer to a complete lack of action, like an inanimate object. Rather, nonaction is acting in a way that is natural, unforced, and unselfconscious. The *Laozi* and *Zhuangzi* both advocate nonaction, but the latter text strongly suggests that it can be achieved only through years of self-conscious practice. Confucians also take nonaction as a goal, but they disagree with Daoists about the means to achieve this goal, and the kinds of activities in which one manifests it. For illustrative uses, see *Analects* 15.5 (in chapter 1 of this volume) and *Daodejing* chapters 2, 3, 10, 38, 43, 47, 63, 64 (in chapter 6 of this volume). The butcher in *Zhuangzi* chapter 3 (in chapter 8 of this volume) is also often taken as an illustration of "nonaction," although that term does not occur in the passage. For more on this concept, see Edward Slingerland, *Effortless Action: Wu-wei as Conceptual Metaphor and Spiritual Ideal in Early China* (New York: Oxford University Press, 2003). See also *ziran*, "natural" (below).

xián 賢 ("worthy"). A term designating a level of cultivation in general somewhere between a *shi*, "scholar," and a *sheng*, "sage" (see above). For most thinkers in this volume, this indicates a level of ethical excellence, but for Han Feizi (in chapter 10 of this volume) the term indicates someone with technical or polit-ical skills.

xīn 心 ("heart," "mind," "disposition," or "feeling"). This term can refer to the phys-ical organ in the chest, but it can also refer to the psychological faculty of thinking, perceiving, feeling, desiring, and intending. (These were not regarded as separate functions by Chinese philosophers, as they sometimes are in West-ern philosophy.) By synecdoche, *xin* can also refer to "feelings," or dispositions to feel or perceive things in a certain way. For illustrative uses, see *Analects* 2.4, 6.7, 14.39 (in chapter 1 of this volume); *Mengzi* 1A7, 2A2, 2A6, 4B12, 4B28, 6A6, 6A7, 6A15, 7A1, 7A27, 7B31 (in chapter 4 of this volume); and *Zhuangzi* chapter 4 (in chapter 8 of this volume).

xìng 性 ("nature" or "human nature"). For most thinkers in the classical period, this term refers to the characteristics of a paradigmatic instance of the sort of creature that one is. (This is much like one of the senses that "nature" has in Western philosophical writings, hence the translation.) These tendencies are more likely to be realized if one is given a healthy environment. Thus, the sprout of a willow tree has a tendency to grow into an adult willow tree, but it may die from a lack of water, or be warped through techniques such as those used to grow *bonsai*. For illustrative uses, see "Robber Zhi" (in chapter 3 of this volume) and *Mengzi* 6A1–4, 6A6–8, 7A1, 7B24 (in chapter 4 of this volume). In contrast, Xunzi insists that *xing* be used only to refer to the characteristics something has innately. See *Xunzi* chapter 23 (in chapter 9 of this volume). In philosophical texts, the nature under discussion is often specifically "human nature" (rén xìng 人性), so the character *xing* by itself will sometimes be translated that way. For more on this concept, see Angus C. Graham, "The Background of the Mencian Theory of Human Nature," in his *Studies in Chinese Philosophy and Philosophical Literature* (Albany, NY: State University of New York Press, 1990), 7–66. See also *qing*, "essence" (above).

yì 義 ("right" or "righteousness"). One early definition states that "The right is the appropriate," where "appropriate" (yí 宜) refers to what is appropriate for one to do and to be, given the situation and one's social role (e.g., ruler, minister, father, son, etc.). However, *yi* can also refer to what is right or appropriate for a person in general. By extension, the term refers to the character of one who does what is *yi* (hence "righteousness"). Note that "human rights" is a very different notion, which belongs to a distinct and unrelated conceptual framework.

yīn 陰 and yáng 陽. In their earliest use, *yin* and *yang* may have referred to the shady and sunny sides of a hill, respectively. Eventually, the terms were associated with *qi* (see above) and understood either as two distinct modes of *qi* or as two fundamental forces that shape and guide *qi*. In general, *yin* and *yang* designate two broad sets of phenomena characterized by associated states, tendencies, or qualities. For example, day, hot, above, active, masculine, speech, Heaven, etc. are *yang;* night, cold, below, still, feminine, silence, earth, etc. are *yin*. The various phenomena and the states, tendencies, and qualities within each set are thought to be related to one another and are all regarded as natural aspects of different situations, things, or events. *Yin* and *yang* are thought to be complementary forces or qualities and a given situation, thing, or event can often be described in terms of one or the other. Used early as technical terms in Chinese medicine, the pair eventually became part of the standard vocabulary of Chinese cosmology.

zhì 智 (sometimes written 知, "wisdom," or "cleverness"). *Zhi* typically has a positive connotation and refers to a virtue that manifests itself in such things as good judgments about the consequences of various actions. For a passage that illustrates the characteristics of someone with wisdom, see *Mengzi* 5A9 (in chapter 4 of this volume). Sometimes, however, *zhi* refers to amoral intelligence or cleverness, and in other contexts is clearly regarded as a human vice or defect. For passages illustrating this sense, see *Daodejing* chapters 3, 18, 19, 65 (in chapter 6 of this volume).

zǐ 子 ("Master"). An honorific term, often used after someone's family name, typically referring to a teacher who has disciples (e.g., "Kongzi" = "Master Kong"). It may be used by someone in reference to teachers who are not one's own "master."

zìrán 自然 ("natural"). Literally meaning "self-so," this term describes anything that occurs of its own accord, without external coercion. A number of thinkers of this period regard such unselfconscious spontaneity as a mark and necessary constituent of a well-lived life. See also *wuwei*.

IMAGE CREDITS

Front matter map: © Hugo Lopez –Yug / Wikimedia Commons / CC-BY-SA-3.0.

Ch. 1: Confucius, Illustrations of The Classic of Filial Piety. Unknown artist, Song dynasty. National Palace Museum.

Ch. 2: Chinese stamp featuring Mozi. Charlesimage. Shutterstock 167796167.

Ch. 3: Bonsai tree. sirtravelot. Shutterstock 207655471.

Ch. 4: Mengzi. Yuan dynasty. From *Half Portraits of the Great Sage and Virtuous Men of Old*.

Ch. 5: *Night Shining White*. Han Gan. Tang dynasty. Metropolitan Museum of Art.

Ch. 6: Laozi riding an ox. National Palace Museum.

Ch. 7: From *The Nine Dragons*. Chen Rong. Song dynasty. Museum of Fine Art, Boston.

Ch. 8: *Zhuangzi Dreaming of a Butterfly*. Lu Zhi. Ming dynasty.

Ch. 9: Xunzi. Shutterstock 1829046137. Creative Vector Artist.

Ch. 10: Han Feizi. Naci Yavuz. Shutterstock 2064753407.

Ch. 11: Tainan Confucian Temple. Reproduction of a calligraphy of *Great Learning* by Yuan calligrapher Zhao Mengfu at the Confucian temple in Tainan, Taiwan. M. Weitzel. Wikimedia Commons. CC Attribution Share-alike 2.5.

Ch. 12: Calligraphy. Yishan Wang.